HOBBESIAN MORAL
AND POLITICAL
THEORY

STUDIES IN MORAL, POLITICAL, AND LEGAL PHILOSOPHY

General Editor: Marshall Cohen

HOBBESIAN MORAL

AND POLITICAL

THEORY

Gregory S. Kavka

PRINCETON UNIVERSITY PRESS
PRINCETON, NEW JERSEY

Copyright © 1986 by Princeton University Press
Published by Princeton University Press
41 William Street
Princeton, New Jersey 08540
In the United Kingdom:
Princeton University Press, Guildford, Surrey

All Rights Reserved

Library of Congress Cataloging in Publication Data
will be found on the last printed page of this book.

ISBN 0-691-07718-5 (cloth)   0-691-02765-X (pbk.)

This book has been composed in Linotron Aldus.

Clothbound editions of Princeton University Press books
are printed on acid-free paper, and binding materials
are chosen for strength and durability. Paperbacks,
although satisfactory for personal collections,
are not usually suitable for library rebinding.

Printed in the United States of America
by Princeton University Press
Princeton, New Jersey

For Virginia, and all who helped

CONTENTS

CONTENTS

CONTENTS

PREFACE

Both conflict and cooperation are ubiquitous features of human social life. Interests of individuals conflict with those of their neighbors because (among other reasons) material resources are scarce, ideals and values are diverse, and people care about their reputations and relative standing among their fellows. At the same time, individuals share a number of common interests and concerns, and this makes social cooperation possible. Among the most important of these common interests are the prevention and limitation of violent conflict and the protection of personal possessions. When these interests are secured and when environmental and economic conditions are reasonably favorable, people generally can live out their lives and engage in cooperative (and competitive) social activities without constant concern for their own survival and that of their loved ones. But it is not easy to secure persons and possessions when others may gain by attacking the former or seizing the latter. In fact, it requires two major social institutions—morality and government—working in a coordinated fashion to do so. This is one of the main themes of Hobbes's philosophy that will be developed in this book.

Another main theme concerns the age-old problem of the relationship between morality and self-interest. Since self-interested concerns play such a large role in motivating human actions, we must seek an account of morality that allows such concerns a significant place; otherwise we risk constructing abstract moral systems that people are generally incapable of consistently following and that hence have little bearing on social reality. Hobbes's own project was to ground morality in long-range rational self-interest. It will be argued here that he was more successful in this than is generally believed, and that a modified version of his program may, to a considerable extent, succeed.

In recent years, a number of serious attempts have been made to systematize and develop the moral and political themes of great philosophers of the past. Kant, Locke, Marx, and the Classical Utilitarians all have their current defenders and are taken seriously as expositors of fundamentally sound moral and political views. It is the aim of this book to introduce Hobbes into this select group, since his insights on morals and politics are as profound, as systematic, and as close to being true as those of any philosopher. However, it is clear that if Hobbes's philosophy is to be taken seriously today, it must be modified in certain respects. Some of his arguments must be repaired or discarded. And, most important, three basic empirical assumptions usually attributed to Hobbes must be rejected as unsound. Hobbes's apparent view that all human acts are motivated by self-interest cannot be accepted.[1] Fortunately, a plausible substitute assumption about motivation suffices for the purposes of Hobbes's arguments, when it is conjoined with Hobbes's other major assumptions about human nature. Two other false assumptions ground Hobbes's political absolutism. He holds that a sovereign's interests will coincide with those of his people and that divisions of, or limitations on, sovereign power inevitably lead to civil war. In the course of this work, these assumptions are analyzed and discarded, leaving us with a version of Hobbes's philosophy that reaches considerably more liberal conclusions than he himself did, while retaining some of Hobbes's conservative insights. The resulting view is not Hobbes's own, but it is derived largely from his methods and arguments and may fairly be dubbed "Hobbesian."

In presenting this version of Hobbes's moral and political philosophy, *Leviathan* is taken as our basic text, for it is Hobbes's final systematic presentation of his moral and political views. Hobbes's other writings are relied on mainly when they are useful for clarifying obscurities in *Leviathan* or when differences be-

---

[1] Whether this was Hobbes's real view is discussed in section 2-3.

tween works suggest interesting changes in Hobbes's views over time. (First references to Hobbes's works are to title, volume, chapter [if any], section [if any], and page number in *The English Works of Thomas Hobbes*, ed. Sir William Molesworth, 9 vols. [London: John Bohn, 1839; reprint, Scientia Aalen, 1962]. Later references shorten the titles and omit the volume numbers.)

This book makes no pretense of being complete. It focuses only on the doctrines and arguments of Hobbes that contribute to its main themes or that seem to be of special philosophical interest. And it departs from previous tradition by dividing the exposition of Hobbes's philosophy into two parts—concerning, respectively, a descriptive theory of interaction patterns among (idealized) rational individuals and a normative theory concerning rights, obligations, and moral ought-judgments. This occasionally results in some repetition, but it has two compensating advantages. It clearly separates questions about motivation and obligation that tend to get confused by Hobbes and some of his commentators,[2] and it provides separate treatment for groups of issues that may be of special interest to some readers. For example, analytical political scientists or other social scientists with little initial interest in moral philosophy may nonetheless find Part I of this book, on descriptive theory, to be highly relevant to their concerns.

A book such as this risks offending doubly. Some will wonder why the presentation is so closely linked to Hobbes's texts and line of argument, while others may wish there were more discussion of the details of the text and its historical context. (Historical context is largely ignored here.) To the former, it can only be said that my approach has been so heavily influenced by *Leviathan* that it would be both unprofitable and misleading to separate my argument from the structure that Hobbes provides. At the same time, it is hoped that this book may serve as a model of one way in which a classic text can be used to contribute to contemporary philosophical debate. To those who might prefer a more textual or historical approach, these clarifying remarks are

[2] Other commentators, such as Howard Warrender, emphasize this distinction but use it to reach very different conclusions from those drawn here. See section 9-3.

offered. This book is less concerned with what Hobbes said for its own sake than with what may be learned from what he said. In particular, it is concerned with his moral and political ideas insofar as they are relevant today. So the text corrects, modifies, and departs from Hobbes where necessary, always trying to make clear that this is being done, and why. Further, there are three recent, superb books on Hobbes—by Howard Warrender,[3] David Gauthier,[4] and F. S. McNeilly[5]—and several very good ones, to which readers are often referred for discussion of textual details, contrasting interpretations, and so forth.[6] Finally, except where it explicitly modifies Hobbes, the present reconstruction tries to give as accurate a picture of *Leviathan* as any in the literature. It is not a perfect picture, but a perfect picture should not be expected, for as Melville wrote (in a different context), "Anyway you may look at it, you must needs conclude that the great Leviathan is . . . one creature . . . that must remain unpainted to the last. True one portrait may hit the mark nearer than another, but none can hit it with any very considerable degree of exactness."[7]

A main contention of this book is that a Hobbesian analysis of morality is an illuminating one. It explains, in a general way, why morality exists, why it has the content it does, and why beings such as ourselves are—or can be made—capable of acting morally. At the same time, it lays out reasons for being moral that most rational persons should be willing to accept. However, Hobbesian theory does all this only for a part of morality, the morality of requirements. It explains and defends the minimal

[3] Howard Warrender, *The Political Philosophy of Hobbes: His Theory of Obligation* (Oxford: Clarendon Press, 1957).

[4] David Gauthier, *The Logic of Leviathan: The Moral and Political Theory of Thomas Hobbes* (Oxford: Clarendon Press, 1969).

[5] F. S. McNeilly, *The Anatomy of Leviathan* (London: Macmillan, 1968).

[6] Jean Hampton's *Hobbes and the Social Contract Tradition* (Cambridge: Cambridge University Press, forthcoming) is not referred to because it was not available at the time this book was written. Some of my major disagreements with Warrender, Gauthier, and McNeilly are set out in sections 9-3, 10-1, and 4-5, respectively.

[7] Herman Melville, *Moby Dick*, ed. Alfred Kazin (Boston: Houghton Mifflin, 1956), p. 215.

standards of conduct that we are required to follow in our interactions with others and that we can reasonably expect and require
others to follow. But there is another more intractable and less
systematic area of morality—that of ideals, both personal and social, which we aspire to emulate, though we are not required to
do so. There are no doubt many interesting things to be said
about this aspect of morality, but few if any of them are said in
Leviathan or in this book.

ACKNOWLEDGMENTS

Portions of some sections of this book originally appeared in the following articles:

"Hobbes's War of All Against All," *Ethics* 93 (January 1983). © 1983 by The University of Chicago. All rights reserved.

"Deterrence, Utility, and Rational Choice," *Theory and Decision* 12 (March 1980).

"Rule by Fear," *Nous* 17 (November 1983).

"Two Solutions to the Paradox of Revolution," *Midwest Studies in Philosophy* 7 (1982).

"Right Reason and Natural Law in Hobbes's Ethics," *The Monist* 66 (January 1983).

"The Reconciliation Project," in *Morality, Reason, and Truth,* ed. David Copp and David Zimmerman (Totowa, N.J.: Rowman & Allanheld, 1984).

My research was generously supported by fellowships from the National Endowment for the Humanities, and the School of Humanities, University of California, Irvine (UCI). UCI's Department of Philosophy provided me with an ideal personal and intellectual atmosphere in which to work and temporarily lightened my teaching load to facilitate revision of the manuscript. A number of people made helpful comments on drafts of single chapters: Richard Brandt, Jean Hampton, Thomas E. Hill, Jr., Christopher Morris, Warren Quinn, Holly Smith, and David Zimmerman. Several others read and offered very useful advice about pieces of the manuscript ranging from two to twelve chapters: David Braybrooke, Carlos Colombetti, Rob Content, David Gauthier, Russell Hardin, Jerry Santas, and Gary Watson. I thank all of them, together with others I may have failed to list, and invite them to suffer the inevitable reviews with me. Responsibility for remaining errors I share with no one but Hobbes.

My initial interest in philosophical ethics, which I developed as an undergraduate, was stimulated by the fine teaching of Joel Feinberg, Thomas Scanlon, Robert Solomon, and Gregory Vlastos. Later, in graduate school, Richard Brandt taught me the importance of systematic thinking in moral theory, William Frankena demonstrated how much can be learned from the history of ethics, and Robert M. Adams provided a model of how to extract ideas and arguments from classic philosophical texts. In my early years of teaching, I received crucial philosophical and personal support from Tyler Burge (and his family). This book on Hobbesian theory owes much to the inspiration provided by these individuals, as well as to the fine and quick work of Sandy Thatcher and the staff at Princeton University Press.

Finally, I am grateful to physicians and staff at the UCI Medical Center, Fermilab Neutron Therapy Facility, and M. D. Anderson Hospital for prolonging my life in the face of a grave threat, thereby enabling me to complete this book. During this difficult period, the support of numerous colleagues, friends, and relatives and the love of my parents and sister sustained me. In sickness and in health, the contributions of my wife, Virginia Warren, defy description. To all these good people, and to her especially, I dedicate this book.

Irvine, California
September 14, 1985

INTRODUCTION

O N E

METHOD—HOBBES'S
AND OURS

1-1. Hobbesian Theory

Though he has been more than three hundred years in the grave, Thomas Hobbes still has much to teach us. His works identify enduring problems of social and political life and suggest some promising solutions for them. Yet, at the same time, they contain important errors in method, assumptions, reasoning, and conclusions. To learn the most from Hobbes, we must correct or avoid these errors, while preserving and building upon the fundamentally sound philosophical structure that they infest.

With that aim in mind, this book offers an explicitly revisionist interpretation of Hobbes's moral and political philosophy. This interpretation takes clarification of Hobbes's own position as but part of a larger process of understanding, evaluation, and modification. The ultimate goal of this process is to explicate and defend a plausible system of moral and political hypotheses suggested and inspired by Hobbes. Throughout, an attempt is made to indicate clearly which of the views discussed are Hobbes's and which are proposed alterations or improvements of his position. Because the modifications offered are not trivial, it would be misleading to describe the theory propounded here as that of Hobbes. Even where it departs from his position, however, the theory resembles his in critical respects: in its adoption of a nonoptimistic view of human nature, in its analysis of the perils of anarchy, in its use of the social contract idea to ground political obligation, in its emphasis on the risks of revolution, in its attempt to reconcile morality and prudence, and so on. Thus, while not Hobbes's own

3

theory, the theory set forth in this book surely is a *Hobbesian* theory.

Hobbes's political conservatism is well known. It will be argued that many of his extreme conservative conclusions are derived from faulty empirical assumptions, so the Hobbesian theory that emerges here is considerably more liberal than Hobbes on such issues as revolution and the rights of individuals against the State. Yet it retains, in modified form, some of the more defensible aspects of the conservative view on these questions.

The general method of Hobbesian moral and political theory is the method that Hobbes himself uses—logical and conceptual analysis combined with empirical observation and probabilistic reasoning. While Hobbes's method is fundamentally sound and appropriate to his subject matter, there is more than a little confusion in what he *says* about method. To clarify matters, let us begin our inquiry with a look at Hobbes's professed method.

1-2. Hobbes's Method

Hobbes strongly rejected the practices of the scholastic philosophers who dominated the English universities during the period of his education at Oxford. These philosophers, in his eyes, were guilty of two sins. They tended to support their conclusions by appeals to the authority of earlier writers (especially Aristotle), rather than by reasoning from acceptable first principles. And because they did not clearly define and consistently use their key philosophical terms, these Schoolmen often ended up uttering nonsense. They would employ contradictory expressions such as "immaterial substance," which for Hobbes—who equated substance and matter—was on a par with "round quadrilateral." Often their terms (e.g., "consubstantiate" and "hypostatical") were empty ones signifying no conception and referring to no object. And they frequently committed what we now call *category mistakes* by ascribing to things of one sort (e.g., physical objects) properties that can be possessed only by things of a different sort (e.g., linguistic expressions).

For an alternative method, Hobbes turned to science, which he regarded as being identical with philosophy, properly understood. He was especially impressed with geometry, apparently for two reasons. The conclusions of geometry appeared to be demonstrably certain. Though not self-evident, they could be derived by clear steps of reasoning from seemingly uncontroversial principles and definitions. Thus, from a well-known passage in Aubrey's *Brief Lives* we learn that Hobbes fell in love with geometry after reading in Euclid the proof of a proposition he initially took to be false and impossible.[1] Here, Hobbes must have thought, was a method that would not only allow one to discover the truth, but would enable one to demonstrate it to others and might force their assent even if they originally disagreed. So he adopted a version of it as his professed philosophical method. That is, he advocated starting, in philosophy, from clear definitions of one's terms and then spelling out, step by step, their logical consequences.

Hobbes was equally taken with another feature of geometry, its utility. In *Leviathan*, he describes geometry as "the mother of all natural science"[2] and ascribes to it "infinite other uses"[3] in addition to measuring land and water. *De corpore* spells out some of these uses: measuring mass, velocity, and time, transporting heavy objects, and constructing instruments.[4] The Epistle to *Philosophical Rudiments* goes even further, crediting geometry with producing all the advantages of civilization.[5] It was apparently Hobbes's hope to preserve the primary benefits of civilization by convincingly applying the same method that created those benefits to a new domain—that of moral and political philosophy.[6]

The social utility of a theory, however, is dependent on the

[1] *John Aubrey's Brief Lives*, ed. Oliver Lawson Dick (Ann Arbor: University of Michigan Press, 1975), p. 150. Note the strikingly similar account of a great scientist's introduction to Euclidean geometry in Albert Einstein, "Autobiographical Essay," in *Albert Einstein: Philosopher Scientist*, ed. Paul A. Schilpp (Evanston, Ill.: Library of Living Philosophers, 1949), pp. 8–11.

[2] *Leviathan*, vol. 3, chap. 46, p. 668.

[3] Ibid., p. 664.

[4] *De corpore*, vol. 1, chap. 1, sec. 7, pp. 7–8.

[5] *Philosophical Rudiments Concerning Government and Society*, vol. 2, p. iv.

[6] Ibid. See also the Epistle to *Human Nature*, vol. 4; *De corpore*, chap. 1, sec. 7, pp. 7–8.

acceptance of its conclusions. And this obviously posed a problem for Hobbes's moral and political theory, for while he aspired to demonstrative certainty, Hobbes realized that even well-proven conclusions would be resisted should their acceptance threaten people's interests. Thus, he wrote:

> For I doubt not, but if it had been a thing contrary to any man's right of dominion, or to the interest of men that have dominion, *that the three angles of a triangle, should be equal to two angles of a square;* that doctrine should have been, if not disputed, yet by the burning of all books of geometry, suppressed, as far as he whom it concerned was able.[7]

Given, however, the content of Hobbes's moral and political philosophy, he hoped to overcome this problem of persuasion. He believed that his conclusions and prescriptions were consonant with everyone's true long-range interests and that his arguments would show that this was so. Further, since virtually unconditional obedience to those in power was a main tenet of his civil philosophy, civil authorities might adopt his philosophy and have it taught in the universities.[8] The reception that his writings actually received and the subsequent banning and burning, rather than teaching, of his books at Oxford showed these hopes to have been as vain, in the short run at least, as the philosophy of the Schoolmen.[9]

From a modern perspective the gravest problems with Hobbes's professed method are problems he does not recognize. His paradigms of demonstrably certain truths—the theorems of Euclidean geometry—depend upon postulates or assumptions which modern physics tells us may not be fully descriptive of the real universe. More significant, our current understanding of the differences between mathematical, empirical, and moral discourse makes it evident that Hobbes could not proceed far into the moral and

[7] *Leviathan*, chap. 11, p. 91; see also *Human Nature*, Epistle.
[8] *Leviathan*, "A Review, and Conclusion," p. 713.
[9] See Samuel Mintz, *The Hunting of Leviathan* (Cambridge: Cambridge University Press, 1962).

political realm if he followed his professed method.[10] At the very least, he would need empirical assumptions or evidence about human motives, actions, and interactions to arrive at substantive and interesting conclusions about morals and politics.

In his discussions of method, however, Hobbes generally denigrates the obvious source of such assumptions and evidence—observation and experience. He does allow that we have observational knowledge of particular facts, and he honors with the title "prudence" the remembrance of such facts and the making of predictions about the future based on them. Furthermore, as Ian Hacking has noted,[11] Hobbes possesses the rudiments of a theory of probabilistic prediction. Occurrences that have in the past preceded or followed a given event Hobbes calls "signs" of that event, and he holds that the future appearances of the sign should produce expectation of the event in proportion to the degree of past conjunction of the two. But Hobbes denies observational knowledge the status of being scientific or philosophical because it does not jointly satisfy the criteria of universality and certainty.[12] Either it is knowledge of past events—which if certain is merely particular—or it is conjectural (i.e., probabilistic), rather than certain knowledge concerning the connection of events of various types. In addition, one's prudential knowledge is a function only of the amount and range of one's experience. It is not based on learned and demonstrable skills and expertise, as is science.[13]

Preferring the apparent certainty of the geometric method to probabilistic conjectures based on observation, Hobbes borrowed from burgeoning Galilean science an ontological first principle from which, in conjunction with clear definitions, he hoped to construct a complete deductive philosophical system. This is the

[10] In *The Anatomy of Leviathan*, McNeilly makes an imaginative and heroic attempt to reconstruct the argument of *Leviathan* in conformity with Hobbes's professed method. My reasons for thinking that this attempt fails are given in section 4-5.

[11] Ian Hacking, *The Emergence of Probability* (London: Cambridge University Press, 1975), p. 48.

[12] See McNeilly, *Anatomy of Leviathan*, pp. 48–51.

[13] *Leviathan*, chap. 5, pp. 35–37; chap. 8, p. 60.

principle of motion, according to which the universe is composed of matter in motion and all observable changes consist in changes in the motions of physical objects and their parts. By determining, in order, the patterns of motion of three progressively narrower classes of objects—bodies in general, human persons, and multiple human persons joined into a civil society—Hobbes aspired to construct a deductive science of physics, ethics, and politics.

This aspiration is unfortunately grounded in a mass of methodological confusions.[14] Most fundamentally, Hobbes fails to distinguish properly between logical and empirical relations.[15] Thus, for example, Hobbes's discussion of signs, noted above, contains the roots of a sensible Humean constant-conjunction analysis of causal relations among events. But Hobbes defines causation—the subject matter of science—as logical necessitation of the effect by its causes and correspondingly indicates that the test of whether a given set of accidents (properties) causes an effect is "whether the propounded effect *may be conceived to exist*, without the existence of any of those accidents."[16] This confusion between the logical and the empirical is carried over into Hobbes's views on mathematics. He indicates that geometry is the science of motion concerning figures[17] and that it consists in knowledge of the causes and effects of geometric figures. Thus, he mistakenly treats the defining property of a circle—being the set of points on a plane equidistant from a given point—as a proposition about how such a figure can be caused or generated by the process of rotating a body around a fixed point.[18]

It was only by conflating logical deduction and causal reasoning that Hobbes could have dreamed of a purely deductive politics derived solely from definitions and the principle of motion. But

---

[14] A detailed discussion of some of the confusions and inconsistencies in Hobbes's method may be found in McNeilly, *Anatomy of Leviathan*, part I.

[15] Many modern philosophers, following W. V. O. Quine, doubt that there is a hard-and-fast theory-independent distinction between empirical and logical truths. Hobbes, on the other hand, simply overlooks the distinction.

[16] *De corpore*, chap. 6, sec. 10, p. 77 (emphasis supplied). For definitions of "cause," see ibid., p. 77; chap. 9, sec. 3, pp. 121–22.

[17] *Leviathan*, chap. 9, p. 73.

[18] *De corpore*, chap. 1, sec. 5, p. 6.

he did construct an interesting moral and political theory, from whence we may infer that his actual method did not correspond to this geometric method. Hobbes concedes as much himself. In the preface to *Philosophical Rudiments*, he admits to grounding his arguments on "principles sufficiently known by experience."[19] But this is described as only a temporary measure forced on him by the need to inform his readers quickly concerning vital political issues at a time of incipient civil war. Later, in *Leviathan*, he comes closer to recognizing the necessity of relying on observational data, for while in the chapters on method he still endorses the geometric method, he indicates in the introduction that the psychological principles that ground political philosophy are known by introspection and can be demonstrated no other way.[20] As we shall see as we reconstruct Hobbes's arguments in the remainder of this book, even this statement about the role of empirical evidence in *Leviathan* is too limited. Hobbes actually relies on empirical data about other people's minds and bodies and about the natural environment, as well as on introspective data. Further, many of his arguments are most plausibly interpreted as probabilistic rather than purely deductive. So even in *Leviathan* there remains a significant gap between methodological theory and practice.

This gap, and the confusion that it engenders, is exemplified in the closing paragraph of chapter 20 of *Leviathan*. There, having just argued for unlimited sovereign power, Hobbes considers the objection that sovereigns have seldon been accorded such power in practice. He responds that few commonwealths have been free long from civil war and that in those which were, the sovereign's powers have not been disputed. These are empirical historical claims that, if true, would support the desirability of absolute sovereignty. Yet rather than backing the claims with evidence, Hobbes

---

[19] *Philosophical Rudiments*, p. xx.

[20] *Leviathan*, pp. xi–xii. It is interesting in this regard to compare Hobbes with Freud, who initially adopted the introspectionist method in psychology because he (correctly) believed that our biological knowledge of brain processes was too rudimentary to offer much insight into psychological processes.

goes on to suggest that historical data and generalizations based on them are really irrelevant to the matter at hand:

> But howsoever, an argument from the practice of men . . .
> is invalid. For though in all places of the world, men should
> lay the foundation of their houses on the sand, it could not
> thence be inferred, that so it ought to be. The skill of mak-
> ing, and maintaining commonwealths, consisteth in certain
> rules, as doth arithmetic and geometry; not, as tennis-play,
> on practice only.[21]

Here Hobbes pays continued lip service to using the geometric method in politics, at the cost of directly undermining a potentially significant argument that he has just presented.[22]

It may be concluded that in interpreting Hobbes's method we are well advised to look more at what he does than at what he says. Each argument should be scrutinized in its own right to see whether, where, and how it depends on empirical observations and probabilistic reasoning. Following this procedure, we will find some pure deductions from definitions, but in most important cases we will be dealing with arguments that do not conform to the geometric method. Before closing our discussion of Hobbes's method, though, we must consider whether that other cornerstone of his professed method—the principle of motion—has significant consequences within his ethics and politics.

It has been suggested that Hobbes's principle of motion, and the theory of human action which it inspires, have significant consequences within his moral and political philosophy.[23] This is in a sense true, for there are a few substantial conclusions about

---

[21] Ibid., chap. 20, pp. 195–96.

[22] We shall see in sections 4-4 and 5-5 that this argument, though empirically implausible, is essential to Hobbes's case for unlimited sovereignty.

[23] For a recent but moderate version of this thesis, see J. W. N. Watkins, *Hobbes's System of Ideas* 2d ed. (London: Hutchinson & Co.: 1973), pp. xiii, 13–14, 69, 83. See also Leslie Stevenson, *The Study of Human Nature* (New York: Oxford University Press, 1981), p. 86; George Croom Robertson, *Hobbes* (Edinburgh: William Blackwood and Sons, 1910; reprint, St. Clair Shores, Mich.: Scholarly Press, 1970), p. 216; and Marjorie Grene, "Hobbes and the Modern Mind," in *Anatomy of Knowledge*, ed. M. Greene (London: Routledge & Kegan Paul, 1969), p. 3.

human psychology that Hobbes appears to have drawn from the mechanistic features of his theory of action. Whatever role mechanism plays, however, it is a nonessential one, for the conclusions that Hobbes derives from mechanism, insofar as they are worth preserving, are easily supported by independent considerations. Hence, Hobbesian political theory need not be committed to materialism, mechanism, or even determinism; it can remain neutral with respect to these ontological and metaphysical positions.

The key to the dispensability of Hobbes's principle of motion lies in the theory of voluntary action presented in *Leviathan*, which in broad outline goes as follows.[24] Voluntary acts, as opposed to "vital motions" such as the coursing of the blood, are movements of the body preceded by thoughts of whether and how to move. This thinking, or deliberation, process, which precedes the act, consists of an alternation of desires for and aversions to an external object. Desires and aversions are two species of *endeavors*, infinitesimal beginnings of motion within the agent's body. The last endeavor which carries the day and blossoms forth into voluntary action is the will. Endeavors are caused by motions passed to the heart from the external object via the air and the agent's sensory and other organs (i.e., the nervous system). Whether sensory stimulation from an object produces desire or aversion is a function of the agent's past experience with objects of that kind.[25]

Inasmuch as it treats desires, the will, and deliberation as motions, or complexes thereof, this is a mechanistic theory, but it is a defective theory in several obvious respects. First, it covers only premeditated acts, leaving out of account habitual action and other cases of acting without thinking which cannot be classed with the autonomic bodily processes that Hobbes calls "vital motions." The theory is too narrow in another respect, for it characterizes desires and actions as aimed at physical objects, when in general

[24] *Leviathan*, chap. 6, pp. 38–42.

[25] In *Human Nature* (chap. 7, secs. 1-2, pp. 31–32), Hobbes says that sensory stimulations cause desires or aversions according to whether they help or hinder vital motion. However, McNeilly (*Anatomy of Leviathan*, pp. 106–17) argues convincingly that this is not part of the *Leviathan* theory of action.

11

their targets are states of affairs. Thus, when I desire to win a volleyball game, it is not a physical object that I want; and even when I desire a chocolate cupcake, I seek the occurrence of a certain state of affairs involving myself and it, typically my consuming it.[26] Hobbes's theory also fails to acknowledge that deliberation usually terminates in a *decision* to act, either now or at some future time.[27]

Finally, and most important, deliberation consists not of alternating desires and aversions to perform an act but of cumulative consideration of reasons for and against performing an act. Even if we identify, or assume a one-to-one correspondence between, reasons for (against) doing an act and desires (aversions) to do it, the above account leaves out the cumulative element. We do not simply forget previously canvassed reasons for doing something when we think of a reason not to do it. And unless the negative reason (by itself or in conjunction with previously considered negative reasons) in some sense outweighs the previously considered positive reasons, the agent will not assume an overall aversive posture toward the act upon discovery of the negative reason. During deliberation there may be, as Hobbes suggests, alternations in our attitude toward an action, but this will typically be a function of the shifting weight of all reasons so far considered as new ones are brought to bear, not a simple function of which reason has last entered the agent's mind.[28] This more plausible notion is probably what Hobbes meant to convey, using "desire" and "aversion" to mean something like "the current vector sum of endeavors toward and away from a state of affairs," the individual endeavors having been generated by successive consideration of different features of that state of affairs.

[26] In many cases, simply specifying the desirer and the object desired will not suffice to tell us what the desire is. If the cupcake is a prizewinner, e.g., I may desire to own it or to eat it, and to know what desire I have we must know which of these states of affairs I seek.

[27] The origin of this oversight apparently lies in Hobbes's insistence upon reading the word "deliberate" in parts. See *Leviathan*, chap. 6, p. 48.

[28] It might be that the most recently considered reasons tend to have disproportionate weight in determining our current action dispositions. But previously considered reasons surely have some weight, and time of consideration should play no role in the action selections of a purely rational agent.

If we modify (or reinterpret) Hobbes's theory of voluntary action to correct these apparent defects, what emerges is an account of premeditated actions that is not wholly implausible. A premeditated act, or bodily movement, is one preceded by thoughts of the nature of the state of affairs consisting of the movement and its consequences. Typically the agent will desire the occurrence of some aspects of the resulting state of affairs and be averse to other aspects of it. (The nature and strength of these desires and aversions will depend on the agent's past experience with like aspects of other states of affairs.) He will see the presence of these attractive or aversive features in the state of affairs as, respectively, reasons for and against performing the action.[29] His consideration of each reason will produce in him an endeavor, or infinitesimal increment of motion, to do or not do the act. As various reasons are considered, their corresponding endeavors add together to produce a *net endeavor*. If it is a motion that tends toward doing the action, it is a desire to do the act (and bring about the resulting state of affairs). If it is a motion that inhibits the performance of the act, it is an aversion to the act and its results. Depending upon the nature, strength, and order of the reasons considered and their corresponding endeavors, the agent's attitude toward doing the act may alternate between desire and aversion. The process of considering reasons pro and con and the corresponding changes in net endeavor (which may take the form of alternating desire and aversion) is called *deliberation*. When all the reasons for and against the act are considered, or when the agent perceives that further consideration cannot change the direction of his current net endeavor, deliberation ceases. The current net endeavor at the time is called the agent's *will* or *decision* and produces either the action (or its nonperformance, if the net endeavor is an aversion) or the intention to perform it at some future time.[30]

[29] Here and in the sequel, terms such as "he" and "man" are sometimes used in their generic sense to mean "he or she" and "man or woman." The substantive question as to whether Hobbes's theory applies equally to males and females is discussed in sections 2-1 and 3-6.

[30] Cf. *Human Nature*, chap. 12, sec. 9, p. 70, where Hobbes defines an intention as the last desire in an interrupted deliberation.

13

This is an incomplete theory of premeditated action. It ignores, for example, the fact that deliberation involves weighing the merits of alternative courses of action and taking account of different sets of possible consequences of each one. Yet, within its own limited domain, it both makes sense and preserves the fundamental relationships among the main concepts of Hobbes's account. And while it adds the psychological concept of a *reason* to Hobbes's story, this is compatible with Hobbes's generally materialistic stance. For one could simply identify reasons with (or reduce them to) the endeavors they correspond to, and these—as the theory stands—are simply motions within the agent's body. What is critical to note, though, and what the revised account makes clear, is that this identification of endeavors with motions does no real work in the theory. It does not, for example, explain how the direction of net endeavors is determined, for the idea of "summing" endeavors—in the absence of a specification of the underlying physical processes—is no less metaphorical than that of "weighing" reasons. Thus, if we interpret endeavors simply as dispositions to perform (or not perform) actions, as F. S. Mc-Neilly suggests,[31] we remove the mechanistic element while retaining whatever coherence and plausibility the repaired Hobbesian account possesses. Since such dispositions might conceivably be interpreted in a mentalist, functionalist, or physicalist manner, the account is ontologically neutral.

It does not yet follow that Hobbesian theory can do without mechanism, for while Hobbes's theory of premeditated action can survive the loss of its mechanistic elements, there might be conclusions that Hobbes derived from these elements which are worth retaining and are not independently supportable. In fact, however, this is not the case. There are two potentially significant psychological theses that Hobbes's clearly attempts to derive from his mechanism, and two others that certain commentators have suggested he did. Yet each of these, insofar as they are needed for Hobbesian moral and political theory, can be sufficiently grounded in other ways.

[31] McNeilly, *Anatomy of Leviathan*, p. 106.

Consider first Hobbes's assertion that "because the constitution of a man's body is in continual mutation, it is impossible that all the same things should always cause in him the same appetites, and aversions."[32] This is a significant claim, for Hobbes, since he views intrapersonal variation in desires over time as rendering lasting interpersonal agreement on what is desirable highly improbable in the absence of an enforced public standard. But must the notion of desire variation over time be supported in mechanistic terms? Hardly. It is made quite evident by our observations of people's speech and behavior. And if this alone does not satisfy us, we can throw in two plausible explanations of such variation that are not inherently mechanistic and that are suggested by Hobbes himself only two paragraphs earlier.[33] As biological creatures, we have certain physical drives that require satisfaction periodically but not continually, such as the appetite for food. Further, our desires are altered through our lives by learning, as experience teaches us more about the effects of various objects and actions. On the basis of these observations and explanations, we can reasonably assert intrapersonal desire variability without committing ourselves to mechanism.

According to Hobbes's theory of action, the inevitable effect of sensory stimulations interacting with an agent's vital motion (especially the activity of the heart) is the production of motions that are the beginnings of actions—endeavors. If this is so, from the presence of an environment providing sources of such stimulation and from the absence of any desires or aversions in the agent, one may infer the absence of vital motion in the agent, that is, one may infer the agent's death. Hobbes makes this inference, noting that "life itself is but motion, and can never be without desire,"[34] and he attempts to draw a further conclusion: that during life no state of tranquility is possible. Here he is taking issue with the Greek philosophers who imagined people finding perfect contentment in the contemplation of God or of Goodness. For Hobbes, no such perfect fulfillment is possible in

[32] *Leviathan*, chap. 6, pp. 40–41.
[33] Ibid., p. 40. See also McNeilly, *Anatomy of Leviathan*, p. 120.
[34] *Leviathan*, chap. 6, p. 51; see also chap. 8, p. 62; chap. 11, p. 85.

15

this life; the best that can be attained is the successive satisfaction of the unending series of desires one has as a living being—what he calls *felicity*.

There are two main questions to address here. Must the claim that living humans constantly possess unsatisfied desires rest on mechanistic premises? And does this claim support the further assertion that there can be no tranquility in human life? The first question may be firmly answered in the negative. Part of the explanation of our constantly possessing unsatisfied endeavors is biological. We have physical needs that must be satisfied periodically, rather than once and for all, and we have constant aversions to objects we believe may kill or injure us. Now if we view biology as a system of mechanistic explanations of the structure and behavior of living creatures, we might interpret this point as but a variation of Hobbes's mechanical theme. But two *intellectual* features, which Hobbes stresses that we possess, are at least as important in explaining our possession of unsatisfied desires.[35] We are forwardlooking, in the sense of caring about our future as well as our present well-being. Hence, we are sure to have desires concerning the future that cannot be satisfied until later. Also, humans, unlike other animals, are naturally curious creatures—and since there are an unlimited number of things to be discovered and learned, one's desire to know is never likely to be fully satisfied. So from certain general biological and psychological facts about human beings that Hobbes would not challenge, we can derive, without any appeal to mechanism, his conclusion about unsatisfied desires.

Does this conclusion imply that there is no tranquility in this life? This depends on what we take it to be. Three forms of tranquility may be distinguished. A person is in a state of *present tranquility* if and only if all that person's desires concerning the present are satisfied. *Future tranquility* requires, in addition, that the person now be confident that all his desires concerning later times will be satisfied at the appropriate later times. *Present-future*

[35] See ibid., chap. 3, pp. 13–14; chap. 11, p. 85; chap. 12, p. 95.

tranquility is a state in which all of one's desires concerning the present and future are satisfied now. Since present satisfaction of desires concerning future states of affairs is impossible, present-future tranquility is possible only if an agent has no desires concerning the future, in which case it coincides with present tranquility. Hobbes's mechanical theory of desire implies that a living person always has some future-directed desires, and hence that present-future tranquility is impossible.

But this is a weak and uninteresting conclusion that leads nowhere. For when Hobbes makes use of the "no tranquility" claim in his arguments about conflict in the state of nature, it is the version concerning future tranquility that he must, and does, rely on.[36] But this cannot be derived from his mechanism. Future tranquility is perfectly consistent with one desire (i.e., object-directed endeavor) succeeding another throughout an agent's life, as the mechanical theory of action postulates. So long as each new desire is satisfied at the appropriate time, and the agent confidently expects this to be the case, he can go through life in a state of constant future tranquility. Such tranquility is precluded, in fact, by scarcity of resources and competition from others,[37] not by people being bodies in motion.

In addition to the two psychological claims we have discussed, Hobbes may be viewed as basing a key *definition* on his mechanism. Specifically, Jean Hampton has suggested (in correspondence) that Hobbes's materialism and mechanism are essential to an understanding of his concept of liberty, which is developed in chapter 21 of *Leviathan*. In one sense, this is true, for both Hobbes's general definition of liberty as "absence of . . . external impediments of motion"[38] and his classic soft determinist stance in chapter 21 are clearly premised on and motivated by his materialist-mechanist metaphysics. However, as will be explained in section 7-3, it is Hobbes's more specific concept of *moral* or *political* liberty, thought of as absence of external impediments of

---

[36] See section 3-3.
[37] See sections 3-4 and 3-6.
[38] *Leviathan*, chap. 21, p. 196.

certain kinds (i.e., moral rules or laws[39]), which plays a significant role in Hobbes's moral and political theory, and this concept presupposes no mechanistic or materialist doctrines.

In three places, then, where Hobbes relies on the mechanistic elements of his theory of action, these elements turn out to be superfluous or unhelpful as regards the development of his moral and political theory. There are two other main theses—that people are purely selfish and that they will avoid death at any cost—which major commentators have suggested Hobbes derives from his mechanism.[40] Each of these theses will be discussed in some detail later.[41] Essentially the same conclusions are drawn about each thesis. (1) Hobbes's commitment to it is ambiguous. (2) The thesis is false and must be modified. (3) The modified version of the thesis suffices to support any moral and political conclusions worth retaining that are derived by Hobbes from the original thesis. On the assumption that these conclusions will prove to be accurate, we can proceed to construct a Hobbesian moral and political theory that is wholly independent of the mechanistic aspects of Hobbes's philosophy.

Having argued that Hobbes did not follow his professed geometric method and that his mechanism plays no essential role in his moral and political philosophy, should we conclude that Hobbes's philosophy in no way benefited from his interest in scientific method? Not really. The clarity of his reasoning, and the care he takes to formulate clear and consistent definitions of his central moral and political terms, are fruits of Hobbes's exposure to geometrical method. While his mechanism is not needed to support his main conclusions and line of argument, it may have inspired him to discover them. Further, there is one bit of scientific method that Hobbes borrowed from his contemporaries and used to good effect in his political philosophy.[42] This is the reso-

---

[39] See ibid., pp. 197–99, for Hobbes's (implicit) definition of this more specific variety of liberty.

[40] See Gauthier, *Logic of Leviathan*, p. 7, on selfishness; and Watkins, *Hobbes's System*, pp. 80–84, on death.

[41] In sections 2-1 through 2-5 and section 2-6, respectively.

[42] As is noted by a number of commentators. See, e.g., Watkins, *Hobbes's System*, pp. 32–34, 47–50.

lutive-compositive method, which involves understanding a system by breaking it down—in thought—into its basic constituent elements and imagining how these elements must be joined together to allow the system to operate properly. Hobbes, in his political theory, applied this method to nations. He imagined them decomposed into the human individuals that make them up and sought to discover the principles of interaction of such individuals. This led him to the theory of rational conflict and cooperation developed in Chapters 3 and 4 of this book. Hobbes's social contract theory represents the composition step in his political application of the resolutive-compositive method. Before making some preliminary remarks about that theory, we must explain a novel feature of the present approach to Hobbes's philosophy.

1-3. Our Problems and Plans

Leviathan contains two distinguishable theories woven together into what appears to be a single line of argument. There is a *descriptive* theory of human behavior, which identifies the primary motives and patterns of human action and interaction, and there is a *normative* theory of human behavior, which prescribes proper, or morally permissible, modes of action both within civil society and outside it. Departing from tradition, this book separates these two theories and treats them in succession. This facilitates identification and analysis of the fundamental relationships between the two and—within limits—allows for their separate evaluation.

The relationships of dependence between Hobbesian descriptive theory and normative theory run primarily, though not entirely, in one direction. While some features of Hobbesian descriptive theory are selected with normative applications in mind, this theory can plausibly stand on its own. But Hobbesian normative theory cannot. It is specifically designed to deal with, and ameliorate, the human situation as set out in the descriptive theory. Its problems, its limits, and its possibilities are constrained by what Hobbesian descriptive theory tells us about human motives and manners. We shall see, however, that these constraints may al-

19

low the Hobbesian theorist to maneuver around the fabled fact-value gap and construct a moral theory that has both normative and persuasive force.

Hobbesian descriptive theory comes first, then, and will be developed in Part I of this book. To avoid confusion, however, it should be noted at the outset that in two respects this theory is not purely descriptive. While it bases its fundamental principles of human motivation and conduct on observation, it often considers the interaction patterns of *ideally* rational individuals under *hypothetical* circumstances. Such abstraction and idealization allows for general and manageable analysis of interpersonal behavior in contexts thought to be of special practical or theoretical significance. Insofar as people do for the most part act rationally, it may provide considerable insight into how they would behave in the relevant circumstances. And if these circumstances resemble reality in important respects, or play an important role in a normative theory, such insight may be extremely valuable.

Before turning to descriptive theory, though, it will be useful to outline the central problems in ethics and political philosophy that Hobbes addresses from the perspective provided by that theory. This will allow us to reconstruct the theory with an eye to its eventual normative applications.

The attempt to clarify the relationship between moral requirements and the well-being, good, or self-interest of the individual agent has been perhaps the central undertaking of the Western tradition in moral philosophy. Hobbes devoted a good deal of attention to this issue. Offering a novel view of the requirements of both morality and prudence, he argues that the two are not really in conflict. (Here and in the sequel, the term "prudence" is used in its standard modern sense, rather than in the special sense defined by Hobbes and noted above in section 1-2.) Hobbes was not the first, or the last, philosopher to try to reconcile prudence and morality, but in recent times this project has fallen into disfavor, and it is apt to be regarded as a confused and hopeless enterprise. It shall be argued here that Hobbes's version of the project is more successful than modern skeptics might think and that a suitably modified version of it is even more promising.[43]

In a wider sense, Hobbes's moral philosophy may be viewed as an attempt to reconcile four types of potentially insistent demands upon the individual—those of prudence, morality, the State, and religion. The last-named area, religion, is largely ignored here because it plays little role in Hobbes's moral and political system[44] and because this book is an attempt to contribute to secular ethical theory. But the Hobbesian edifice which unites and reconciles the other three spheres deserves serious consideration.

In presenting his reconciliation of prudential, moral, political, and religious requirements, Hobbes had a very practical aim. He sought to persuade people to obey civil authorities rather than follow the deceptive callings of apparent gain, supposed conscience, or self-appointed spokesmen of God. This book's aim, by contrast, is theoretical. It seeks to promote understanding of some central problems in moral and political philosophy and certain solutions to them. Its only persuasive intent is to persuade readers that the interpretation of Hobbes's philosophy is a useful means to that end.

Just as the relationship between morality and prudence lies at the center of Western ethics, so the relationship between the individual and the State forms the core of Western political philosophy. In particular, questions about the existence, nature, ground, and limits of the individual's obligation to obey civil authorities have dominated political theory since Socrates' *Apology*. Hobbes's views on such issues concerning political obligation are generally and correctly[45] thought to be too conservative to withstand rational scrutiny, but his general method for dealing with political obligation—the construction of a social contract theory of a certain type—holds greater promise.

---

[43] See also my "The Reconciliation Project," in *Morality, Reason, and Truth*, ed. David Copp and David Zimmerman (Totowa, N.J.: Rowman & Allanheld, 1984), pp. 297–319.

[44] See section 9-3.

[45] See, however, section 6-4.

Social contract theory suggests that we view citizens' obligations to political authorities as grounded somehow in agreement. The nature of the grounding, and the content and consequences of the agreement, vary greatly from theorist to theorist. Like certain modern writers, for example, John Rawls,[46] Hobbes is essentially a *hypothetical* contract theorist. For him, the social contract is not an actual historical event, but a theoretical construct designed to facilitate our understanding of the grounds of political obedience.

The common logical form of hypothetical contract theories is represented by the following schema:

(1) If people were rational and in such-and-such circumstances,[47] they would choose or agree to social arrangements of a certain kind.

(2) Therefore, people actually living under social arrangements of that kind ought to obey the rules of these arrangements and the officials designated to enforce the rules.

Looking at this schema, it is apparent that a hypothetical contract theorist faces a number of distinct problems. Since (2) does not follow logically (or inductively) from (1), the theorist must somehow justify this inference in the context of the particular theory. That is, he must explain how the fact that one *would* agree to something under admittedly counterfactual circumstances can constitute a compelling moral reason for doing it. And insofar as the theory is supposed to have motivational as well as justificatory force, he must explain how one's acknowledgment of merely hypothetical consent should motivate one's obedience to the resulting arrangements. In addition, each theory must provide an interpretation of what the relevant "circumstances" and "arrangements" in (1) are, as well as an argument that those arrangements would be chosen in those circumstances.

Hobbes presents a hypothetical contract theory that solves all

[46] John Rawls, *A Theory of Justice* (Cambridge, Mass.: Harvard University Press, 1971).

[47] To simplify the schema, the set of alternatives selected from and the characteristics of the people (besides their rationality) are treated as aspects of the circumstances of choice.

these problems, save the last ones, reasonably well. He imagines rational and predominantly self-interested persons living in a situation of anarchy choosing among remaining in that situation, living under a government with limited or divided powers, or living under a government with unlimited and undivided powers. His arguments that people would favor unlimited government over limited government rest on faulty sociological-historical premises and therefore fail. But suppose we replace these premises with more plausible ones that are in accord with other principles of Hobbes's philosophy. Then we emerge with a Hobbesian hypothetical contract theory that justifies obedience to limited governments of certain sorts on grounds of common advantage and utility, motivates obedience to such governments on a prudential basis, uses circumstances of choice that are appropriate to the problem of political obligation, and argues plausibly that limited government of the indicated sort would be selected under the specified conditions. Such a theory is worth taking note of, especially since, as will emerge in due course, it plays a significant role in the Hobbesian strategy for reconciling morality and prudence.

Before embarking upon the presentation of Hobbesian moral and political philosophy, it will be useful to preview the topics to be covered and some of the general points to be made.

Our discussion of descriptive theory begins, in Chapter 2, with human nature. Some suggestions are offered about what a theory of human nature is, and the common idea that Hobbes's theory of human nature is simply Psychological Egoism is challenged on two grounds. First, other assumptions about human beings and their living conditions are of at least equal importance in Hobbes's argument. Second, Psychological Egoism is a false doctrine that Hobbes does not really need and to which his commitment is ambiguous. For the purposes of Hobbesian theory, Psychological Egoism is explicitly replaced by another view about human motivation called Predominant Egoism, which is milder and which accords well with common sense and scientific evidence.

In Chapters 3 and 4 of this book, with Predominant Egoism assumed as a premise, Hobbes's famous arguments against anarchy are reinterpreted and developed. It turns out that Hobbes's

23

arguments are more subtle and complex—and more spread out in the text of *Leviathan*—than is usually thought. We point out that the absence of reliable interpersonal cooperation is as important a negative feature of anarchy, for Hobbes and in fact, as is the presence of violent conflict.[48] Further, there are really two different, though related, complexes of arguments at work, one against individualistic anarchy, the other against anarchy among small groups. In the course of analyzing these various arguments, some of the relevant parts of elementary game theory are introduced and employed, for example, various versions of the game prisoner's dilemma. Also, a novel (and Hobbesian) principle of rational choice under uncertainty is offered, and a new way of looking at the differences between Hobbes and Locke on what life outside civil society would be like is suggested. In the end, Hobbes is credited with brilliantly perceiving the fundamental problem of social interaction—the potential divergence between individual and collective interests—and with having produced a strong argument against anarchy based on this perception.

Hobbes's solution to this fundamental problem, the creation of the absolute State, "that great LEVIATHAN . . . to which we owe . . . our peace and defence,"[49] is critically examined in Chapters 5 and 6. Hobbes properly analyzed the central functions of the State—to protect individuals from one another and to facilitate their mutually beneficial cooperation by promulgating and enforcing reasonable rules of interpersonal conduct. And, as indicated above, he presents a version of social contract theory that has the potential of being motivationally efficacious. When, however, this theory is revised by jettisoning some false empirical hypotheses about social stability and the interests of rulers and citizens, Hobbes's defense of absolutism collapses, and the remaining pieces of his theory point toward a more limited and more liberal State. Further, Hobbes's earlier arguments against anarchy spell trouble for the State, with regard to both its formation and its sustenance. How this is so is spelled out in a dis-

[48] Cf. my "Hobbes's War of All Against All," *Ethics* 73 (January 1983): 291–310, where this is not sufficiently noted.
[49] *Leviathan*, chap. 17, p. 158.

cussion of two opposed paradoxes concerning revolution under conditions of oppression. One, the paradox of perfect tyranny, says that under certain oppressive conditions revolution must occur; the other, the paradox of revolution, says that it cannot.[50] Neither conclusion is sustainable, but study of the two paradoxes helps determine how much of Hobbes's own theory of the State should be retained.

Part II of this book deals with normative theory. In Chapter 7 we explore Hobbes's analysis of key moral concepts, such as "rights" and "obligation," and his qualified endorsement of the "ought implies can" principle. This principle figures heavily in Hobbes's arguments concerning the right of self-defense. These arguments, which are discussed in Chapter 8, are insightful but in desperate need of repair. Sufficient modifications are made in them to allow the right of self-defense to stand as a partial foundation of Hobbesian moral theory.

It is argued, in Chapter 9, that this theory is best viewed as a rule-egoistic theory.[51] That is, it asserts that particular actions are to be justified by appeal to a specific set of rules (the laws of nature in Hobbes's system), while the rules themselves are justified because general adherence to them best promotes each agent's interests. This interpretation of Hobbes's ethics is supported by an analysis of the logical form of his laws of nature and the justification he provides for them.[52] Metaethical issues concerning the meaning of the concept of morality are sufficiently broached to support the claim that a rule-egoistic system of Hobbes's sort may properly be classified as a moral system. Further, close connections between Hobbes's rule egoism and certain plausible forms of rule utilitarianism are shown to exist.

Hobbes's rule-egoistic moral theory provides the moral foun-

---

[50] Further discussion of these paradoxes may be found, respectively, in my "Rule by Fear," *Nous* 17 (November 1983): 601–20; and "Two Solutions to the Paradox of Revolution," *Midwest Studies in Philosophy* 7 (1982): 455–72.

[51] This point was first suggested in print in Stanley Moore, "Hobbes on Obligation, Moral and Political," *Journal of the History of Philosophy* 9 (January 1971): 43–62; 10 (January 1972): 29–41.

[52] See also my "Right Reason and Natural Law in Hobbes's Ethics," *The Monist* 66 (January 1983): 120–33.

dation for his theory of the State and political obligation. The fundamental rule of this moral theory is to seek peace, and the Hobbesian analysis of anarchy implies that lasting peace requires the establishment of a commonwealth. Hence, in Chapter 10 we arrive at the normative side of Hobbesian social contract theory, in which the State that we should obey is identified with the sort that would emerge by agreement of rational and predominantly self-interested individuals seeking lasting peace. In addition to dealing with issues of motivation and justification mentioned above, this chapter develops a major insight of Hobbesian methodology—that while social contract theory is too weak to generate conceptions of the ideal or just society, it is strong enough to generate sufficient conditions of political obligation.

Hobbes holds that the individual's obligations to the State are limited only by the right of self-defense. He applies this claim, in complex and inconsistent ways, to persons charged with crimes, battlefield soldiers, prisoners of war, and revolutionaries. An attempt is made in Chapter 11 to correct Hobbes's errors on these questions and sketch a plausible Hobbesian view on the limits of political obligation. It will be suggested that certain of Hobbes's principles support a considerably narrower right of non-self-incrimination, and a broader right to revolt, than he explicitly allows.

The most serious apparent shortcoming of Hobbesian moral and political theory, its failure to deal with nonreciprocal obligations, is discussed at the start of the final chapter. Suggestions are offered as to how obligations of economic justice, both domestic and international, might plausibly be supported by Hobbesian appeals to long-range prudence. Obligations to future generations pose a tougher problem. But even here the Hobbesian has some points to offer, and it is noted that he can perhaps take solace in the manifest failure of other moral theories to adequately deal with this issue. Finally, some of the main insights of Hobbesian theory are summarized and significant differences between the viewpoint of this book and earlier interpretations of Hobbes, and social contract theory, are reviewed.

26

I

DESCRIPTIVE THEORY

T W O

HUMAN NATURE

2-1. Theories of Human Nature

Traditionally, Hobbes's theory of human nature has been identified with Psychological Egoism, the doctrine that all human action is selfishly motivated. It shall emerge in this chapter that
this identification is doubly erroneous—it overemphasizes the role
that Psychological Egoism plays in Hobbes's philosophy, and it
ignores the important role played by other claims about human
motives and capacities. Prior to developing this theme, however,
something must be said about what a theory of human nature is
supposed to be.

A theory of human nature is a *descriptive* theory that ascribes
certain general properties or features to human beings. Therefore, it may err by including features that people do not possess
(e.g., perfect wisdom and perfect benevolence) or by not taking
into account features that people do possess. But a theory of human nature need not include all features that most people possess—this would yield a long and relatively useless list. In fact,
the theory must select a certain subset of these features, but which
subset? An initial proposal is that as a theory of *human* nature it
must select properties that are possessed by all (or nearly all)[1]
human beings. The combination of features selected must be possessed by humans alone, or else we would have a theory of the
nature of a wider class of beings. Also, the properties in question
must be very difficult or impossible to alter by changing the natural or social environment, or else they cannot plausibly be at-

[1] Certain general categories of "abnormal" people might not be covered: the
severly retarded or handicapped, the permanently comatose, young children, etc.

29

tributed to our *natures*. In sum, a theory of human nature picks out those features that are unalterably possessed by (nearly) all human beings and are together possessed by them alone.

Following this proposal, we would search for Hobbes's theory of human nature among his remarks, scattered primarily in the early chapters of *Leviathan*, about how humans differ from the beasts, that is, other animals. Humans, according to Hobbes, possess the capacity for language—they assign names to ideas and combine these into propositions which they are capable of understanding and communicating.[2] As a result, humans are capable of discovering general truths and, less fortunately, of uttering absurdities.[3] People are also inherently curious; they desire to know the causes of various observed effects and the effects of observed causes.[4] This curiosity produces religion, the desire to know the ultimate cause of things.[5] Desires that go beyond the mere drives for sex, food, and rest are also unique to humanity, as is concern for one's future well-being.[6] Man is therefore the linguistic, curious, forwardlooking being, and all that flows from that. Note that each of these features involves, or presupposes, our possession of higher mental capacities. It is these that, at bottom, truly distinguish humans from the lower orders. Hence, Hobbes's account of people's peculiar features is both roughly on target and not far removed from the classical definition of man as rational animal.

We cannot, however, settle for this account of Hobbes's theory of human nature. Our initial proposal concerning what such a theory is must be modified. As it stands, for example, it allows us to identify human nature with "featherless bipedity," for these two features are universal, (relatively) unalterable properties of humans that are, in combination, peculiar to humans. Clearly this will not do. Our initial proposal has missed something. Among

---

[2] *Leviathan*, chap. 2, p. 11; chap. 3, p. 16; chap. 4, pp. 18, 28; chap. 5, p. 33.
[3] Ibid., chap. 5, p. 33.
[4] Ibid., chap. 3, pp. 13–14; chap. 5, p. 33; chap. 6, pp. 44–45; chap. 12, p. 94. See also *Human Nature*, chap. 9, sec. 18, pp. 50–51.
[5] *Leviathan*, chap. 12, pp. 94–96.
[6] Ibid., pp. 94–95; chap. 6, pp. 44–45.

(nearly) universal and unalterable properties of people, a theory of human nature selects only a group of *important* properties, where importance is determined relative to the uses to which the theory is to be put. Thus, a theory of human nature to be used to place humans in biological categories for purposes of medical research will appropriately focus on features that are different from those that a theory of human nature designed to ground a normative political philosophy will focus on. Further, the properties of such a theory are *interrelated*, in the sense of implying or supporting one another, or jointly implying or supporting useful corollaries or applications. As a result, theories of human nature can suffer from a variety of deficiencies: they may be too broad (encompass nonhumans), inaccurate (ascribe to humans properties that most of us do not have), disjointed (the features do not relate to one another), incomplete (important features are left out), or useless (for the further purposes we have in mind when we construct them).

Theories of human nature are often proposed with normative applications in mind. This is the case as regards Hobbes's theory. But modern readers impressed with the oft-drawn distinctions between facts and values, and is-statements and ought-statements, may wonder how a descriptive theory of human nature could possibly have normative implications. Later, in sections 7-1, 9-1, and 9-4, we will see how Hobbes deals with this problem in the context of his moral theory. For the moment it will suffice to demonstrate the potential relevance of descriptive theories of human nature to normative political theory, without trying to bridge the fact–value gap.

To begin, let us acknowledge that appeals to human nature are often used illegitimately to support questionable normative conclusions. For example, it is often said that we are heterosexual (or acquisitive, etc.) by nature, so we ought to encourage people to be heterosexual (or acquisitive, etc.) and to discourage them from being otherwise. This pattern of inference—"We are Z by nature, so we ought to encourage being Z"—may be called the Naturist Fallacy. That it is a fallacy can be seen by simply noting that if we were fully Z by nature, there would be no need to encourage being Z. But if we are less than fully Z, it does not follow that we should become more so, unless we assume that if we are (somewhat) Z by nature, it is good to be Z (and as much Z as possible). But this is absurd. Some have argued, for example, that humans are somewhat aggressive by nature.[7] Would anyone infer from this that we should be encouraged to be even more aggressive? Or, to take a Hobbesian example, if people tend to be somewhat shortsighted, does it follow that we should encourage and support this harmful trait? Surely not. We must therefore be suspicious of any argument from human nature having the form of the Naturist Fallacy.

But there are other, and better, arguments from human nature that lead to normative conclusions. The form of a typical valid argument of this sort is:

(1) Certain social conditions C are undesirable.

(2) People are X by nature.

(3) A group of people that are X will be in social conditions C, unless they live under social arrangements of kind Y.

(4) Therefore, other things being equal, social arrangements should be of kind Y.

An argument of this form starts from a normative premise concerning what sort of social conditions are undesirable. Thus, it does not attempt to deduce values from facts alone. But the value premise, (1), may be uncontroversial, in which case the descriptive theory of human nature expressed in (2) may play a critical role in deriving a possibly controversial normative political conclusion from an uncontroversial normative premise.

Note that there are a number of equally valid variants of this argument. We may, for example, replace (1) with a premise about *desirable* social conditions and correspondingly alter (3) so that arrangements Y are necessary for X-people to attain these conditions. Or by strengthening (1) so that conditions C are designated as "the *most* undesirable for people," we can remove the *ceteris paribus* clause from our conclusion (4). This last maneu-

---

[7] See Konrad Lorenz, *On Aggression*, trans. Marjorie Kerr Wilson (New York: Bantam Books, 1966), chap. 13.

ver yields the form of the fundamental argument of *Leviathan*. If we read "much violence and insecurity combined with low economic development" for C, and "unlimited and undivided power in the hands of a single individual or assembly" for Y, we obtain Hobbes's argument by plugging in, for X, the characteristics picked out by his operative theory of human nature.

There are six such characteristics, described below, three applying primarily to individuals and three describing relations among individuals. Only one, forwardlookingness, is from the above list of features that Hobbes took as distinguishing humans from other animals. All play a substantial role in Hobbes's arguments against anarchy, and several play a further role in other of his arguments. Our possession of each of these features, save Egoism, is so obvious from common sense and observation[8] that we are unlikely to view a theory based on them as powerful enough to generate interesting and controversial conclusions. But in Hobbes's hands they do just that. The six features are:

1. *Egoism.* Individuals are primarily concerned with their own well-being, and act accordingly.
2. *Death-aversion.* Individuals are strongly averse to their own death, and act accordingly.[9]
3. *Concern for Reputation.* Individuals care about their reputations, about what others think of them, and they act accordingly.[10]
4. *Forwardlookingness.* Individuals care about their future, as well as present, well-being, and act accordingly.[11]
5. *Conflicting Desires.* Satisfaction of one person's desires often interferes with, or precludes, satisfaction of another person's.[12] This may result from material scarcity, opposed claims to the same particular objects, incompatible ideals or values,

---

[8] No explicit derivation is offered for the ascription of any of the six features to people. This confirms our view, set out in section 1-2, about the role of observation in Hobbes's actual method. On a possible implicit (and fallacious) derivation of a form of egoism by Hobbes, see section 2-3.

[9] See discussion and references in section 2-6.

[10] *Leviathan*, chap. 13, p. 112.

[11] See esp. ibid., chap. 11, p. 85.

[12] Ibid., chap. 13, p. 111.

competing aspirations for domination or preeminence, and so on.

6. *Rough Equality*. People are fairly equal in their intellectual and bodily powers. They are equal enough, in any case, that each is vulnerable to death at the hands of others.[13]

Three of these elements of Hobbes's account of human nature require special treatment, both because of their importance for Hobbesian philosophy and because of ambiguities in Hobbes's own position concerning them. We close this section with a brief discussion of the Rough Equality assumption as applied to the two sexes. Then in the next several sections of this chapter we shall consider Egoism, turning to Death-aversion in the final section.

Does rough equality characterize the natural relationship between the sexes? Despite the greater average physical strength of men, it surely does. The ranges of both brain and brawn of members of the two sexes overlap considerably, with many men being weaker and/or less intelligent than many women. And any individual—man or woman—is vulnerable to death at the hands of members of either sex who may band together or take the individual by surprise. At one point, Hobbes acknowledges this rough equality of the sexes, observing that "there is not always that difference of strength, or prudence between the man and woman, as that the right [of dominion over their child] can be determined without war."[14] But he is apparently ambivalent about this, and when he comes to apply the assumption in his argument against anarchy, he sometimes speaks as if only men are roughly equal agents, who compete with one another over possessions, including women.[15] Hobbesian theory does not share this ambivalence. It endorses the applicability of the Rough Equality assumption to both sexes, while attending (in section 3-6) to the possibility that remaining differences between the sexes may affect the Hobbesian argument against anarchy.

[13] Ibid., p. 110. Also *Philosophical Rudiments*, chap. 1, sec. 3, pp. 6–7.
[14] *Leviathan*, chap. 20, p. 187.
[15] See ibid., chap. 13, p. 112. Hobbes's ambivalence about women's equality is noted in Susan Moller Okin, *Women in Western Political Thought* (Princeton: Princeton University Press, 1979), pp. 197–99.

2-2. Psychological Egoism

Ultimately, we wish to determine the degree of Hobbes's own commitment to Psychological Egoism and to evaluate the doctrine itself as a candidate for inclusion in Hobbesian theory. But before undertaking these tasks, we must define Psychological Egoism. This is by no means easy. It requires laying out several sets of distinctions and examining a number of different egoistic doctrines.

However, two features of Psychological Egoism emerge immediately from its most general characterization as the thesis that all human actions are motivated by self-interest. Psychological Egoism is a *descriptive* thesis about human psychology which is intended to be empirically informative. It is also a *universal* thesis, purporting to characterize the motives of all human agents on all occasions of action. From the conjunction of these two features, it follows that Psychological Egoism is potentially vulnerable to refutation by counterexample. Before examining its fate in this regard, let us further clarify its nature by considering two pseudo-egoistic doctrines that are too often confused with genuine Psychological Egoism.

Tautological Egoism[16] is the view that people always act to satisfy their own desires. This is a truism, without empirical content, if we interpret "desire" in a broad sense, so that it refers to whatever motivational feature within the agent produces the action. Tautological Egoism would be of little interest, save for the possibility of its grounding confused arguments for genuine Psychological Egoism. Thus, one might fallaciously slip from the true but tautological claim that all acts originate in desires of the self to the claim that all acts originate in selfish desires. This fallacy is tempting to beginning philosophy students, but not to them alone. Below we shall see that Hobbes himself may have fallen victim to a slightly subtler version of it.

Another doctrine, Causal Egoism, is pseudo-egoistic because it

---

[16] I borrow this term from Bernard Gert, Introduction to Thomas Hobbes, *Man and Citizen* (Garden City, N.Y.: Doubleday, 1972), p. 7.

concerns the origins, rather than the objects, of our desires. According to Causal Egoism, we desire (are averse to) states of affairs according to the amount of pleasure (or pain) that we have experienced in conjunction with similar states of affairs in the past. But whether a desire is self-interested or not depends upon the nature of the *object* of the desire, not on its causal etiology. For example, if Mother Teresa's genuine objective in helping poor people is to make them better off, then she is acting unselfishly even if her concern for the poor was caused by rewards she received as a child from her parents for being kind to others. Thus, Causal Egoism is logically compatible with some (or even all) of our desires being non-self-interested and hence is not a genuine form of Psychological Egoism.

The reason this is not always understood is that the story the causal egoist tells may lead us to suspect that what the seemingly altruistic agent really desires is not to help others but to receive another dose of the reward that he associates with helping others. This may be true in some cases, but it need not be, either logically or empirically. There are distinct logical criteria that allow us to pick out the real object of an agent's desire in a case of this kind, and these operate in such a way that the real object of desire need not coincide with the cause of that desire.

Two criteria of the real object of a desire might be used here. The weaker criterion is that of *hypothetical choice*. If an agent associates reward R with the satisfaction of a desire whose apparent object is O, the theoretical test of whether the real objective is O or R is which the agent *would* select if O and R were separated.[17] Suppose, for example, that I plan to buy life insurance so my family could financially weather my premature demise. My apparent objective here is the financial well-being of my family after my death, but a cynic might suggest that my real objective is obtaining the satisfying peace of mind I expect from (and associate with) knowing my family is thus protected. How, in principle, might we determine whether the cynic is correct? We can

---

[17] McNeilly would seem to agree. See his discussion of the patriot in *Anatomy of Leviathan*, p. 99.

imagine my being offered a choice between (1) my family's being protected but my not knowing it and thus not having peace of mind and (2) my family's not being protected while I peacefully and falsely think that they are. If in these circumstances I would choose (1), the well-being of my family is my real objective; if I would choose (2), I really desire peace of mind. Admittedly, the choice between (1) and (2) would be possible only if I believed at the time of choice that my memory of it would be quickly[18] and permanently altered afterward (e.g., by drugs or hypnosis), so that I would come to believe that my family was protected if and only if they were not. But this is conceivable and empirically possible. (Since the test is a hypothetical one, the empirical difficulties of instantiating the required choice situation do not matter.) Now there is no apparent logical or empirical reason for supposing that if Causal Egoism is true, these hypothetical choices must always come out as the cynic supposes. By using the hypothetical choice test of the real object of a desire, it becomes clear that Causal Egoism neither is a form of nor entails Psychological Egoism.

One might, however, impose a stricter test on the genuineness of an apparently altruistic desire.[19] Allowing that the hypothetical choices specified above might often result in the selection of the altruistic alternative, one might attribute this to the difficulty of breaking the psychological association between altruistic behavior and personal reward. Thus, if one chooses altruistically, it is because—in the face of contrary evidence—one retains the unconscious belief that one will be rewarded (e.g., with peace of mind) if and only if one acts altruistically (e.g., purchases the insurance). Since this belief is stronger than your contrary conscious belief, the selection of the apparently altruistic alternative does not yet reveal which is your real objective. On this view,

---

[18] If the belief-altering process follows the choice soon enough, the amount of guilty suffering I expect to endure in the interim if I make the selfish choice is not likely to be large enough to influence my choice substantially.

[19] See Michael Slote, "An Empirical Basis for Psychological Egoism," in *Egoism and Altruism*, ed. Ronald Milo (Belmont, Calif.: Wadsworth, 1973), pp. 100–107.

the altruistic desire can be presumed genuine only if it retains its motivating force after its association with the personal reward is broken. Hence, the test of its genuineness is whether it survives a sufficient number of extinction trials in which its satisfaction is not accompanied by the familiar personal rewards.

We should be reluctant to adopt this stricter test of genuineness for an apparently altruistic desire, for it is difficult to see how the test can be made plausible without positing, in the manner suggested above, the existence of a relevant unconscious belief.[20] And we should be cautious about attributing such beliefs. For present purposes, however, it suffices to note that even on this stricter test, Causal Egoism is compatible with the falsity of Psychological Egoism; it does not follow logically from our altruistic desires and aversions being initially caused by personal rewards and punishments that they are always extinguishable by the withdrawal of same. Further, some psychologists hold that there are in fact higher-order nonselfish desires which are nonextinguishable or "functionally autonomous."[21] So even if we adopt the stricter test of the object of an apparently nonegoistic desire, there remains a gap between Causal Egoism and genuine Psychological Egoism.

Turning to real varieties of egoism, we may begin by distinguishing between Maximizing and Nonmaximizing Egoism. According to Maximizing Egoism, of the acts available at a given time, a human agent will always perform the one which he expects will on balance best promote his long-run self-interest. One version of this doctrine pictures people as rational calculators who weigh the personal pros and cons of each prospective action and choose to perform the act promising the greatest personal good (or, in the case in which all the options are bad, the least personal evil). This version of egoism is quite implausible because the calculations it describes do not precede most, much less all, human acts. A weaker version of Maximizing Egoism claims that people

---

[20] Slote, in ibid., does not posit such beliefs, leaving, in my view, a gap in the defense of his test.

[21] See Gordon Allport, *Personality: A Psychological Interpretation* (New York: Henry Holt, 1937), chap. 7. Slote refers to Allport's discussion.

always act *as if* they had undertaken such calculations and followed their dictates. This view is unacceptable because it does not allow for the fact that human agents are sometimes carried away by strong particular desires like anger, greed, or lust and as a result perform clearly imprudent actions.

That people are weak of will, in this sense, can be accepted with equanimity by the nonmaximizing egoist. This theorist contends, simply, that the ultimate aim of every human action is to obtain some personal benefit for the agent.[22] Nonmaximizing Egoism is thus a doctrine about the nature of agents' reasons or motives for acting as they do, about what they are trying to accomplish or bring about through their actions. It is divorced from the claim that human agents are always rational calculators or maximizers and hence is more plausible than Maximizing Egoism.[23]

But our formulation of Nonmaximizing Egoism lays bare the central difficulty involved in defining Psychological Egoism. Which aims or ends of action count as "personal benefits" to the agent and which do not? What general principle or criterion enables us to distinguish between personal benefits or advantages and other possible goals of action? Answering these central questions in a way that is both consistent with common-sense views about self-interested desires and immune to devastating objections is a difficult task. A representative sample of the relevant difficulties emerges from consideration of the two most popular answers in the literature.

One could interpret "personal benefits" hedonistically as pleasure or the avoidance of pain. This leads us to Psychological Hedonism, a doctrine whose problems are legion. If we use "plea-

---

[22] The term "ultimate" is used to exclude the possibility that the end in question is desired only as a means to some further end or ends.

[23] Gary Watson has pointed out that the present analysis implies that the *brute*, the person who has no second-order desires but acts unreflectively on his strongest desire of the moment, is an egoist if his desires are all self-interested. Upon reflection, this turns out to be a strength, rather than a weakness, of our analysis, for though one paradigm of an egoist is the coldhearted calculator who deliberately puts his own interests ahead of those of others, this is not the only sort of egoist. Young children and most animals are egoists in much the same way as the brute, and a correct analysis will allow for this.

sure" as a catchall term for whatever state the agent aims at, we are back to a form of Tautological Egoism. If instead we think of pleasure as a certain kind of phenomenological sensation, it seems obvious that many of our desires and drives—even clearly self-interested ones such as the desires for power or reputation—are not for pleasure per se. Perhaps, as the causal egoist claims, the etiology of these desires is to be found in our past pleasure-pain reinforcement schedules, but as we have seen, this does not imply that pleasure is the real object of these desires. Furthermore, insofar as the point of hedonism is to reduce the objects of all our desires to a common item, termed "pleasure," there is an inherent tendency to treat its degrees or amounts as determinative of action. This produces a hedonistic form of Maximizing Egoism, which flies in the face of facts about weakness of will.

As an alternative to hedonism, we might define self-interested desires as those aimed at some state of, or essentially involving, the agent himself. In this vein, F. S. McNeilly characterizes egoistic desires as aimed at "bringing about some preferred state of himself,"[24] and Mark Overvold suggests that the agent must be "an essential constituent"[25] in the desired state of affairs. Interpreted as supplying necessary and sufficient conditions for a desire being self-interested, this proposal yields results that do not fit our firm pretheoretic views. It is at the same time too broad and too narrow—too broad because it would classify desires to be humiliated, tortured, or killed as self-interested desires if an agent ever preferred these things on other than instrumental grounds. But surely our concept of self-interest or personal benefit contains an objective component based on what people normally want and have reason to want, not simply on the particular agent's preferences. An agent's preferences play a considerable role in determining his interests and what benefits him, but if they diverge too drastically from the normal in certain directions, common sense would not allow them to be decisive. So the perverse desires mentioned above, though conceivably for a "preferred (by the agent) state

[24] McNeilly, *Anatomy of Leviathan*, p. 99.
[25] Mark Overvold, "Self-Interest and the Concept of Self-Sacrifice," *Canadian Journal of Philosophy* 10 (March 1980): 117n–118n.

of the agent," are aimed at personal *harm*, not benefit, and are not the sorts we want included in an egoistic theory of motives.

The present proposal is also too narrow. It excludes, for example, the desire for posthumous fame from the class of self-interested desires. This is clear from Overvold's spelling out of what it is for an agent to be an essential constituent of a state of affairs: "The proposition asserting that the agent exists at t is a logically necessary condition of the proposition asserting that the feature or outcome obtains at t."[26] Since one's existing (i.e., living) at time t would logically preclude one's being posthumously famous at t, an agent is not an essential constituent, in the relevant sense, of the state he desires when he desires posthumous fame. But surely the desire for posthumous fame is, or can be, a self-interested one.[27] Certainly, if its pursuit led to the neglect of one's duties to others, we would not hesitate to characterize it as selfish, which generally means self-interested and wrongfully detrimental to others.

A final problem with the proposed analysis of self-interested desire concerns relational states. Are these to be included as states of oneself? If not, as McNeilly's wording might suggest, we leave out many self-interested desires, for example, for power and dominance over others. Suppose, on the other hand, we do count relational states, as Overvold's above-quoted criterion implies we may. Then we encompass a whole new range of nonegoistic desires, for example, to be less well-off than others, within our category of self-interested desires. We may conclude that, all things considered, it is best to approach the problem of defining self-interested desires, or desires aimed at personal benefits, in another way.

Let us abandon the hope of providing a general criterion for separating self-interested desires from non–self-interested desires, and personal benefits from other ends of action. Instead, we may partially explicate the distinction by providing a list of the

---

[26] Ibid., p. 118n.

[27] At *Leviathan*, chap. 11, p. 87, Hobbes notes the existence of such desires, though his words may be read as suggesting that the agent's real object in such cases is the present pleasure of contemplating future fame.

sort of aims that count as personal benefits, and of the sort that do not, and by noting possibly relevant distinctions within the first list. This was roughly the strategy pursued by C. D. Broad,[28] and we will make use of some of his distinctions.

Starting from the negative side, it seems there are three sorts of aims that cannot be ultimate ends of action according to Psychological Egoism: harming the agent, doing what is morally right, and promoting the well-being of others. Acts having ultimate ends in these categories are non-self-interested because, respectively, they are self-destructive, morally motivated, or altruistic. Aims of action that do count as personal benefits, in the relevant sense, include the agent's pleasure, pain, wealth, power, security, liberty, glory, possession of particular objects, fame, health, longevity, status, self-respect, self-development, self-assertion, reputation, honor, and affection.[29] Other items might be added to this list, and there might be borderline candidates whose status with respect to inclusion is unclear. Putting this last worry aside, let us call desires having items on the list as their ultimate objects *self-directed*, and call the doctrine that all human desires are self-directed *Narrow Egoism*.

The claim that self-directed desires are self-interested, as that latter notion is normally understood, should be relatively non-controversial. But there is another whole class of desires whose status is more ambiguous. Suppose the ultimate object of an agent's desire is a state of someone or something besides himself but that this desire exists, or is as strong as it is, only because the agent stands in a certain preexisting relationship to that someone or something. For example, one wants a certain horse, child, amateur athlete, and professional athlete each to win (different) races. The explanation of this is that these four are, respectively, one's property, offspring, friend, and countryman. Such desires we call *self-relational*.[30] As Broad notes, they typically arise from rela-

---

[28] C. D. Broad, "Egoism as a Theory of Human Motives," in *Egoism and Altruism*, ed. Milo, pp. 88–100.

[29] Cf. ibid., pp. 89–90.

[30] Broad, ibid., p. 90, uses the term "egoistic motive stimulants." See also Andrew Oldenquist, "Loyalties," *Journal of Philosophy* 79 (April 1982): 173–93.

tionships of biological kinship, love or friendship, ownership, or common membership in an institution to which one feels committed. *Wide Egoism* (the temptation to say "Broad" Egoism shall be resisted) is the claim that all human desires are self-directed or self-relational.

Wide Egoism is Broad's favored interpretation of egoism. There are, however, four good reasons for preferring Narrow Egoism. First, genuine concern for others is usually taken as the hallmark of a nonegoistic view, it being assumed that a genuine egoist must explain away such concern, even for friends and family, in terms of narrowly self-interested motives such as display of power, hope for reciprocation, and so on.[31] Second, Narrow Egoism classifies desires solely by their *objects*; hence, via the hypothetical choice test it is, in principle, subject to empirical test and evaluation. Wide Egoism, on the other hand, invokes both objectual and causal criteria for classifying desires. This adds a level of complexity, and possible confusion, to the task of evaluating the veracity of Psychological Egoism. Third, the Wide interpretation of egoism gains some of its attraction from the misguided notion that our motivational stance must either be one of selfishness or one of impartiality with respect to the interests of all. This leads to the assimilation of favoritism toward our relations—a clear form of partiality—into the egoistic category. Once it is realized, however, that group loyalty and various forms of altruism of limited scope are possible and are distinguishable from both pure self-interest and universal altruism,[32] we may simply reject the assimilation and preserve the useful distinctions between different types of motivations. Fourth, and most important, Wide Egoism, interpreted literally, threatens to obliterate the basic distinction between altruistic and self-interested motivation. There are religious and humanistic people who love, or claim to love, all mankind because we are creatures of the same God or members of

---

[31] See, e.g., McNeilly's discussion, on p. 118 of *Anatomy of Leviathan*, of Hobbes's egoistic analysis of charity in *Human Nature*, chap. 9, sec. 17, pp. 49–50.

[32] See Oldenquist, "Loyalties," and, from a different perspective, Peter Singer, *The Expanding Circle* (New York: Farrar, Straus, & Giroux, 1981).

the same species. Acts motivated by such universal love are among the paradigms of altruistic, non-self-interested action. Yet the existence or strength of these altruistic desires seems to be causally dependent, at least in part, on the agents' perceptions that they stand in certain preexisting relations to those toward whose welfare these desires are directed. So, according to Wide Egoism, these desires turn out to be self-interested! There is no apparent way of avoiding this problem save by arbitrarily restricting the nature or scope of the relationships that may figure in the definition of self-relational desires. The better course is to reject Wide Egoism in favor of Narrow Egoism.

In the sequel, then, unless otherwise specified, Psychological Egoism shall mean Narrow Nonmaximizing Egoism,[33] that is, the doctrine that all human actions have as their ultimate objects items on our list (or a suitably expanded list) of personal benefits. Before discussing whether this doctrine is true or false, we must consider whether Hobbes was committed to it, or any other version of Psychological Egoism.

2-3. Was Hobbes a Psychological Egoist?

According to traditional interpretations, Psychological Egoism is one of the central elements of Hobbes's philosophy. It is derived from his mechanistic theory of human action and serves as a vital premise in Hobbes's famous arguments against anarchy, which ground his entire political theory. Recently, however, this interpretation has been challenged by Bernard Gert and by F. S. McNeilly, who contend that Hobbes, at least in *Leviathan*, did not endorse or use Psychological Egoism.[34] This challenge has

---

[33] And the terms "self-interested" and "self-directed" may be used interchangeably, as they could not be had we adopted Wide Egoism.

[34] Bernard Gert: Introduction to *Man and Citizen*; "Hobbes and Psychological Egoism," in *Hobbes's Leviathan: Interpretation and Criticism,* ed. Bernard Baumrin (Belmont, Calif.: Wadsworth, 1969), pp. 107–26; and "Hobbes, Mechanism, and Egoism," *Philosophical Quarterly* 15 (October 1965): 341–49. F. S. McNeilly: *Anatomy of Leviathan,* chaps. 5–6; and "Egoism in Hobbes," *Philosophical Quarterly* 16 (July 1966): 193–206. For our purposes, we need not attend to the differences between Gert's and McNeilly's views.

gained enough support to inspire one recent writer to refer to it as a "refutation" and to declare that the traditional interpretation "has rarely appeared in serious discussions of Hobbes's philosophy since."[35] In this section, we will assess to what degree, and in what respects, Gert's and McNeilly's interpretation of Hobbes as a nonegoist can be sustained.

One point is beyond dispute. In *Leviathan*, and elsewhere, there are numerous passages which contain either explicit assertions of Psychological Egoism or egoistic analyses of specific classes of actions. Some of these passages express Nonmaximizing Egoism, as when Hobbes writes, "Of all voluntary acts, the object is to every man his own good."[36] Other passages, such as the following discussion of punishment, suggest some form of Maximizing Egoism: "When men compare the benefit of their injustice, with the harm of their punishment, by necessity of nature they chuse that which appeareth best for themselves."[37] And some passages in the earlier works can be read as expressing either of these two forms of egoism.[38] No systematic pattern of development is discernible here; apparently Hobbes appeals to whichever version of egoism seems to best support the point he is trying to make at the time.

Gert is satisfied to dismiss such assertions by Hobbes as "a kind of rhetorical exaggeration."[39] McNeilly suggests more cautiously that these claims are carelessly transported into *Leviathan*—where they do not fit the general approach—from earlier, more egoistic works.[40] Neither, then, places much weight on

[35] Robert Fogelin, review of *Hume's Moral Theory*, by J. L. Mackie, *Journal of Philosophy* 79 (April 1982): 211n.

[36] *Leviathan*, chap. 15, p. 138; see also chap. 14, p. 120; chap. 25, p. 241. In *Philosophical Rudiments*, chap. 1, sec. 2, p. 5; chap. 1, sec. 10, p. 10; chap. 1, sec. 13, p. 12; chap. 2, sec. 8, p. 19; chap. 6, sec. 11, p. 78; chap. 9, sec. 3, p. 116. In *Elements of Law*, (*De corpore politico*) vol. 4, part 1, chap. 1, sec. 12, p. 85; chap. 3, sec. 6, pp. 98–99; chap. 4, sec. 8, p. 107.

[37] *Leviathan*, chap. 27, p. 281; see also chap. 4, p. 127. In *Philosophical Rudiments*, Epistle, p. xvi; chap. 6, sec. 4, p. 75; chap. 13, sec. 16, p. 180. In *Human Nature*, chap. 12, sec. 6, pp. 69–70.

[38] *Philosophical Rudiments*, chap. 1, sec. 7, p. 8. *Elements of Law*, part 1, sec. 6, p. 83; chap. 4, sec. 14, p. 109.

[39] Gert, Introduction to *Man and Citizen*, p. 7.

[40] McNeilly, *Anatomy of Leviathan*, pp. 128–129.

Hobbes's explicit assertions of egoism, preferring to take indirect counterevidence as overriding. Here they depart from a methodological principle of interpretation that Hobbes offers in *Human Nature*:

> When it happeneth that a man signifieth unto two *contradictory* opinions, whereof the *one* is *clearly* and directly *signified*, and the *other* either *drawn* from that by *consequence*, or not known to be contradictory to it; then, when he is not present to explicate himself better, we are to take the *former* for his opinion.[41]

Perhaps, however, Gert and McNeilly are wise to ignore Hobbes's methodological advice, since the reasons for rejecting a straightforward egoistic interpretation of *Leviathan* may be strong.

What are those reasons? First, certain definitions offered in *Leviathan* are less egoistic than their counterparts in earlier works. Second, Psychological Egoism is not implied by Hobbes's mechanistic theory of action, as the traditional interpretation of Hobbes's philosophy supposes. Third, and finally, Psychological Egoism does *no work* in Hobbes's moral and political theories; no significant conclusions are derived from, or presuppose, it. Let us consider each of these claims in turn.

In *Human Nature*, first circulated around 1640,[42] pity is defined as "*imagination* or *fiction* of *future* calamity to *ourselves*, proceeding from the sense of *another* man's calamity."[43] According to *Leviathan*, begun after 1647 and published in 1651, "Grief for the calamity of another, is PITY; and ariseth from the imagination that the like calamity may befall himself."[44] The former definition is, as both Gert and McNeilly note,[45] clearly more egoistic in that it defines pity as a form of concern for oneself, while the latter definition (correctly) characterizes pity as a form of concern

[41] *Human Nature*, chap. 13, sec. 9, pp. 75–76.
[42] See Robertson, *Hobbes*, p. 51. See also McNeilly, *Anatomy of Leviathan*, pp. 13–14, for dates of composition of *Leviathan* noted below in the text.
[43] *Human Nature*, chap. 9, sec. 10, p. 44.
[44] *Leviathan*, chap. 6, p. 47.
[45] Gert, "Hobbes and Psychological Egoism," p. 114; and McNeilly, *Anatomy of Leviathan*, pp. 118–19.

for another. Similar points can be made about the definitions in *Human Nature* and *Leviathan* of "benevolence" and "indignation."[46] We may accept this observation by Gert and McNeilly, but we should add that Hobbes's definitional changes over time are not always away from egoism. For example, while in *Elements of Law* a free gift is defined as a transfer of right "without consideration of reciprocal benefit,"[47] *Leviathan* characterizes it as a nonmutual transfer of right, in which the transferring party hopes "to gain thereby friendship, or service from another, or from his friends; or . . . the reputation of charity, or magnanimity; or to deliver his mind from pain of compassion; or in hope of reward in heaven."[48] Here we find the nonegoistic definition of an earlier work replaced in *Leviathan* by a straightforwardly egoistic definition.

Let us next consider the relationship between Hobbes's theory of action and Psychological Egoism. Both Gert and McNeilly suggest that only Tautological Egoism, a pseudo-egoistic doctrine, follows from Hobbes's theory of action.[49] Since by that theory each voluntary act is generated by the last endeavor in deliberation, the objective of the act is the object of a desire which the agent has. Unless the nature of the objects of desire is restricted (e.g., to personal benefits), this is only Tautological Egoism. Nor can we validly progress toward Psychological Egoism via Hobbes's subjectivist definition of good and evil, "Whatsoever is the object of any man's appetite or desire, that is it which he for his part calleth *good*: and the object of his hate and aversion *evil*,"[50] for this definition places no limitations on what states of affairs may be objects of desire or aversion.

It does, however, follow from this definition and Hobbes's theory of good that the agent would call the object of his action

[46] See Gert, "Hobbes and Psychological Egoism," pp. 113–15; and McNeilly, *Anatomy of Leviathan*, p. 118.

[47] *Elements of Law*, part 1, chap. 2, sec. 7, p. 89.

[48] *Leviathan*, chap. 14, p. 121.

[49] Gert, Introduction to *Man and Citizen*, pp. 6–7; and McNeilly, *Anatomy of Leviathan*, p. 117.

[50] *Leviathan*, chap. 6, p. 41. For further discussion of this definition, see section 7-2, below.

"good." While this conclusion is in no way egoistic, there are certain fairly natural ways of restating it which have both an innocent reading and an egoistic reading. For instance, one might say that a corollary of Hobbes's theory of action is that the object of every action is something good to the agent. Reading "something good to the agent" as "something regarded as good by the agent, something he would call 'good,'" we get the correct non-egoistic reading. But if we read "something good to the agent" as "some good for the agent, some personal benefit for him," we get Nonmaximizing Egoism. Hence, if one gets confused over the use of various idioms involving the concept of good, one might fallaciously conclude that Nonmaximizing Egoism is a corollary of Hobbes's theory of action and his analysis of good and evil.

Is there any reason to suppose that Hobbes may have been taken in by this fallacy? There are three such reasons. First, in making egoistic statements, Hobbes often makes use of ambiguous phrases such as "good to," "good unto," and "good for," which have both egoistic and nonegoistic readings.[51] Second, there is part of a sentence in *Philosophical Rudiments* in which Hobbes may commit the very fallacy in question: "Now because whatever a man would [do], it therefore seems good to him because he wills it, and either it really doth, or at least seems to him to contribute towards his preservation."[52] Here Hobbes reasons from the performance of the action, to the act of will, to the object seeming good to the agent, and then apparently commits the fallacy by reading "good to" egoistically as "promoting the agent's conservation."

Third, and finally, note that just as Nonmaximizing Egoism can be fallaciously "deduced" from Hobbes's stated theory of action, Maximizing Egoism can similarly be "deduced" from the modified Hobbesian account of action sketched in section 1-2. This account held action to be determined by the vector sum of the agent's desires and aversions, as Hobbes himself probably intended. If objects of desire and personal benefits for the agent are

[51] See, e.g., *Leviathan*, chap. 15, p. 138; *Elements of Law*, part 1, chap. 3, sec. 6, pp. 98–99; *Philosophical Rudiments*, chap. 1, sec. 13, p. 12.
[52] *Philosophical Rudiments*, chap. 1, sec. 10, p. 10.

confused, this account would seem to imply that agents act to maximize personal benefits (or minimize personal losses).

With this in mind, we can see how the hypothesis that Hobbes was himself confused about the implications of his theory of action can explain some puzzling facts about chapter 14 of *Leviathan*. There Hobbes uses Nonmaximizing and Maximizing forms of egoism to ground two distinct arguments for the inalienability of the right of self-defense.[53] The puzzle is that in each argument he simply asserts the egoistic premise without any pretense of supporting it. This suggests that he took these premises to have been established earlier or to be obvious corollaries of earlier conclusions. His first assertion of egoism in chapter 14 is virtually the first mention of voluntary action since chapter 6,[54] and this suggests that he was relying on his chapter 6 theory of voluntary action. Thus, the hypothesis that Hobbes mistakenly thought that Psychological Egoism followed from his theory of action could explain something otherwise perplexing—namely, why Hobbes felt free in chapter 14 to twice assert, and use, controversial versions of egoism without supporting them.

Admittedly, none of these three reasons for supposing Hobbes to be confused about the implications of his own theory of action is conclusive. That he mistakenly took Psychological Egoism to be a corollary of his theory of action is only a speculation, but there are sufficient grounds supporting this speculation to call into question the significance of Gert's and McNeilly's observation that egoism does not follow from Hobbes's theory of action. This observation, without evidence of Hobbes's recognition of it, tells us little about Hobbes's own stance with regard to Psychological Egoism.

There remains to be considered the most telling point raised by Gert and McNeilly: that Psychological Egoism is not used in, or needed for, Hobbes's moral and political theories.[55] This is

---

[53] See sections 8-2 and 8-3.

[54] *Leviathan*, chap. 14, p. 120. The only intervening mention of "voluntary action" I have found is in a combined assertion of egoism and forwardlookingness at ibid., chap. 11, p. 85.

[55] Gert, Introduction to *Man and Citizen*, p. 8; and McNeilly, *Anatomy of Leviathan*, pp. 150–54.

true as regards the centerpiece of Hobbes's theory which Mc-
Neilly and Gert focus on: the argument that people in the state
of nature are in a war of all against all. As will emerge in the
next two chapters, this pivotal argument rests on various elements of Hobbes's theory of human nature noted in section 2-1,
including a motivational assumption considerably weaker than
Psychological Egoism.[56] On the other hand, as McNeilly acknowledges, Psychological Egoism serves as a premise in Hobbes's
argument that the right of self-defense is inalienable.[57] Further,
McNeilly fails to note that there are two such arguments resting
on different versions of egoism. But the inalienability of the right
of self-defense grounds Hobbes's answer to the central political
question of the limits of government authority over the individual.[58] In view of this, we may be skeptical of claims that Psychological Egoism plays absolutely no role in Hobbes's political philosophy.

In summary, there is evidence on both sides of the question of
whether Hobbes is committed to Psychological Egoism in *Leviathan*. Gert and McNeilly are correct that some definitions are less
egoistic in *Leviathan* than in earlier works, that Psychological
Egoism is not validly derivable from Hobbes's theory of action,
and that Psychological Egoism is not a premise in Hobbes's *central* political arguments. The force of each of these points is
weakened, however, by other considerations. Some definitions are
more egoistic in *Leviathan* than in earlier works. There is some
reason to suspect that Hobbes may have (wrongly) believed Psychological Egoism to be a corollary of his theory of action. And
one significant, though not central, political doctrine of Hobbes—
the inalienability of the right of self-defense—does derive from
egoistic premises. In addition, there are the various explicit assertions of two versions of Psychological Egoism that can be found
in *Leviathan*.

What are we to conclude from all this? Gert's verdict about
Hobbes, "that the evidence *against* his holding psychological ego-

[56] On this assumption, see section 2-5.
[57] McNeilly, *Anatomy of Leviathan*, p. 127.
[58] See Chapter 11.

50

ism overwhelmingly outweighs the evidence for his holding it,"[59] seems too extreme. On the other hand, the points raised by Gert and McNeilly have sufficient force to undermine the traditional view of *Leviathan* as a work unambiguously committed to Psychological Egoism. To a large extent, how we pigeonhole *Leviathan* with respect to egoism is a function of the relative weight we place on different criteria of classification. If we put greatest weight on explicit statements, as the author of *Human Nature* suggests doing, we shall be more inclined to regard *Leviathan* as an egoistic work. If, instead, we focus on the dispensability of the doctrine with respect to the argument structure of the work, or the apparent trend in Hobbes's views over time, we shall more likely deny that *Leviathan* is egoistic. Having said this, and having noted what the considerations are on both sides of the question, it is difficult to see what further illumination might be gained by simply attaching an egoistic or nonegoistic label to *Leviathan*.

This does not mean that the whole controversy, and Gert's and McNeilly's raising of the issue, has been without value and importance. Their suggestion that Hobbes's commitment to egoism is at best tenuous and ambiguous, and their observation that Psychological Egoism plays at most a limited role in the argument structure of *Leviathan*, together have considerable significance, for they imply that a Hobbesian moral and political theory may not need to rely on Psychological Egoism, and would not be abandoning the core of Hobbes's philosophy if it did without this doctrine. This frees builders of Hobbesian theory to evaluate Psychological Egoism on its own merits and to discard or modify it if necessary. We turn now to this task of evaluation.

2-4. *Evaluating Egoism*

Bishop Joseph Butler, whose *Sermons* were published some seventy-five years after *Leviathan*, is often said to have decisively refuted Psychological Egoism.[60] Yet many of his arguments touch

---

[59] Gert, Introduction to *Man and Citizen*, p. 13.
[60] See, e.g., C. D. Broad, *Five Types of Ethical Theory* (London: Routledge & Kegan Paul, 1956), p. 55.

only pseudo-egoism or weaker forms of egoism and have no direct bearing on the truth of more plausible forms of the doctrine, such as Narrow Nonmaximizing Egoism.

Consider Butler's famous comment that we can, if we wish, apply the term "selfish" to all our motives, on the ground that they are all motives of the self. But, he continues, we would then have to invent new terminology to express the apparently useful distinction we now draw between selfish and nonselfish motives.[61] This observation exposes as illicit the tempting but confusing slide from Tautological Egoism into genuine egoism. Aside from removing this one possible illicit prop for egoism, however, it does not in any way imply that the doctrine, when properly understood, is false.

Butler's other main arguments against egoism rest on his identification of self-interest or happiness with the satisfaction of one's first-order desires for particular objects or states of affairs—what Butler calls "particular passions."[62] On his view, then, the desire for happiness or personal well-being is a regulative or second-order desire concerned with securing maximum possible fulfillment of one's particular passions. Within this framework, Butler argues on two grounds that people do not solely pursue self-interest. First, there is the phenomenon of weakness of will. People are often carried away by strong particular passions and act in ways they know to be detrimental to their interests. Second, people could not solely pursue self-interest and hope to succeed, for happiness or well-being requires the satisfaction of particular passions, getting the particular things one really wants for their own sake. Without particular aims to give content to one's interests, one's pursuit of happiness is empty, aimless, and necessarily unsuccessful. So to be happy, one must care about and aim at things

[61] Joseph Butler, *Sermons*, Preface and Sermon XI, in *Ethical Theories*, ed. A. I. Melden (Englewood Cliffs, N.J.: Prentice-Hall, 1967), pp. 238, 259–60.

[62] This view that each particular end is sought as part of one's happiness is close enough to Tautological Egoism to suggest a certain tension between Butler's various lines of criticism of Psychological Egoism.

other than one's own happiness. Modern philosophers sometimes call this second point the paradox of hedonism.[63]

The psychological egoist can readily accept much of the substance of these two arguments, however, without having any reason to abandon his position. The point about weakness of will shows only that Maximizing Egoism is false. Nonmaximizing Egoism is unaffected by it. The paradox of hedonism indicates at most that successful pursuit of self-interest presupposes having first-order desires. It says nothing about the content of these first-order desires. A person whose first-order desires were all on our list of self-directed (i.e., self-interested) desires could achieve happiness if enough of those desires were satisfied to a sufficient degree. So there is nothing necessarily self-stultifying, or pragmatically contradictory, about the stance of the purely self-interested individual. The practical attitude ascribed to all of us by the psychological egoist is a perfectly consistent one.

But is this ascription accurate? Are our desires, in fact, always of the sort that are on our list of self-directed desires? Butler's observations about Tautological Egoism, weakness of will, and the necessity of having particular passions do not begin to tell us. But common sense and experience do. These sources inform us, as they did Butler,[64] that people have non-self-interested desires (in particular, benevolent desires aimed at promoting the well-being of other individuals and groups) and that these desires motivate concrete actions. Such non-self-directed desires appear to be at work in actions varying from the routine (e.g., buying life insurance to protect one's family) to the heroic (e.g., sacrificing one's life to protect one's country). Psychological Egoism, as a *universal* doctrine, cannot acknowledge the existence of altruistic motivation in any of these cases. Its supporters must attempt to explain away the appearance of such motivation in every case.

In general, the tools available for use in such explanations are *sanctions*—internal and external, positive and negative. Accord-

[63] See, e.g., Joel Feinberg, "Psychological Egoism," in *Reason and Responsibility*, ed. Joel Feinberg, 4th ed. (Encino, Calif.: Dickenson, 1978), p. 533.
[64] See, e.g., Butler's Sermon I in *Ethical Theories*, ed. Melden, pp. 241–43.

ingly, it is claimed that the real aim of an altruistic act is to gain the pleasure of knowing one has helped someone, or to avoid the guilt one might feel for not having done so. Or one simply wants the approval and future help of others, rather than their disapproval or punishments, and hopes to win the former by acting "altruistically."

Now it must be admitted that such sanctions play a considerable role in the motivation of many apparently altruistic acts. Brutally honest introspection of one's own motivations, and careful probing of the motivations of others, generally reveal complex and mixed motivations for most significant actions that we undertake. Nor will it do to dismiss the explanatory role of the internal sanctions, as is sometimes done, on the grounds that one would not enjoy helping, or feel guilty for not doing so, unless one already desired to help for its own sake.[65] Pleasures for helping and guilt for not helping can be inculcated by training and may at some stage in moral development be initiating causes of a desire to help that did not previously exist. (Indeed, if this were not so, it is difficult to see how one could be taught altruism by punishment and reward, as the dominant theory of moral education—Social Learning Theory—suggests we are, in part.[66])

On the other hand, there are a significant number of actions, both routine and heroic, which cannot plausibly be understood as motivated solely by concern about sanctions. Either the degree of self-sacrifice is so great, or the behavioral evidence and testimony of the actor (whom we know from past experience to be honest) is so clear and consistent, that we must accept the presence, and decisive motivational role, of non-self-interested desires. Or perhaps the act is an altruistic one of our own and hence open to careful scrutiny of motives by introspection, without having to worry about deliberate deception on the part of the agent.

The psychological egoist, then, if honest, is forced to acknowledge that insofar as agents themselves can tell, some of their actions are motivated by non-self-interested desires. To cling to

[65] Feinberg, "Psychological Egoism," p. 532.
[66] See, e.g., Thomas E. Wren, "Social Learning Theory, Self-regulation, and Morality," in *Ethics* 92 (April 1982): 409–24, esp. p. 409.

egoism in the face of this admission, one must appeal to unconscious (or subconscious) self-interested motives (or to unconscious beliefs that appropriately hook up with conscious self-interested motives—for example, the belief that if I do not help, my dead grandmother will beat me severely). But there are serious difficulties here. If one's ground for asserting the existence of such motives or beliefs is that "they must be there, or else the agent would not have performed the action," one has confused the necessity of having some motivation with the necessity of having a self-interested motive, that is, one has fallen back into Tautological Egoism. Or if one posits the existence of such motives solely because they are needed to save Psychological Egoism, one is treating that doctrine as a dogma, rather than as a genuine empirical hypothesis subject to disconfirmation by evidence.

The respectable alternative for the psychological egoist is to link his view up to some psychological theory that involves unconscious or subconscious desires and is independently motivated and supported by evidence. There are two obvious candidate theories, each presenting its own special problems for the egoist. Freud's theory is partly nonegoistic, in its later form, in that it posits a death instinct as one of the primary human drives.[67] Also, its status as a testable empirical theory is subject to controversy.[68] On the other end of the psychological spectrum, Skinnerian behaviorism might serve as a vehicle for the egoist to ride on, if behavior-dispositions caused by past rewards and punishments were identified with subconscious beliefs concerning similar future rewards and punishments.[69] But such an identification is entirely foreign to the spirit of behaviorism. Further, Skinnerian behaviorism is probably too simplistic and too suspicious of innate structures to accurately capture the complexities of human

[67] However, many followers of Freud reject the death instinct. See Alan Rosenblatt and James Thickstein, *Modern Psychoanalytic Concepts in a General Psychology* (New York: International Universities Press, 1977), p. 55; and Frank Sulloway, *Freud: Biologist of the Mind* (New York: Basic Books, 1979), p. 393.

[68] See, e.g., the essays in *Psychoanalysis, Scientific Method and Philosophy*, ed. Sidney Hook (New York: New York University Press, 1959).

[69] See section 2-2.

learning and behavior. And finally, if learned desires can become autonomous, in the sense defined in section 2-2, a form of behaviorism could be true, while Psychological Egoism was not.

Psychological Egoism is rendered implausible, then, by common sense. But it is not refuted, since it could be seen as a corollary of certain revised versions of some psychological theories that still have their adherents and have not been proven false. Fortunately, however, we need not rely on common sense alone in rejecting Psychological Egoism and denying it a role in Hobbesian theory. There is confirmation from another source—the theory of sociobiology.

Sociobiology is a growing movement in biological and social science that seeks to use the theory of evolution to understand aspects of the social behavior of organisms. There is a great deal of controversy concerning the extent to which its concepts and findings may reasonably be applied to human behavior,[70] and there has been a tendency on the part of some of its more enthusiastic exponents to make serious errors in attempting to assess the ethical implications of the theory.[71] Nonetheless, we shall here cautiously apply its most central hypotheses to human beings, trying to avoid the errors of the enthusiasts and dealing with relevant objections as they arise.

According to the theory of evolution by natural selection, genes that produce physical structures or behaviors that promote an organism's chances of survival and reproduction will, on average, increase their representation in a species' gene pool from generation to generation, compared to genes that produce less advantageous (or detrimental) structures or behaviors. Hence, at first glance, the theory would seem to predict the elimination, over time, of genes leading to behaviors that risk the organism's life or use up its energy and resources while benefiting other organisms of the same species. Let us call such behaviors *altruistic in*

[70] See, e.g., the essays in *The Sociobiology Debate*, ed. Arthur Caplan (New York: Harper & Row, 1978); and *Sociobiology Examined*, ed. Ashley Montagu (New York: Oxford University Press, 1980).

[71] See, e.g., Singer's discussion of E. O. Wilson in Singer, *Expanding Circle*, chap. 3.

the behavioral sense, or *altruistic*$_B$. Then the prima facie lesson of the evolutionary approach to social behavior would be a form of Behavioral Egoism: altruism$_B$ does not exist.

But as common sense and observation of people call Psychological Egoism into question, observation of animals even more clearly undermines Behavioral Egoism. Animals frequently engage in altruism$_B$—they share hard-won food, defend co-specifics, utter warning calls that can focus predators' attention on themselves, and even evolve into castes of sterile workers who devote their lives and energies to raising and protecting other individuals' offspring rather than their own. The existence of such altruism$_B$, in apparent contradiction to the predictions of evolutionary theory, is the puzzle that spurred the development of sociobiology.[72]

One initially attractive solution to this puzzle appeals to group selection. Organisms often live and breed in groups, and altruism$_B$ helps other members of one's group to survive. As a result, in harsh environments, groups made up mainly of altruistic$_B$ individuals are more likely to survive, while other groups in the species go extinct. Thus, over time, genes that produce altruism$_B$ become fixed in the gene pool.

However, this solution is subject to a free-rider problem.[73] If there are any nonaltruistic$_B$ individuals in the largely altruistic$_B$ group, they will ride free on their fellows' efforts and will increase their relative numbers in the group from generation to generation. Since selection and extinction among groups proceeds on a slower scale than among individuals within a group, by the time the initially altruistic$_B$ groups are the only surviving groups, their members will largely be nonaltruists. Thus, group selection can operate effectively only in conditions that prevent nonaltruistic$_B$ genes from invading and taking over the gene pool of the originally altruistic$_B$ group (and that allow such an altruistic group to

[72] See Edward O. Wilson, *Sociobiology: The New Synthesis* (Cambridge, Mass.: Harvard University Press, 1975), p. 1; and Richard Dawkins, *The Selfish Gene* (New York: Oxford University Press, 1976), pp. 2, 4.

[73] Dawkins, *Selfish Gene,* pp. 8–9. See also George Williams, *Adaptation and Natural Selection* (Princeton: Princeton University Press, 1966), p. 113.

form in the first place).[74] The groups must be small, so that altruism_B can become fixed in some groups by random variation, and they must be isolated, so that free-riding nonaltruists_B do not often join altruist_B groups. Further, selection pressures must be severe, so that group selection does not proceed at a very much slower pace than individual selection, for otherwise even a low rate of migration into the altruist_B group would suffice to transform it into a nonaltruist_B group. Since these restrictive conditions are not often satisfied in nature, sociobiologists downplay the importance of group selection for explaining altruism_B.

Instead, they appeal primarily to two alternative phenomena: kin selection and reciprocal altruism.[75] To understand kin selection, consider first parental care for offspring. Since it involves investment and risk by parents, it fits our definition of altruism_B. But it is easy to see how this form of altruism_B can be preserved genetically. Tokens of a gene-type producing parental care will be better represented in future generations than tokens of a gene-type producing parental abandonment of offspring, provided the survival advantages gained from such care by the offspring offset the disadvantages (measured in terms of survival and future reproductive potential) suffered by the parent.

Looked at abstractly, as if from the point of view of the genes themselves,[76] parental care consists in genes of a certain type producing behaviors in one organism (i.e., the parent) that promote the survival of another organism that is likely to possess genes of the same type. But parents and children are not the only organisms possessing many of the same genes. Full brothers and sisters share, on average, the same percentage of genes as do par-

[74] On the conditions for group selection, see Williams, *Adaptation*, pp. 111–13; and J. Maynard Smith, "Group Selection," in *Readings in Sociobiology*, ed. T. H. Clutton-Brock and Paul Harvey (San Francisco: W. H. Freeman, 1978), pp. 20–31. For a mathematical treatment, see Scott Boorman and Paul Levitt, *The Genetics of Altruism* (New York: Academic Press, 1980), chaps. 10–11.

[75] The ground-breaking articles on these are, respectively, W. D. Hamilton, "The Evolution of Altruistic Behavior," *American Naturalist* 97 (September–October 1963): 354–56; and R. L. Trivers, "The Evolution of Reciprocal Altruism," *Quarterly Review of Biology* 46 (March 1971): 35–57. Both are reprinted in *Readings in Sociobiology*, ed. Clutton-Brock and Harvey.

[76] As in Dawkins, *Selfish Gene*.

ents and children (½), aunts and nieces share half as many genes (¼), first cousins half again as many (⅛), and so on for more distant relatives. Now, if the "loss to actor/gain to recipient" ratio for a kind of altruistic$_B$ act is smaller than the fraction of genes shared by the two, performance of the act in question will increase the expected number of copies in the next generation of the gene-type that produces the act. (To take a stock example, a gene that caused you to sacrifice your life to save nine cousins would fare better, on average, than one causing you to refrain from such a sacrifice.) So genes leading to altruism$_B$ toward relatives could survive natural selection, since cost-benefit ratios for altruistic$_B$ acts in the real (animal and human) world are often small enough to make altruism$_B$ toward fairly close relatives "pay" in terms of preserving one's genes over generations.

Reciprocal altruism consists in organisms helping, or cooperating with, one another—hunting together, sharing food, picking parasites off each other, and so on. It is a pattern of action consisting of acts of altruism$_B$ that are individually costly to the performing organism, with the costs likely to be more than repaid by later reciprocal action on the part of the recipient organism. Under these conditions, a gene that produces altruistic$_B$ behavior can survive and prosper in the gene pool—for different organisms carrying that gene help each other to mutual advantage. Note that "reciprocity" implies behavior that is responsive to past behavior of others. This is necessary to avoid a free-rider problem. If altruists$_B$ continued to help others who did not return their favors, the latter would prosper more than the former and would pass on *their* (free-rider–behavior-causing) genes in greater numbers to the next generation.[77] Such reciprocity, however, requires an ability to recognize other individuals of the same species, so that the organism is able to aid past reciprocators but not past free-riders. Such recognition capacities are generally characteristic of species thought to practice reciprocal altruism.[78]

Applying the concepts of reciprocal altruism and kin selection

[77] For a fuller analysis, see ibid., pp. 197–201.
[78] See Wilson, *Sociobiology*, p. 120; and Singer, *Expanding Circle*, p. 17.

to human beings hardly seems farfetched. Anthropologists tell us that reciprocity is a norm of behavior in virtually every human society,[79] and people everywhere are notoriously partial to their relatives, especially their close relatives. As Hobbes puts it, "Men are presumed to be more inclined by nature, to advance their own children, than the children of other men; . . . [and] it is always presumed that the nearer of kin, is the nearer in affection."[80]

We must, however, deal with three objections before we can even tentatively attribute the generation of human altruism to the mechanisms described by sociobiology. The first objection is that human altruism is learned, rather than governed by genes. In response to this, we may first acknowledge that there is an essential learning component in the etiology of altruistic feelings and behaviors in human individuals. But the universality of kin-favoritism and norms of reciprocity across cultures, taken in conjunction with the sociobiologists' evidence about kin selection and reciprocal altruism in other animals, suggests an underlying genetic component as well. Further, to the extent that we are altruistic$_B$ we can at least be sure that our genes do not prevent our learning altruism$_B$. This may seem to be a trivial observation, but in the face of our initial puzzle about altruism$_B$, it is not, for a gene, or combination of genes,[81] could conceivably inhibit or destroy our capacity to develop altruistic feelings in even the most favorable social environment. To explain why possession of such "altruism$_B$-inhibiting" genes did not spread throughout the gene pool, we might need to appeal to the concepts of kin selection and reciprocal altruism.[82] So even if social learning plays a key role in the development of altruism, there is an important sense in

[79] See Alvin Gouldner, "The Norm of Reciprocity," *American Sociological Review* 25 (April 1960): 161–78.

[80] *Leviathan*, chap. 19, p. 183.

[81] Critics of sociobiology point out that selection probably works on combinations of genes. The implications of this are unclear. See James King, "The Genetics of Sociobiology," in *Sociobiology Examined*, ed. Montagu; and Dawkins, *Selfish Gene*, pp. 37–42.

[82] The alternative would be to suppose that no such genes ever entered the gene pool or that they were eliminated by "bad luck" whenever they did.

which sociobiological concepts may help explain why we are altruistic.[83]

A second objection notes that the concept of behavioral altruism used in sociobiology is different from our ordinary concept of altruism, which characterizes an act as altruistic according to its motive or objective.[84] An act is altruistic in this latter sense, altruistic$_M$, if and only if its ultimate objective is to promote the well-being of another person or persons. Hence, sociobiological explanations of altruism$_B$ do not explain why we are sometimes altruistic$_M$.

There is no doubt that the classes of human acts that are altruistic$_B$ and altruistic$_M$ are distinct, though overlapping. Still, an explanation of altruism$_B$ can contribute to the explanation of altruism$_M$. No one supposes that genes *directly* cause altruistic$_B$ actions in humans or other animals. Genes act by producing proteins and influence animal behavior only through a complex series of biochemical and physiological processes. In humans, much behavior is, as Hobbes saw, premeditated action. Hence it is determined, or influenced, at the proximate level by individuals' motives and objectives. Altruistic$_M$ motivation tends systematically, as few other motives do, to produce altruistic$_B$ behavior that is initially costly to the actor. Therefore, there is a prima facie evolutionary puzzle about the existence of altruism$_M$, just as there is about the existence of altruism$_B$.[85] The concepts of kin selection and reciprocal altruism provide a solution to the former puzzle as well as to the latter. (However, they do not explain why altruism$_M$ is a primary proximate mechanism of altruism$_B$ in humans. This presumably has to do with general facts about the evolution of the nervous system and consciousness, and their relations to behavior.)

A third objection focuses on reciprocal altruism. It points out

[83] The now familiar subscript has been left off because, in talking of "feelings," we introduce another sense of "altruism." See the next paragraph in the text.

[84] This objection is suggested by a paragraph in Mary Midgley, *Beast and Man* (New York: New American Library, 1978), p. 117.

[85] Assuming that kinds of motives, or tendencies to develop them, are long-lasting enough in the human species to have selective pressures operate on them (indirectly through the behaviors they produce).

that an act undertaken in order to obtain beneficial reciprocation later is not altruistic$_M$, but self-interested. This seems to suggest that what the sociobiological concept of reciprocal altruism can explain in humans is a form of sophisticated egoism, not any form of altruism, but this objection, like the previous two, draws the wrong conclusion from a sound observation.

Whether an act is genuinely altruistic$_M$ depends on the agent's aim or objective in performing it. If the ultimate aim is beneficial reciprocation to the agent, the act is self-interested.[86] If, on the other hand, the agent seeks to promote the welfare of another for the other's sake, the act is altruistic$_M$. This would remain true even if the agent's possession of this aim is contingent upon certain relations holding between him and the other person. Thus, my concern for your welfare can be genuine and altruistic$_M$, even if it would cease if you betrayed me or stopped being friendly. As a result, I may feel and act genuinely altruistically$_M$ toward you, this being conditional upon your responding in certain ways. The "conditionality," however, is outside the scope of my concern for you: I care for you *so long as* you care for me, not *so that* you will care for me.

We may look at this distinction between two types of caring as paralleling two behavioral rules that our genes might conceivably make us tend to follow:

1. Help others, unless and until they fail to reciprocate.
2. Help others only if their past behavior gives you reason to expect that they will reciprocate.

The attitude corresponding to the first rule would be one of genuine altruism$_M$, while that corresponding to the second rule would be a form of sophisticated egoism. There is a key operational difference between the two rules. A population of individuals following rule 2 would never get started helping each other—in every dyadic interaction each party would wait for the other to make the first move. Individuals following rule 1, on the other hand, would easily get started on mutually beneficial cooperation, both

---

[86] This was our basis for treating the *Leviathan* definition of free gift (quoted in section 2-3 above) as egoistic.

among themselves and in interactions with followers of rule 2. Following rule 1 rather than rule 2 would thus, on theoretical grounds, seem to be more beneficial to the individual in question. There is some empirical confirmation of this as well. Robert Axelrod ran an experiment involving iterated plays of a game with a choice on each play between a cooperative and noncooperative move. With a variety of sophisticated players using all sorts of complex strategies, the most successful strategy (in terms of long-run overall payoffs when matched against every other strategy) turned out to be a simple strategy fitting the general pattern of rule 1.[87] All this suggests that if we are genetically predisposed toward reciprocally altruistic behavior, it is the sort corresponding to genuinely altruistic$_M$ motivations.

Might we deny that such altruism$_M$ is genuine on the grounds that it explains altruistic$_M$ feelings, at the genetic level, on the basis of self-interest? No, for several reasons. The evolutionary explanation is ultimately based on relative frequencies of genetypes in a species' gene pool and makes no real appeal to the self-interest of genes, whatever that might be.[88] Further, it is the *objects* of desires that determine their status as altruistic$_M$ or nonaltruistic$_M$, not their causes. The reciprocal altruism hypothesis of the sociobiologists explains how behavior-inducing desires aimed at the welfare of others might arise, without violating the precepts of evolutionary theory. This causal explanation no more undermines the status of those desires as altruistic$_M$ than does the competing causal explanation of the causal egoist.[89]

In the end then, we have uncovered no telling objection to cautiously applying the findings of sociobiology to human altru-

---

[87] Robert Axelrod, "Effective Choice in Prisoner's Dilemma," and "More Effective Choice in Prisoner's Dilemma," *Journal of Conflict Resolution* 24 (March and September 1980): 3–25, 379–403. On the importance of using a rule like 1 rather than like 2, see pp. 9–10, 389–90. The game "prisoner's dilemma" is discussed in Chapter 3 of this book.

[88] Unless we take Dawkins' selfish gene metaphor literally, as he himself has been accused of sometimes doing. See Mary Midgley, "Gene Juggling," in *Sociobiology Examined*, ed. Montagu, pp. 108–34.

[89] To transform this causal explanation into an egoistic analysis of the desire in question, we would have to ascribe to the apparent altruist the unconscious desire to maximize in the gene pool the number of genes of the same type as his own!

ism. When we do this, we find theoretical confirmation of our common-sense conclusion that Psychological Egoism should be rejected. Here, then, is our first major departure from Hobbes, whose view on this controversial doctrine was not, as we saw in section 2-3, one of clear rejection (or clear acceptance). In place of Psychological Egoism, we need a more plausible hypothesis about human nature upon which to build a Hobbesian theory.

2-5. Predominant Egoism

We indicated in section 2-1 that some sort of egoistic assumption about human motivation is needed to support Hobbes's arguments against anarchy, which must be a centerpiece of any Hobbesian political theory. But our discussion in section 2-4 has revealed that Psychological Egoism, interpreted as a universal empirical claim, is (to say the least) a highly dubious motivational assumption. What is needed, then, for Hobbesian theory, is an alternative assumption about self-interested motivation that is weak enough to ground Hobbes's antianarchist arguments. In this section, we will set out, and defend as plausible, such an alternative assumption. It is a much modified and qualified version of egoism that will be called *Predominant Egoism*.

In most general form, Predominant Egoism says that self-interested motives tend to take precedence over non-self-interested motives in determining human actions. That is, non-self-interested motives usually give way to self-interested motives when there is a conflict. As a result, we may say that human action in general is predominantly motivated by self-interest.

This idea can be spelled out more precisely as the conjunction of four propositions:
1. For most people in most situations, the "altruistic gain/personal loss" ratio needed to reliably motivate self-sacrificing action is *large*.[90]
2. The *number of people* for whom altruism and other non-self-

---

[90] Cf. Howard Margolis, *Selfishness, Altruism, and Rationality* (Chicago: University of Chicago Press, 1984), chap. 4.

64

interested motives normally override self-interested motives is *small*.

3. The *number of situations*, for the average person, in which non-self-interested motives override personal interest is *small*.

4. The *scope of altruistic motives* that are strong enough to normally override self-interest is, for most people, *small*, that is, confined to concern for family, close friends, close associates, or particular groups or public projects to which the individual is devoted.[91]

Proposition 1 recognizes that most people are sometimes willing to make genuine sacrifices to produce gains for others, but it contends that this occurs frequently only in cases in which the net sacrifices required are quite small, compared to the benefits produced.[92] Propositions 2–4 spell out the sense in which it is "usual" for self-interest to take precedence over other motives—it does so for most all people most always, except when the well-being of close associates or relations is involved.

Two further points are worth noting about the doctrine characterized by these four propositions. It does not deny that non-self-interested motives typically exist and have some weight in the deliberative process. In many cases, overall self-interest and altruism will agree in the course of action they recommend, and the latter will add an increment of motivational force. In other situations, altruistic concerns may break a tie, or near tie, between different self-interested motives pointing toward different courses of action. And even when overridden by self-interest, altruistic motives may inhibit or delay action, motivate a search for new alternatives that serve both selfish and altruistic ends of the agent, and so on. Second, the doctrine represented by these prop-

[91] The "situations" referred to in proposition 3 encompass those with the large gain-loss ratios of proposition 1. But the latter situations are among those meant to be excluded by the term "normally" used in propositions 2 and 4.

[92] Actually, proposition 1 is an oversimplification. Willingness to sacrifice is probably a complex function of cost-benefit ratio, absolute level of cost to the agent, and the specific nature of the benefits and costs. Large sacrifices may be quite infrequent even if the payoff ratio is large.

ositions does not make universal claims[93] and hence is not vulnerable to counterexample in the way Psychological Egoism is. Each of the four propositions allows for exceptional individuals and situations with respect to which the usual dominance of self-interested motives does not hold.

It will be convenient, in the sequel, to summarize the content of our four propositions with the formula "self-interest tends to be overriding." To define Predominant Egoism, we must weaken this formula by substantially restricting its potential scope. Predominant Egoism, then, is the doctrine that self-interest tends to be overriding in people's motivational structures (in the sense of the four propositions), at least until they have reached a stable and satisfactory level of well-being and security. Adding this restriction allows for the possibility that many, most, or even all people would be largely altruistic (or otherwise non-self-interested) if they were well-off enough in the present and expected to continue to be so in the future.

There are two sorts of reasons for writing this restriction into our definition of Predominant Egoism. We need nothing stronger to reconstruct Hobbes's arguments against anarchy, for these, as we shall see, concern how people would act in the absence of "sufficient security."[94] Further, there is some evidence that attainment of material and physical security does increase the tendency to engage in altruistic behavior. Economists have noted that altruistic and group-interest-promoting actions are what they call "superior goods," that is, those with higher incomes (who presumably are more secure) are willing to spend a higher percentage of their income on them.[95] And Abraham Maslow, in a much-noted theory that attempts to synthesize the viewpoints of

[93] But it fits the account of "egoism" as a feature of Hobbes's theory of human nature offered in section 2-1. That account was deliberately constructed with this in mind.

[94] *Leviathan*, chap. 15, p. 145.

[95] See Howard Margolis, "A New Model of Rational Choice," *Ethics* 91 (January 1981): 271, 274; and Russell Hardin, *Collective Action* (Baltimore: Johns Hopkins University Press), pp. 119–20. Note, however, that declining marginal utility of income might provide an alternative explanation of these patterns of behavior.

a number of schools of psychology, posits the existence of a hierarchy of needs such that the drive to satisfy needs at each level presupposes adequate satisfaction of lower-level needs. In his hierarchy, physiological and safety needs are at the foundation level, with social and affiliative needs coming after.[96] This implies a stronger tendency toward social, affiliative, and altruistic behavior among those whose basic material and security needs are satisfied.

Before turning to the question of evidence for Predominant Egoism, we must confront the objection that this doctrine is too vaguely defined to be supported, or refuted, by evidence. This charge might arise out of the observation that there are a number of imprecise terms involved in the definition, for example, "large," "small," "close associates," and "satisfactory level," but it is unconvincing for several reasons.

The doctrine is, in principle, falsifiable, since the evidence might conceivably show altruism to be so widespread as to violate the conditions of the doctrine on *any* reasonable specification of the vague terms. Now we might seem to render the doctrine more suitable for direct testing by plugging in precise mathematical values for "large," precise anthropological definitions for "close friends and associates," and so on. But choice of specific values and details of definition would be relatively arbitrary. Further, it would not really enhance our ability to assess the plausibility of Predominant Egoism, since, as we shall see, the available evidence we may draw on is itself a general and not mathematically precise kind. In view of the additional fact that the present "imprecise" definition will suffice for the purposes of Hobbesian theory, in retaining this definition we shall be following Aristotle's sound advice not to impose more precision on a subject than is suitable to it.[97]

---

[96] Abraham Maslow, *Motivation and Personality*, 2d ed. (New York: Harper & Row, 1970), chap. 4. See also Martin Hoffman, "Empathy, Role Taking, Guilt, and Development of Altruistic Motives," in *Moral Development and Behavior*, ed. Thomas Lickona (New York: Holt, Rinehart & Winston, 1976), pp. 124–43, esp. 126.

[97] Aristotle, *Nicomachean Ethics*, trans. Martin Ostwald (Indianapolis: Bobbs-Merrill, 1962), book I, chap. 3, p. 5.

In principle, Predominant Egoism must be defended against foes on each side: the psychological egoist[98] and those who hold that Predominant Egoism—while an improvement over Psychological Egoism—is still too pessimistic and cynical a view about human motivation. However, having already offered reasons for rejecting Psychological Egoism in section 2-4, our defense will focus on the kind of evidence which supports Predominant Egoism as against more optimistic portrayals of human nature. Some will undoubtedly find the very idea of defending Predominant Egoism morally repulsive, but there is considerable evidence that supports this doctrine. And while some might choose to disregard this evidence, or to interpret it more charitably, we follow the eighteenth-century theological utilitarian John Brown in holding that "with regard to human Nature, as well as Individuals, 'Flattery is a Crime no less than Slander.' "[99]

Predominant Egoism makes a claim about the motivational springs of most all human behavior. Hence, in principle, the findings of all disciplines dealing with human action are relevant sources of evidence. All that can be done here is to indicate the *kinds* of evidence that tend to support the doctrine and to urge others to consult also their own judgment and knowledge of human behavior in drawing conclusions. The evidence is divided into five categories: common sense, introspection, history and anthropology, explanation of social behavior, and sociobiology. This way of categorizing and presenting the evidence may not be the best way, but it allows us to note the different kinds of evidence that Hobbes himself appeals to in defending his pessimistic view of human motivation.

Common sense and ordinary observation of human actions lend initial credibility to Predominant Egoism. Part of our growing-up process involves learning to identify hidden motives of people's

---

[98] Our definition of Predominant Egoism would be logically compatible with Psychological Egoism if zero and infinity, respectively, were possible values for "small" and "large" in propositions 1–4. However, the definition is not to be read this way, but rather as asserting the existence of some altruistic acts.

[99] John Brown, *Essays on the Characteristics*, Essay II, sec. 7, reprinted in *A Guide to the British Moralists*, ed. D. H. Munro (London: Fontana, 1972), p. 116.

behavior—very often concealed self-interested motives. In the public realm, it is generally more reliable to rest our expectations of others' behavior on discernment of their interests than on hopes of their altruism. As Adam Smith put it, "It is not from the benevolence of the butcher, the brewer, or the baker, that we expect our dinner, but from their regard to their own interest."[100] Analysis of everyday social practices reveals an underlying presumption that people cannot be trusted to refrain from self-interested conduct that is harmful or unfair to others. What do we imply about our families, servants, and neighbors, Hobbes asks, when we lock up our valuables and travel armed on the highways?[101] Similar and additional distrustful practices pervade modern life—credit checks, surveillance cameras, tax audits, and so on. Even in the relatively benign halls of academia, we often find people locking up final-examination questions, reading cynically between the lines of administrative and departmental memos, and concealing their ideas and discoveries from colleagues. Hobbes would ask them to consider what they imply, in doing so, about the motives and character of their students, superiors, and colleagues.[102]

As observation of others' behavior may, over time, inform us about their motives, so may introspection inform us about our own motives. And if we assume, as seems reasonable, that we are not fundamentally different from others in motivation, we can make appropriate inferences about the predominant motives of our fellows. As Hobbes says, "Whosoever looketh into himself, and considereth what he doth, when he does *think, opine, reason, hope, fear,* &c. and upon what grounds; he shall thereby read and know, what are the thoughts and passions of all other men

---

[100] Adam Smith, *The Wealth of Nations* (Chicago: Henry Regnery, 1953), book I, chap. 2, p. 25.

[101] *Leviathan,* chap. 13, p. 114. *Philosophical Rudiments,* Preface, xv.

[102] These sorts of examples do not, however, prove that we believe most people are too selfish to be trusted most of the time. They imply only the weaker belief that enough people are too selfish to be trusted enough of the time to make distrust and protective measures worthwhile, given what we have to lose by misplaced trust. The pervasiveness of such practices does, however, suggest how widespread we take selfishness to be.

upon the like occasions."[103] Furthermore, if we take advantage of other people's introspective reports of their desires and motives offered in situations in which they have reason to be truthful, we may be able to make systematic generalizations about human motivation. This was the procedure followed by the greatest of the introspectionists, Sigmund Freud. He listened to the introspective reports of patients in therapeutic situations, in which the patients were (at least at the conscious level) highly motivated to be truthful, so as to obtain relief from their psychic disorders. His observations initially led him to a view of human motivation as fundamentally reducible to two sorts of self-interested drives or instincts—the self-preservative and the sexual.[104] Even if we are skeptical of some of the details of Freud's early theory, or question whether his patients were a representative sample of humanity, the fact that the introspective data from patients has led Freud and his followers to view certain self-interested drives as dominating the human motivational structure lends some credence to the predominant egoist's claims.

Introspective data and observations of people's behavior provide a degree of direct confirmation of Predominant Egoism by exhibiting instances of motivation that conform to that doctrine. A hypothesis like Predominant Egoism may also be *indirectly* confirmed if it enables us to explain phenomena that we cannot otherwise adequately explain. Hobbes provides a primitive prototype of such indirect confirmation in *Philosophical Rudiments*. He offers a hypothesis to explain both the general fact that people

[103] *Leviathan*, Introduction, p. xi. Hobbes is ambivalent about generalizing here. He cautions that we cannot know the "objects" of others' desires in this way, though we should take him to mean here the *particular* objects, rather than the general kinds of objects, such as power and glory.

[104] Sigmund Freud, "Instincts and Their Vicissitudes," in *General Psychological Theory* (1915; reprint, New York: Collier Books, 1963), pp. 83–103. Freud later merged these two categories and, as noted in section 2-4, introduced a "death instinct" to create a new duality. To the extent that one takes the death instinct seriously and ascribes considerable force to it, one weakens the support that Freudian introspective theory provides to Predominant Egoism. Note, however, that positing a strong death instinct does not imply that people are more altruistic than Predominant Egoism says, only that they are more self-destructive. Also, as indicated in note 67 of this chapter, many Freudians reject the death instinct.

seek one another's company and various specific facts about how they interact when in one another's company (e.g., each tries to outdo the others with stories concerning himself). Hobbes's hypothesis is the egoistic one that we seek society for gain or glory, which are forms of self-love.[105]

Hobbes's proposal is crude, but it exemplifies a pattern in modern social theory. People are postulated to be purely, or largely, self-interested, in all or a significant subset of their activities, and a theory of their interaction patterns in certain types of situations is constructed on the basis of this postulate. To the extent that these theories succeed in providing explanations of actual social behavior in such situations, the egoistic doctrines expressed in the postulates are indirectly confirmed.

Economics, the most systematic, developed, and successful of the social sciences, is notorious for assuming purely self-interested behavior on the part of individuals.[106] And even some economists who explicitly reject the pure egoism postulate tend to replace it with motivational assumptions along the general lines of Predominant Egoism.[107] Further, in recent years, there has been a trend toward constructing theories of noneconomic social behavior, using self-interest postulates. Thus, for example, Anthony Downs puts "rational behavior directed primarily toward selfish ends" as one of the axioms in his trailblazing economic theory of democracy.[108] Applying this axiom to the behavior of voters and office-seekers, Downs constructs a theory of democratic politics that contains plausible explanations of a variety of observed phenomena—for example, that in a two-party system the parties tend to converge on the center without becoming ideologically identical. Similarly, in his theory of bureaucracy Gordon Tullock starts from the assumption that "we can normally treat the individual [bureaucratic] politician *as if* he were behav-

---

[105] *Philosophical Rudiments*, chap. 1, sec. 2, pp. 3–5.

[106] See, e.g., Hardin, *Collective Action*, pp. xiv–xv.

[107] See, e.g., David Collard, *Altruism and Economy* (Oxford: Martin Robertson, 1978), p. 9; Serge-Christophe Kolm, "Altruism and Efficiency," *Ethics* 94 (October 1983): 18, 26; and Margolis, "New Model of Rational Choice."

[108] Anthony Downs, *An Economic Theory of Democracy* (New York: Harper & Row, 1957), p. 27.

ing out of selfish motives,"[109] and he proceeds to explain such things as why bureaucracies tend to be conservative, nonresponsive to clients' needs, and inclined to coverup their members' mistakes. The success of these various social theories in explaining observed social phenomena provides considerable indirect support for Predominant Egoism as a theory of human motives.

Various direct and indirect evidence about the motives and behavior of ourselves and our fellows may render Predominant Egoism plausible, but to accept it as a reasonable account of human motivation, we must have reason to believe that we and our fellows are not idiosyncratic in our motivational patterns. If we are to accept Predominant Egoism, we must have reason to believe that it applies not just in contemporary urban, industrialized societies, but in other times and places as well. Therefore, the disciplines of history and anthropology are relevant to the assessment of Predominant Egoism. Hobbes was aware of this. His first published work was an English translation of Thucydides' *History of the Peloponnesian War*.[110] The view of human nature expressed there stresses the motives of "fear, greed, and ambition" while treating "considerations of justice . . . [as] at best, pretexts."[111] In Thucydides, Hobbes probably found historical confirmation of his own pessimistic view of human motivation, or was encouraged to form such a view if he had not already.[112]

Hobbes even indulges in some amateur (and inaccurate) anthropology. Having argued (using an egoistic premise, among others[113]) that without government people would be in a war of all against all, in which life is "solitary, poor, nasty, brutish, and short,"[114] he observes:

---

[109] Gordon Tullock, *The Politics of Bureaucracy* (Washington, D.C.: Public Affairs Press, 1965), pp. 29–30.

[110] Hobbes, "The History of the Grecian War Written by Thucydides," vols. 8–9.

[111] P. A. Brunt, Introduction to Thucydides, *The Peloponnesian Wars*, trans. Benjamin Jowett (New York: Washington Square Press, 1963), pp. xxix–xxx.

[112] See *Hobbes's Thucydides*, ed. Richard Schlatter (New Brunswick, N.J.: Rutgers University Press, 1975), Introduction, pp. xviii–xxiii.

[113] See sections 2-1 and 3-3 through 3-6.

[114] *Leviathan*, chap. 13, p. 113.

It may peradventure be thought, there was never such a . . . condition of war as this; . . . but there are many places, where they live so now. For the savage people in many places of America, except the government of small families, . . . have no government at all; and live at this day in that brutish manner, as I said before.[115]

The writings of modern anthropological observers, based on their experiences living in underdeveloped communities, are more reliable than these second- or third-hand reports about American Indian life which Hobbes offers. But some of them definitely echo our Hobbesian theme: predominantly egoistic motivations are characteristic of human beings, they are not a mere artifact of advanced industrial cultures. Consider two examples. Edward Banfield studied an extremely poor Southern Italian village in the 1950s and concluded that the continued poverty and backwardness of the town was primarily attributable to the inhabitants' "amoral familism."[116] This term is used by Banfield to describe behavior in accordance with the rule "Maximize the material, short-run advantage of the nuclear family; assume that all others will do likewise."[117] The conformity of Banfield's observations with the claims of the predominant egoist is obvious.

A more notorious example is Colin Turnbull's description of life of the Ik, former wandering hunter-gatherers who were forced by drought and new political boundaries to adopt a farmer-gatherer mode of life in an extremely hostile climate.[118] The Ik, according to Turnbull, who lived among them for eighteen months, are openly and utterly selfish. They lie, cheat, and steal from each other and laugh at each other's misfortunes. They do not share food with others; in fact, they would feel outrage at someone who shared food with starving kin. The tribal structure and

[115] Ibid., p. 114.
[116] Edward C. Banfield, *The Moral Basis of a Backward Society* (Chicago: The Free Press, 1958), esp., pp. 10, 85–127.
[117] Ibid., p. 85.
[118] Colin Turnbull, *The Mountain People* (New York: Simon & Schuster, 1972); and "Rethinking the Ik: A Functional Non-social System," in *Extinction and Survival in Human Populations*, ed. Charles Laughlin, Jr., and Ivan Brady (New York: Columbia University Press, 1978), pp. 49–75.

family structure have broken down. The old are left to die help-lessly, without aid from their children or others. Children are abandoned by their mothers at the age of three and live together in food-gathering packs until they are adolescents. Even hus-bands and wives do not cooperate much, or share food, or act affectionately toward each other.

The case of the Ik is admittedly an extreme one, but it is suggestive of how the predominance of self-interest in people's motivational structures can make itself manifest in those circum-stances in which self-interested and moral modes of behavior are consistently nonoverlapping. In addition, it provides further evi-dence that predominantly egoistic motivation and behavior is not an idiosyncrasy of advanced industrial cultures.

However, to feel satisfied enough with Predominant Egoism to use it as a foundational principle of Hobbesian theory, we need more than scattered observational confirmation of its general ap-plicability. We need some general theoretical reason for suppos-ing that it applies to human beings in all societies. Fortunately, such a reason is already available in the findings (and specula-tions) of the sociobiologists, as discussed in section 2-4.[119] By way of the mechanisms of kin selection and reciprocal altruism, sociobiology provides an evolutionary explanation of the origins of altruism, but this explanation suggests that, as proposed by Predominant Egoism, the strength and scope of altruism will be restricted. Kin selection directly explains significant altruism toward close kin only, and reciprocal altruism is likely to be directed pri-marily toward close associates or others who may be in a position to reciprocate when this is needed. This fits well with proposition 4 in our above characterization of Predominant Egoism. Further, the logic of both concepts implies, in line with proposition 1 of that characterization, that individuals are considerably less con-

[119] Sociobiology is one source of evidence that Hobbes did not consider. How-ever, he does feel called upon to discuss and explain the cooperative sociality of bees, one of the social insects (*Leviathan*, chap. 17, pp. 156–57). As we have seen, sociobiology derives much of its central impetus from the need to explain such sociality, and the social insects provide some of the critical evidence for its main claims.

cerned about the welfare of others than about their own welfare. In the case of kin selection, this is due to the nonperfect genetic overlap among relatives, and in the case of reciprocal altruism to the uncertainty of reciprocation. Finally, since natural selection depends on survival and reproduction rates rather than on quality-of-life considerations, there is no real tension between sociobiological accounts of the foundations of altruism and our restriction which allows for greater altruism once sufficient security is achieved by the individual in question.

We thus find support for Predominant Egoism from a variety of sources: common sense, ordinary observation of others' behavior, introspection and introspective psychology, economics and politics, history and anthropology, and sociobiology. No one of these sources is alone sufficient to establish the correctness of Predominant Egoism, but taken together they appear to render the doctrine plausible and probable enough to allow its inclusion in Hobbesian theory.

Yet to be considered, however, is the most significant objection to Predominant Egoism. This is *not* the claim that humans are predominantly altruistic (or otherwise non-self-interested) by nature. Rather, it is that they are extremely motivationally plastic by nature, with their degree of altruism being (almost) entirely determined by the social environment in which they are raised and with there being no significant upper limit on this degree of altruism. The most interesting form of this objection, the Marxist version, is the one that will be dealt with here. According to that version, the observational data cited above do provide an accurate picture of the egoistic orientation of human behavior in *certain societies*. In societies dominated by the institution of private property, especially capitalist societies, human actions are motivated by individual self-interest. Theories of social, economic, and political interactions that start from egoistic assumptions will be able to correctly describe and predict much about behavior in these societies.[120] But if raised in a different sort of

---

[120] See, e.g., C. B. Macpherson, *The Political Theory of Possessive Individualism* (Oxford: Clarendon Press, 1962); and Marshall Sahlins, *The Use and Abuse of Biology* (Ann Arbor: University of Michigan Press, 1976), chap. 4.

social environment—one emphasizing sharing of resources, promoting common interests, fraternal solidarity, cooperation, and other socialist values—people would not have predominantly self-interested motivational structures.[121]

This line of objection is important and widespread enough to take seriously, but for several reasons it does not pose a successful challenge to Predominant Egoism.

If the objection were correct we would expect not to find self-interested motives dominating life in socialist countries, but evidence suggests that this expectation is not borne out.[122] It is well known that socialist governments that have tried to remove private gain as the primary motive of economic activity have often been forced, by subsequent production failures, to reverse themselves. Thus, for example, we read reports of an official of the People's Republic of China who has "unorthodox ideas about tempering Chinese socialism with competition, material incentives and other forms of capitalism" and who is being appointed to a very high position because "his whatever works philosophy has produced results."[123] Perhaps the most successful modern experiment in replacing the profit motive has been in Cuba, where, in theory, workers are being taught to work for the common or public good. In a book "written without an ideological axe to grind,"[124] Robert Bernardo describes the actual operations of the Cuban system in these terms:

Although material rewards are still given, rewards are now moral titles which bestow public praise and social status on its recipients. Workers are urged to compete for and earn moral prizes in exchange for work. In place of the old market system of responding to a scale of differential prices for labor, workers are taught to respond mainly to a scale of

[121] Kai Nielsen, "Impediments to Radical Egalitarianism," *American Philosophical Quarterly* 18 (April 1981): 123.

[122] As is conceded, in effect, by Nielsen, ibid., p. 128.

[123] Linda Mathews, "Zhao—How He Bounced Back," *Los Angeles Times*, September 8, 1980, part 1, p. 4. See also Thomas Pyle, "Bringing Management to China," *Princeton Alumni Weekly*, February 23 and March 9, 1981, p. 59.

[124] Irving L. Horowitz, Introduction to Robert N. Bernardo, *The Theory of Moral Incentives in Cuba* (University, Ala.: University of Alabama Press, 1971), p. xviii.

moral titles or prizes of different social ranks. The greater is the worker's effort and improvement of his skills, the higher is the social grade of the prize he receives. Moral prizes are given also in exchange for direct voluntary and overtime labor.[125]

If this description is accurate, we have not, in Cuba, had a system of altruistic or public-spirited motivation replacing private rewards. Instead, what we have had is a system in which one of the private rewards emphasized by Hobbes in *Philosophical Rudiments*—gain—is largely replaced by the other—glory, here in the form of public praise, status, honors, and titles.

Defenders of the objection under consideration may acknowledge that socialist countries have not yet eradicated or contained egoistic motives among their citizens, but they may contend that citizen egoism is a carryover from the capitalist past and/or is a result of socialist governments having to use capitalist motivational techniques in the short run to develop their countries and to protect them against capitalist competition, aggression, and interference.[126] This may conceivably be true, even if it has the appearance of an excuse or an ad hoc explanation. But its mere possibility or conceivability poses no real threat to Predominant Egoism. If the objector wishes us to believe that predominantly egoistic motivation and behavior is an artifact of capitalist (or private property) systems, he must provide evidence of its absence elsewhere. To concede its presence but to attribute this to alleged factors that distort socialist society does not succeed in rebutting the positive descriptive evidence for Predominant Egoism. In effect, the objector who adopts this line is like a defense attorney who concedes that both prosecution and defense witnesses confirm the State's charges against the accused but rests the defense on the unsubstantiated claim that defense witnesses have been unduly influenced by the prosecution.

One way, then, of answering the Marxist objection to Predominant Egoism is to suggest that the burden of proof is on its sup-

---

[125] Bernardo, *Moral Incentives*, p. 58.
[126] A suggestion along these lines is made by Nielsen, "Impediments," p. 128.

porters to answer the prima facie observational evidence that confirms this doctrine. And this burden has not been discharged. But there is an alternative approach to dealing with this objection. We may point out that Predominant Egoism is really compatible with much of what the Marxist says, so there is less direct conflict between the two than might appear.

There are two points to notice here. First, Predominant Egoism allows that people may no longer be predominantly self-interested once they have reached a state of sufficient safety, well-being, and security. But such a secure condition is, according to traditional Marxism, what awaits us in a fully developed communist society.[127] In fact, it is because this condition of society requires sufficient productivity to provide for everyone's material needs that Marx regards capitalism as a necessary stage on the road to communism.[128] But it is only in a fully developed communist society that the new community-oriented altruistic individual is supposed to emerge; until then, people are largely motivated by private interests or shared class interests. So standard Marxist doctrine asserts the predominance of non-self-interested motivation only in a social state in which Predominant Egoism allows for it.

Second, remember that we intend to employ Predominant Egoism as one element in a Hobbesian theory of human nature. In section 2-1, we said that such a theory is to focus on "unalterable" properties of human nature, but what counts as unalterable depends on context. Even genetically based properties are theoretically alterable by evolution or genetic engineering. On the other hand, features of human nature that are determined by the cultural or social environment may appropriately be treated as "unalterable" if that environment cannot be changed at all or cannot be changed without excessive or disproportionate cost. History has not yet shown that a transition to a socialist system

[127] Karl Marx, "Critique of the Gotha Programme," in *Karl Marx: Selected Writings*, ed. David McLellan (Oxford: Oxford University Press, 1977), pp. 564–70. See also Nielsen, "Impediments," p. 123.

[128] See, e.g., G. A. Cohen, *Karl Marx's Theory of History: A Defence* (Princeton: Princeton University Press, 1978), chap. 7, esp. pp. 201–2.

peopled by predominant altruists can be accomplished. And, as we shall see in section 6-4, there are reasons within Hobbesian theory to question the general rationality and desirability of attempts at effectuating such changes by revolution, which is the necessary means of doing so according to traditional Marxist theory. So even if we acknowledged—for the sake of argument—the Marxist objector's main point that degrees of altruism are a function of social environment, it would not follow that Predominant Egoism is an inappropriate assumption to use in political theory, for it seems to be descriptive of human motivation in current social environments and in those that appear to be feasibly attainable. The fact that this assumption need not apply in some ideal socialist utopia is irrelevant, if there is "no way to get there from here" or no way whose costs do not exceed the benefits that would thereby be obtained.

At this point, it is worth noting in passing another objection to Predominant Egoism. Because that doctrine admits that some individuals are not predominantly self-interested, someone might suggest that this shows that predominant altruism is possible and that we could, or would, *all* be predominant altruists if we were raised the way those individuals were raised. However, even if we set aside the possibility of relevant genetic differences between individuals, there is a fallacy of composition lurking behind this suggestion, for it may well be that the kind of social environment that produces predominant altruism is one that cannot be provided for everyone. Suppose, for example, that growing up altruistically depends on consistent training, parental security and confidence, sufficient parental attention and care to foster a continual sense of well-being during one's early years, generally altruistic behavior by parents, and so on. Society may simply lack the resources to provide this to everyone. There is not enough money to make all families secure, there are not enough knowledgeable, emotionally stable, and altruistic parents to consistently provide the right sort of modeling and direction, and so forth. The upshot is a repetition of a point noted above: even if we concede that the social environment determines the degree to which people are self-interested, it does not follow that most peoples' predominant egoism is readily (or even ultimately) alterable or eliminable.

Some may not be satisfied with these responses to the Marxist objection to Predominant Egoism. Others will regard degrees of altruism as purely environmentally determined, on different grounds than those offered by Marxists. Yet others will interpret the observational evidence about human motivation quite differently from the way we have and will on that basis reject Predominant Egoism. To those who for these or other reasons decline to accept Predominant Egoism, a final alternative may be offered: Treat the arguments and conclusions that follow as conditional or hypothetical. Regard them as having the form "If people were (or are) predominantly egoistic, then. . . ." This will allow you to follow the reasoning of, and discern the structure and content of, Hobbesian moral and political theory. The only difference will be in the lessons drawn. You will see, through your relatively rose-colored glasses, the implications of what you take to be an erroneous pessimism. Hobbesians, by contrast, will see a system of plausible moral and political hypotheses emerging from a realistic portrayal of human nature.

2-6. Death-Avoidance

One particular self-interested endeavor plays a special role in Hobbes's philosophy: the aversion to death. That people have a very strong aversion to death (or alternately a very strong desire to preserve their lives) is a vital premise or presupposition of Hobbes's arguments about anarchy and the State, his account of moral rights and moral principles, and virtually every other main thesis of his moral and political philosophy. Before proceeding to consider these arguments and theses in later chapters, it will be useful to clarify two aspects of Hobbes's views about the human inclination to avoid death.

First, there is the question of whether prople always regard death as the greatest of all worldly evils. J. W. N. Watkins asserts that Hobbes holds this position, and there are passages in *Elements of Laws* and *Philosophical Rudiments* where Hobbes does indicate that death is regarded as the greatest of natural evils.[129] Further, Hobbes says in *A Dialogue of the Common Laws* that one who commits suicide is to be presumed insane. On the other hand, Hobbes refers twice in *Philosophical Rudiments* to fates people regard as worse than death: suffering slander and living "infamous and hated of all the world."[130] As for killing oneself, the *Dialogue* passage describes the suicidal person as distracted "by some inward Torment or Apprehension somewhat worse than Death."[131] And in *De homine*, Hobbes writes, "Though death is the greatest of all evils . . . , the pains of life can be so great that, unless their quick end is foreseen, they may lead men to number death among the goods."[132] This passage suggests that Hobbes's real view is that death is worse than any other *single* evil (according to ordinary schemes of individuating evils), but will not exceed all *combinations* of other evils. In any case, the evidence against Watkins' interpretation is strong; Hobbes is simply unclear and inconsistent on the matter. We are therefore free, in reconstructing his arguments, to adopt the more realistic view of peoples' attitudes toward death: that death is nearly universally shunned as a very great, but not necessarily the greatest possible, worldly evil.

A second issue concerning our aversion to death is whether this aversion is intrinsic or extrinsic. That is, do we avoid death because of its own nature or because of other evils that generally or inevitably accompany it? The correct answer seems to be "both." We, like other animals, have a natural fear of death itself programmed into us by natural selection and manifested in "fight or flight" behavior when confronted by imminent danger.[133] But as reasoning, goal-directed beings, we also have a rational, or extrinsic, fear of death as something which typically involves great

[129] Watkins, *Hobbes's System*, pp. 80–83. *Elements of Law*, part 1, chap. 1, sec. 6, p. 83; *Philosophical Rudiments*, chap. 1, sec. 7, p. 8.
[130] *Philosophical Rudiments*, chap. 3, sec. 12, p. 38; chap. 6, sec. 13, pp. 82–83.
[131] *A Dialogue Between a Philosopher and a Student of the Common Laws of England*, vol. 6, pp. 88–89.
[132] *De homine*, chap. 11, sec. 6, in Hobbes, *Man and Citizen*, pp. 48–49.
[133] See *Philosophical Rudiments*, chap. 2, sec. 18, p. 25.

suffering and leaves many of our hopes, plans, and goals unful-
filled. Thus, in his fullest explanation of why we fear death, Hobbes
describes death as, "the terrible enemy of nature, . . . from whom
we expect both the loss of all power [i.e., means to accomplish
our ends], and also the greatest of bodily pains in the losing."[134]

It is vitally important to recognize the *rational* element in
Hobbes's account of death-avoidance, for this makes clear that
self-preservation solely for its own sake, that is, mere survival, is
not the guiding value of Hobbes's philosophy. Survival is prized
as well as a prerequisite of the attainment of other human goods.
Thus, Hobbes's view of the importance of survival does not commit him to ignoring quality-of-life considerations in favor of mere
longevity. Further, as we shall see in the three chapters immediately following, it is the rational fear of death that plays a critical role in Hobbes's political philosophy. This fear is the source
of both the greatest threat to humankind—the war of all against
all—and its greatest hope, the commonwealth, "that great LEVI-
ATHAN . . . to which we owe . . . our peace and defence."[135]

[134] *Elements of Law*, chap. 1, sec. 6, p. 83. Note that while the fear of the pains
accompanying death is a rational fear, in our sense, there is a close connection
here to the natural fear of death: pain presumably evolved as a signal to avoid
stimuli and situations that threaten death or injury.
[135] *Leviathan*, chap. 17, p. 158.

T H R E E

CONFLICT IN THE STATE
OF NATURE

3-1. The Structure of the Argument

In the preface to *Philosophical Rudiments*, Hobbes describes his application of the resolutive-compositive method to the State:

> For as in a watch, or some such small engine, the matter, figure, and motion of the wheels cannot well be known, except it be taken insunder and viewed in parts; so to make a more curious search into the rights of states and duties of subjects, it is necessary, I say, not to take them insunder, but yet that they be so considered as if they were dissolved, that is, that we rightly understand what the quality of human nature is, . . . and how men must be agreed among themselves that intend to grow up into a well-grounded state.[1]

Hobbes's plan is to break the commonwealth up into its constituent elements, human individuals, and examine the operations and interactions of these elements in the absence of the commonwealth, that is, in the state of nature.[2] The primary purpose of doing this is to determine what the proper *function* of the State is, what undesirable conditions or features of the state of nature it serves to ameliorate. This, in turn, can provide guidance for improving existing States, by indicating what purposes they should be serving and by providing a contrasting model of a situation

---

[1] *Philosophical Rudiments*, preface, p. xiv.

[2] Hobbes uses the term "state of nature" in *Philosophical Rudiments*, while in *Leviathan* he uses "condition of mere nature" or "natural condition." We shall employ the former term.

83

(the state of nature) in which these purposes are not being served. In addition, to the extent that existing States are carrying out the proper function of States, we thereby provide a potential *justification* for them and legitimize some of the powers exercised by their officials.[3] However, this last purpose of Hobbes's state-of-nature theory is purely normative and will not directly concern us until the second part of this book.

Hobbes's theory of life in the state of nature is idealized in two senses. It is essentially a *hypothetical* theory concerning what (counterfactually) would happen if the social and political ties between persons were suddenly dissolved.[4] Such a theory is called for because actually dissolving society to observe the result would likely be disastrous and irreversible, if not impossible.[5] Equally important, the individuals whose behavior and interaction patterns are the content of the theory are not real people, but *idealized* persons assumed to possess certain properties—rationality, certain background beliefs and ways of reasoning, and so on. In the absence of the capacity for direct experimentation, such idealization is necessary if it is to be possible to derive any general conclusions about what would occur in a state of nature. At the same time, if the individuals of the theory resemble real persons in enough important respects, their interaction patterns in the state of nature might provide considerable insight concerning how real people would be likely to behave in similar circumstances. Further, to the extent that the idealized individuals of our theory have features that actual individuals should strive to approximate (e.g., perfect rationality, possession of full information), their behavior may be relevant to normative issues concerning the proper organization of society, government, and so on.

[3] See Robert Nozick, *Anarchy, State, and Utopia* (New York: Basic Books, 1974), chap. 1.
[4] In addition to the above-quoted passage, see *Philosophical Rudiments*, chap. 8, sec. 1, pp. 108–9.
[5] Watkins (*Hobbes's System*, p. 48) quotes Sextus Empiricus reporting on a Persian custom of practicing five days of lawlessness after the death of a king. While the reported unhappy results are consistent with Hobbes's views, they provide only limited support for them, since the results of a known *temporary* removal of law enforcement might be very different from those of permanent removal.

The idealized individuals of Hobbes's theory are, with exceptions noted later, assumed to be rational. This means, among other things, that in interactive situations—where outcomes depend on the actions of both oneself and other agents—they take into account, in deciding what to do, how other relevant agents are likely to act. Let us express this point by saying that Hobbesian agents are *planners*. It will be convenient, for the purposes of reconstructing and analyzing certain of Hobbes's arguments, to distinguish between three sorts of planners according to how they predict other relevant agents' likely behavior. (Ideal, as well as real, planners may be mixtures of the three sorts.) The inductive planner, or inductivist, predicts the behavior of others by generalizing from their past behavior, or the past behavior of people like them, in similar situations. Deductive planners, or deductivists, predict the behavior of others by attempting to place themselves in other agents' shoes (or heads) and recapitulating other agents' reasoning. Thus, the deductivist assumes or posits that other parties have certain goals or values and certain beliefs about the present situation, and attempts from these data to deduce the optimum course of action for each party according to some appropriate rule of rational choice (e.g., expected value maximization). However, in the course of his calculations, the deductivist assumes that the other parties are themselves inductivists, who use only inductive techniques to predict the behavior of others.

On the other hand, the strategic planner, or strategist, while attempting to recapitulate other parties' reasonings and to deduce the outcomes of these reasonings, assumes that these parties are deductivists or other strategists. That is, the strategist assumes that others predict their fellows' behavior (including possibly the original strategist's own) by hypothetical recapitulation and deduction. This means that the strategist's calculations, unlike those of the inductivist and deductivist, may terminate in indeterminacy due to circularity, because successful completion of strategist A's reasoning about how strategist B will act might require recapitulating strategist B's reasoning about strategist A's own reasoning. In some cases, such completion is not possible. For example, imagine a simple game of penny-matching in which each

85

player secretly writes "heads" or "tails," with strategist B winning one cent if they do not match, and strategist A winning one cent for a match on tails and two cents for a match on heads. Strategist A may initially reason that B will write "tails" because he expects A to write "heads" due to the larger potential payoff. So A may first conclude that he should also write "tails." But given *this* reasoning, and the assumption that strategist B will recapitulate his reasoning, it follows that B will anticipate this and write "heads." So, second, A should conclude that he should write "heads." But on the assumption that B recapitulates *this* reasoning, A should write "tails"; and so on, ad infinitum.

Below we shall see that a similar indeterminacy of strategic reasoning infects one interpretation of Hobbes's classic argument concerning the grave disadvantages of anarchy. Turning now to that argument, we may begin with the observation that while it is Hobbes's central and most famous contribution to political philosophy, it rarely receives detailed examination and analysis in the literature.[6] There seem to be two quite opposite reasons for this curious fact. On the one hand, many apparently regard the argument as so straightforward and correct as to require little detailed analysis.[7] On the other hand, some take the argument to be so dependent on the false doctrine of Psychological Egoism as to be readily dismissible.[8] Neither of these reactions is justifiable. Hobbes's argument neither presupposes Psychological Egoism nor is straightforward. Its difficulty and complexity, and its presuppositions, have not been clearly identified because of insufficient analysis of what the argument is.

There has not even been a clear enough understanding of *where*, in the text of *Leviathan*, Hobbes's argument against anarchy oc-

---

[6] The treatment in McNeilly, *Anatomy of Leviathan*, discussed in section 4-5, is a notable exception.

[7] Thus, e.g., Gauthier (*Logic of Leviathan*) devotes but a few pages to the argument, and Warrender (*Political Philosophy of Hobbes*) none at all.

[8] A recent suggestion along these general lines may be found in Alan Wertheimer, "Disrespect for Law and the Case for Anarchy," in *Anarchism, Nomos XIX*, ed. J. Roland Pennock and John Chapman (New York: New York University Press, 1978), p. 177.

curs. It is frequently assumed to be wholly contained in chapter 13, "Of the Natural Condition of Mankind as Concerning Their Felicity and Misery," but there we find only the first part of a multipart argument against anarchy. This first part deals with interactions among individuals in the state of nature, while an equally vital second part, presented primarily in chapter 17 of *Leviathan*, concerns interactions among and within groups of individuals, and a third part—spread over part II of *Leviathan*—deals with the relative advantages of the State. Further, a revealing version of the first part of the argument, which contains important clues to its basic structure, is previewed in one paragraph of *Leviathan's* chapter 11.

Before commencing our analysis of the first part of the *Leviathan* argument, we should note in passing that earlier versions of that argument appear in *Elements of Law* and *Philosophical Rudiments*.[9] The *Leviathan* argument differs from the earlier versions in two main respects. Greater and clearer emphasis is placed on people acting out of concern for their *future* well-being, and the Hobbesian "right to all things" appears as a corollary, rather than a premise, of the first part of the argument. In the latter respect, the *Leviathan* version spearates descriptive and normative issues in a way that fits well into the structure of this book— basing conclusions about rights on a previous purely descriptive analysis. In addition, the *Leviathan* argument was published later and is a bit more sophisticated than other versions. Hence, we shall take it as the definitive form of the argument against anarchy.

3-2. State of Nature and State of War

The second part of Hobbes's argument against anarchy concerns interactions among and within groups and is the focus of the next chapter. Our present concern is the first part of the argument,

[9] See *Elements of Law*, part 1, chap. 1, pp. 81–86; part 1, chap. 6. secs. 1–6, pp. 117–21. Also, *Philosophical Rudiments*, chap. 1, pp. 1–13; chap. 5, pp. 63–71.

which deals with individuals. The conclusion of this part is the notorious proposition that the state of nature is a state of war of all against all. To understand the argument, we must have a firm grasp of the meaning of this conclusion, and especially its key terms "state of nature" and "state of war."

People are in a state of nature (or condition of mere nature), according to Hobbes, when there is no "common power to keep them all in awe."[10] Later elaboration of this formula indicates that what is required in order to be out of a state of nature is the existence of an earthly power capable, by threats of sufficient punishments, of compelling each party in question to keep their agreements with the other parties and to obey other moral rules ("laws of nature") concerning nonaggression and so forth.[11]

Two points should be noted about this conception of the state of nature. "State of nature" is, strictly speaking, a relational concept. Two parties are in a state of nature with respect to one another if there is no single party that can compel each to keep its agreements with, and not commit aggression against, the other. So a given individual may be in a state of nature with respect to another individual, but not with respect to a third individual. For example, if sovereigns A and B do not intend to forcibly settle disputes between subjects of A and of B, a subject of A is in a state of nature with respect to the subjects of B, but not with respect to other subjects of A.

A certain looseness enters the concept of being in a state of nature when that concept is applied to groups of three or more parties. Is such a group outside the state of nature if most pairs in it are under a single common power? Or if most individuals are under some common power with some other member of the group? Must all pairs, or all individuals, be so linked? Must the common power that links the various different pairs be the same for all pairs? (Or, for example, may agreements between A and B be enforced by power 1, while those between B and C and A and C are enforced by powers 2 and 3 respectively?) These ques-

[10] *Leviathan*, chap. 13, p. 113.
[11] Ibid., chap. 15, p. 131; chap. 17, p. 153.

tions reveal that a collection of individuals may be more or less in a state of nature according to how few of them are linked to how few others by common powers and how many different common powers are involved. It seems, however, that the state of nature initially envisioned in the first part of Hobbes's argument is the extreme one in which no pair of individuals is under a power common to them,[12] and we adopt this conception in our first reconstructions of this part of the argument.

There is another problem concerning the concept of a common power, in terms of whose absence the state of nature is defined. Due to limited personnel, resources, wisdom, knowledge, and the irrationality of potential aggressors, no power can successfully punish or deter all criminal acts and violations of citizen rights. How much protection must a power provide before it has removed those subject to it from the state of nature? Hobbes recognizes this problem at one point. He indicates that the state-of-nature right of self-protection, including the right to attack and conquer others, may be exercised "if there be no power erected, *or not great enough for our security.*"[13] But security too varies by degree, and we need at least some notion of what constitutes the "sufficient security"[14] that removes us from the state of nature.

There is an appropriate (though still vague) Hobbesian answer to this question, but to find it we must first consider the concept of a state of war. Hobbes writes: "WAR, consisteth . . . in a tract of time, wherein the will to contend by battle is sufficiently known: . . . so the nature of war, consisteth not in actual fighting; but in the known disposition thereto, during all the time there is no assurance to the contrary."[15] There are three points worth noting about this characterization of war. First, being in a

---

[12] As Hobbes may view some of the parties in the state of nature as heads of small groups based on family ties or conquest, this may not be strictly true. However, it is analytically most convenient to deal with such groups in our reconstruction of the second part of the argument (Chap. 4) and in our discussion of objections (section 3-6).

[13] Ibid., chap. 17, p. 154 (emphasis supplied).

[14] Hobbes uses this term in a related context, ibid., chap. 15, p. 145.

[15] Ibid., chap. 13, p. 113.

state of war, like being in a state of nature, is a relational concept. Two parties are at war with one another if the will of each to battle the other is sufficiently known (presumably to the other).[16] Thus, one may be at war with some parties and at peace with others, at the same time. Second, parties need not actually be fighting each other to be in a state of war at a given time. All that is required is a known willingness to fight, under appropriate or opportune conditions. Third, Hobbes's account contrasts with Locke's view of a state of war as "declar[ed] by Word or Action, not a passionate and hasty, but a sedate settled Design, upon another Mans Life."[17] The key difference is that while Locke requires an active sign of hostility, Hobbes assumes a disposition to fight unless there are assurances to the contrary. Hence, Lockean and Hobbesian individuals start from different presumptions about the attitudes of others and in the absence of all specific evidence about such attitudes consider themselves at peace and at war, respectively. In section 3-5, we shall see that this divergence between Locke and Hobbes underlies one interpretation of the first part of the latter's argument against anarchy.

For Hobbes, the supposed outcome of returning people to a state of nature is a war of each individual against every other individual. Given the above analysis of a state of war between two parties, what is the nature of such a war? All that directly follows from Hobbes's definition of war is that a war of all against all is a condition in which each individual knows that every other individual is willing to fight him. Yet Hobbes's famous description of the war of all is considerably richer than this, and worth quoting at length:

In such condition, there is no place for industry; because the fruit thereof is uncertain: and consequently no culture of the earth; no navigation, . . . no knowledge of the face of the

---

[16] This account leaves open certain questions not directly germane to the Hobbesian argument: Are two parties at war if only one is willing to fight, or if only one knows of the other's willingness to fight?

[17] John Locke, *Two Treatises of Government* (New York: New American Library, 1965), Second Treatise, chap. 3, sec. 16, p. 319.

earth; no account of time; no arts; no letters; no society; and which is worst of all, continual fear, and danger of violent death; and the life of man, solitary, poor, nasty, brutish, and short.[18]

Notice that this very sorry state of affairs that Hobbes describes would not likely arise out of a war of all (by his definition), unless there was a good amount of actual fighting taking place, because insofar as people reason as inductivists, as all to some extent do, the willingness of others to fight them would not paralyze them with fear and prevent their engaging in productive activities if they observed over a period of time that no (or very little) fighting ever occurred.[19] Just as a rational woman with a fiancé who has been "willing" to marry her for many years but has never found the right occasion for it would eventually stop planning for a married future with this man, so would even timid individuals in a violence-free war of all eventually stop fearing violence. So if Hobbes, or a Hobbesian, wishes to argue that the state of nature would degenerate into a state of war *with the described consequences*, he must show that the state of war in question contains substantial actual violence.

In recognizing this, we should not be led into the error of supposing that violence, and the injury, death, and fear that it engenders, is all that is wrong with the war of all. For the absence of the fruits of social cooperation and of the incentive to labor productively are equally important negative effects of that war. This observation points toward a solution to an earlier problem: How much security must a common power provide to remove those under it from the state of nature? The Hobbesian answer is enough security of person, property, and contract fulfillment that individuals need not be preoccupied with security concerns and may go on with the normal tasks of life. This requires enough security from violence that reasonably cautious individuals will

[18] *Leviathan*, chap. 13, p. 113.
[19] As Hobbes writes in *Philosophical Rudiments*, chap. 13, sec. 17, p. 181: "We esteem the future by what is past, seldom expecting what seldom happens."

not be discouraged from taking part in normal social life, enough security of property that people will have incentives to work hard and productively, and sufficient reliability of agreement enforcement to allow cooperative economic and social ventures. It also requires that most people most of the time feel secure enough in all these respects that they do not feel compelled to violate the rights of others to protect their own interests adequately—for example, by engaging in preemptive violence or in cheating and theft prompted by others' doing so.

We now understand all the major elements in Hobbes's famous conclusion that the state of nature is a state of war of all against all. To imagine people in a state of nature is to imagine them in a condition in which there is no power over any pair of them that can reliably protect each from the other by threats of punishment. To say that this state is a state of war of all against all is to say that each individual knows that every other individual is willing to fight him. But the conclusion of the first part of Hobbes's argument against anarchy goes further than this. It says that the state of nature is what we may call an *active* war of all against all, that is, a war in which there is much actual violence, enough to render people so fearful for life and property that productive work and social cooperation—the prerequisites for producing the benefits of civilization—are hardly present. Our next task is to reconstruct the argument by which Hobbes arrives at this devastating antianarchist conclusion.

3-3. Preliminary Version of the Argument

"I put for a general inclination of all mankind, a perpetual and restless desire of power after power, that ceaseth only in death."[20] This notorious statement from chapter 11 of *Leviathan* is a key element in the first part of Hobbes's argument against anarchy. It leads some to attribute to Hobbes the view that people are selfish and power-hungry by nature and that social life is always

[20] *Leviathan*, chap. 11, pp. 85–86.

filled with conflict.[21] Such a reading entirely misses the point that
Hobbes is trying to make. To understand this important statement properly, we must look both at its main constituent concept—power—and at the surrounding text.

Hobbes defines a person's power as "his present means; to obtain some future apparent good."[22] This is a broad, plausible, and
purely formal definition. It identifies powers as means or capacities to attain one's ends or objectives, without any restriction on
what those ends may be.[23] On this definition, it would follow
that people, as rational purposive beings, will be inclined to seek
to obtain and retain power. All this amounts to is that they tend
to pursue the means necessary to the attainment of their ends.

Hobbes goes on to divide powers into two exhaustive classes:
natural powers, "eminence[s] of the faculties of body or mind:
as extraordinary strength, form, prudence,"[24] and *instrumental*
powers, "means and instruments to acquire more [power]: as riches,
reputation, friends."[25] Characterizing natural powers compara-
tively, as eminences, is a mistake. It does not fit with the formal
definition, since even people's below-average faculties are means
to the accomplishment of many of their ends.

What apparently prompts this error is an underlying insight
about power, both in its natural form and its instrumental form.
It is *inflationary*, in the sense that the same absolute amount of
power tends to become less effective in achieving one's ends as
the power of other agents grows. For example, my fishing skills
represent the same absolute power or capacity to catch fish today
as they did yesterday, but if fish are scarce in our common fishing ponds and you have increased your fish-catching skills, the
effective power of my fishing skills have decreased. Further, if
you have more power than others, you can often coerce them to

---

[21] See, e.g., Wertheimer, "Disrespect for Law."

[22] *Leviathan*, chap. 10, p. 74.

[23] This follows from Hobbes's definitions of "good" (see section 2-3) and "apparent good" (ibid., chap. 6, p. 50). See also McNeilly, *Anatomy of Leviathan*,
pp. 137, 144–45.

[24] *Leviathan*, chap. 10, p. 74.

[25] Ibid.

use their powers to accomplish your ends rather than their own. Thus, my fishing skills also represent less effective power to catch fish for me if you increase your power by buying a machine gun and force me to turn over a portion of my catch.

As the above example shows, power over others can have multiplicative effects. If I can force or entice you to exert your powers toward my ends, I can roughly double my power,[26] which I might never be able to do by developing my own faculties. If I can thus influence a number of agents, I can quickly increase my power severalfold. Further, as Hobbes points out in characterizing instrumental power, power related to one's influence over others is self-reinforcing: increases in this sort of power lead to further increases. Wealth breeds opportunities for gaining more wealth, coercive power over some allows you to use them to coerce others and entices into submission those seeking a protector, having many friends leads to favor among their friends and those who seek the friendship of the many-friended, and so on.

We may summarize these points by reworking Hobbes's categories. Natural powers are simply bodily or mental capacities of a person. *Social powers* are means of influencing others to aid in the attainment of one's ends.[27] Hobbes's key insights are that powers of both sorts are subject to inflationary effects[28] and that social powers tend to be self-reinforcing and vastly more effective than unaided natural powers.

With these observations about power in hand, we may return to Hobbes's claim about our restless desire for power. The most relevant parts of the passage containing that claim read as follows:

> The object of man's desire, is not to enjoy once only, and for one instant of time; but to assure for ever, the way of

---

[26] If there are efficiencies of scale or coordination involved, my power may increase by an even larger factor.

[27] These categories are not exclusive; intelligence, e.g., is both a natural power and a social power.

[28] Social power is subject to inflationary effects because one's means to influence another will tend to be less effective, the stronger the contrary influences that others may exert on him.

his future desire. And therefore the voluntary actions, and inclinations of all men, tend, not only to the procuring, but also to the assuring of a contented life; . . .

So that in the first place, I put for a general inclination of all mankind, a perpetual and restless desire of power after power, that ceaseth only in death. And the cause of this, is not always that a man hopes for a more intensive delight, than he has already attained to; or that he cannot be content with a moderate power: but because he cannot assure the power and means to live well, which he hath present, without the acquisition of more.[29]

As noted earlier, it follows from Hobbes's formal concept of power that all purposive beings will seek to accumulate some of it. The present passage throws in a substantive assumption about people—that we are forwardlooking in the sense of being concerned with our own future (as well as present) well-being—and extracts the stronger conclusion that people naturally tend to constantly seek ever greater power. This expanded power is sought not necessarily as a means to a better future life but simply to assure maintaining one's satisfactory present standard. Why must *greater* power be accumulated for this purpose? Hobbes does not explicitly say, but based on our earlier observations about power we may assume that he is not solely concerned with hedging against natural disaster. It is because power is inflationary, and because social power is so effective and self-reinforcing, that one cannot stand still on the treadmill of power without falling so far behind as to threaten one's retention of the means necessary for living a satisfactory life. In other words, to protect himself from potentially successful competitors or conquerors, even a "moderate" forwardlooking individual, who seeks only to retain a modest level of welfare, will be forced to increase his power. But "competition of . . . power, inclineth to contention, enmity, and war."[30] Hence, in conclusion, there is a natural tendency for all people

---

[29] Ibid., chap. 11, pp. 85–86.
[30] Ibid., p. 86.

(even "moderates") to seek expanded power and as a consequence end up at war with one another.

By adding the last part of this conclusion, we present the chapter 11 passage from *Leviathan* as a preliminary version of the argument that the state of nature is a state of war of all against all. Read in this way, the passage highlights three elements that will help us understand the more developed argument of chapter 13. First, the assumption that people are forwardlooking is central to the argument. Second, there is no presumption that people are purely selfish, or naturally power-hungry, or have infinitely expanding desires, or the like. The main motivational assumption is the highly plausible one that people are concerned with obtaining and securing a reasonable level of well-being. Third, and finally, people's reasons for pursuing power are primarily defensive and preemptive—they seek more power to retain the effectiveness of their present power and to stay ahead of competitors who can weaken or destroy them. With these three clues from chapter 11 before us, we may proceed to decipher chapter 13 of *Leviathan*.

3-4. The Basic Argument

Hobbes's argument that the state of nature is a war of all against all starts from a number of assumptions about the parties in the state of nature. In accordance with the theory of human nature laid out in section 2-1 above, the parties are all taken to be death-averse, concerned with their reputations, forwardlooking, in possession of desires that conflict with those of others, roughly equal in natural endowments, and egoistic. Their egoism, however, is *predominant* in the sense explicated in section 2-5, rather than pure. Further, in line with the aims of state-of-nature theory, as explained in section 3-1, the parties are rational planners: in interactive situations they take account of how other relevant agents may act. (As we shall see, different versions of the argument may involve different assumptions about what *sort* of rational planners some or all of them are—inductive, deductive, or strategic.)

Alike in all these respects, the parties in the state of nature are assumed to vary in one respect: some are *dominators* who desire conquest, dominion, and power over others for its own sake, while the rest are *moderates*,[31] who desire power over others, if at all, only as a means to protect and secure themselves and their possessions. Finally, there is a plausible factual assumption about the probable outcomes of conflicts among the parties. Anticipation—striking first or gathering power over others so that one will be in a stronger relative position when battle erupts—generally improves one's chances of success in a potential conflict situation.[32]

From these reasonable and for the most part realistic[33] assumptions about human beings, Hobbes constructs an elegant and insightful argument for the state of nature being an active state of war of all against all. The core of the argument goes as follows. Imagine people in a state of nature in which there is no common power over them to punish them for robbing, assaulting, and killing one another. As forwardlooking creatures vulnerable to death at the hands of virtually any of their fellows, they will rightly be quite concerned about their future security. Lacking a system of law enforcement, they cannot expect potential attackers to be effectively deterred by fear of counterviolence, for because of the rough equality of people's natural powers and the advantages of striking first, potential attackers will realize that they have a good chance of success. Nor can one expect potential attackers—whose altruism is, at most, limited—to refrain from attack out of concern for their potential victims. Thus, each person in the state of nature must fear violence by others who may attack for any of four reasons.[34] First, dominators may attack simply because they enjoy conquest. Second, competitors may attack to remove one

---

[31] For passages suggesting this term, see *Elements of Law*, part 1, chap. 1, sec. 3, p. 82; and *Leviathan*, chap. 11, p. 86.

[32] See *Leviathan*, chap. 11, p. 88; chap. 13, p. 111.

[33] The rationality assumption is not intended to be entirely realistic.

[34] Ibid., chap. 13, pp. 111–12.

as an obstacle to the satisfaction of their desires. Third, those you may have insulted or undervalued may attack to preserve or improve their reputation and standing in the eyes of others. Fourth, and most important, even moderates, who have no desire for power for its own sake and who may have no specific quarrel with a person, may for defensive purposes engage in anticipatory violence against that person. That is, they may attack to remove one as a potential future threat to themselves, or to conquer one to use one's power to defend against future attacks by others, or to gain a reputation of power that will awe and deter others. In these circumstances, eventual involvement in violent conflict is not unlikely. And since anticipation generally improves one's chances of success, it is the most reasonable course of action for rational persons caring about their future well-being (and caring much less, if at all, about the well-being of most others). In Hobbes's words, "There is no way for any man to secure himself, so reasonable, as anticipation; that is, by force, or wiles, to master the persons of all men he can."[35]

We have not yet brought the argument to its final conclusion that the state of nature is an active war of all against all, but it is worth stopping midway to note that the argument for anticipation being the most reasonable state-of-nature strategy does not depend upon unrealistically pessimistic or cynical assumptions about human nature.

Psychological Egoism, for example, is not needed for the argument. Assuming Predominant Egoism suffices to insure that the parties—caught up in the insecurities of the state of nature and with their very lives at stake—will not refrain from attacking others if this seems to provide the best prospects for their own safety. In fact, predominant egoists may even be more aggressive than psychological egoists in many state-of-nature situations. The former may slightly discount the value of personal power gains due to successful conquest because of the losses they impose on others and the risk that retaliation may be carried out against their friends as well as themselves, but they will also generally *augment* the value of their power gains by a significant factor,

[35] Ibid., p. 111.

because these gains enable them to better promote the well-being of those besides themselves whose welfare most concerns them.[36]

Hobbes's argument need not assume that people are purely selfish, and neither does it assume that they are power-hungry. This latter feature characterizes only the dominators, and they are a minority amid the moderates, who seek power only as a means of security.[37] Thus, while the two different sorts of agents in the

---

[36] Consider the simplest possible case presented in slightly more formal terms. Imagine a potential conqueror C of a stranger S. Suppose that the expected personal welfare payoff to C of conquering S is a. If C were a psychological egoist, he would compare only a to the expected personal welfare payoffs of alternative acts in deciding whether to conquer S. But suppose that C is a predominant egoist who values each unit of a friend F's welfare at some fraction f of the value he (C) places on a unit of his own welfare, and who values each unit of stranger S's welfare at some very much smaller fraction s of the value he (C) places on a unit of his own welfare. C must consider three additional and potentially significant factors in evaluating the conquest of S. These are the expected loss S would suffer if conquered, the expected welfare increment (in addition to his own "consumption" of a) that C would be able to pass on to F in virtue of his conquest of S, and the expected loss to F due to the danger that S's friends will retaliate *against* F for his friend C's action. Let y, x, and z stand for the values of these three factors respectively. Then C would value the conquest of S at $a + [f(x-z) - sy]$. If the additional "others' welfare" factor, $[f(x-z) - sy]$, is positive, the rational predominant egoist is—because of his concern for others—*more likely* to undertake conquest than a rational psychological egoist would be in similar circumstances.

This factor will be positive when f/s, the ratio of C's concerns for his friend and the stranger, exceeds $y/(x-z)$. It is given that the former ratio is very large. What of the latter ratio? In most state-of-nature circumstances, z is likely to be very small, for it is the *product* of F's average losses if retaliated against and the probabilities of three events: S's friends deciding to retaliate against C's friends, their identifying F as such a friend, and their being able to locate F and carry out the retaliation. One or more of these probabilities is likely to be quite low, rendering z quite small, if not negligible. Still, the ratio $y/(x-z)$ may be rather large, for S would be unlikely to produce as much utility (x) for F as he loses for himself (y) even if assigned by C to be F's slave or servant. And the danger of S being killed or injured in the conquest must be factored into y. Nonetheless, the "others' welfare" factor is likely to be positive in many cases, and even when negative it is unlikely (given the very high f/s ratio) to be substantially so. Hence, we should not expect predominant egoists to be significantly more inclined, on average, than psychological egoists to refrain from attack and conquest in the state of nature.

[37] Hobbes may have changed his view on this matter. Cf. *Elements of Laws*, part 1, chap. 1, secs. 3–5, p. 82, with *Philosophical Rudiments*, preface, p. xvi. At *Leviathan*, chap. 13, p. 111, Hobbes indirectly endorses the *Philosophical Rudiments* view by suggesting that "conservation" rather than "delectation" is the primary end that leads to conflict.

state of nature follow the same general line of conduct—attack and conquest—the reasoning that leads them to it is different. We may clarify this by employing our earlier distinction between inductive, deductive, and strategic reasoning.

In the argument offered above, four different reasons for attacking others in the state of nature are noted: the enjoyment of conquest, competition, response to insult, and defensive anticipation. What sort of reasoning is involved in establishing each of these as a reason for attack? (Note that we are not concerned with how one might reason about carrying out the attack successfully, but rather with how one reasons to the discovery that one has a reason to attack.) The main point to notice is that for the first three sorts of reasons—enjoyment of conquest, competition, and insult response—we need to posit nothing more than inductive reasoning on the part of the agent. For example, if A and B are in competition over the same piece of land, to perceive that he has a reason to kill or conquer B, A need only generalize from B's past behavior ("B is going to keep on using this land, as he has before, unless someone stops him").

But when it comes to anticipation, we enter the realm of deductive and strategic reasoning. In discussing anticipation, we will first focus on the moderate, returning to the dominator later. Moderate M attacks party X either to remove him as a future threat or to use him in defense against a future threat posed by party Z. Why does he expect a future attack from party X or Z? If it is simply because X or Z or others like them have attacked M (or others like him) before, M's reasoning is still only inductive. Relying on such reasoning only, we certainly could not conclude that each moderate (much less each party) in the state of nature is at war with every other. What justifies this conclusion is the observation that M can expect X or Z, even if they are moderates rather than dominators, to attack him *from anticipatory motives*. Thus, M may reason as a deductivist and note that X and Z have a reason to conquer him to strengthen themselves against future attacks by others who have attacked people in the past. More important, M may reason as a strategist and note that X and Z have reason to attack him and other moderates, because they will realize that he and other moderates have similar reasons to attack them. In other words, a strategic moderate will realize that if he has reason to anticipate, so do other strategic moderates, and this realization gives him a new reason to anticipate and adds urgency to the task of beating the others to the punch.

This way of looking at the matter provides us with one way of filling in a critical gap in Hobbes's argument. Hobbes jumps from the subconclusion that anticipation is the most reasonable course to follow in the state of nature to the conclusion that the state of nature is a state of war of all against all. But that latter conclusion implies that every party *knows* that every other has good reason to attack him, which goes beyond the previously established claim that everybody has good reason to attack anyone else. A further assumption that would neatly close this gap is that all the parties are rational strategists and know that the other parties are. A strategist will not only recapitulate the argument that *he* should anticipate, but he will also attribute appreciation of the same argument to his strategist fellows and correspondingly assume that they are inclined to anticipate against him.

This way of proceeding to the conclusion that the state of nature is a war of all against all is especially attractive because it immediately sustains the needed further inference that the war of all is active, that is, involves substantial actual violence. For if anticipatory attack is the most reasonable way to defend oneself in the state of nature, and all parties are rational and realize that the others understand the arguments for anticipation, there will be much actual anticipatory violence in addition to whatever violence is generated by power-hungry dominators. And given this level of violence, the known willingness of each to attack any other, and the corresponding lack of trust among parties, there would be constant insecurity of person and property, and insufficient incentives and cooperation to spur economic development.

This concludes our initial survey of the first part of the Hobbesian argument against anarchy. The pivot point on which that argument hinges is the claim that anticipation is the most reasonable strategy for rational parties to follow in the state of nature. Objections to this claim focus on two sorts of alternative strategies: more passive individualist strategies and cooperative strategies. Various forms of these objections will be considered in the next two sections and in the following chapter. In sketching the Hobbesian response to these objections, we will develop and clarify the Hobbesian argument against anarchy.

3-5. War or Peace?

Anticipation is an active strategy that involves seeking to expand one's power by forcibly taking control of other persons and/or their material resources. It is also a risky strategy which exposes one to the dangers of defensive force applied by those one seeks to conquer or steal from, retaliatory force applied by their friends, and so on.[38] Surely if enough others are determined to anticipate, prudence may require trying to beat them to the punch. But given the dangers of anticipation, might it not be more reasonable in the state of nature to lie low, strengthen one's defenses, and hope the others do the same? That is, given a choice of strategies between "anticipate" and "lie low," is not the latter the most reasonable one to adopt in the state of nature?

A useful way to approach this question is to imagine that all parties in the state of nature are moderates and strategists, who are aware of one another's basic features (i.e., that they are moderates, strategists, predominant egoists, etc.) and the characteristics of their situation (no common power, rough equality including mutual vulnerability, conflicting desires due to scarcity, etc.) and who possess no special knowledge that differentiates them from one another.[39] In this homogeneous state of nature, what strategy will the similarly situated parties choose to follow—"anticipate" or "lie low"? The answer is indeterminate, as the following argument shows.[40]

Consider such a party P. As a predominant egoist, he will an-

[38] For further dangers associated with anticipation, see section 3-6.
[39] It is, in Hobbes's words, "as if [they were] but even now sprung out of the earth, and suddenly, like mushrooms, come to full maturity." *Philosophical Rudiments*, chap. 8, sec. 1, p. 109.
[40] There are similar arguments in D. H. Hodgson, *Consequences of Utilitarianism* (Oxford: Clarendon Press, 1967), chap. 2.

ticipate if he believes that anticipating is necessary for self-defense. As a moderate, he will attack only out of defensive motives. But since the others are moderates, it will be necessary for him to anticipate for defensive purposes only if the others anticipate. As a strategist, P predicts whether the others will anticipate by recapitulating their reasoning. But, being similarly situated, the others will reason precisely as P does. Another party P' will have reason to anticipate[41] if and only if he expects P and others like him to anticipate. And he expects P (and the others) to anticipate only if they have reason to anticipate, which they will have only if they expect P' (and others) to have reason to anticipate. We have here a reflexive circle and an indeterminate outcome.

We can see this more clearly, by noting that P cannot escape the problem by simply assuming, for the sake of argument, that the others have reason to choose a certain one of these strategies (or will expect others to choose it), because such an assumption is a self-fulfilling prophecy, *whichever assumption it is.* If P assumes that the others have reason to anticipate, then he has reason to anticipate, everyone (including him) will anticipate, and each does have reason to anticipate (because the others all are). If P assumes that the others have reason not to anticipate, then he also has reason not to, no one will anticipate, and it turns out that each does have reason not to (because no one else is). Either assumption is self-confirming. Similarly, suppose P assumes that each of the others assumes that the other parties have reason to anticipate. It follows that each of the others has reason to anticipate, and hence that P does. But the opposite result follows in the same way from P's assuming that each of the others assumes that the other parties have reason not to anticipate. Hence, there is no satisfactory argument for (or against) anticipation here— only two equal but opposite arguments, with the "success" of each disconfirming the "success" of the other.

Recall from section 3-2 that Hobbes's and Locke's definitions

---

[41] In this context, "having a reason to" is short for "having more reason to than not to."

of a state of war may be viewed as embodying competing presumptions about the aggressive intentions of other parties. Hobbes's definition suggests that, in the absence of other evidence, one should presume that others are disposed to fight. Locke's definition suggests the opposite. Suppose we identify the disposition to fight with the disposition to anticipate, and the disposition not to fight with the disposition to lie low. Then we could view the divergence in Hobbes's and Locke's opinions about the prevalence of war in the state of nature as flowing from application of opposite forms of the self-fulfilling arguments sketched in the previous paragraph.

These competing presumptions were undoubtedly present in Hobbes and Locke, and they quite possibly had a nonnegligible influence on their differing conceptions of life in a state of nature. But in the absence of strong empirical evidence that human beings are inherently inclined to prefer active defense (i.e., anticipation) to passive defense (i.e., lying low), Hobbesian philosophy cannot safely assume such an inclination without being vulnerable to a charge of arbitrariness. Fortunately, however, Hobbes provides us with a device besides mere presumption for knocking the moderates off the fence between anticipation and lying low.

The dominators are this device. In a population of strategic moderates, there is no determinate strategy choice. The situation might spiral either to peace or to all-out war, depending upon arbitrary presumptions of the parties or the direction of random perturbations in their early behavior. Adding a significant minority of dominators to the mix, however, arguably biases the process in the direction of war. Other things being equal, the dominators will attack simply because they enjoy conquest, and if there is a significant minority of them, each moderate may reasonably fear that he is likely to eventually be a victim of such an attack if he simply lies low. So he may now perceive himself as having good reason to anticipate. Further, as a strategist, he will expect other moderates to reason similarly and to be likely to anticipate. This given him a *new* reason to anticipate and to expect other moderates to anticipate, which is yet a further reason to anticipate, and so on.

Another way of looking at the matter is this: The introduction of dominators into the population gives strategic moderates several new reasons to anticipate against others who in fact are moderates. (1) In attempting to strike first against dominators, they may attack some moderates by mistake, "because [they] cannot distinguish them."[42] (2) A moderate may seek to conquer other moderates to use in future battles against dominators. (3) A moderate may strike first against other moderates he expects might otherwise attack him for reasons of type 1 or 2. (4) A moderate may strike against another who may anticipate against him for reason 3, and so on. The higher-level reasons are self-reinforcing among strategic moderates; hence an active war of all against all is a likely outcome of mixing strategic moderates and a substantial minority of dominators in the state of nature.

Introducing dominators into the population also allows us to relax the assumption that all moderates reason strategically. We can now assume a mix of inductive, deductive, and strategic reasoning among the moderates. Consider first the extreme case in which all the moderates are assumed to be inductivists. Suppose that there were no dominators and that each moderate started with resources adequate to sustain a decent life indefinitely (assuming no losses to attackers). Then there would not be any initial acts of violence to begin a spiral toward general war, for a moderate will attack only in anticipation against future attacks, but an inductivist will expect future attacks only if there have been past ones.

Once we mix a substantial minority of dominators in with the inductivist moderates, however, things change. Moderates will vary along a continuum in their initial estimates of the relative gains and losses of anticipating and lying low, but it is reasonable to assume that for every moderate (1) the relative attractiveness of anticipating (compared to lying low) increases monotonically along with the number of attacks expected in the future (per time period) and that (2) the relative attractiveness of anticipating ex-

[42] *Philosophical Rudiments*, preface, p. xvi.

ceeds zero for some number of expected attacks.[43] Let us call the number of expected attacks for which the individual's relative attractiveness of anticipating is exactly zero that individual's *anticipation threshold*. (Anticipation thresholds need not be whole numbers, by this definition. Some dominators will have an anticipation threshold of zero.)

In this state-of-nature situation, attacks by dominators only will generate some level of violence, v_1, in the initial time period. Assume that the inductivist moderates follow the simplest inductive rule and expect the level of violence in the next time period, v_{n+1}, to equal the level of violence in the last period, v_n. So each inductivist moderate expects a level of violence equal to v_1 in time period two. But v_1 will very likely exceed the anticipation thresholds of some moderates, for as the dominators are a significant minority, v_1 will be fairly high, and it is quite unlikely that every moderate will regard it as best to accept (or defend against) this much violence purely passively. As a result, some moderates anticipate during time period two, and $v_2 > v_1$. But as the participation thresholds vary continuously across the population of moderates, this will cause the expectation of violence in the next period to exceed the anticipation threshold of more moderates and will produce yet more violence in the next period, and so on. For most plausible distributions of anticipation thresholds, this escalation process will continue until everyone's threshold has been passed. (This will be the case, for example, for a normal bell-shaped distribution centered at a threshold corresponding to less than half the population engaging in attacks.) At that point we have an active war of all against all, or nearly all against all.

This argument is based on a number of simplifying assumptions, but for the most part these assumptions *underestimate* the tendency toward escalation of violence. Thus, for example, inductivists following less simple inductive rules would expect violence to increase in future periods, if it had done so over a few past

---

[43] This last is the sum of expected attacks by dominators and by moderates who anticipate. Monotonicity here means that an increase in this sum always corresponds to an increase in the expected net gain of anticipating (relative to the expected net gain of lying low).

periods. This expectation would fuel the spiral of violence faster than the corresponding expectations in the above argument.

More important, the tendency toward a war of all is increased if we suppose that some of the moderates are deductivists or strategists. Deductivist moderates, by applying the above arguments to their inductivist fellow moderates, will early on predict future high levels of anticipation by these inductivists and will have all the more reason to anticipate themselves. Strategists, in turn, will recapitulate this last deductivist line of reasoning and correspondingly will expect much anticipation by deductivists as well as by inductivists. And in view of this, strategists will expect the anticipation strategy to be followed early by their fellow strategists, who presumably have gone through the same reasoning process and will anticipate themselves. As a result, dominators are even more effective catalysts of war when applied to a mixture of strategic, deductive, and inductive moderates than when applied to the latter alone.

3-6. Objections

In the last three sections, we have developed a Hobbesian argument concerning the interactions of rational persons in a state of nature, with no common power over them to make and enforce laws. This argument purports to show that suitably characterized persons in such circumstances will end up in an active war of each against every other. In this section, we will consider four major objections to this argument. This will force us to clarify and modify the argument and further explain its role in the overall Hobbesian critique of anarchy.

The first objection is that the argument is, in effect, self-refuting. It claims that anticipation is the rational strategy to follow in the state of nature,[44] but it explains that (and why) the ultimate result of the parties following that strategy is insecurity, poverty, and misery for them all. But rational parties should be

---

[44] Throughout this section, when speaking of rational or reasonable strategies, we mean *for moderates*. It is simply assumed that the rational strategy for dominators is at least as aggressive.

able to foresee this, and hence they will not adopt the anticipation strategy in the first place.

To assess this objection, we may begin by considering what the three general *alternatives* to anticipation are for the parties in the state of nature. (1) Each, or any, party could lie low. (2) Groups of them could, by agreement, form defensive alliances. (3) Acting in concert, all (or nearly all) the parties could institute a civil society and leave the state of nature. A look at how Hobbes deals with each of these alternatives reveals the overall structure of his argument against anarchy. He views the last alternative—forming a civil society—as the proper solution to the problem of insecurity in the state of nature. But since this course of action involves leaving the state of nature by establishing a common power, it is not an alternative to anticipation within the state of nature. Forming a defensive alliance, on the other hand, *is* a strategy within the state of nature. Hobbes does not necessarily regard this strategy as inferior to individual anticipation. Rather, he believes that such alliances would be unreliable and that essentially the same logic of anticipation would apply to the defensive groups in the state of nature as applies to isolated individuals there. Thus, as we shall see in the next chapter, if the parties follow the defensive-alliance strategy, there will ensue a devastating war of each group against every other, with consequences for individuals only somewhat less severe than the consequences of universal war among individuals.

Given this, we can provide a preliminary outline of the overall Hobbesian argument against anarchy:

(1) Anticipation is a more reasonable strategy for individuals to follow in the state of nature than is lying low.

(2) But universal war and misery is the inevitable result of the individuals in the state of nature following the anticipation strategy.

(3) The parties in the state of nature joining together into defensive groups merely moves the main anticipatory violence from the interpersonal level to the intergroup level.

(4) Only leaving the state of nature by forming a civil society

can provide security to the parties and avoid the problems posed by the logic of escalating anticipation.

(5) The problems encountered in an appropriate kind of civil society are less severe than the problems of insecurity and anticipation in the state of nature.

(6) Therefore, rational parties in a state of nature would form a civil society of an appropriate kind in order to leave that state of nature.

Looking at the argument this way reveals that the only comparative claim that Hobbes really needs concerning anticipation is that it is more reasonable than lying low (or following some similar passive strategy). However, even such a limited claim might be challenged on the grounds stated in our first objection: anticipation foreseeably leads to misery for all and hence cannot be more reasonable than lying low. But this challenge involves the critical error of failing to distinguish between what it is rational for each of the parties in the state of nature to do *individually* and what it would be rational for them all to do *collectively*, (that is, if they acted in concert).

Of course, as noted in section 3-5, the parties are all much better off if they all lie low than if they all anticipate. Nonetheless, if—as Hobbes plausibly supposes—anticipation provides its practitioners with advantages over those who lie low and do not anticipate, it will pay individuals to anticipate to gain advantages over nonanticipators and to prevent other anticipators from gaining advantages over them. As a result, if the parties in the state of nature each follow the *individually* more rational course of action, they ironically end up, each and all, with a result worse than they would have obtained had they all adopted the less rational course. Pointing out this apparent divergence between the courses recommended by individual and collective rationality was one of Hobbes's major contributions to social and political philosophy.

Hobbes's idea has been rediscovered and reexpressed by modern game theorists in the form of the well-known game pris-

FIGURE 1

Player 2

	Cooperate	Don't cooperate
Cooperate	x_2 x_1	w_2 z_1
Don't cooperate	z_2 w_1	y_2 y_1

Player 1

oner's dilemma.[45] Acquaintance with this game will help us deal with the present objection and will later facilitate the explication of other Hobbesian arguments. Two-party prisoner's dilemma involves two players who must each choose (independently and without knowledge of what the other is choosing) between a cooperative move and a noncooperative move. Each combination of moves determines a payoff to each player. The payoffs are such that each player ranks the outcomes in the following order, from most preferred to least: unilateral noncooperation, mutual cooperation, mutual noncooperation, unilateral cooperation. Two-party prisoner's dilemma is illustrated in Figure 1, with Player 1's payoffs listed in the lower left corner for each combination of moves, and with $w_1 > x_1 > y_1 > z_1$ and $w_2 > x_2 > y_2 > z_2$.

In prisoner's dilemma, both players do better if they both cooperate than if they both do not, for in the former case they receive payoffs x_1 and x_2, and in the latter case they receive less-preferred payoffs y_1 and y_2. But noncooperation is the rational move for each individual to make because it is a *dominant* move. That is, each does better, playing this move, against either move the other may make. (By not cooperating rather than cooperating, player 1 obtains w_1 rather than x_1 if player 2 cooperates, and y_1 rather than z_1 if player 2 does not cooperate. Similarly, by not

---

[45] The name "prisoner's dilemma" comes from the story first used to illustrate the puzzle. On the history of prisoner's dilemma, see *Rational Man and Irrational Society*, ed. Brian Barry and Russell Hardin (Beverly Hills: Sage, 1982), Preface and Introduction, pp. 11–12, 24–25.

FIGURE 2

Player 2

	Lie low	Anticipate
Lie low	0 0	+5 −5
Anticipate	−5 +5	−1 −1

Player 1

cooperating, player 2 obtains w_2 rather than x_2 if player 1 cooperates, and y_2 rather than z_2 if player 1 does not cooperate.) Hence, if each does what is *individually* rational, each will not cooperate. This will result in their reaching outcome (y_1 , y_2), rather than the collectively preferred outcome (x_1, x_2).[46]

We can see the relationship between Hobbes's point and prisoner's dilemma even more clearly by actually casting his problem in game theoretic form. Imagine a state of nature with two equal parties. Because of the advantages of surprise, if one anticipates while the other lies low, the anticipator conquers; he correspondingly makes large gains while the defender suffers large losses. If both lie low, neither gains or loses. If both anticipate, neither conquers, but each suffers small losses (e.g., injury, resource expenditure) in the exchange. Assuming symmetry, the game matrix summarizing this information might look like that in Figure 2.

Figure 2 illustrates an instance of two-party prisoner's dilemma in which lying low is the cooperative move and anticipating is the noncooperative move. The divergence between individual and collective rationality is apparent. Anticipating is a dominant, hence rational, move for each party, as $5 > 0$ and $-1 > -5$.

[46] In other terms, (y_1,y_2) is an (the only) *equilibrium* in the game (i.e., it is the only position from which neither gains by unilaterally defecting), but is *Pareto-inferior* to (x_1,x_2) (i.e., at least one prefers the latter to the former, and none prefers the former to the latter).

But each does better if they both lie low (0) than if they both make the rational move and anticipate (-1).

Now there are multiparty as well as two-party versions of prisoner's dilemma. Imagine a game involving simultaneous choice between a cooperative and noncooperative move by each of n players. Such a game will be a multiparty prisoner's dilemma if, and only if, (1) universal cooperation is better for all players than universal noncooperation and (2) each player does better not cooperating, no matter how many (and which) other players are cooperating. Condition 2 amounts to noncooperation being a dominant move for each player individually, while condition 1 states that cooperation is the collectively rational move for the group. Hence, the divergence between individually and collectively rational moves is virtually built into this definition of multiparty prisoner's dilemma.

Multiparty prisoner's dilemma is of special interest to us because it resembles the structure of the choice between anticipation and lying low in the state of nature. We have shown the two-person version of this choice to be a two-party prisoner's dilemma. Similarly, the state of nature as described by Hobbes can be viewed, on first approximation, as fitting the above definition of a multiparty prisoner's dilemma. First, the result of universal anticipation is misery, insecurity, and relatively quick death for all. But if all lay low, each would live in peace and security (except for natural shortages and natural disasters). As the latter outcome is better than the former for all, condition 1 in the definition is satisfied. But because anticipating gives one an advantage over those who do not anticipate, and keeps other anticipators from gaining an advantage over one that they otherwise would have, it may be argued that condition 2 is satisfied as well.

Viewing the choice between anticipation and lying low in the state of nature as a multiparty prisoner's dilemma allows us to pinpoint what is wrong with the first objection to our argument. Anticipation leading to a worse outcome for all does not imply, as the objection assumes, that it is not the "most reasonable" strategy for each to follow. In a multiparty prisoner's dilemma, the most reasonable individual strategy must, if universally followed, produce a suboptimal outcome. And Hobbes's very point about the state of nature is that it has this multiparty prisoner's dilemma structure and hence must be abandoned. For so long as individuals remain in that state and act rationally, they will inevitably produce worse outcomes for themselves than they could obtain under other conditions.

This answer to our first objection leads immediately to a second objection: the multiparty prisoner's dilemma analysis of the state of nature is inconsistent with the section 3-5 analysis based on anticipation thresholds and escalation. In holding that anticipation is a dominant strategy, the former analysis implies that it pays anyone to anticipate even if all others do not; in other words, each party has an anticipation threshold of zero. But the dynamic analysis of section 3-5 assumes that nearly all moderates, at least, have higher anticipation thresholds. Hence, both analyses cannot be right.

This objection is, strictly speaking, correct. The dynamic analysis shows that Hobbes's war-of-all conclusion follows from assumptions that are weaker than those needed to picture the state of nature as a multiparty prisoner's dilemma. We can make the relationship between the two arguments clearer by introducing some general definitions.

Let us say that a move by one party in an n-person game is *quasi-dominant* if and only if that move yields a higher payoff for that player than any other move for every likely, plausible, or reasonably expectable combination of moves by other players. This is a weaker notion than dominance. Dominance implies quasi-dominance, but not vice versa. This is because a quasi-dominant move might not yield the best possible payoff against some unexpected or implausible combination of moves by the other players. In effect, it only dominates against the plausible or likely moves of others. But given that it does, it is reasonable to suppose that a quasi-dominant move is the rational one to choose, if one is available.[47]

---

[47] There may be an exception to this. If a quasi-dominated move would produce a *massively* better result if others play in an unlikely way, and only a slightly worse result otherwise, it might be rational to choose it rather than a quasi-dominant alternative.

We may now define a multiparty (or *n*-person) *quasi prisoner's dilemma* as a game in which (1) universal cooperation is better for all players than universal noncooperation, and (2) noncooperation is a quasi-dominant move for each player. The following is a good example of a quasi prisoner's dilemma.[48] One thousand strangers (unable to communicate with one another) will each receive ten dollars if and only if every one of them sends in one dollar. All do better (i.e., gain nine dollars each) if all cooperate by sending in their dollar than if none does (in which case there is no net gain). But this is not a prisoner's dilemma, since the noncooperative move of not sending your dollar fails to yield your best outcome if (and only if) the other 999 do. It is, however, a quasi prisoner's dilemma in that one can be quite confident that at least one of the other 999 will not cooperate (since he or they expect some others not to cooperate), so that the noncooperative move is quasi-dominant. Consistent with our view that quasi-dominant moves are rational, we would advise against sending in your dollar.

The concepts of quasi-dominance and quasi prisoner's dilemma are useful in allowing us to deal with cases, like the above, which resemble but are not quite prisoner's dilemmas. Many such cases involve threshold phenomena, where a large difference in total (and individual) payoffs exists if p people cooperate rather than $p-1$. The above case, where we equally share ten thousand dollars if one thousand cooperate, but share nothing if 999 do, is an extreme example. The provision of various public goods may exemplify this pattern, and the concept of quasi prisoner's dilemma may sometimes help us understand problems associated with such provision. For example, the famous irrationality of voting paradox, based on the extreme statistical unlikelihood that your single vote will make the difference in an election, may profitably be viewed as a quasi prisoner's dilemma.

Our present purpose, however, is to use the quasi-dominance notion to render the dynamic and prisoner's dilemma analyses of

---

[48] Somewhat similar cases are discussed in Douglas Hofstadter, "Metamagical Themas," *Scientific American* 248 (June 1983): 14–28.

the state of nature consistent. We may do this by noting that, on the Hobbesian analysis, the individualist state of nature need not constitute an actual multiparty prisoner's dilemma situation. It may be only a *quasi* prisoner's dilemma with at least the moderates perferring not to anticipate if all others similarly refrain. But the analysis of section 3-5 shows that, when dynamic tendencies toward escalation are taken into account, anticipation is a quasi-dominant strategy even for moderates, that is, even moderates will expect their anticipation thresholds to be eventually crossed. So that if the state of nature situation is represented as a one-time choice between a cooperative move or strategy ("never anticipate") and a noncooperative one ("anticipate at some time"), it constitutes a quasi prisoner's dilemma. This suffices to establish the general rationality of anticipation and the resulting war of all individuals.[49]

In the sequel, we will for convenience often ignore these complications and speak simply of prisoner's dilemmas, leaving open the possibility that on closer analysis some of these may turn out to be merely quasi prisoner's dilemmas. Hence, the reader should be prepared to substitute the notion of a quasi prisoner's dilemma in contexts where stated assumptions render it unlikely that a genuine prisoner's dilemma exists.

A third set of objections to the Hobbesian analysis of the individualist state of nature revolves around the dominators, who play a crucial role in that analysis. An initial worry is that our account of dominators as those who intrinsically value power over others does not fit with Hobbes's instrumental definition of power as means to people's ends. This worry is readily countered by noting that, as a matter of psychological fact, some people do come to value intrinsically what is originally a purely instrumental good. The miser's love of that paradigm instrumental good—money—is a clear instance of this. Similarly, Hobbes's dominators are supposed to intrinsically value a certain specific kind of power: power over others. Since goods may be valued both as

[49]Given, as seems plausible, that the exception to the rationality of choosing the quasi-dominant strategy noted in note 47 of this chapter does not apply.

means and as ends, there is no real conflict here with the instrumental definition of power.

A more serious issue concerns why dominators, as characterized, would anticipate in the state of nature. Even if they love power over others, won't they generally value safety even more and hence hesitate to start a cycle of escalation? Probably most will value safety more. But lying low is the safer course only if enough others do likewise. Yet no *one* dominator controls the actions of his fellow dominators (or the moderates). Hence, none can assume that his refraining from anticipation will restrain enough of his fellows, some of whom can be expected to anticipate to his detriment. This may well make it prudent for him to anticipate, even if he would prefer that no one anticipate. In other words, dominators—even if they prefer safety to conquest—will be in a (quasi) prisoner's dilemma with respect to their fellows in which anticipation is a (quasi) dominant strategy. Further, we saw in section 3-5 that the relative rationality of anticipating and lying low may be equal or indeterminate *even in a population of moderates*. If considerations of safety alone (the primary motive of the moderates) thus balance out between the two courses of action, the desire for power over others of the dominators should tip the balance toward actions that lead to the satisfaction of that desire, that is, toward anticipation.

This response makes clear that we need not view dominators as irrational. They may simply be people who possess, or possess to an unusual degree, a kind of intrinsic desire or preference that others lack—the desire for power over other people. The presence, or strength, of this desire may make it rational for them to undergo greater risks to their safety in pursuit of conquest than it would be rational for people who lack this desire to undergo. So while it is possible that some dominators are irrationally aggressive (i.e., get carried away by their lust for power to the extent of taking risks that outweigh expected power gains by their own "cool moment" calculations), the Hobbesian argument in no way depends on this.

A final point about dominators adds a gloss to our earlier dynamic analysis. Since the rationality of anticipation depends on

116

one's expectations about how others will behave in the future, a "credible (but false) rumor" of the existence of a sufficient number of dominators can lead to a war of all, provided the rumor cannot be disconfirmed until it is too late (i.e., too far into the escalatory process). Given the likelihood of a sufficient number of real dominators, Hobbesian theory need not rely on this "false belief" version of the escalation argument. Taking note of this version of the argument is nonetheless helpful, for it reminds us that moderates' *expectations* of the anticipations of others lie at the heart of the argument, and it identifies a feature—exaggeration of the threat posed by dominators—that can easily accelerate the escalation process.

Turning from the dominators, who are especially prone to conquest, we run into a fourth objection based on the likely existence of a class of persons who are especially prone to avoid violence. According to this objection, people of below-average physical strength, including most women, and people who are squeamish about attacking others even when their security interests seem to require it will be inclined to lie low rather than anticipate in the state of nature. Hence they will dampen or prevent the escalating cycle of violence postulated in the dynamic Hobbesian analysis. There are two ways of replying to this objection. First, it will be in the interests even of those weaker than average to anticipate—hoping thereby to build their aggregate power—if violence by dominators and the strong has grown to sufficiently threatening levels, as it is likely to. Similarly, even initial squeamishness about using violence will often be overcome when one's security is threatened and there seems to be no safe alternative to anticipation. Admittedly, a few may be so squeamish (or principled) as to abjure anticipation, or even all defensive violence, no matter what. This indicates that the individualist state of nature might end up only in a war of *nearly* all against all, but it hardly vitiates the general force of the escalation argument. Second, and more important, endangered individuals who are too weak or squeamish to anticipate are likely to soon find themselves under the control of those who are not. That is, they are likely to either

117

seek the protection of the strong[50] or be conquered by the strong. Then the war of all will continue in the form of a war among small groups (e.g., families) with equally unhappy consequences.[51] (See section 4-4.)

This second reply takes us into new territory. Until now, we have explicitly deferred consideration of courses of action involving group formation, but according to a fifth objection, our presentation has not been perfectly consistent in this respect. While we have claimed to be analyzing interactions among individuals in the state of nature, our earlier argument has implicitly presupposed coordinated actions and the formation of groups within the state of nature, in two ways. First, universal vulnerability of each individual to loss of life and property depends upon the assumption that others may *join together* to overpower even the strongest individual. Thus, Hobbes writes, "The weakest has strength enough to kill the strongest, . . . by confederacy with others" and "If one . . . possess a convenient seat, others may probably be expected to come prepared with forces united, to dispossess, and deprive him."[52] Second, anticipation, the recommended Hobbesian strategy for the state of nature, involves conquering others to increase one's power. But surely this implies the formation of a kind of group, with the conqueror as its leader. So even the argument to the war of all among individuals is, at bottom, an argument concerning group actions as well as individual actions.

The only fair response to this objection is to concede it, while noting that this does not undermine the substance of the arguments so far considered. After all, the division of the argument against anarchy into separate parts involving individuals and groups is merely an analytical convenience. What the present objection shows is that the possibility of at least temporary group forma-

---

[50] At *Leviathan*, chap. 10, p. 74, Hobbes writes: "Reputation of power . . . draweth with it the adherence of those that need protection."

[51] Hobbes sometimes portrays the war of all as a war among small family groups (*Leviathan*, chap. 13, p. 114; chap. 17, p. 154). However, he views such groups as bound together by "natural lust" rather than the need of the weaker (e.g., women and children) for protection.

[52] *Leviathan*, chap. 13, pp. 110–11.

tion already plays a role in generating the war of all individuals. It suggests that a more accurate description of the two parts of the argument discussed in this and the next chapter might involve other distinctions besides the individual-group dichotomy, for example, the distinction between natural (familial or conquest-based) and artificial (contractual) groups.

This need not worry us, even if we cannot find neat and appropriate titles for the two parts of the argument. But the objection before us draws our attention to the group-forming aspects of anticipation, and this raises some genuine substantive difficulties. Anticipation involves mastering others by "force, or wiles."[53] Hobbes is not explicit about how wiles may lead to dominion over others in the state of nature. Let us assume that they are used to reduce others' physical powers, or to trick them into making themselves vulnerable to your physical power, or to convince them that you (or your henchmen) are so much more physically powerful than they that they had better submit. On this assumption, force or the apparent threat of it remains the ultimate arbiter in the Hobbesian state of nature.[54]

But in what does even forceful mastery of others consist? If such mastery is to increase one's power usefully, it must imply the future capacity to dictate or strongly influence the mastered party's actions. Perhaps when you have once physically overpowered someone, he is likely to obey you in the future in the state of nature (if you can find him), out of fear of being overpowered again and punished. Or perhaps upon the initial conquest you can extract a promise of future obedience.[55] (Though independent of the last consideration, the threat of future punishment, promises are not, according to Hobbes, worth much.[56]) And once you have reliably subdued some, maybe you can use them to subdue others and keep these others in line. The key point to

[53] Ibid., p. 111.

[54] This remains so even if wiles are used by one subordinate to "master" another by winning their common superior's favor, for whatever power the subordinate exercises over others is ultimately based on the perceived coercive power of his master.

[55] See ibid., chap. 20, p. 189.

[56] See sections 4-1, 4-3, 9-1, and 9-2.

notice, however, is that even a successful anticipator in the state of nature will have problems exercising and maintaining power over those he has once mastered. Escape, defiance, rebellion, and assassination attempts are all potential actions by subordinates that state-of-nature conquerors, as well as political authorities in civil society, are likely to face.

The upshot of this is to diminish further the net expected pay-offs of following an anticipation strategy in the state of nature, for even the gains of anticipation, once won, are precarious and possibly difficult and expensive to retain. Acknowledging this leads to our sixth, and most significant, objection to the war of all argument: that the costs and dangers of anticipation are so high as to render lying low a more rational strategy after all. Let us begin consideration of this objection by stating it in its strongest form.

Whatever the advantages of anticipation in the state of nature, there are many dangers and disadvantages of pursuing such a strategy. As indicated earlier, you expose yourself to the defensive violence of those you attack and to the retaliatory violence of the victims and their friends. Equally important, by anticipating you make yourself an especially tempting target for other anticipators, for you identify yourself as one of those who is definitely inclined to anticipate and—compared with those who have not yet anticipated—this makes you a graver threat to attack others in the future. Further, with anticipation, even success carries special dangers. The more power you amass, the more power a dominator or anticipator can expect to win if he conquers you. Also, as noted two paragraphs above, successful conquest may expose one to violence at the hands of one's own subordinates. Given all these dangers that result from following an anticipation strategy in the state of nature, it seems that lying low—whatever its disadvantages—would have to be safer and "more reasonable."

There is some indirect empirical support for this objection drawn from observation of animal behavior and human behavior in certain primitive societies. The relevant observation concerns the relative lack of violence observed, compared to what one might expect if anticipation were a superior strategy to lying low in a state of nature. Thus, Turnbull, for example, having noted the extremely selfish and asocial behavior of the Ik, also observes that there is practically no violence in Ik society.[57] And observers of animal behavior have frequently noted that violent contests within species are relatively rare and are typically highly conventionalized so that little damage is done to participants.[58] Since this animal behavior is presumably influenced by genes and in the long run should accurately reflect the relative gains and losses of aggressive fighting and more passive strategies,[59] the low incidence of aggressive violence suggests that active aggression is not an optimal strategy in a state of nature.

In reply, let us first clarify the difference between the two strategies to be compared—anticipation and lying low. The difference is *not* that following the former involves being constantly engaged in violence, while the latter is a nonviolent strategy. Rather, the rational anticipator will use force aggressively *on occasions when it seems worth the risk*, while those who lie low avoid use of force except in immediate defense. Thus, an anticipator will engage in violence more often, but perhaps not that much more often than one who lies low, and—if rational—will not use violence unless success is likely (or the immediate alternatives are all quite bleak). Further, successful anticipation, by increasing one's power and demonstrating one's prowess, has very important deterrent advantages. Others now have more to gain by conquering you, but they are less likely to be able to do so and are running greater risks in trying to do so. This deterrence-enhancing feature of successful anticipation largely offsets the ex-

---

[57] Turnbull, *The Mountain People*, p. 261.

[58] See S. A. Barnett, "Attack and Defense in Animal Societies," in *Aggression and Defense*, ed. Carmine Clemente and Donald Lindsley (Berkeley: University of California Press, 1967), pp. 35–56, esp. the summary on p. 45; and Konrad Lorenz, *On Aggression* (New York: Bantam Books, 1966), chap. 7. Cf. E. O. Wilson, *Sociobiology*, pp. 246–47.

[59] See G. A. Parker, "Assessment Strategy and the Evolution of Fighting Behavior," in *Readings in Sociobiology*, ed. Clutton-Brock and Harvey, pp. 271–92.

tra dangers, listed above, to which an anticipator exposes himself in the state of nature.

Nor will it do, as the objector suggests, to extrapolate the relative payoffs of anticipation and lying low in the state of nature by observing levels of violence among animals, for there are special features of human beings that appear to make the anticipation strategy more attractive and viable for them. As Hobbes emphasizes, people are concerned with their reputations, and this creates an additional source of conflict that might lead to others' attacking them. People are forwardlooking, and hence will not be inclined to rely on a strategy like lying low that provides no assurance of safety other than the hope that no one stronger will ever have the occasion to attack them. People are also intelligent and have language; hence they are generally much more capable of coordinated action than are other animals. As a result, humans are especially vulnerable to others of their own kind acting in concert. This provides even the strongest with the incentive to anticipate and increase their power beyond their natural powers. Because of these distinctive human features, then, even if it generally pays other animals to lie low in dealing with co-specifics, it may well pay *people* to anticipate in the state of nature.

Though these replies reduce the force of our sixth objection, that objection still makes a valid and important point. Anticipation is both more costly and more dangerous in some respects, and more beneficial in others, than lying low. Correspondingly, which strategy is better overall probably cannot be determined a priori for all state-of-nature situations. Instead, it will depend upon the specific values of a number of important variables and parameters, which will vary according to the version of the state of nature in question. Broad limits on the values of these variables are imposed by some of the explicit assumptions of the argument: rough equality of persons, the presence of a significant minority of dominators, conflicting desires due to some degree of resource scarcity, and so on. But assignment of different values within these limits might well produce different optimal strategies—anticipation for one assignment, lying low for another. Further, there are variables not yet mentioned which probably have significant influence on which of these two is the better strategy. Population density is an obvious example; lying low becomes a more promising strategy for survival if the population is more sparsely distributed.

The upshot of this is that lying low may, after all, be the "most reasonable" strategy in some hypothetical states of nature and in some real situations approximating the state of nature. In such situations, an active war of all will not result. The Ik, for example, do not appear to be in an active war of all—they practically never use violence against one another. There is a plausible explanation for this. They are so poor and malnourished that no one has much to steal or defend, and they cannot afford the energy expenditure of violent conflict.[60] Perhaps, then, anticipation and the resulting active war of all are characteristics of state-of-nature environments that are neither too poor nor too rich—there is sufficient abundance to make theft, conquest, and defense worthwhile, but not so much as to remove material scarcity as a source of conflict.

The question now arises as to how much these admissions about the possible optimality of lying low affect the force of the Hobbesian argument against anarchy. It is interesting that they do not affect it much. One may preserve accuracy by simply incorporating further needed restrictions on relevent variables (e.g., at least moderate population density) into the assumptions of the argument and weaken the conclusion to read "people in a state of nature are *very likely* to end up in an active war of all against all." Such changes would not interfere with the role the argument plays in Hobbesian moral and political theory, for the primary function of the argument is to explain and justify the role that the State plays in modern civilized societies. The state of nature is used, in Hobbesian theory, as a model of what would happen to *us* if central political authority were removed, and its purported negative features serve as reasons for us not to pro-

---

[60] See T. H. Clutton-Brock and Paul Harvey, "Evolutionary Rules and Primate Societies," in *Readings in Sociobiology*, p. 295; and Morton Fried, *The Evolution of Political Society* (New York: Random House, 1967), p. 67.

mote or allow such removal, for example, by provoking a civil war.

Therefore, what matters for the explanatory and normative uses of Hobbesian state-of-nature theory is what would happen in the state of nature whose occupants and background conditions resemble those of modern societies.[61] But modern civilizations clearly satisfy the additional assumptions needed to infer that the state of nature would likely become an active war of all—nonextreme scarcity, substantial population density, people who are concerned for their reputations and have a capacity for coordinated action, and so on. Hence, given the intended uses of the war of all argument, the aforementioned modifications in that argument would not negatively affect the construction of Hobbesian political theory.

The seventh and final objection we shall consider proposes a novel alternative to anticipation in the state of nature: tacit agreement. The parties in the state of nature use up energy, resources, and time, and risk life and injury, attacking and defending against one another. Hence, they could all do better, in terms of wealth and security, if they mutually limited their aggressive behavior.[62] In the next two chapters, we will consider efforts to do this by explicit agreement. But, the current objection urges, such limitation can develop as a tacit convention involving mutual behavioral restraint, as all parties realize that mutual gains can thereby be obtained. No explicit agreement is needed, only implicit acknowledgment of the genuine mutual interest in maintaining and observing constraints.

This objection need not be dealt with at length because the main problems with the tacit agreement alternative are discussed elsewhere. First, there is the prisoner's dilemma aspect of the matter: in the absence of an enforcement mechanism, individual

---

[61] Hence, even if C. B. Macpherson's *The Political Theory of Possessive Individualism* (London: Oxford University Press, 1962) were correct that Hobbes read features of his society back into the state of nature, this would not necessarily constitute an error, *given the aims of Hobbesian theory.*

[62] See, e.g., James Buchanan, *The Limits of Liberty* (Chicago: University of Chicago Press, 1975), pp. 23–27.

parties would seem to have reason to violate the restricting convention even though it is collectively beneficial.[63] Second, tacit
agreements in the state of nature face all the enforcement difficulties of explicit agreements. As we shall see in the next chapter,
these include the problems of identifying violators and getting
others to share the costs and risks of enforcement. Third, there
are special enforcement difficulties associated with the vagueness
and inexplicitness of conventions or tacit agreements: the possibility of honest differences about what the agreement or convention is, corresponding difficulties of convincing others to punish
an apparent violation, and dangers of escalating conflicts due to
divergent interpretations of the tacit agreement.[64] So while we
cannot say, a priori, that tacit agreements could never be a good
road to peace and security in any state-of-nature situation, explicit agreements would appear to be a much more promising road.
In the next three chapters, we will explore that road and discover
that it leads somewhere but is dotted with traps and pitfalls.

[63] For some complications, see the discussion in the next chapter concerning
iterated prisoner's dilemma.

[64] This last difficulty is hinted at by Locke in his *Second Treatise*, sec. 13, p.
316.

F O U R

COOPERATION IN THE STATE
OF NATURE

4-1. Defensive Cooperatives

In the last chapter, we focused on comparing two primarily individualistic strategies for getting by in the state of nature: lying low and anticipating.[1] It seems evident, however, that a strategy of group formation and collective defense would offer the individual greater protection and security against "forces united, to dispossess, and deprive him"[2] in the state of nature, than would either individualistic strategy. Nor would Hobbes himself deny this. Rather, in the second part of his argument against anarchy, he contends that any group-formation strategy that falls short of establishing a commonwealth will not provide the parties with "sufficient security" to lead decent lives. In the course of developing this part of the argument, Hobbes relies on some highly implausible empirical assumptions about political societies and reaches conclusions that are stronger than warranted. Thus, it will be our task in this chapter to correct, as well as explicate and develop, the second part of the argument against anarchy. Along the way, we shall learn something about the possibility of, and limits on, cooperation in the state of nature.

Defensive groups in the state of nature may originate in various ways—by family ties, conquest and submission, tacit agreement, explicit agreement, or some combination thereof—and they

[1] As we saw in section 3-6, however, even anticipating is not a purely individualistic strategy, in that it involves attempting to improve one's defenses by amassing a group of followers.
[2] *Leviathan*, chap. 13, p. 111.

126

may take a variety of forms, such as helping one another build defensive fortifications or having a specialized subgroup of defenders whose sole task is to deter and repel invaders. For simplicity and convenience, we shall take as our paradigm of the state-of-nature defensive group the *defensive cooperative*. This consists of an explicit agreement, among some group of individuals in the state of nature, that each will come to the aid of any other in the group whose person or property is attacked or threatened. Though they are simple, defensive cooperatives have sufficient structure to allow us to use them to investigate the primary obstacles to cooperation in the state of nature.

The main such obstacle that Hobbes emphasizes is the problem of compliance. This applies to state-of-nature agreements in general and to the defensive cooperative agreement in especially acute form. Hobbes labels agreements calling for the parties to perform later, and in sequence, *covenants of mutual trust*. He contends that in the state of nature, where there is no common power to enforce the agreement, it would not be rational for the first party to such an agreement to perform, because he lacks assurance that the other party will perform in turn.[3]

Defensive cooperative agreements may profitably be viewed as covenants of mutual trust (though until the first attack the parties may not know which of them will be called on to perform first). If you help another party to such an agreement when he or his land is threatened by an invader, you risk your life without any assurance that the person you help will not simply hide or flee when you or your property is attacked. As first performer, therefore, it may be irrational for you to comply with the agreement.

We can put this problem in a familiar perspective if we assume that each party to a two-person state-of-nature defense agreement firmly decides on a strategy for dealing with the first attack before it comes, and thus before either knows who will be the victim (that is, each now decides whether to keep the agreement and come to his partner's aid should the partner be attacked first).

---

[3] Ibid., chap. 14, pp. 124–25. For some complications, see sections 4-3 and 9-2.

FIGURE 3

Party 2

	Keep (aid)	Break (don't aid)
Keep (aid) (Party 1)	$-2b$ ⟍ $-2b$	$-b$ ⟍ $-(a+b)$
Break (don't aid) (Party 1)	$-(a+b)$ ⟍ $-b$	$-a$ ⟍ $-a$

We assume further that the parties are purely self-interested[4] and have equal chances of being the victim of the attack when it comes, and that each would suffer a loss represented by $-2a$ if attacked and not aided. On the other hand, if the attacked party is aided, both he and his helper will suffer a loss of $-2b$ defending against the attack, with their combined payoff ($-4b$) being a smaller loss than $-2a$. (This last point implies that the defense arrangement works if kept—it would reduce the losses from attack of the two taken together.)

From these assumptions we can construct a game matrix representing the parties' choices to keep or not keep the agreement should the other be attacked. Each party's expected payoff for each combination of choices is calculated by adding his payoff (for that combination) if he is the attack victim times the probability of his being that victim (1/2), and his payoff if the other is the victim times the probability of that (1/2). The resulting matrix is presented in Figure 3, which can readily be seen to be a prisoner's dilemma matrix. Since $-4b$ is a smaller loss than $-2a$, it is a larger (less negative) quantity, that is, $-2a < -4b$. So $-a < -2b$, and each is better off if both Keep rather than both Break. But Break is a dominant strategy for each, as $-2b < -b$ and $-(a + b) < -a$. As a result, it appears that defense pacts among rational agents in the state of nature are extremely vulnerable when first put to the test, so vulnerable as to be worthless. Note,

[4] This simplifying assumption is carried over into section 4-3. Its significance is discussed at the end of that section.

however, that in calculating costs and benefits we have considered only the short-term results of keeping or breaking the defense pact on the first occasion. A more sophisticated analysis must take into account that such agreements are intended to apply to a number of similar, but distinct and successive, situations. That is, they are intended to secure reciprocal cooperation among agents *over time*. The implications of this are of critical importance for the theory of rational cooperation and for Hobbesian political theory.

4-2. Cooperation over Time

By focusing only on the first attack suffered by parties to a state-of-nature mutual-aid pact, we have so far overlooked a significant motive that rational forwardlooking individuals would have for adhering to such a pact. In coming to the aid of an attacked partner, you encourage others to offer similar aid to you in the future, while by not coming to his aid you would place your credibility and your membership in the coalition in jeopardy. Thus, if you aid a coalition partner today, you can expect him to aid you tomorrow to increase the chances that you and others will aid him the day after tomorrow. To put the point in more general terms, the fear of losing credibility and hence future opportunities for beneficial cooperation can suffice to motivate rational self-interested parties in the state of nature to keep their agreements with one another. This is an important point about rational cooperation to which Hobbes did not devote sufficient attention.[5]

If, however, we conceive the parties in the state of nature as highly rational and knowledgeable strategists, there is a theoretical objection against founding defensive cooperatives on their expectations of benefiting from future cooperation with their partners. This objection consists in applying to defensive cooperatives the following general argument about situations having the structure of iterated plays of the game prisoner's dilemma.

We have noted that noncooperation is the rational, because

[5] Except, perhaps, in his answer to the Fool. See section 4-3.

129

dominant, move for each party in a single-play prisoner's dilemma game. Suppose, now, that we have a game of *iterated* prisoner's dilemma of some definite number of moves, n, to be played by two players who are rational and interested solely in maximizing their personal payoffs and who will remain so throughout the game. It is assumed that this is all common knowledge among the players, that is, each knows it, knows the other knows it, knows the other knows he knows it, and so forth. Given the assumptions of self-interest and rationality, and the dominance of noncooperation on a single play, it follows that a player will cooperate on a given play only if he believes that doing so may induce his partner to cooperate on some later play or plays. Since each party, being rational, knows this, each party knows his opponent will not cooperate on the nth (i.e., last) play, for there are no later plays on which cooperation by one's opponent could be induced by a cooperative move on the nth play. But then each party knows that a cooperative move on the $n -$ 1st play could not induce future cooperation by his opponent and, being rational, he will not cooperate on the $n -$ 1st play. But his opponent, knowing this, will have no reason to cooperate on the $n -$ 2nd play and will not so cooperate. By similar reasoning, we work our way back step-by-step (or by mathematical induction) to the very first play and conclude that each party will make the noncooperative move on every play.[6] This argument can be generalized in two ways. First, it can be extended to cover *multiparty* versions of prisoner's dilemma. (Recall from section 3-6 that a game with two possible moves on each play is an instance of multiparty prisoner's dilemma if one move, the noncooperative move, is dominant for every player [i.e., each does better playing that move no matter what combination of moves the others make], and if universal play of the other, cooperative, move yields higher payoffs to every player than universal play of the dominant move.) Second, the argument can encompass cases in

[6] An early version of this argument may be found in R. Duncan Luce and Howard Raiffa, *Games and Decisions* (New York: John Wiley & Sons, 1957), pp. 97–99.

which the players do not know the exact number of plays there will be but do know that some specific and definite number, u, is an *upper bound* on the number of plays and that how they play the game will have no influence on the number of plays there are.[7] For assuming that the conditions specified (plus the ability and propensity of each to accurately perceive and count plays) are common knowledge among all the players, *each* knows that if there is a uth play, each of the others will make the noncooperative move. Each therefore knows that if there is a $u - 1$st play, each will have no reason to cooperate on that play, for each will know that this play will either turn out to be the last play or will be followed by a uth play on which the others will all make noncooperative moves. It follows that each knows his opponents will not cooperate on the $u - 1$st or uth plays, if there are such, and by reasoning similar to the above we work back to the conclusion that none will cooperate on any play.

This argument that rational and sufficiently knowledgeable players will never cooperate in bounded iterated multiparty prisoner's dilemma can be applied to try to show that mutual-aid pacts will never be kept by such parties in the state of nature. Prior to any given attack, an aid-pact member prefers universal adherence to the pact to universal nonadherence, because this protects him if he should be one of the attacked parties. But—taking the single instance in isolation—he prefers his own noncompliance with the pact because of the dangers of compliance. Hence, the aid-pact compliance problem has the structure of a multiparty prisoner's dilemma. Assume that each party accurately identifies and counts attacks as they occur and that the parties will, between them, suffer at most a definite number of attacks, u,[8] with the actual number determined by the propensities of external attackers and not in any way by their own behavior. If all this is common knowledge among the parties, the as-

---

[7] As far as I know, this generalization of the argument was first noted in my "Hobbes's War of All Against All," *Ethics* 93 (January 1983): 302.

[8] This is apparently not an unrealistic assumption, as u may be chosen as large as we wish. But see note 9 and the text accompanying note 11 in this chapter.

sumptions of the above argument are satisfied, and we may infer that the parties will never comply with the aid pact.

The conclusion of the argument, that aid pacts are hopeless in the state of nature, is counterintuitive, even paradoxical. It seems that truly rational parties so situated would at least *try* aiding their fellows a few times in hopes of creating a practice of beneficial reciprocal aid. Nevertheless, the argument, or some more precisely stated variant of it, seems to be valid. The implausible conclusion derives not from fallacious reasoning but from the argument's extremely strong assumptions.

For the argument to go through, the parties must be assumed to all be rational strategists who will replicate the line of reasoning contained in the argument itself. If we throw in even a few inductivists, we ruin the argument, for we now have a subpopulation that will not predict the future acts of others by the recapitulative-deductive process represented in the argument. Some of these inductivists would aid others in hopes of inducing reciprocation, which gives even the strategists a possible rational incentive for helping to stave off attacks.

A further degree of unrealism is introduced into the argument by the assumption that each rational strategist knows that each of the others is thus rational, that each knows each of the others knows all are thus rational, and so forth, up to high orders of knowledge.[9] Furthermore, the kind of knowledge of the circumstances and the other parties that is required for the argument to work is "certain" knowledge, that is, true beliefs about whose truth the believers have not the slightest doubts. This is because the rational parties' chains of reasoning invoke a large number of (relatively) independent premises, and their degrees of belief in the conclusion of the argument at each stage will not (since they are rational) exceed their degrees of belief in the conjunction of the premises used up to that point. So, if their beginning degrees of belief in the premises about the risks of aiding others, in the rationality of their partners, and so on, were significantly less

---

[9] Some formal investigation suggests that the parties must have uth order knowledge of the relevant facts of the situation, where u is the known upper bound on the number of attacks.

than "certainty," they would not conclude that their partners surely will not cooperate. And they might rationally attempt cooperation on common-sense grounds.[10]

In addition, the critical assumption that there is a known upper bound u on the total number of attacks has an odd status. It is plausible only because we may simply choose u as high as we like, high enough to greatly exceed our realistic estimates of the number of attacks.[11] But if the rational parties to an aid pact ever got to within a few attacks of a uth one, they would likely begin to doubt that u was an appropriate upper bound and would no longer possess the required "certain" knowledge that it was. Thus, in a way that is not apparent on the surface, the upper bound assumption introduces yet another unrealistic element into the present model of state-of-nature defense pacts.

Finally, the assumption that the number of attacks by outsiders is independent of the behavior of the pact members is almost certainly mistaken. The more the parties band together to successfully repel early attacks on members, the less likely they are to be attacked in the future, other things being equal. Common defense acts as a deterrent against potential aggressors. Since it is to the advantage of each partner to minimize the total number of attacks (because he may be among the victims), each thus has an additional self-interested reason for coming to the defense of attacked coalition partners.

We must conclude, then, that the iterated prisoner's dilemma argument for the futility of defense pacts (and, more generally, cooperative agreements) in the state of nature would hold only under the most restricted and unrealistic conditions. Nonetheless, the argument establishes an interesting theoretical point about cooperation in the state of nature. Such cooperation is possible only for creatures, such as ourselves, possessing *nonextreme* lev-

[10] I adapt this point from Tyler Burge, who applies it in a different context in "Reasoning About Reasoning," *Philosophia* 8 (December 1978): 651–55. See also Hardin, *Collective Action*, pp. 148–49, which, like the present treatment, emphasizes the uncertainty of the assumptions underlying the reasoning that noncooperation is rational in iterated prisoner's dilemma.

[11] See note 8 above. Cf., however, note 9, where it is noted how choosing a high u requires strengthening other assumptions of the argument.

els of knowledge and rationality. If we were as rational and knowledgeable as the assumptions of the iterated prisoner's dilemma argument assumes, certain highly beneficial forms of cooperation might be closed to us. If, on the other hand, we were *ir*rational in various ways—for example, devaluing long-term benefits relative to short-term ones, risking necessities to obtain uneeded gains—we might also miss out on the potential fruits of cooperation. This latter point is one of the main themes of Hobbes's argument against the Fool, to which we turn in the next section.

First, however, it will be useful to make some general observations about the rationality of cooperating in those situations modeling state-of-nature defense pacts, that is, iterated prisoner's dilemmas. The above argument, because of its highly restrictive assumptions, fails to demonstrate that cooperation is irrational in realistic iterated prisoner's dilemma situations. And both common sense and experiments in which many pairs of players achieve a rewarding pattern of mutual cooperation on most plays[12] suggest that it is often rational to cooperate in such situations to induce future cooperation by one's partner(s).

When is it rational to play an iterated prisoner's dilemma cooperatively and when is it not rational? And what pattern of cooperation is best? Unfortunately, there are no easy rules to follow here, and whether (and how) it is rational to cooperate in a given iterated prisoner's dilemma is influenced by a variety of very complex factors. Below are seven features of an iterated prisoner's dilemma that increase the rationality of making early cooperative moves, other things being equal. This listing is simply to give an idea of the many dimensions of the problem.

1. *Relative benefits of cooperation and noncooperation.* The higher the per-play rewards of mutual cooperation compared to those of mutual noncooperation, and the lower the per-play rewards of successful exploitation (and penalties of being exploited),

[12] See Anatol Rapoport and Albert Chammah, *Prisoner's Dilemma* (Ann Arbor: University of Michigan Press, 1965), pp. 63–66.

the more rational it is to cooperate in order to induce future co-operation by others.[13]

2. *Number of plays.* The greater the number of iterations, the more potential gains there are to be reaped by mutual coopera-tion, and hence the more rational it is to try early cooperation.

3. *Uncertainty about the number of plays.* Greater certainty about the number of plays can produce end game effects as the likely end of the series of interactions approaches. That is, play-ers may make noncooperative moves because they confidently ex-pect to have little to lose thereby (given the few opportunities for cooperation remaining) and because they expect the other to react likewise and cease cooperating. Such potential end game effects can reverberate forward if players try to stop cooperating before others do so. Our earlier argument assuming complete certainty about the number of plays (or an upper bound thereof) carries this process to its theoretical limit—anticipatory noncooperation by all parties from the first play onward.

4. *Unforgivingness.* The less forgiving the other parties are (i.e., the more severely they are inclined to punish your non-cooperation with their future noncooperation), the more it is ra-tional to cooperate. Imagine, for example, that all others use some common version of this strategy in dealing with you: "Cooperate initially, but follow any noncooperative move by the other (i.e., you) with, on average, n noncooperative moves." The higher n is, the more unforgiving the particular strategy (and the party following it) is toward you. When n equals zero, your partner is totally forgiving—a pure saint (or sucker)—and you gain most by continually exploiting him. When n equals infinity, your partner is totally unforgiving and you lose all chance of future coopera-tion if you cross him just once. For values in between, the higher the number, the more opportunities for beneficial cooperation you

---

[13] Let P_{CC}, P_{NN}, P_{CN}, P_{NC} stand for a player's payoffs for mutual cooperation, mutual noncooperation, unilateral cooperation, and unilateral noncooperation, re-spectively. Then we may represent the relative benefits of cooperation and non-cooperation by the ratio: $(P_{CC} - P_{NN})/([P_{NC} - P_{CC}] + [P_{NN} - P_{CN}])$. For the pris-oner's dilemma matrix of Figure 3, e.g., this reduces to $(a - 2b)/2b$.

forgo with each noncooperative act, and the more reason you have to cooperate on any given play.

5. *Reactivity.* Others may become less inclined to cooperate with you in the future, not because you cheat them but because they learn of your cheating third parties. People who are like this may be called *reactive.* The more reactive the people you may want future cooperation with are, the more rational it is for you to cooperate in a given iterated prisoner's dilemma situation.

6. *Detectability.* So far, we have implicitly assumed that your move (cooperation or noncooperation) will certainly become known to your partner and perhaps to others. But in the real world, information problems of various sorts (including deliberate deception on your part) may prevent your partner or others from knowing what you have done. The more likely they are to know, the more detectable your move is, and the more you have to gain by cooperating.

7. *Accuracy of Reputation.* Even if your moves are detectable, information about them may not be available to those who interact with you in the future, unless there are accurate and accessible records of how you acted and others are able to identify you as the person who performed the recorded acts. To the extent that you are reidentifiable and your past is correctly and accessibly on record, we may say that you have an *accurate reputation.* The more you expect to have an accurate reputation in the future, the more rational it is to cooperate now, since you will be more able to reap the future benefits of present cooperation and less able to avoid the future penalties of present noncooperation.

There are doubtless other important variables that influence the rationality of cooperation in iterated prisoner's dilemma situations, and even the seven features listed are too vague, complex, and various to integrate readily into a precise model of rational cooperation over time. Nonetheless, Hobbes does present an important argument concerning cooperation in the state of nature that may be interpreted as taking several of these features into account. We must now consider that argument.

4-3. Cooperation and the Fool

Hobbes defends the possibility of rational cooperation in the state of nature most fully in his response to the Fool. The Fool, an atheist who does not fear divine punishment, contends that it is in one's interests, and hence reasonable, to violate agreements in the state of nature. Hobbes's reply is worth quoting at considerable length, with parts numbered for ease of later reference.

(1) For the question is not of promises mutual, where there is no security of performance on either side; as when there is no civil power erected over the parties promising; for such promises are no covenants: but either where one of the parties has performed already; or where there is a power to make him perform; there is the question whether it be against reason, that is, against the benefit of the other to perform, or not. (2) And I say it is not against reason. (3) For the manifestation whereof, we are to consider; first, that when a man doth a thing, which notwithstanding any thing can be foreseen, and reckoned on, tendeth to his own destruction, howsoever some accident which he could not expect, arriving may turn it to his benefit; yet such events do not make it reasonably or wisely done. (4) Secondly, that in a condition of war, wherein every man to every man, for want of a common power to keep them all in awe, is an enemy, there is no man who can hope by his own strength, or wit, to defend himself from destruction, without the help of confederates; (5) where every one expects the same defence by the confederation, that any one else does: and therefore he which declares he thinks it reason to deceive those that help him, can in reason expect no other means of safety, than what can be had from his own single power. (6) He therefore that breaketh his covenant, and consequently declareth that he thinks he may with reason do so, cannot be received into any society, that unite themselves for peace and defence, but by the error of them that receive him; nor when he is received, be

137

FIGURE 4

Second party

		Keep	Break
First party	Keep	5 5	8 −3
	Break	−3 8	0 0

retained in it, without seeing the danger of their error; (7) which errors a man cannot reasonably reckon upon as the means of his security: and therefore if he be left, or cast out of society, he perisheth; and if he live in society, it is by the errors of other men, which he could not foresee, nor reckon upon; and consequently against the reason of his preservation.[14]

This central passage of Leviathan begins, in part 1, with the sorting out of cases of keeping agreements into three categories: a first party performing his part of a state-of-nature agreement, a second party performing in the state of nature when the corresponding first party has already performed, and either party performing in civil society. For the moment, let us limit our attention to the first two categories. Since it benefits one party if the other complies, but is costly for either to comply himself, we can represent a typical state-of-nature agreement as a prisoner's dilemma matrix as in Figure 4 (symmetry is assumed only for simplicity). If the parties perform in sequence, the first party must break the agreement, assuring himself a payoff of 0. Keeping would leave him open to the rational second party's maximizing his own payoff to a level of 8 by breaking, leaving the first party with −3. Hobbes apparently accepts this reasoning, agreeing (with the

[14] Leviathan, chap. 15, pp. 133–34.

FIGURE 5

		Second party	
		Keep	Break
First party	Keep	5 / 5	8 − p / −3
	Break	−3 / 8 − p	−p / −p

Fool) that the first party should not perform.[15] We may say that Hobbes approves of *defensive* violations of state-of-nature agreements, that is, violations motivated by the desire to avoid being taken advantage of, to avoid becoming a unilateral complier.

But suppose some naive first party does not break a state-of-nature agreement? How should the second party respond? In particular, should he *offensively* violate the agreement, obtaining his maximum payment of 8, by betraying his partner who has complied? The Fool thinks so, but Hobbes disagrees; he refuses to endorse offensive violations. We will best understand his reasons for rejecting such violations if we first consider why he rejects violating agreements in civil society. The obvious reason is that civil authorities, as part of their function, will impose penalties on contract-breakers that exceed the benefits obtainable by breach.[16] Let p be the magnitude of that penalty (or, if its application is uncertain, its magnitude discounted by its probability). Then the state-of-nature matrix in Figure 4 is transformed, by the threat of penalty, into the matrix in Figure 5. Provided that $p > 3$, keeping the agreement is a dominant strategy for each party, and mutual compliance with the agreeement yields a Pareto-optimal result. Thus, the introduction of a sufficient threat of penalties for breach removes possible offensive and defensive motives for

---

[15] Ibid., chap. 14, pp. 124–25, 128–29. Later in this section we shall discuss some problems this poses for Hobbes.

[16] Ibid., chap. 15, p. 131; chap. 27, pp. 281, 299.

violation and changes a prisoner's dilemma situation into one in which the two parties' interests no longer substantially conflict. (It is worth noting that the same result could have been obtained by offering a *reward* of more than 3 to any party that kept the agreement. In general, however, a reward policy is a less-promising method for authorities to use in securing compliance with agreements. Not only is it costly to pay the rewards, doing so also provides parties with incentives to enter into nonproductive agreements just to earn the rewards of compliance.)

We are now in a position to understand Hobbes's disagreement with the Fool over second-party compliance with state-of-nature agreements. The Fool, looking only at the immediate payoffs available, sees the situation depicted in Figure 4. He therefore proclaims breach (i.e., offensive violation) as the most reasonable response of the second party to first-party compliance. Hobbes, however, views the second party's response as having long-term effects on that party's prospects of future cooperation with others. Specifically, he suggests in parts 4–6 of the reply to the Fool, quoted above, that a particularly vital sort of cooperation, inclusion in defense confederations, will be denied known offensive violators of agreements, since other members will not trust them to keep their promises of aid (part 5). Because the alternatives to confederation in the state of nature—the individualist strategies of lying low or anticipation—are so bleak (part 7),[17] the net long-run penalty one suffers from not performing as a second party will exceed the gains of breaking the agreement. In other words, with long-term effects figured in, the choice the second party faces is represented by the matrix in Figure 5 with $p > > 3$. The danger of being excluded from future cooperative defense arrangements here has a function that is analogous to that of civil punishments within the commonwealth: it transforms a situation in which noncooperation is a dominant strategy into one in which cooperation is dominant.

One difficulty with Hobbes's reply to the Fool, as so far inter-

[17] This supports our earlier claim that Hobbes regards forming defensive cooperatives as a better state-of-nature strategy than anticipation.

preted, is that it *assumes* that viability of defense cooperatives in the state of nature. If one is to count nonmembership in defense cooperatives as a substantial *cost* of reneging on a state-of-nature agreement, it must be that such structures exist and are stable enough that a person could reasonably hope to join one and gain substantial benefits from it if he does not renege on the agreement. In the last section, we rejected as unrealistic an argument designed to show that state-of-nature defense cooperatives are impossible, but we did not show that the existence of such cooperatives is guaranteed, or even highly likely. And the key considerations advanced in the general argument—each party's lack of assurance of the other party's future compliance—does seem to raise questions about the availability and stability of such cooperatives in a state of nature.

However, Hobbes's reply implicitly and effectively deals with this source of concern, for suppose one takes it seriously and doubts that state-of-nature defense pacts are viable and can provide substantial security benefits. In that case one may simply read "society" in parts 6 and 7 of the reply to the Fool as standing for civil society, or the commonwealth. Then Hobbes may be viewed as pointing out that founders, or preserving members, of a commonwealth will not accept unreliable parties, such as offensive violators of agreements, as members. Second-party state-of-nature agreement violators are thus not simply risking future membership in shaky state-of-nature defense cooperatives, they are risking their chances of permanent escape from the state of nature via the only effective mechanism thereof, membership in a commonwealth. And commonwealths possessing sovereigns with the power to enforce agreements among their members are not subject to the potentially worrisome assurance and compliance problems of state-of-nature defensive cooperatives.[18]

We have so far assumed that one's offensive violations of state-of-nature agreements will surely be known to potential fellow citizens or defense-coalition partners. Hobbes's more realistic assumption—that there is a *risk* that an offensive violator will be-

[18] See section 6-1, where this claim is somewhat modified.

141

come known as such to relevant parties—introduces a further element of complexity, and ambiguity, into his reply to the Fool (parts 3, 6, and 7). In fact, it allows us to interpret the reply as based on any of three principles of rational choice: expected utility maximization, maximin, or disaster-avoidance.[19]

Consider first the expected utility interpretation. It begins from the assumption that the cost, c, of being excluded from defensive cooperatives or commonwealths (i.e., likely destruction) is very large relative to the gains, g, to be made by violating a state-of-nature agreement as second party. Assuming, further, that defense-pact members will surely exclude a known second-party violator,[20] the argument continues with the claim that there is a significant probability, q, that a second-party violation will become known to potential pact members. Given these assumptions, the expected utility of violating a state-of-nature agreement as second party equals the expected utility of keeping it plus $g - qc$ (gains minus potential cost discounted by the probability of suffering the cost). But since q is significant, and $c >> g$, the quantity $(g - qc)$ is quite likely to be negative, in which case breaking the agreement has lower expected utility for the agent and is thus irrational.

The other two interpretations of Hobbes's reply rely on principles of rational choice under uncertainty, that is, when probability estimates are not available. The maximin principle, which can be applied under complete uncertainty (i.e., when there is *no* probability information), says to choose the alternative with the best worst outcome. The disaster-avoidance principle, which can be applied only when certain ordinal[21] probability data are avail-

[19] On disaster-avoidance, see my "Deterrence, Utility, and Rational Choice," *Theory and Decision* 12 (March 1980): 41–60. For application to the Fool, see my "Right Reason and Natural Law in Hobbes's Ethics," *The Monist* 66 (January 1983): 120–33, sec. 4. On Hobbes's apparent use of disaster-avoidance reasoning, see section 5-3. In discussing these three principles, I do not mean to suggest that Hobbes was explicitly aware of them or the differences between them.

[20] This assumption is relaxed later in this section.

[21] These ordinal data are of the form "A is more (or less) likely than B," where A and B are events, outcomes, or outcomes conditioned on the performance of certain actions.

able, recommends choosing the course of action that maximizes your chances of avoiding all disastrous outcomes. These principles agree in their prescriptions when the best worst outcome is nondisastrous.[22] Then the course of action possibly leading to this outcome has a probability of one of avoiding disaster and will be selected by the disaster-avoidance principle as well as the maximin principle. When, however, each course of action risks disaster, the two principles may diverge in their implications, as the following reading of the nuclear balance of terror illustrates.

Superpower S is deciding whether to continue nuclear deterrence against superpower rival R. S believes that continuing deterrence risks a worse disaster—large-scale nuclear war—with indeterminant probability p_1. S's disarming unilaterally (of nuclear weapons) would risk a lesser disaster—domination of the world by R—with indeterminant probability p_2. While S cannot assign even approximate numerical values to p_1 and p_2, it is confident that $p_1 < p_2$. In this situation, the maximin principle recommends disarming unilaterally, since the worst outcome this could produce—world domination by R—is not as bad as the worst possible outcome of the alternative course, nuclear war. The disaster-avoidance principle, by contrast, recommends continuing deterrence, for this yields a higher probability of avoiding all disasters than does the alternative course (i.e., $[1 - p_1] > [1 - p_2]$).

Hobbes's reply to the Fool could be viewed as an instance of *either* maximin or disaster-avoidance reasoning under uncertainty, for on the natural reading of the situation Hobbes describes, the implications of the two principles coincide with each other and with Hobbes's own conclusion (parts 2 and 7 of the reply). Consider the alternatives of breaking and keeping the agreement. The former, according to Hobbes, risks being left to

---

[22] This is not strictly true. When more than one alternative guarantees disaster-avoidance, the disaster-avoidance principle does not discriminate among them, while the maximin principle may. It is worth noting that Rawls's use of the maximin principle in his theory of justice can be viewed as an application of the disaster-avoidance principle in a special case. See my "Right Reason and Natural Law in Hobbes's Ethics," sec. 4.

go it alone in the state of nature and one's subsequent destruction. The latter risks only the extra gains one might get (3 and g in our earlier examples) by unilateral violation of the agreement. Forgoing these gains in favor of the still-positive gains of mutual compliance is not going to be disastrous for the agent.[23] Hence, by keeping his state-of-nature agreement after the first party complies, the second party opts for the alternative with best worst outcome (missed opportunity for gain is better than going it alone in the state of nature). And he selects the one alternative that maximizes the probability (in fact, assures him) of obtaining a nondisastrous outcome.

All of our three principles of rational choice yield Hobbes's conclusion about second-party compliance in the state of nature (given his assumptions). The text of the passage itself is not explicit enough to allow us to discern which, if any, of these principles Hobbes himself employs. The expected utility and maximin principles are, of course, widely known and often used choice rules. By contrast, the disaster-avoidance principle is a concoction of the author created to deal with certain choice problems such as the disarmament decision noted above. The principle is at the same time Hobbesian in that it serves, as we shall see in section 5–3, to explicate other arguments of Hobbes's concerning revolution, the social contract, and obedience to political authorities. It is therefore worth noting that it, as well as the more familiar maximin and expected utility principles, can be employed to derive the conclusion of Hobbes's reply to the Fool.

Whatever principle of rational choice it presupposes, Hobbes's reply is subject to some significant objections. Hobbes assumes that there is a significant probability that your second-party violation of a state-of-nature agreement will be known to members of a defense group that you later may wish to join or stay in, and that the members will certainly exclude or expel you if they do know of this. It may be objected that these assumptions are un-

---

[23] Except in the very special case in which the agent needs the ill-gotten gains to survive and lead a decent life.

realistic, that defense groups will not care enough about past violations to investigate members and exclude past violators.

There may be some truth in this objection, but not enough to upset Hobbes's argument. Admittedly, it is not certain that state-of-nature defense groups would expel known past second-party contract-breakers. But given the known potential instabilities of state-of-nature defense pacts (as discussed in the last section), and the need for reliable intragroup cooperation in the war of all groups (to be discussed in the next section), pact members would have strong incentives to allow only reliable parties in their groups and to deter agreement-breaking by applying strong exemplary punishments, such as banishment, to known violators. And if excluding potential cheaters is an important goal, soliciting and collecting information on the past behavior of potential members would be worth some effort. Further, cheated first-party compliers in a state of nature would have reasons of vengeance, as well as deterrence, for making the behavior of those who cheated them widely known. This reduces the information-gathering costs of defense groups.

Most important, Hobbes's conclusion does not require certainty of expulsion if discovered or a high absolute probability that the violation will become known. The expected utility interpretation of Hobbes's argument is the one that is most vulnerable to the present objection.[24] But all it really requires to reach a conclusion in favor of the rationality of keeping state-of-nature agreements is that the following condition be satisfied: the products of the probability of the violation becoming known to relevant parties and the probability of these parties expelling a known violator exceeds the gains of breaking the agreement divided by the cost of being left in the state of nature. Or, symbolically, $(qe) > g/c$, where e, the probability of expulsion, is the probability that a known violator would be excluded or expelled, and the

---

[24] This is because the other principles—maximin and disaster avoidance—aim exclusively at avoiding or minimizing losses and pay no attention to maximizing potential gains. As long as there is a significant risk of cheaters being isolated in the state of nature, these principles will recommend against cheating.

145

other terms are as defined above, page 142.[25] Since going it alone in the state of nature is so dangerous, the latter ratio (g/c) will be very small. And as rational defense-group members have very good reasons, noted above, for keeping unreliable people out of their groups, the former product (qe) is unlikely to be very small. Hence, it is not unreasonable to suppose, as Hobbes in effect does, that the above condition is satisfied.

A different objection to Hobbes's reply to the Fool is based on recent work by Robert Axelrod.[26] Axelrod had a number of experts on decision theory devise strategies for playing two-party iterated prisoner's dilemma. When employed pairwise against all the other strategies, the most successful strategy was a simple "tit-for-tat" strategy: cooperate on the first play, and on subsequent plays do whatever your partner (opponent) did on the previous play. Now someone playing "tit for tat" will keep a state-of-nature agreement as a second party; that is, respond to the first party's cooperative move with one of his own. And, according to our objector, doing so is rational because, as Axelrod's results show, it leads on average to the best long-run payoffs for the individual involved. Threats of exclusion from defense groups, on which Hobbes bases his reply, are therefore not needed to establish the rationality of second-party cooperation: they are entirely superfluous.

The trouble with this objection is that it assumes that the state

---

[25] The expected gain of breaking a state-of-nature agreement (relative to keeping it) is the weighted sum of the potential gains (g) and losses ($-c$) of unilateral noncompliance, with the weights being the respective probabilities. The former probability is assumed to be 1 and the latter is (qe), or the probability of being discovered times the probability of being expelled if discovered. So the expected gain of breach, EG_B, equals $g - [c(qe)]$. Keeping an agreement pays if and only if EG_B is negative, i.e.,

$$g - [c(qe)] < 0 \qquad (1)$$

Adding $[c(qe)]$ to both sides of (1) yields:

$$g < [c(qe)] \qquad (2)$$

Dividing both sides by c yields:

$$(g/c) < (qe) \qquad (3)$$

This is the condition specified in the text.

[26] Robert Axelrod, "Effective Choice in Prisoner's Dilemma" and "More Effective Choice in Prisoner's Dilemma." See also Axelrod's *The Evolution of Cooperation* (New York: Basic Books, 1984).

146

of nature is modeled by each individual playing independent games of iterated two-party prisoner's dilemma with every other individual. If this assumption were correct, Axelrod's results would go a long way toward establishing the rationality of second-party cooperation in the state of nature. But the assumption is wrong. The model in question fails to reflect at least three relevant features of the state of nature: that particular pairs of individuals may interact directly very few, if any, times; that it may be difficult to identify your opponent in a previous non-cooperative encounter (e.g., an attack or a theft); and that one party may reasonably take account of another's previous behavior toward third parties as well as toward himself. As a result of the first two features, second-party cheating may pay in the state of nature because your victim may not know you were the cheater or because you may not need to interact with him in the future. As a result of the third feature, cheating may *not* pay because, irrespective of what your victim does, others may react by withdrawing future cooperation. Unlike the independent two-party prisoner's dilemma model, Hobbes's reply to the Fool does take account of these features. It relies on the individual's need for future cooperation with *some* others (rather than specific others), takes account of the problem of identifying noncooperators, and assumes that defense groups will tend to exclude cheaters of third parties. Because it reflects the three relevant features, while the two-party prisoner's dilemma model does not, it is a superior account of why second-party state-of-nature cooperation is rational.

A third objection to Hobbes's reply to the Fool, raised by Jean Hampton,[27] is more serious. The basic idea is that if Hobbes is right that it is rational for second parties to keep state-of-nature agreements, then it must be rational for *first* parties to keep them as well. The argument is that the latter, following the logic of Hobbes's argument, will not expect rational second parties to cheat

---

[27] Jean Hampton, "Hobbes, Contracts, and the Wisdom of Fools "(unpublished paper presented at the University of Colorado, Boulder, 1979). See also her "Hobbes's State of War," *Topoi* 4 (March 1985): 47–60. David Zimmerman has raised a similar objection in a letter to me.

them, and that even if they are cheated, first parties can expect to gain more than compensating advantages by proving themselves trustworthy partners in future defense cooperatives or commonwealths.

The clear response to the first part of Hampton's objection, suggested by passages in chapter 14 of *Leviathan*,[28] is that first parties to state-of-nature contracts cannot count on second parties acting rationally. It is in the long-term interest of second parties to comply with state-of-nature agreements, as the reply to the Fool shows, but their short-term interests (and strong passions, like greed) dictate a different course. Given the frequent tendency for people to be carried away by short-term interests and immediate passions and to act against their longer-term interests, it is not safe to be a first-party complier with a state-of-nature agreement because of the substantial risk of *irrational* noncompliance by the second party.

This reply raises the question of whether it is appropriate to treat some parties as irrational in certain ways, in the context of a state-of-nature theory. After all, in section 3–1 it is suggested that the state of nature is a hypothetical realm populated by similarly and purely rational parties. Given this, we need special justification for allowing irrational tendencies, or parties, to figure in the argument for first-party noncompliance.

Several considerations provide such a justification. First, as noted in section 3-1, the state of nature is supposed to function as a model of societies of real people dissolved by civil disorder or removal of the State. Insofar as specific but highly common irrational tendencies would contribute to problems in such a situation, they must be taken into account if we want our state-of-nature theory to explain correctly the dangers of anarchy and the function of the State. Second, there is no general reason why the state-of-nature population must be regarded as perfectly homogeneous, with regard to rationality or anything else. We have, for example, already considered several arguments in which diversity between dominators and others—or between inductivists,

---

[28] *Leviathan*, chap. 14, pp. 124, 128–129.

deductivists, and strategists—was assumed. Third, there is no real conflict between our earlier assumption that people are forwardlooking and the present observation that they tend to be irrationally shortsighted. The former assumption says that they are concerned about their future well-being; the latter says that this concern is sometimes lost in, or overcome by, the force of immediate passions or interests. Fourth, the assumption that people tend to be irrationally short-sighted is hardly an ad hoc assumption invented to serve the needs of the present argument. It is a commonplace recognized by Hobbes's critic Bishop Butler,[29] among others, and it plays a role elsewhere in Hobbes's philosophy in explaining revolution and crime.[30] Finally, Hobbes would not be playing fast and loose by inserting the assumption here and ignoring it elsewhere (e.g., in the first part of the argument against anarchy), for in those other places it would merely reinforce, rather than contravene, the conclusions drawn from assuming that the parties are all rational. Thus, for example, assuming that many individuals tend to be shortsighted and often carried away by greed and anger, rather than perfectly rational, would merely strengthen the spiral toward the active war of all in the first part of the Hobbesian argument against anarchy. Taking all these considerations into account, we may regard appeal to potential second-party irrationality as a legitimate part of the analysis of the rationality of first-party compliance in the state of nature.

It is less clear how Hobbes would deal with the second part of Hampton's objection. The objection says that the same long-range consideration that Hobbes uses to justify second-party compliance—preserved credibility resulting in a greater prospect of joining a defense group[31]—could also be used to justify first-party compliance. We can deny this only if we hold that defense-group members are likely to react *differently* to first-party and second-

[29] See Butler, Sermons 1 and 11 in *Ethical Theories*, ed. Melden, pp. 241–48, 258–66.

[30] *Leviathan*, chap. 18, p. 170; chap. 27, p. 279.

[31] The term "defense group" is intended to encompass both commonwealths and state-of-nature defensive groupings.

party violators of state-of-nature agreements. In particular, the defender of Hobbes's view must believe that defense-group members will regard first-party violators as more reliable and desirable partners than second-party violators.

There are some plausible grounds for this belief. Second-party violators are offensive violators, while first-party violators are defensive violators. Members of an already operating defense group may rightly fear the disruptive effects of offensive violations more than defensive ones, for if the present state within the group is one of cooperation, there is little motivation for undertaking defensive violations. But offensive violations will always be a threat and would have the potential of undermining or destroying the present condition of cooperation within the group. In addition, the immediate victims of first-party noncompliance (i.e., second parties whose agreements thereby collapse) are normally harmed less than the cheated victims of second-party noncompliance (i.e., first parties who have borne the cost of keeping their end of the bargain). So the costs to others of having a first-party violator in their midst is less, on average, than the costs of having a second-party violator there. Finally, some defense-group members may even regard first-party compliers with state-of-nature agreements as *undesirable* candidates for membership, for they may fear that, as group members, these first-party compliers may urge dangerous first compliance policies on the group in its dealings with other groups, with respect to which it is in the state of nature. This would, to some extent, counteract any entrance advantage that first-party compliers would earn by proving their reliability.

There are plausible reasons, then, why defense-group members might regard first-party violators of state-of-nature agreements as less undesirable candidates for group membership than second-party violators. And if parties in the state of nature were aware of this, they would have stronger long-term incentives to keep state-of-nature agreements as second parties rather than as first parties. This takes us a considerable way toward answering the second part of Hampton's objection.

Note, however, that this Hobbesian reply assumes that defense-group members reason as inductivists: they do not analyze *why* people have violated agreements, they just expect them to be likely to engage in the same type of violations in the future. It also assumes that potential state-of-nature violators are deductivists (in their reasonings about defense-group members): they calculate defense-group members' likely reactions by assuming that the latter are inductivists. Perhaps these assumptions could be grounded by the claim that adding members to a defense group typically requires consensus and that, hence, decisions on such matters must be made on grounds intelligible to all. Then, even if defense groups have strategic and deductivist, as well as inductivist, members, reasoning about admitting members must be carried out in the only terms intelligible to all—inductivist terms. Knowing this, rational individuals in the state of nature will adopt a deductivist stance in predicting the admissions policies of defensive groups; they will expect these policies to be based on inductivist reasoning.

Even if we thus agree that the characterization of group members as inductivists, and individual contract-makers as deductivists, has a plausible rationale, it is worth noting that our argument requires a further assumption about the group members' reasonings. The group members must regard the circumstances of state-of-nature agreements, and of agreements within a defense group, as enough alike that an individual's actions in the former circumstances constitute *evidence* of his likely actions in the latter circumstances. To see that this assumption is required, let us imagine that the (inductivist) group members made the opposite assumption—that the context of the two kinds of agreements are so different that behavior cannot be extrapolated from one context to the other. If the state-of-nature contractors knew this, they would correctly deduce that their present behavior had no effect on their later admittance to defense groups, and they would violate those contracts whenever (e.g., as second parties) they thought they could gain an immediate advantage thereby.[32] Here, the group members' assumption of *unlikeness* functions as

[32] Setting aside the possible negative effects on their ability to make other beneficial agreements in the state of nature.

151

a self-fulfilling prophecy. By effectively removing the threat of the main sanction (i.e., nonadmittance to defense groups) that could make the incentive structure for compliance with state-of-nature agreements like that for agreements within a defense group, that assumption renders itself true.

The same, unfortunately, is true of the assumption we have used above. Group members' assuming that the contexts of state of nature and within-group agreements are alike provides individuals with an incentive for keeping state-of-nature agreements, thus making the contexts alike in the relevant respects. Does this mean we are trapped in indeterminancy, with Hobbes's case for state-of-nature agreement-keeping no better supported than the case for violation? No, because there is an independent reason for preferring the assumption of the Hobbesian reply to its equally self-fulfilling rival assumption. The Hobbesian assumption is *weaker*, requiring only the (positive) *relevance* of behavior in one agreement context to the prediction of behavior in another context. The opposite assumption denies *any* such connection; it is strong and very implausible. Our knowledge of human behavior tells us that important traits, such as honesty and reliability (i.e., keeping one's word), have some significant degree of intersituational consistency—or else we would never ascribe these features to people as traits at all, or rely on the behavioral predictions implied by such ascriptions.[33]

There is a cost, however, to dealing with this problem for Hobbes's reply in this manner. We have in effect acknowledged that knowledge of one's past violations of state-of-nature agreements will have only *some* influence on defense-group members' decision whether to admit one to their fold. In our earlier terminology, we are saying that *e* will not necessarily be very large, much less equal to one. This means that there may be more sit-

[33] Of course, our knowledge is of human behavior within civil society. However, there are many contexts within civil society that resemble the state of nature in the most relevant respect—there being no effective enforcement of norms by authorities. Thus, e.g., lying or breaking promises in everyday private life is not punished by law. Yet we still observe considerable consistency of such behavioral traits between situations containing and not containing threats of formal sanctions.

uations than we previously allowed in which a second-party violation has a higher expected utility than compliance (i.e., more cases in which $[g/c] > [qe]$). This gives us reason, perhaps, in interpreting Hobbes's argument, to prefer the disaster-avoidance or maximin interpretation to the expected utility interpretation, for so long as (1) second-party compliance makes it *somewhat* more probable that one will gain admittance to a defense group and (2) having to go it alone in the state of nature is regarded as disastrous, the disaster-avoidance principle (as well as the maximin principle) will recommend second-party compliance.

Let us briefly recapitulate what we have learned from consideration of Hampton's objections. The rationality of first-party noncompliance to state-of-nature agreements rests on the significant possibility of irrational action on the part of second parties. The rationality of second-party compliance depends on the reasonable expectation that defense-group members will favor state-of-nature compliers for admission over noncompliers. While defense-group members extrapolate the state-of-nature behavior of both first-party (defensive) and second-party (offensive) violators, they are less inclined to admit the latter because of the greater costs and dangers of offensive violations within a cooperative group. It is this fact (together with the possibility of being damaged by an irrational partner if you act first) that makes it likely that second-party compliance is rational in the state of nature while first-party compliance is not. At the same time, the rationality of compliance in either case depends on a number of situational variables that will depend on the way the state of nature is characterized and on the specific features and context of the agreement in question. It also may depend on the specific notion of rationality that one has in mind, for example, expected value maximization, maximining, or disaster-avoidance. Thus, for example, if one can afford to be cheated on this state-of-nature agreement, and if there is some significant chance of noncompliance becoming known and counting against you in a defense-group admissions decision, then it will be rational, in disaster-avoidance or maximin terms, to comply *even as a first party*.

Ultimately, then, consideration and analysis of the Fool pas-

FIGURE 6

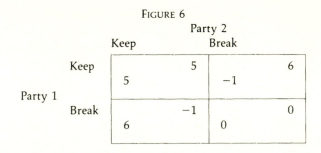

Party 2

	Keep	Break
Keep	5 5	−1 6
Break	6 −1	0 0

sage reinforces the general conclusion reached in the previous section: cooperation in the state of nature is possible, but it is precarious because of each party's lack of assurance of the other's reliability. In the last section, the possibility of cooperation based on the hope of future cooperation was explored. The reply to the Fool offers an extension of this basis—hope of the benefits of entry into an organized group. Before proceeding to consider some important problems concerning such groups, we should note that cooperation in the state of nature has another possible contributory source, altruism.

So far in our discussion of cooperation in this chapter, we have treated the parties as though they were purely self-interested. But in Chapter 2 we suggested that people are not purely self-interested, only predominately so. This introduces additional possible grounds for cooperation in the state of nature: one party may cooperate with another to benefit that other as well as himself. We illustrate this with a state-of-nature contract matrix (Figure 6) similar to the one we introduced at the beginning of this section. We assume, for simplicity, that the parties move simultaneously and that the entries in the matrix represent levels of *personal benefits* to the parties. If the parties are purely self-interested, these levels of personal benefits represent their payoffs. And we have a typical prisoner's dilemma matrix, with breaking the agreement as the dominant move for each.

But let us now allow for altruism. Suppose the two care about one another's well-being, so that each values a unit of personal

FIGURE 7

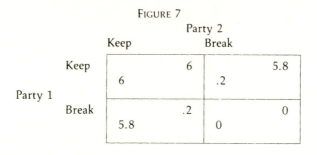

Party 2

	Keep	Break
Keep	6 / 6	5.8 / .2
Break	.2 / 5.8	0 / 0

Party 1

benefit to the other at one-fifth the value of a unit of personal benefit to himself. Then each values a given outcome of the game at $P_I + .2P_O$, where P_I and P_O are the levels of personal benefit which that outcome provides to himself, and the other, respectively (i.e., P_I and P_O are the payoffs assigned to himself and the other in the corresponding quadrant of the matrix in Figure 6). We represent the payoffs to the altruistic players in this contract situation in Figure 7.[34] Here *keeping* the contract is the dominant move for each party. The parties' concern for each other has transformed a largely conflictual situation in which violation is rational into a situation in which compliance is assured if the parties are rational. This result is, of course, dependent upon the specific payoffs we started with and the degree of altruism assumed. If, for example, each party valued benefits to the other at one-tenth the value of benefits to himself, we would have the situation depicted in Figure 8. The situation of these less-altruistic parties remains a prisoner's dilemma, with breaking the contract the dominant move for both. Here the problem is *not enough* altruism. But where parties' beliefs about what benefits people differ, prisoner's dilemmas can occur when each gives the other's welfare equal consideration with his own, or even when each seeks

[34] The payoff for each player in each quadrant of this matrix is his payoff in the corresponding quadrant of the matrix in Figure 6 plus one-fifth of the other party's payoff in the same quadrant of the matrix in Figure 6. For instance, party 1's payoff in the lower left quadrant = $6 + [(1/5)(-1)] = 5.8$.

FIGURE 8

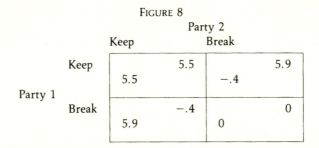

solely to maximize the other's welfare and ignores his own.[35] On the whole, however, most realistic cases are likely to be like those illustrated above, in which the more altruism the better, as far as facilitating mutually beneficial cooperation is concerned.

We are led by various different paths, then, to the possibility of rational cooperation in the state of nature. This was something Hobbes himself recognized: he regarded the war of each individual against every other as an extreme limiting case. And the generation of even this war, we have seen, presupposes at least temporary cooperation among some people, for example, invaders, or successful anticipators and their "subjects." The form of cooperation that is most rational in the state of nature, because it is most desperately needed, is defensive cooperation, banding together for purposes of security. Hobbesian philosophy acknowledges the possibility, even the rational necessity, of the formation of such defense groups. But in the second part of the Hobbesian argument against anarchy, to which we now proceed, their sufficiency for purposes of security is called into question.

[35] See my "Deterrence, Utility, and Rational Choice" for an example of a situation in which equal consideration but differing beliefs could lead to a prisoner's dilemma type of problem. See also J. Howard Sobel, "The Need for Coercion," in *Coercion*, ed. J. Roland Pennock and John W. Chapman (Chicago: University of Chicago Press, 1972), pp. 148–77; Derek Parfit, "Prudence, Morality, and the Prisoner's Dilemma," *Proceedings of the British Academy 1981*, pp. 539–64; and Bernard Grofman, "The Prisoner's Dilemma Game and the Problem of Rational Choice," *Frontiers of Economics* 1 (1975): 101–19.

4-4. Groups and the State

The first part of Hobbes's argument against anarchy establishes that a reliance on individual self-protection by rational parties in a state of nature would be likely to result in an active war of each against every other. This suffices to establish the rationality of state-of-nature parties joining with others for mutual defense. Such defensive groupings may have various origins—conquest of some by others, family ties,[36] or contractual agreement. In the last three sections, we have seen that state-of-nature defensive groupings of the last sort, at least, are possible, though precarious. Hence, as the second part of his argument against anarchy, Hobbes must explain why non-State (i.e., state-of-nature) defense groups fail to provide adequate protection for their members; or else he will not have shown the most plausible form of anarchistic life—existence within state-of-nature defense groups—to be unacceptable and will not have provided grounds for regarding the State as necessary.[37]

Before examining Hobbes's explanation (centered in chapter 17 of *Leviathan*),[38] we must clarify the task he faces. In particular, it is necessary to say something about how the State is to be defined or characterized, so that it is distinguishable from state-of-nature defense groups. While there probably is no single definition of the State that is appropriate in all contexts, we can provide one that will serve adequately in the Hobbesian argument against anarchy.

Max Weber's oft-cited definition of the State says that it must claim a monopoly on the legitimate use of force in a given terri-

[36] See *Leviathan*, chap. 13, p. 114, where Hobbes wrongly reduces these ties (as they exist among American Indians) to "natural lust."

[37] Strictly speaking, completion of the argument against anarchy requires also showing that life in the State will be acceptable. The basis of the Hobbesian argument for this is developed in Chapters 5 and 6.

[38] See also *Elements of Law*, part 1, chap. 6, secs. 3–6, pp. 119–21; *Philosophical Rudiments*, chap. 5, secs. 3–6, pp. 64–68.

tory.[39] Recent writers have noted some obvious flaws in this account: any person or group can claim such a monopoly without having it; yet we cannot require actual possession of a monopoly of force in the definition, since even the officials of paradigmatic States do not have complete monopolies of this kind[40] (think of uses of force by street gangs or the Mafia). Yet there is a core of truth in Weber's definition—what characterizes a State is the existence of a government with something like an effective monopoly of power in a given territory. To be a State, an organization must be *preponderant* in power, in a given geographic region, in the sense that it can physically overpower internal competitors and generally discourage aggression by outsiders. This means it can successfully enforce its rules and judgments against any public internal opposition if it chooses to do so, except possibly in the special case of its being replaced in accordance with established and recognized internal procedures, for example, elections. And it provides sufficient actual enforcement against internal and external transgressors that its citizens are seldom forced to resort to anticipatory action or private vengeance (individually or in small groups) to protect themselves. In other words, a government consists of a subgroup or subsystem that possesses a substantial concentration of the group's power—enough power to discourage self-help (save for immediate self-defense) among its citizens, to put its rulings into effect against any domestic opposition or rival (save for the above caveat about removal), and to generally deter outside aggression. And a State is simply an organized society with a territory and government.

Some points of clarification are in order concerning this account of the nature of the State. It is an account that can be satisfied in *varying degrees* by political entities, because the cri-

[39] Max Weber, *Theory of Social and Economic Organization* (New York: Free Press 1947), p. 156 (cited by Nozick, *Anarchy,, State, & Utopia*, p. 23). A useful gloss on Weber's notion, which brings it close to the account of the State offered below, may be found in Arthur Stinchcombe, *Constructing Social Theories* (New York: Harcourt, Brace & World, 1968), pp. 158–63.

[40] See, e.g., Michael Taylor, *Community, Anarchy, and Liberty* (Cambridge: Cambridge University Press, 1982), p. 5; and Nozick, *Anarchy, State, and Utopia*, p. 23 (citing Marshall Cohen).

teria it contains (e.g., discouraging self-help and deterring out-side aggression) can be satisfied in varying degrees and will not always be satisfied together. This, however, is appropriate. There are borderline cases of States (e.g., contemporary Lebanon), and we should have an account that recognizes this and reveals the complexity of the concept of statehood that leads to it. Also, the requirement concerning enforcing judgments against internal op-position does not mean that a government could enforce all (or even nearly all) its judgments, if they were substantially op-posed. Probably no government possesses the political and eco-nomic resources to do this. Instead, it means that the government can enforce *any* (or practically any) *particular* judgment or direc-tive that it deems to be of sufficient importance. This applies es-pecially to cases of opposition that challenge the government's legitimacy or authority while it still holds office according to pro-cedures generally recognized within the society. If a political en-tity lacks sufficient power to forcibly put down open challenges of this kind, it can hardly be a government (though a government well might *choose* to ignore or deal nonforcibly with many such challenges). Note also that the government's power must be de-cisive only against actual or likely internal opposition groups. It is not required, for example, that the government could forcibly resist the combined opposition of all citizens who are not func-tionaries of the government.[41]

Finally, there is a tricky problem concealed in the requirement that the government provide enough actual enforcement that cit-izens generally need not resort to self-help for protection. We do not normally believe that a State ceases to exist if it contains a persecuted minority group,[42] but often the government apparatus of a State fails to adequately protect minority group members (e.g., blacks in the old South) from depredations by members of favored groups, or actively attacks the group itself (as in the Nazi government's treatment of Jews). There is an important sense in

---

[41] Though this is not a logical impossibility, as has often been suggested. See the discussion of perfect tyranny in section 6-2.

[42] The persecuted "minority" may actually be a majority, as, e.g., in South Africa.

which the persecuted group members are not citizens, in which the State is not a State *with respect to them*, because its government patently fails to carry out the primary function of the State and government—providing protection and security—with regard to these people. Nonetheless, so long as the apparatus in question possesses dominant power in a given territory, provides basic protection to many or most inhabitants, and fails to provide protection for certain groups only because it chooses not to (rather than because it lacks the power to do so), it is least misleading to classify the society ruled by that apparatus as a State. We simply must realize that States may be discriminatory, persecutory, even genocidal. Thus, in characterizing a human organization as a State, we imply that it possesses certain important descriptive features, but we do not necessarily honor it—except in Hobbes's special sense, in which to honor something is to signal recognition of its great power.[43]

Our account of the State resembles Hobbes's own in that it requires a sufficient concentration of power to provide security against internal and external dangers. There is this important difference, however. Hobbes in effect defines the State, or commonwealth, as a complete concentration of unlimited power in the hands of a sovereign individual or group.[44] The two accounts are roughly equivalent on the assumption that completely concentrated and unlimited sovereign power is necessary, and generally sufficient, for citizen protection. Hobbes makes this assumption, but in our second main departure from him (the first being our definite rejection of Psychological Egoism), our Hobbesian theory will reject it, for reasons to be elaborated later in this section. Hence, we must also reject Hobbes's definition of the State and proceed on the basis of the account offered above.

Having fixed upon a working definition of the State, we may begin reconstruction of the second part of Hobbes's argument against anarchy. The Hobbesian acknowledges that defense coalitions are possible in the state of nature, as are family groups.

[43] *Leviathan*, chap. 10, pp. 76, 79.
[44] Ibid., chap. 17, pp. 157–58; chap. 18, pp. 167–68.

But will such groups provide their members with sufficient security? Consider first the simplest case, in which we have a large number of small but equal-size groups in the state of nature. Because of their equality, essentially the same logic of anticipation applies to these groups as applies in the case of individuals.[45] Some groups will consist of dominators who seek conquest for its own sake, and each group is vulnerable to any other, which may conquer it by surprise or by forming a temporary aggressive coalition with another group. Since anticipating yields advantages, each group is forced to seek to increase its power by conquering other groups or by entering into defense alliances with other groups (just as individuals had to anticipate or form defense groups). The result is an active war of all groups, with a tendency for groups to increase in size over time (either through defensive merger or through conquest and absorption). Thus, a state-of-nature structure consisting of small equal-size groups is not in equilibrium.

Now suppose that we start with small groups of *unequal* size. Hobbes astutely observes that security rests primarily on *deterrence*, which—in a system of defense groups—requires that one's group be large enough so that potential attackers cannot be reasonably sure of victory.[46] But, he suggests, a small advantage in numbers is a reliable sign of victory in conflicts between small groups.[47] (He presumably means "small" in absolute numbers, which in small groups is a large percentage advantage.) If this is so, small groups cannot adequately deter attack and provide their members with security. The result is that they are conquered and absorbed by somewhat larger groups, or that they merge with other groups in an attempt to guard against this threat. (Even the initially largest group is subject to defeat at the hands of a coalition of smaller groups.) The result, as in the case of initially equal-size groups, is an inherent instability in state-of-nature defense groups and a strong tendency for them to grow in size. Empirical confirmation for this theoretical result may be found in

---

[45] Thus, Hobbes refers to a war of all small families among American Indians at ibid., chap. 13, p. 114.

[46] Ibid., chap. 17, pp. 154–55.

[47] Ibid.

the historical tendency for human political units to grow in size over time.[48]

This line of argument raises an interesting question that Hobbes never addresses. What puts a stop to increases in group size? Why should those in the state of nature not opt for a grouping of all persons, worldwide, or at least try to form a group containing the majority of mankind? Why would they settle for a group smaller than this when doing so would provide others with the incentive and opportunity to form a larger group and defeat them? There are two sorts of reasons. First, for large groups, being the largest is not always necessary for deterrence and defense. So many variables interact to determine victory in conflicts between large groups that even a substantial advantage in numbers cannot begin to assure one group victory over another. Also, some geographical barriers (e.g., oceans, mountains) will reliably deter a larger group from attacking smaller ones. Second, there are disadvantages associated with increasing group size. It is difficult to coordinate the actions of large numbers of people spread over large distances. The larger the group, the greater the potential for internal conflict, for there is likely to be greater variation in beliefs and values among the members, less group cohesion based on personal attachments and personal contacts, and greater difficulty identifying and controlling malefactors. Given these and other inefficiencies of scale, coupled with the fact that deterrence capabilities are not primarily a function of size for large groups, we would not expect rational inhabitants of the state of nature to seek to increase the size of their groups without limit. Rather than the grand (or a majority) coalition of all mankind forming, we would expect rational parties to gather in large groups, with the exact sizes varying in accordance with particular circumstances.

Technological advances generally tend to increase the optimal size of defensive groups, for they make transportation and com-

---

[48] This argument roughly parallels what Taylor calls the "secondary" theory of state formation. See his *Community, Anarchy, and Liberty*, pp. 130, 136–39.

munication over long distances, and the organization and direction of large numbers of persons, faster and more efficient. At the same time, technological advances tend to make armed conflicts more devastating and costly, thus placing significant inhibitions on empire-building via conquest. Thus, while in recent centuries technological advances have facilitated the formation of giant, continent-spanning nation-states, they will not necessarily lead to even larger (e.g., intercontinental or worldwide) commonwealths.

Suppose that the parties in the state of nature coalesced into a number of large groups for security reasons, as we have argued they would. Wouldn't the state-of-war argument apply to the relations among these groups as it does to individuals and small groups? Hobbes allowed that it would, claiming that the nations of the world are in a constant state of war of each against the others. But this war is largely inactive, and its consequences are not so bleak as those of war between individuals and small groups. Even while known to be willing to fight each other, nations are able to "uphold . . . the industry of their subjects."[49] The import of this cryptic remark may (charitably) be interpreted as follows.

Nations are large enough and orderly enough to secure a man's life and property against those he is likely to come in direct contact with, and to provide him with enough reliable "partners" to make his productive activities worthwhile. Further, the state of war between his nation and others constitutes a much smaller threat to his life than would a war of all individuals (or small groups). Because of the problems of organizing large groups for combat, the uncertainty of the outcome in battles between States, the geographical barriers between States, and the relatively small number of agents on the international scene, actual fighting between States is relatively infrequent and directly involves only a small segment of a warring nation's population when it does occur. Hence, there is much less fighting and killing per capita in

[49] *Leviathan*, chap. 13, p. 115.

the war of all nations than there would be in a war of all individuals (or small groups). [50]

Up to this point, our Hobbesian argument has focused on group size. It establishes that rational parties seeking long-run security would form themselves into *large* defense groups to protect themselves against actual and potential external adversaries. But a large group will surely need specialized organizations, procedures, and functionaries to effectively and efficiently provide security against internal and external dangers. Hobbes emphasizes this point by considering the extreme case in which a large group has no such specialization, no concentration of power. He plausibly claims that, no matter how large, a group in which each individual acts in accordance with his own desires and opinions can provide little security, for it will be ineffective against external enemies because its members will not agree on and coordinate their defensive efforts. Also, having conflicting interests, group members will fight among themselves when threats from outside the group are not imminent. [51]

These considerations convincingly establish the need for some concentration of power in large groups, in the form of organizations and arrangements to provide police and judicial services (internal defense) and military services (external defense). In the absence of the former, the situation within the group itself will be, in effect, a state of nature and will be likely to degenerate eventually into an active war among individuals or small groups. In the absence of the latter, the group is constantly in danger of falling prey to the depredations of other groups that do possess organized military forces.

How much concentration of power is it rational for the parties in a large defensive group to adopt? We shall consider this question in greater detail in later chapters, but some general observations are in order at this point. Since people's primary end is *lasting* security (as follows from their forwardlookingness and

---

[50] For remarks bearing on whether the current danger of nuclear war alters this conclusion, see my "Nuclear Weapons and World Government," *The Monist* 70 (July 1977, forthcoming).

[51] *Leviathan*, chap. 17, p. 155.

predominant egoism), they would opt for a concentration of power that is sufficient to do at least three things: (1) field and support enough military forces to deter or repel likely external invaders; (2) authoritatively settle disputes within the group and put down challenges to its own authority (this is necessary to prevent escalating feuds, active fighting between factions in the group, and civil war); (3) provide citizens with enough security against one another that they are not forced (or tempted) into self-help actions that lead to an escalating cycle of violent anticipation and revenge. But, within a large group, the concentration of power required to accomplish these tasks must be substantial. Successful military operations involving large numbers of persons require central planning, coordination, and authority. Also, in a large group most people will not know each other personally. This means that altruism is unlikely to be alone sufficient to keep crime levels down and that identifying and apprehending criminals will require professional police and judicial organizations. Such concentration of law (rule) enforcement power is also necessary if feuds and anticipatory (i.e., defensively motivated) attacks are to be kept to a minimum.

Given these considerations, all that is required for the large defense groups (that rational state of-nature parties would opt for) to qualify as a State[52] is that the group control a territory. If we add reasonable assumptions about nonabundance of resources, population density, and high costs and difficulties involved in maintaining group cohesion if the group is constantly on the move, we can conclude that group members would prefer to have a permanent home base or territory under its control to live on. It would follow, then, from our Hobbesian arguments, that rational state-of-nature parties would opt for security arrangements constituting a State.

As noted above, Hobbes himself goes further than this. He contends that people can obtain real and lasting security only under an absolute sovereign, that is, a single individual or assembly with unlimited authority to act for all members of the group and

---

[52] By our previous account of what a State is.

165

with accompanying unlimited powers of lawmaking and enforcement, taxation and property distribution, command of the army, and so on.[53] He rests this contention on the assertion that such an extreme concentration of power and authority is both necessary and sufficient to prevent civil war.[54] At first, this assertion seems to be a hasty generalization, apparently based on Hobbes's interpretation of the causes of the English civil wars of his time. Later history, we are tempted to say, has disconfirmed the assertion. Systems of government with limited and divided powers have proven to be long-lasting and stable and have provided security to many generations of their citizens.

But this refutation of Hobbes's contention, while on the right track, is a bit too quick. To evaluate his line of argument properly, we must first understand what Hobbes means by absolute sovereignty. This requires distinguishing between two sorts of governmental powers. Powers of *exercise* are such things as the powers to make and enforce laws, command troops, collect taxes, distribute or redistribute property rights, and so on. Powers of *selection* are powers of choosing which persons shall possess powers of exercise, removing unsatisfactory users of powers of exercise, and designating replacements for those who leave—or are removed from—positions of governmental power. Hobbes's predominant view seems to be that, within the State, those who possess only powers of exercise are mere ministers of the sovereign. When direct powers of exercise and powers of selection lie in different hands, the person or group possessing the *selection* powers is the sovereign. (This emerges most clearly when Hobbes says that an elective king for life is sovereign only if he has the power to appoint his successor; otherwise sovereignty currently lies in whoever else possesses that power.[55]) In such cases, the sovereign may be said to *indirectly* possess powers of exercise in virtue of being able to select for governmental office people who will exercise these powers in the manner the sovereign prefers. And selectors *can* directly possess the powers of exercise by ap-

[53] Ibid., chap. 18.
[54] See, e.g., ibid., p. 168.
[55] Ibid., chap. 19, pp. 178–79.

pointing themselves to relevant offices or by simply issuing relevant orders without appointing subordinate ministers.

This interpretation of the Hobbesian notion of sovereignty renders the idea of absolute sovereignty less otiose than it appears at first glance, for now all unlimited and undivided sovereign power amounts to is a single person or assembly being in a position to appoint all those who exercise the various necessary powers of government. Such an arrangement has the apparent advantage of precluding stalemates between branches of government which could lead to civil war, by having an ultimate authority who can break the deadlock by removing and replacing one (or both) of the contending parties, or threatening to do so.

But even on this interpretation, Hobbesian absolute sovereignty is neither sufficient nor necessary for preventing civil war. It is not sufficient because exercisers of significant powers may forcibly resist removal from office by the sovereign, and may even have significant support within the sovereign itself for doing so, if the sovereign is an assembly. This is a prescription for civil war, as when military officers stage coups to prevent being fired, or when political parties start revolts to resist being stripped of a share of power. Further, according to Hobbes's own apparent views, even absolute sovereigns do not necessarily have the power and authority to remove subordinate officials *at will*. Consider the case of the king for life who claims the power to appoint a successor, and the sovereign assembly that refuses to relinquish that power. Here there is no neutral third party or common power to settle the dispute short of civil war.

Nor is absolute sovereignty in Hobbes's sense *necessary* to prevent civil war. Constitutional limits on governmental power are consistent with lasting order, as is the division of power among distinct governmental bodies. This is so even if different constituencies select members of different branches by different procedures. The United States may serve as an example. There are (amendable) constitutional limits on governmental action which are authoritatively interpreted by the Supreme Court. The Court's justices serve for life and are appointed (but not removable) by the president, who is himself selected by electors chosen in accordance with the state-by-state vote of citizens. By different procedures, overlapping groups of citizens elect senators and congressmen. In general, lasting establishment of laws requires the concurrence of two houses of Congress, the president, and the courts. The constitution itself can be amended, but only by action of a large majority of Congress or in state legislatures. And so on. This, like other systems of limited and divided governmental power, has historically proven to be stable. But there is no absolute sovereign (in Hobbes's sense) here, no single assembly that selects exercisers of unlimited powers of government. Though we may be tempted to say that "the people" are the selectors in all cases (and hence are the absolute sovereign), this merely disguises the facts that *who* the people are (and the procedures by which they select) vary according to the branch of government in question and that the powers officials are selected to exercise are constitutionally *limited*.

For purposes of our Hobbesian theory, then, we should reject Hobbes's extreme views about the concentration of political power. Security and order require a sufficient concentration of certain governmental powers of exercise, not a total concentration of the power to select exercisers of unlimited powers. Therefore, we will, in the sequel, present arguments against anarchy as arguments for the State, not as arguments for the Absolute State.

The Hobbesian argument against anarchy has proceeded by showing that lying low, individual anticipation, forming (or joining) a small defense group, and forming (or joining) a large non-State defense group are, as strategies for achieving security from a state-of-nature starting point, inferior to forming (or joining) a State. However, we have not explicitly considered an alternative security system favored by certain libertarian anarchists.[56] This consists in private protective agencies who offer their protective services, and compete for customers, in a free market. The agencies offer to identify, apprehend, try, and punish violators of their clients' rights, thus deterring violations of those rights. Since

[56] See, e.g., Murray Rothbard, "Society Without a State," in *Anarchism*, ed. Pennock and Chapman, pp. 191–207.

"clientship" with respect to each, or any, agency is voluntary, and since a number of agencies are presumably operating and competing for clients within the same territories, a system of independent private protective agencies would not constitute a State in our sense.[57] But, its advocates claim, it would constitute an entirely satisfactory system for ensuring personal security.

Good reasons for rejecting the private protective agency system as a reliable solution to state-of-nature security problems are straightforward and probably familiar. The agencies, if independent, will be less able than a government to protect the territory against outside aggression, because of costs and problems of achieving agreement and coordination among the different agencies. The system will also, for well-known reasons, be likely to undersupply the territory's inhabitants with various public goods[58]—most relevantly in the present context the good of protection against personal economic disaster.

The most important shortcomings of the private agency protection system, however, concern security of persons and property against aggression by other individuals and groups within the territory. Because protection agencies are independent and have nonoverlapping clienteles, they are bound to be subject to violent conflicts and feuds brought on by differing judgments concerning disputes among their clients. Thus, for example, if agency A finds for its client in his dispute with a client of agency B, while agency B renders an opposite judgment, there is no final settlement of the dispute short of fighting or accepting a compromise that neither side is likely to regard as justified. It is sometimes claimed that this problem will not often arise, since agencies will be fair and impartial in their judgments to better compete for clients. This is a wildly optimistic assumption. It seems more reasonable to suppose that predominantly egoistic clients will hire agencies that they expect will lean over backward to interpret and

[57] Unless one agency came to be a dominant agency in roughly the sense of Nozick, *Anarchy, State, and Utopia,* pp. 15–17. See also the third paragraph below.

[58] For a recent comprehensive discussion of public goods, see Hardin, *Collective Action.*

judge disputes in their own clients' favor. If so, to be successful in recruiting and retaining clients, agencies will have to follow such a pro-client policy. And there will be many disputes among agencies that can be settled only by force, threats, or uneasy compromise. Things could be even worse than this if the agencies did not, as we have so far supposed, operate somewhat in good faith. Outlaw agencies could use their clients' resources and their own physical power to aggress against their clients and others. Acting like groups of dominators, they could well set off a spiraling war of each agency against every other that would be hardly a safer environment than the war of all individuals or small groups.

These internal and external security problems could be solved if there were enough cooperation among the various protective agencies. Suppose, for example, there were a joint military command with authority and power to deal with external threats, and a system of appeals courts that settled cases in which agencies disagreed and whose judgments were obeyed by all agencies. Then the territory's inhabitants could be reasonably secure. But the system of protective agencies, including the military command and appeals court, would by our account constitute a government, and the society ruled by them would be a State.

The libertarian anarchist's most promising reply to these complaints is to acknowledge that there are problems with the private protection agency system, but to point out that similar or worse problems are found in States.[59] Thus, for example, an outlaw agency can at least be opposed and constrained by other agencies operating on the same territory,[60] but there are no co-equal domestic powers to constrain a government that oppresses and exploits its own people.

There is a key insight to be found here: the mere formation of a State, just any State, does not reliably provide security to its citizens. Thus, in a sense, the two-part Hobbesian argument against anarchy so far presented is still incomplete. It indicates that, and why, non-State solutions to the problem of individual security

[59] Rothbard, "Society Without a State," p. 195.
[60] See Nozick, *Anarchy, State, and Utopia*, p. 17.

are unsatisfactory, but it remains to be seen what sort of State, if any, does provide a solution to that problem. We take up this question in the following two chapters. Before doing so, however, we must clarify the nature of the Hobbesian argument against anarchy as so far presented.

4-5. A Priori or Empirical?

Let us recapitulate the Hobbesian argument against anarchy as developed so far. The first part of that argument concerns how rational, forwardlooking, roughly equal, and predominantly egoistic parties with conflicting interests and concern for their reputations would interact in the state of nature if they did not form defensive groups and there were a significant minority of dominators among them. Under these conditions, no individual could feel secure in his person or possessions. Opposed interests, competition for reputation, and the dominators' intrinsic love of conquest are potential sources of violent conflict. Given this, and natural equality, each party would reasonably expect eventual attacks on him by dominators or anticipators, since the two main factors that might restrain such attacks are absent: threats of punishment by a common power, or strong and widely spread altruism. Since one's own chances of success in the violent conflicts that are extremely likely to arise in such circumstances are improved by anticipation (striking first or conquering others to use as defenders), following such a strategy is more reasonable than simply lying low. But because the parties in the state of nature are known to be sufficiently rational to appreciate all this, they will not only be ready to anticipate against others when the opportunity arises, but also expect others to take the same stance toward them. Hence, each will be generally known to be willing to fight any other, that is, there will be a state of war of each individual against every other. Further, because of the presence of the dominators and the rationality of the parties (whose best course is anticipation) this will be an active war involving much actual violence. This active war of all against all destroys the prospects of happiness of the parties in a number of ways. It shortens their life spans, fills them with constant (reasonable) fears of death, destroys the incentive for productive work by making possessions insecure, and undermines cooperation to the extent of making the benefits of advanced civilization unobtainable. These, then, are the bitter fruits of pure individualist anarchy.

The second part of the Hobbesian argument against anarchy concerns group defense. Group defense requires cooperation, which in a state of nature is possible, but precarious and unstable because of the absence of a common power and individual members' resulting concerns about others free-riding. Such concerns might be minimal in a *small* group, as the parties may be linked by substantial altruism and cheaters are more easily identified and punished. But small groups are not adequate for defense in a state of nature, since they can, with high probability, be conquered by larger groups. So within a state of nature there is an incentive for defense groups to grow in size, for purposes of both passive defense (deterrence and repulsion of attacks) and active defense (anticipation). But in large groups, strong altruism and likeness of views among group members are highly unlikely. Cheaters and other norm violators are more difficult to identify, apprehend, and punish. And there are increasing returns to scale to be obtained by specialization and by concentration of power in the areas of internal and external security. As a result, a substantial concentration of military power and authority is needed for external defense—to prevent divided domestic opinion from undermining defense efforts and to take advantage of returns to scale that are also being realized by potential enemies. The same is true as regards police power. It must be concentrated to effectively settle disputes, apprehend malefactors, and discourage feuds and anticipatory violence in a large group whose members are not tightly bound to each other by personal acquaintance and strong altruism. But whatever group or organization possesses such a concentration of military and police power, which is sufficient to enforce domestic decisions, discourage self-help, and deter external enemies, is by definition a government of a State. Hence, rational parties in the state of nature would best protect their security by forming, or joining, what amounts to a State or com-

172

monwealth (provided, as will be argued in the next two chapters, that the State, or at least some States, does not itself threaten the individual's security to an even greater extent than do the alternatives). Thus, anarchy is rejected in favor of the State, on the grounds that no state-of-nature strategy—lying low, anticipation, small-group formation, large non-State group formation—can solve the problem of individual security as well or as reliably as the formation of a commonwealth.

Note that the argument as sketched here and as filled in earlier is straightforwardly empirical and probabilistic. Many of its steps and conclusions (and many of the stated replies to objections against it) assert that certain things are *likely* rather than certain, for example, that it is likely that one would eventually be attacked in a state of nature containing a substantial minority of dominators if one laid low. Even these probabilistic assertions depend for their validity on certain empirically based assumptions about human beings, their interaction patterns, and their natural environments.

The argument against individualist anarchy assumes that people are death-averse, concerned with their reputations, forward-looking, roughly equal in natural endowments, predominantly egoistic, and sufficiently rational to appreciate the reasons for anticipating in a state of nature, and that a significant minority of them seek conquest for its own sake. For this part of the argument to work, assumptions about human interaction and the environment are also needed. Striking first must improve one's chances of success in a conflict, there must be nonabundance of the material goods that people need to survive and prosper, population density must be significant, and so on.

The second part of the antianarchy argument relies on various empirical claims concerning sociology and social psychology. Its success requires that among small groups, larger groups will generally not be deterred from attacking smaller ones; that strong altruism and agreement about external defense policies are less likely in larger groups than in smaller ones; that specialization and concentration of power increases the defense effectiveness of large groups; and a number of similar things. Hence both parts of the Hobbesian argument against anarchy contain essential empirical elements.

This point needs emphasis because an important recent commentator on Hobbes, F. S. McNeilly, offers a directly opposed view. He presents a purely *a priori* interpretation of the argument against anarchy, one which treats the argument as a logical deduction from formal definitions.[61] On his view, what the argument shows is that it is a *necessary truth* that human beings not living under a common power (i.e., living in a state of nature) will be in a state of war that constitutes a state of *despair* in Hobbes's sense: a state in which they have no hope of attaining their objectives.[62] The reason for this is that without a common power others' behavior is uncontrolled by threats of penalties, which in turn entails that anticipation is a more reasonable strategy than lying low.[63] But if all anticipate, no one can hope to achieve his objectives.

The keystone of McNeilly's interpretation is the extremely broad conception of what constitutes a common power that is expressed in the following passage: "In order that a society should be describable as having no 'common power' it would have to be positively committed to abstaining from *any* sort of action which could bring any substantial evil on the head of offenders."[64] In other words, a group is out of the state of nature and governed by a common power as soon as it threatens to impose any sort of significant penalties on misbehaving members.[65] McNeilly combines this with the view that it is necessarily true that any group whose members' behavior is controllable without the threat of penalties is not a group of *human* beings. The reason he offers

---

[61] McNeilly, *Anatomy of Leviathan*, pp. 180–91.

[62] Ibid., pp. 180–82, 186–87, 190–91.

[63] Ibid., pp. 165–67.

[64] Ibid., p. 188. Clearly this definition must be toned down to refer to actions that *normally* or *generally* bring substantial evil on the offender, for even society praising an offender *could* result in substantial evil for him, e.g., by making others jealous or resentful of him.

[65] See ibid.: "It is the threat of penalties which compels; and anything may be a penalty if it is an evil, dispensable at the will of those who have it at their disposal, and sufficient to weigh, in the deliberations of a possible offender, against the good to be achieved by the offence."

for regarding this as a necessary truth is that a group whose behavior was controllable without threat of penalties would have to be so homogeneous (in fundamental values) that it would not fit our concept of a human society, and its members would not fit our concept of human beings.[66] From this purported necessary truth, and his definition of a common power, McNeilly draws the conclusion that the behavior of any collection of humans living under no common power would not be controlled by threats of penalty; and that hence the parties would be forced to anticipate to protect themselves and would be reduced to a state of universal war and despair.[67]

This attempt to cast Hobbes's argument in a priori form is ingenious, and it contains some important insights, for example, that it is the rationality of anticipation which generates the war of all individuals, and that Hobbes's parties are not seeking solely to survive, but to attain other ends as well. Yet McNeilly's argument cannot ultimately succeed, either as a useful argument against anarchism or as an interpretation of Hobbes's argument. To see this, let us focus in turn on anticipation and McNeilly's use of the concept of a common power.

For McNeilly's argument to succeed as an a priori argument, it must be a logical truth that anticipation is a more reasonable individualist state-of-nature strategy than lying low. But as our discussions (in sections 3-4 through 3-6) of the various costs and benefits of each strategy have shown, the argument for this depends on a number of empirical assumptions about the parties in the state of nature and their situation.[68] In some consistently describable state of-nature situations, for example, ones with very low population densities and a very small percentage of dominators, lying low is probably a more reasonable security strategy than anticipation. Further, even if universal anticipation were the entailed outcome in the state of nature, would universal despair follow from this outcome by logical necessity, as McNeilly's ar-

---

[66] Ibid., pp. 189–90.
[67] Ibid., pp. 186–87.
[68] Gauthier makes a similar point in his "Yet Another Hobbes," *Inquiry* 12 (1969): 449–65.

gument requires? It would not if it were logically possible for a person's main goal to be to compete in a war of all against all. A person who had such a goal, perhaps an extreme rugged individualist, would be odd, but surely not logically impossible, *as McNeilly himself admits* when he writes: "A person's values might be such that he preferred to live in a situation of maximum danger and uncertainty, rejoicing in the prospect of the frustration of his own and everyone else's values."[69] Suppose we correct McNeilly slightly by noting that this person's main values are *not* frustrated in a war of all (supposing his aim is to live *as long as he can hold out* in a universal war). Then McNeilly's own illustration refutes the claim he needs to make the a priori argument for universal frustration of people's goals in a state of nature work.

Let us turn now to the concept of a common power, which, according to McNeilly, means some threat of social penalty for misbehavior. Is it a necessary truth that the existence of a common power in this sense, the threat of social penalties, must be present if the behavior of a group of human individuals is to conform with social rules and be predictable? Surely not. (It probably is not even a contingent truth.) Habits of cooperative and prosocial behavior may be learned and internalized in such a way that no penalties imposed by society are necessary to control the behavior of most individuals on most occasions. In any case, it surely is not a necessary truth that human behavior cannot thus be controlled by education.

Perhaps McNeilly would reply that such education must itself involve social penalties, but a permanently childless society (e.g., one whose members have been rendered sterile by nuclear accident) could remain a peaceful human society even if social norms were already internalized and no future penalties had to be threatened. In addition, it is not logically impossible that humans could internalize social norms by an educational process involving only *positive* reinforcement. Of course, McNeilly could insist that any society such as this would be "human" in only the uninter-

[69] McNeilly, *Anatomy of Leviathan*, p. 232.

176

esting, biological sense, but this would amount to no more than foisting an implausible persuasive definition of "human" upon us. Because there is much hallowed tradition on the side of identifying the human in us with our capacities for rationality, cooperation, and love, it is doubtful that many would accept such a definition.

Suppose, however, that we ignored all these objections to McNeilly's argument and granted that he had established that a common power, in his sense, is necessary if people are to avoid despair. This would hardly constitute a case against *anarchy*, as it is usually understood. All McNeilly's argument can establish is that some threat of social penalties for misconduct is needed if humans are to live decent lives in proximity to one another. But such threats are present even in situations thought of as anarchistic, for example, in libertarian anarchism, where private protective agencies punish rights violations; in communitarian anarchism, where misconduct is typically punished by the withdrawal of cooperation; and even in Hobbes's own state of nature, where (as we saw in section 4-3) misconduct may be punished by nonadmission to defense groups. So the content of McNeilly's conclusion is so weak as to be of no use within the traditional debate concerning the relative merits of anarchy and the State.

Finally, given McNeilly's broad and weak definition of a common power, his argument can hardly be viewed as an interpretation of Hobbes's argument. Hobbes defined the State implausibly narrowly as a single person or assembly possessing unlimited and undivided (though perhaps indirect) power over a people and territory. We earlier weakened that definition so that only a substantial concentration of power sufficient to protect against certain typical threats is required for there to be a government and a State. This left us with a definition strong enough that the moral defense of the State, in our sense, conflicts with traditional anarchism. And our definition is roughly equivalent to Hobbes's own, given one (false) assumption that he accepts—that security within and of the State requires unlimited and undivided sovereign power. But McNeilly's definition of a common power, or government of a State, is so weak that it loses virtually all contact

177

with Hobbes's definition. Even Hobbes did not believe that unlimited and undivided sovereign power is necessary if there is to be any threat of social penalty for misconduct. (As noted in the last paragraph, Hobbes clearly believed that such threats were present in the state of nature.) Thus, in contrast to our revised Hobbesian argument, McNeilly's interpretation of the argument against anarchy leaves out of the picture altogether the very element Hobbes stresses: the importance of the *concentration* of power for preserving order. This alone is sufficient grounds for rejecting McNeilly's view of the argument against anarchism.

Having revealed several serious problems with McNeilly's a priori interpretation of the argument against anarchy, we may leave in place our own empirical version of that argument, as developed in this chapter and the previous one. In the next two chapters, we complete the descriptive foundation of the Hobbesian case against anarchy by analyzing the (hypothetical) formation and maintenance of commonwealths.

F I V E

FOUNDING THE STATE

5-1. The Hobbesian Social Contract

Rational forwardlooking and predominantly self-interested parties in a state of nature will seek a form of social organization that can "defend them from the invasion of foreigners, and the injuries of one another, and thereby to secure them in such sort, as that by their own industry, and by the fruits of the earth, they may nourish themselves and live contentedly."[1] The first two parts of the Hobbesian argument against anarchy, considered in Chapters 3 and 4, are designed to show that neither non-State defense groups nor a system of individualist anarchy can reliably perform these functions. To complete the argument, it remains to show that the State, or some kinds of States, can carry out these functions, and do so without imposing yet worse deprivations on citizens.

The first part of this proposition—that the State can perform the function of protecting its citizens—follows directly from our definition of the State as an organized society with a territory and a government, that is, a subgroup possessing a substantial enough concentration of power to generally enforce domestic decisions, discourage self-help, and deter external aggression. And we have already seen (in section 4-4) *how* a substantial concentration of power enables a group possessing it to carry out these protective functions. In particular, we noted that the credible threat of sufficient penalties by a common power deters domestic aggression and agreement-breaking by making offensive violations unprofitable and defensive violations unnecessary. Hence,

[1] *Leviathan*, chap. 17, p. 157.

179

to complete the Hobbesian argument against anarchy, it remains only to demonstrate that, and how, a sufficient concentration of power to carry out these various protective functions (i.e., a government by our definition) could come about and be sustained, without likely imposing on its citizens worse costs and harms than they would suffer in the state of nature. This is the third part of the Hobbesian argument against anarchy, which will be developed in this chapter and the next. Our presentation of this third part will diverge much further from Hobbes's text than our presentation of the earlier parts of the argument against anarchy did. This divergence is necessitated by the rejection of certain of Hobbes's main substantive assumptions about political sociology, and by the desire to develop Hobbesian social contract theory in a methodologically explicit and defensible manner.

Let us begin with a sketch of Hobbes's own account of the origin of the State or commonwealth. For Hobbes, commonwealths arise either by acquisition or by institution. A party achieves dominion over a group by *acquisition* when its members, who are in his power, explicitly or tacitly pledge obedience to his rule.[2] Thus, conquerors and family heads acquire dominion over those they conquer, and their family members, respectively. If the group is large enough to deter or repel invasion, then we have a commonwealth by acquisition, with the party in question possessing dominion as sovereign.[3]

Alternately, commonwealths are formed by *institution*, when a number of independent individuals create a common power over themselves by mutual agreement. This State-creating pact, or social contract, is pictured by Hobbes as having a complex structure. It is not really a single agreement, but a set of bilateral agreements linking each contractor with every other. Hence, a single party can rightly demand fulfillment of the agreement by each of the others.[4] Each of these bilateral agreements surrenders

[2] Since dominion is transitive (see ibid., chap. 20, p. 188), pledges (even tacit ones) from all are not required. E.g., a conquered sovereign who pledges obedience to his conqueror thereby places all his previous subjects under the dominion of his conqueror. See ibid., chap. 21, p. 209.
[3] Ibid., chap. 20, p. 191.
[4] Ibid., chap. 18, p. 160.

the individual's right of self-rule to, and authorizes all the actions of, a sovereign person or assembly to be elected later by the parties by majority vote. In this two-stage process, the actual sovereign is selected only after the parties are joined into a social union by overlapping mutual agreements. The parties bind one another to confer on whoever is elected their combined power and authority, in hopes thereby of achieving protection against foreigners and one another. The sovereign is not, qua sovereign, a party to the social contract and is therefore not constrained by it.[5] He in effect receives sovereignty as a free gift, in Hobbes's sense: "When the transferring of right, is not mutual: but one of the parties transferreth, in hope to gain thereby . . . service from another, . . . this is not contract, but GIFT, FREE GIFT."[6]

Now there is no doubt that of these two accounts, the former—sovereignty by acquisition—is a more accurate historical account of the origins of most actual commonwealths. Yet for our purposes it will be best to largely ignore sovereignty by acquisition and to focus on sovereignty by institution. The reason for this is that we wish to construct a normative as well as descriptive Hobbesian political theory. We are concerned with whether the State can be *justified*, on what grounds, and with what limitations or restrictions. And we want our arguments to be persuasive to (or at least speak to) individuals who conceive themselves as morally independent beings. Therefore it is of more interest to us in what manner and form a State might be founded by agreement among independent rational individuals, than how they have actually originated via family ties and conquest. Further, as will be argued later (section 10-2), Hobbes's theory of sovereignty by acquisition is beset with errors—both normative and conceptual. The third part of our Hobbesian argument against anarchy will therefore rely on sovereignty by institution, Hobbes's version of social contract theory.

[5] Ibid., pp. 161–62. Even if the sovereign were, as an individual, one of the original contracting parties, this would not limit his freedom of action as sovereign, for all he is committed to is authorizing, and not resisting, the acts of the sovereign, i.e., himself. See section 10-1.
[6] *Leviathan*, chap. 14, p. 121.

That theory is, as observed in section 1-3, a hypothetical contract theory. It seeks to justify certain social arrangements by claims about what rational people would select or agree on under appropriately specified conditions. It is important to notice, however, that Hobbes's version of hypothetical contract theory differs from the versions of contemporary writers such as John Rawls[7] and David Gauthier[8] in at least one vital respect. While these writers seek to derive principles of social justice from the hypothetical contract, Hobbes (and Hobbesian theory) uses the device for a more modest purpose: to identify the conditions that a political system or State must satisfy in order for its citizens or inhabitants to be obligated to obey its rules, rulings, and officials. In other words, Hobbesian social contract theory seeks to identify necessary and/or sufficient conditions for political obligation. The conditions so identified will be too weak to insure social justice, attainment of the ideal society, or similar lofty goals, but in a world in which the moral legitimacy of various States (or even all States) is frequently disputed or called into question they are still well worth knowing.

With these matters clarified, we may turn back to Hobbes's account of the social contract. Two features of that account stand out in our sketch above: the two-stage sequence in the creation of the sovereign, and the unlimited power and authority bestowed upon him (or them).[9] In section 5-5 we shall reject the latter feature, but there is something of considerable interest in Hobbes's idea of a two-stage social contract. To bring it out, we can use some terminology from elementary game theory.

Consider the two-person game pictured in Figure 9. Assuming the players must play simultaneously, secretly, and without communication, this game constitutes a *coordination problem*. That is, while there is no conflict of interest (indeed, for every outcome the payoffs to the two players are equal), success depends

---

[7] Rawls, *A Theory of Justice*.

[8] Gauthier, "Justice as Social Choice," in *Morality, Reason, and Truth*, ed. Copp and Zimmerman, pp. 251–69.

[9] As noted in section 4-4, the sovereign may exercise some of this unlimited power and authority only indirectly.

FIGURE 9

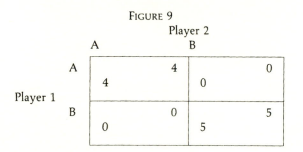

FIGURE 10

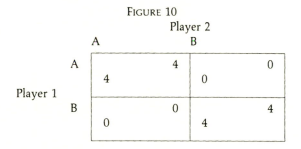

upon coordinating with your partner by selecting a move that produces a good outcome in conjunction with his move. Thus, your selecting move A is advantageous if your partner does the same, but it is disadvantageous if he selects B—and similarly for your selection of B. In view of this, move combinations (or outcomes) AA and BB are said to be *coordination points* of the game.

Perhaps the coordination problem pictured in Figure 9 is easily solvable, as each player can be confident that the other will aim for, and expect him to aim for, the more lucrative coordination point, and each will therefore select B. But if the matrix is as in Figure 10, this reasoning does not apply, and the players will be left to rely on contextual clues, background knowledge, or pure guesses in trying to coordinate.[10] Of course, even this problem is

[10] People are able to coordinate surprisingly well using contextual clues and background knowledge. See Thomas Schelling, *The Strategy of Conflict* (London: Oxford University Press, 1960), chap. 3.

FIGURE 11

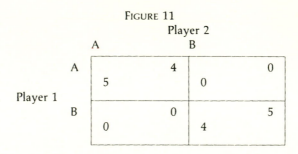

readily solvable if we allow communication among the players. They will simply agree on playing A, or B, and then select accordingly. Since both gain by coordinating and lose by not doing so, each can rely on the other to keep the agreement. There is no incentive to cheat here, as in prisoner's dilemma situations.

Consider, however, a third matrix, as depicted in Figure 11. We shall call problems of the sort displayed in Figure 11 *impure coordination problems*. That is, they are predominantly coordination problems in that each player gains much by winding up at either coordination point rather than at a noncoordination point. But the players have conflicting interests in the sense that they most prefer *different* coordination points, though these preferences are much less strong than the preference for coordination over noncoordination.[11] In the Figure 11 game, for example, player 1 prefers AA to BB by one unit, while he prefers either over AB or BA by an average of 4.5 units. Player 2's preferences are alike, save for his preferring BB to AA by one unit.

The key point about impure coordination problems is that they are not necessarily solvable by communication among the parties. If the players in our last game communicate, they may reach agreement on both playing A (or B), or they may not. Player 1, for example, may declare he is going to play A no matter what,

[11] It is this last feature which differentiates impure coordination problems from *bargaining problems* in general, of which the former form a subclass. On the characterization of bargaining problems, see, e.g., Allan Gibbard, "Human Evolution and the Sense of Justice" *Midwest Studies in Philosophy* 7 (1982): 32.

trying to force player 2 into going along to keep from getting nothing. Player 2 might respond with a similar declaration, and if neither gave in (or *both* did without warning at the moment of play), they would fail to coordinate.

From a Hobbesian perspective, the choice of a sovereign by rational parties in a state of nature is an impure coordination problem. It is primarily a coordination problem because, given the likely miseries of the state of nature (an active war of all individuals or small groups), it matters much more to each *that* there be a sovereign than *who* in particular it is.[12] It is an impure coordination problem, because various individuals would expect to fare better under different sovereigns (e.g., each party might most prefer that he himself were sovereign).

Hobbes's proposal for selection of a sovereign by a two-stage sequence—unanimous endorsement of whoever receives majority support in a subsequent election, followed by such an election—represents a promising and interesting general strategy for solving impure coordination problems. The basic idea is to segregate the coordination and conflict aspects of the problem, to add a procedure for settling the conflict to the coordination aspect, and then to deal with the enlarged coordination aspect first. Thus, in the first stage, we agree to limit the jointly determined outcomes to the set of coordination points, and we adopt some procedure for later selecting one of those points. Then, in the second stage, we carry out the procedure to determine which coordination point is the actual outcome.

This general strategy could be applied, for example, by the players of the game pictured in Figure 11. They could simply agree to flip a coin to determine whether both choose A or choose B, and then actually flip and choose accordingly. In effect, they view their original apparently two-choice game as a three-choice game with the form illustrated in Figure 12 (where some entries

[12] Hobbes writes (*Leviathan*, chap. 18, p. 170): "The greatest, that in any form of government can possibly happen to the people in general, is scarce sensible, in respect of the miseries, and horrible calamities, that accompany a civil war, or that dissolute condition of masterless men, without subjection to laws, and a coercive power."

FIGURE 12

Player 2

	A	B	Decide by flip
A	4 5	0 0	2 2.5
Player 1 **B**	0 0	5 4	2.5 2
Decide by flip	2 2.5	2.5 2	4.5 4.5

now represent *expected* payoffs). This expanded version of the game is still an impure coordination problem, but it is one in which it may be easier to settle on an agreed solution, because it contains a symmetrical coordination point (namely, both deciding by the coin flip with expected payoff of 4.5 each).

Hobbes's two-stage social contract employs a like strategy for dealing with the impure coordination problem of selecting a sovereign. In the first stage, the parties do what is in their common interest: they all agree to authorize a single sovereign and to settle their conflicting interests over who that sovereign is by a specified procedure. The conflict is then played out at the second stage within the specified procedure, which is designed to resolve it: a majority election procedure that picks out a specific sovereign.

Note that it is essential to the entire scheme that the outcome of the process in question—flipping a coin or having a majority election with a large number of voters—be *uncertain* at the time of the first-stage agreement. Otherwise, those who expect the procedure to yield their least-favored coordination outcomes will be no more willing to accept the first-stage agreement than they would be to accept these outcomes directly. Thus, for example, a rational player 1 will not be willing to accept the procedure "let player 2's loyal henchman pick the coordination point" unless he is willing to accept coordination at BB directly.

But uncertainty is gone once the procedure is actually carried out. Why should rational election or coin-flip losers go along then, rather than trying to reopen negotiations? The reason is that in even an impure coordination problem the advantages of coordination are substantially greater than the advantages of reaching a favored coordination point. Therefore, when coordination is virtually assured by carrying out an agreed procedure, it would be foolish to risk an eventual noncoordinated outcome by reopening negotiations. This is especially so if there are a large number of parties and coordination points involved, so that the a priori probability of achieving coordination is low.

In the specific case of Hobbes's social contract, this amounts to saying that having once found a promising way out of the poor and dangerous state of nature, one would be foolish to risk returning there merely in hopes of later finding an even better way out. There is another way to look at the matter. Hobbes has already argued that it is irrational, as a second party, to violate state-of-nature agreements, because this *risks* your later being kept out of a commonwealth (or other defense group). So then it must be more irrational, even foolish, to violate your agreement to enter a commonwealth, for you would thereby turn down the certainty of rescue from the state of nature, make the numerous other contractors mad at you, and make almost everyone less likely to include you in future commonwealths. This would appear to be rational only in the extreme case in which you regard living under the selected sovereign as personally highly dangerous (e.g., he is your sworn enemy).

The *possibility* that losers in the selection procedure may defect from the agreement can help us understand and justify Hobbes's choice of majority election as the method of picking the sovereign. Why majority election rather than some other procedure—for example, drawing lots or having a footrace? Majority election has the advantages of being salient, nonarbitrary, and seemingly fair. Other procedures may share each, perhaps even all, of these features, but majority election is the only procedure that guarantees the least possible number of losers, that is, those who did not prefer the chosen sovereign. Hence, if we desire the fewest possible defectors from the agreement upon selection of a sovereign, we are best off choosing majority rule as a selection procedure.[13]

Does the two-stage idea apply only to the authorization and selection of a sovereign? Obviously not. The parties may unanimously agree at the first stage on a procedure for writing a constitution, enacting legislation, and so on. If there is a common interest in safeguarding certain individual or group rights and interests, they may even agree *at the first stage* on certain substantive principles or procedural arrangements designed to safeguard those rights and interests. Trade-offs and bargaining may even occur at the first stage, so that interests or rights that are not unanimously valued are nevertheless protected. We cannot tell what sort of solution rational parties in the state of nature would find for their impure coordination problems until we say more about these parties and the circumstances we suppose them to be in.

5-2. The Parties

Even to speculate in a plausible way about the likely outcome of negotiations over a social contract, we must specify certain main features of the negotiation and the parties to it. As regards the negotiation, the most relevant features are what is being negotiated (i.e., the *target*), the *rules* for formulation, discussion, negotiation, and adoption of proposals, and the nature of the *no agreement point* (i.e., what happens if agreement is not reached). The characteristics of the parties that are of crucial importance are their knowledge, cognitive abilities, and motivational structures.

---

[13] This assumes a binary choice. As is well known, there are a variety of voting procedures for selecting one winning candidate from a number of alternatives. There is no *guarantee* that a procedure making greater use of majority voting will produce less dissatisfaction than one making less use of it. But, for the reason given in the text, one would expect this to be the case, *other things being equal.*

The *target* of the social contract, for the purposes of Hobbesian theory, is the establishment of a permanent State or commonwealth, perhaps of a specific kind. Thus, at a minimum, the parties aim at adopting rules that create public offices with powers sufficient to perform security functions, and procedures for selecting officials to fill those offices. They may also seek substantive or procedural rules governing or limiting the conduct of private individuals and/or public officials and institutions. Whatever rules are adopted are to be binding on all, and they are to be selected with the goal of stability, or permanence, of the resulting system in mind.[14] The *no-agreement point* is the state of nature; if no social contract is made, the parties all remain in that undesirable condition.[15]

The *rules for negotiations* call for open discussion and debate. All parties are free to offer proposals (which include establishment of sufficient public power to constitute a State) and to give reasons in support of or against any proposal. Sufficient time is allowed for adequate discussion of all proposals. Proposals may be conjoined, modified, and amended as individual parties choose. The formation of coalitions, and agreements among individuals and subgroups, are not allowed during the negotiations. The purpose of this restriction is to prevent arbitrary and contingent features of coalition formation patterns from influencing the ultimate content of the social contract; and in particular to prevent the formation of blocking coalitions that could effectively use the threat to veto any agreement as a way of winning special advantages. Of course, individual parties may perceive, discuss, and publicly make known common interests with others. They may also formulate proposals to appeal to special groups and may point out the advantages and disadvantages of various proposals to those

---

[14] The importance of permanence is suggested in *Leviathan* at chap. 17, p. 155, and chap. 29, p. 308. Problems concerning the stability of the State are discussed in sections 6-2 through 6-4.

[15] Depending upon what they know of their specific situations in the state of nature, and their attitudes toward the kinds of dangers encountered therein, different parties will regard not reaching agreement as undesirable to different degrees. How this may affect the reasonings of "naturally advantaged" parties and "lazy" people is discussed later in this section and in section 5-4.

possessing certain characteristics. But they cannot make binding agreements among themselves (except by adopting a social contract) or form themselves into bargaining units represented by spokesmen, agents, and so forth.

At any time after a number of proposals have been adequately discussed, a member may call for a vote on a proposal. To be adopted, a proposal must receive *nearly unanimous* support, that is, a positive vote exceeding a prespecified cutoff point above 95 percent. (Hobbesian theory thus departs, for reasons that will emerge below, from the complete-unanimity requirement suggested by Hobbes and supported by contemporary contract theorists.[16])

The parties to these negotiations are assumed to be rational, appropriately forwardlooking, and predominantly self-interested. Their rationality is a necessary assumption for any hypothetical contract theory that seeks to display the rationale for, and thereby provide a justification of, the State, for hypothetical agreements, unlike actual ones, can provide reasons for action only if they are rational agreements. The parties' rationality is therefore required if we are to make normative use of Hobbesian social contract theory.

The predominant self-interest assumption, by contrast, is adopted for other reasons. Most important, as argued in Chapter 2, it accurately characterizes human motivation. Further, it simplifies our reconstruction of the parties' reasonings and deliberations. In the negotiation situation the parties have not yet attained a condition of satisfactory security. Hence, according to Predominant Egoism, we may take it that the deliberations of nearly every party will be dominated by concern to promote his own security and well-being.

Our reasons for assuming that the parties are appropriately

[16] Ibid., chap. 18, p. 159. For contemporary theorists, see, e.g., Rawls, *A Theory of Justice*, pp. 122, 139; Gauthier, "The Social Contract: Individual Decision or Collective Bargain?" in *Foundations and Applications of Decision Theory*, vol. 2, ed. C. A. Hooker, J. J. Leach, and E. F. McClennan (Dordrecht: Reidel, 1978), p. 48; and James Buchanan and Gordon Tullock, *The Calculus of Consent* (Ann Arbor: University of Michigan Press, 1962), p. 250.

forwardlooking include both descriptive accuracy and a desire to fit the requirements of normative theory. *Appropriately* forwardlooking parties consider their long-run as well as short-run desires and interests and give their desires and interests at different times equal weights in decision-making. That means they discount temporally more-distant goals or outcomes relative to nearer ones only to the extent justified by uncertainty. We noted earlier that forwardlookingness, in the sense of concern for future well-being, is a general characteristic of human beings. But this feature is compatible with shortsightedness, that is, discounting more temporally distant goals or outcomes because of their distance. Shortsightedness is likely to be minimized when people deliberate at length over important and final commitments that they realize will substantially affect their security and well-being over their entire lifetimes. Hence, we could expect most real people to approximate appropriate forwardlookingness in the context of negotiating a binding social contract. Furthermore, for purposes of *justifying* the permanent and lasting authority of (certain) States, we should be interested in the political arrangements that rational farsighted (i.e., appropriately forwardlooking) people would agree on. (To take a parallel example, we would not consider current environmental policies justified by the observation that they are the policies that rational shortsighted people would agree to, but we might well consider such policies justified if convinced that rational farsighted people would agree to them.) So normative social contract theory requires not merely forwardlooking parties but also appropriately forwardlooking ones.

We now turn to the critical question concerning the characterization of the negotiating parties. What do they know? For purposes of dealing with this question, let us artificially divide up things the parties might want to know into five categories: the negotiating circumstances, general social knowledge, their own particular society's characteristics, individual characteristics, and individual social position. The *negotiating circumstances* are the facts just described: the target and rules of the negotiations, and the specified characteristics of the other parties. Clearly the parties should be assumed to possess this information, so that they know what they are doing in the negotiations and can reasonably argue, bargain, and reach agreement. *General social knowledge* is knowledge of general facts about human psychology and social behavior—the available findings of the social sciences of psychology, economics, sociology, political science, and so on. Since the parties are considering arrangements and institutions to govern a society of human beings, such general social knowledge will be essential to their intelligently carrying out their task, and we shall assume that they have it. A *particular society's characteristics* are its significant features not shared by human societies in general, its history, language, culture, geography, economic system, and so on. Knowledge of these would also be useful in choosing social and governmental institutions. However, we are seeking general criteria of political legitimacy for institutions, and a general justification for the State, that can extend across societies possessing a wide range of particular characteristics. For this reason, it is desirable to abstract from the peculiar features of particular societies by supposing that the negotiating parties do not possess such information about their own society. There are no substantial bad effects of this restriction, for the parties can agree on rules that will take account of particular societal features in their application, and institutions and procedures that will be able to adjust to and accommodate such features.

Matters become more difficult when we turn to the issue of an individual party's knowledge of his own particular features. A person's *individual characteristics* are such things as gender, state of health, appearance, strength, traits of character, skills, level of knowledge, intelligence, goals, ideals, plan of life, and so on. One's *individual social position* is characterized by one's economic and social status within society—one's occupation, level of wealth, membership in groups with high or low status, the power of public and private offices and positions that one occupies, and so forth.[17] Should the negotiating parties be presumed to know their own individual characteristics or social positions?

[17] This distinction between characteristics and social position is *roughly* analogous to that drawn between natural and social powers in section 3-3 above.

192

Two considerations support opposite answers to this question. Agreement would clearly be easier to obtain among parties deprived of information about their individual features and position, for known individual differences can lead to irreconcilable disagreements about the content of the social contract, for example, between the rich who prefer strong property rights and the poor who favor redistribution, or between the clever and aggressive, who want competition for top jobs, and the less clever and more passive, who might prefer a rotation system or random selection. On the other hand, we want our hypothetical contract theory to be motivationally efficacious. We want real people, who know their individual characteristics and social positions, to be persuaded that they should go along with the kind of social institutions and principles that would be agreed on in the hypothetical contract situation. But people are more likely to be thus persuaded if they see the parties in that situation as like themselves, if they are able to identify with the parties. This is facilitated by allowing the parties knowledge of their individual characteristics and situations.

Hobbes is able to avoid facing this trade-off between motivational efficacy and agreement facilitation, but only by relying on highly implausible empirical assumptions. Falsely asserting that limitations on, or divisions of, sovereign power lead inevitably to civil war and anarchy, he concludes that regardless of individual differences virtually all parties inside or outside society have an overriding common interest in establishing the only institution that can bring them lasting peace and security—an unlimited and undivided sovereign power. If we discard Hobbes's false assumption about unlimited and undivided power, we cannot so easily assume that unanimous agreement on a social contract is possible among parties possessing full knowledge of their personal and social characteristics.

In developing Hobbesian theory, then, we shall follow a middle ground between allowing the contracting parties full knowledge of their personal situations and Rawls's strategy of ruling out all such knowledge. In particular, our basic assumption shall be that the parties know their personal characteristics but not their social positions. Thus, a party may know, for example, that she is an intelligent, success-oriented woman, but not that she is an upper-middle-class attorney earning a high income and having substantial status and political influence in her community. Two complications must be noted, however. First, we must rule out knowledge of personal goals, or other characteristics, that presuppose for their existence or fulfillment the existence of a certain specific governmental system or set of institutions. Not doing so would doom us either to begging the question in favor of existing institutions (if all parties had goals presupposing them) or likely ending up with irreconcilable differences among various parties whose goals presupposed incompatible institutional arrangements. Second, there are two ways in which a party's knowledge of his personal characteristics may allow him to make inferences about his social position. He may believe that a certain personal characteristic, for example, aggressiveness or good looks, will *causally* contribute to his attaining a certain social position—by leading him to seize business opportunities or by enabling him to make a socially advantageous marriage. Alternately, knowing that certain personal characteristics tend to *correlate* with social position independently of the former causing the latter, he may take his known possession of a personal characteristic (e.g., belief in a laissez-faire ideology) as a *sign* of his likely social position (e.g., being economically well-off).[18] The former sort of inferences are allowable, as they concern the parties' deliberations about how they will or may fare under various arrangements in the postagreement society. The latter kind of inferences are not legitimate—they merely allow known personal characteristics to serve as probabilistic proxies for the information we have explicitly denied the parties, knowledge of their actual personal social position.[19] We therefore assume (or stipulate) that the negotiating

[18] On the distinction between causes and signs in the context of the theory of rational decision, see Brian Skyrms, "Causal Decision Theory," *Journal of Philosophy* 79 (November 1982): 695–711.

[19] This apparently differentiates our position from that of Gauthier ("The Social Contract as Ideology," p. 56), in which any knowledge of social position inferred from personal characteristics seems to be allowed.

parties do not make inferences of this latter kind, that their present individual social positions remain a mystery to them despite their knowledge of their own individual characteristics.

Why allow the parties to know their personal features but not their social positions? One reason is that the absence of knowledge of social position is implicit in Hobbes's own resolutive-compositive procedure of dissolving society into its atomic elements, individuals, and reconstructing it from those elements. Why not then go further, as Rawls explicitly does, and exclude knowledge of personal features so as to make the atoms of social theory indistinguishable? One reason concerns motivational efficacy. It is much easier for most people to identify with hypothetical contractors pictured as ourselves deprived of knowledge of our social positions, than with such contractors pictured as devoid of all individuating features. Also, remember that our fundamental concern is with the justification of the State as an alternative to anarchy and with establishing minimal conditions of government legitimacy. In this context, abstracting from differences in social position, which are created or facilitated by the very institutions being called into question, seems entirely appropriate. But differences in personal characteristics are in part natural and are influenced more indirectly and to a lesser degree (than is social position) by existing institutional structures. Since these differences would remain at least partly as they are under various institutional arrangements, it is appropriate to view the institutions of the State as designed to accommodate these differences. This is achieved by allowing the parties to retain knowledge of their personal characteristics while they negotiate the social contract.

To explain how our limited restrictions on the parties' knowledge are intended to operate, it will be useful to contrast them with Rawls's restrictions on knowledge. In his early contractarian theory, presented in two articles,[20] Rawls imposed no knowledge restrictions. He believed that even without them self-interested

---

[20]"Justice as Fairness," *Philosophical Review* 67 (April 1958): 164–94; and "Justice as Reciprocity," in *Utilitarianism with Critical Essays*, ed. Samuel Gorovitz (Indianapolis: Bobbs-Merrill, 1971), pp. 242–68.

contractors could reach unanimous agreement on principles of social justice designed to maximize the prospects of a representative
member of the worst-off social group. Those higher up in the
social order would agree to such principles as insurance against
the possibility that they themselves or their loved ones would
end up at the bottom of the social heap.[21] In his later contractarian theory, however, Rawls changes his mind and imposes severe
knowledge restrictions to obtain agreement among the parties—
he deprives them of all knowledge of their personal characteristics
and social position (and even of the probabilities of their possessing various such characteristics).[22] Under these conditions of
complete uncertainty, he contends, the parties will opt for principles that maximize the prospects of a representative member of
the least-advantaged social group, for under moderate scarcity this
assures them a decent level of well-being, and the parties do not
care much for the additional advantages they (individually) might
gain under a less egalitarian system.[23] Further, this maximin arrangement best insures adherence to the agreement by not requiring anyone to make intolerable sacrifices for others.[24]

There are useful elements in both early and later Rawlsian
contractarian theory that can be incorporated into Hobbesian theory. From the early Rawls comes one of the two main reasons
that we would expect Hobbesian parties with knowledge of their
(differing) personal characteristics (but not their social positions)
to reach agreement on a social contract that treats the less advantaged decently: even those with most of the characteristics useful
in a laissez-faire social system would know there was a significant
possibility that they (or those they cared much about) might end
up in some badly off social group. Later Rawlsian theory notes
the second main reason for the favorably endowed to agree to
terms that provide for the well-being of the worst-off. Long-run
social stability, which is the primary aim of the social contract
and the prerequisite of the secure well-being of each, will be un-

---

[21] Rawls, "Justice as Fairness," p. 171–72.
[22] Rawls, *Theory of Justice*, pp. 137, 155, 168–69.
[23] Ibid., p. 154.
[24] Ibid., pp. 175–78.

likely if the least advantaged are treated too badly and are hope-less and desperate. Hobbes emphasizes this point when he ob-serves that needy people will foment rebellion if they are strong enough to hope for success or are deprived of the necessities of life.[25]

Later Rawlsian theory also provides the promising idea that under great uncertainty and with so much at stake it is reason-able for the contracting parties to pursue a conservative strategy designed to assure themselves, insofar as possible, a decent out-come. But Rawls is wrong that his principle of maximizing the prospects of the representative person in the least-advantaged group does this. Many individual members of the least-advantaged group (and some members of other groups) will be worse off than this representative person,[26] and they might end up, under Rawlsian principles, with a supply of needed social goods that was too small to support a decent life. Hence, rational contractors focusing their main attention on assuring themselves a decent life would prob-ably opt for some guaranteed social minimum (perhaps with ap-propriate work incentives) rather than a Rawlsian maximin prin-ciple.

Note further, as various critics have pointed out,[27] that Rawls has no good grounds for supposing that the parties care little for the extra advantages they might obtain in a less egalitarian social system. If, quite plausibly, we suppose the opposite, we have an-other reason for thinking the Hobbesian contractors would be more likely to agree on a guaranteed minimum than on Rawlsian max-imin principles, for at least in relatively wealthy societies a guar-anteed minimim system is likely to leave the advantaged better off, other things being equal, than a Rawlsian system. Hence,

[25] *Leviathan*, chap. 11, pp. 86–87; chap. 15, p. 139.

[26] It is assumed here that Rawls's "representative" is as well off as the average member of the worst-off group. The present objection is avoided if one assumes that Rawls's representative is supposed to be the "least advantaged of the least advantaged." But there is no textual support for this view, which in addition runs into problems (noted in sections 5-3 and 5-4) concerning the enormous costs of maximizing the prospects of the very worst-off individuals.

[27] See, e.g., Thomas Nagel, "Rawls on Justice," in *Reading Rawls*, ed. Norman Daniels (New York: Basic Books, 1976), p. 12.

contractors knowing that they possess personal characteristics likely to bring success in relatively competitive and inegalitarian systems are more likely to agree to a guaranteed social minimum than to maximizing the prospects of the representative member of the least-advantaged group.

It might still be objected that allowing negotiating parties knowledge of their personal characteristics will preclude the possibility of their reaching agreement on a social contract, for those with personal characteristics likely to produce success in a highly competitive environment will be unwilling to agree to the social insurance or redistributive measures demanded by those possessing less-favorable characteristics. Note, however, that personal characteristics (with social position left out) are at best unreliable and uncertain indicators of success even in specific known societies.[28] They will be even more unreliable and uncertain indicators of success for our negotiating parties, since they do not know the particular features of their own society. Also, many personal features that may tend to lead to success in any sort of society, such as robust good health, are subject to alteration due to natural or social contingencies, for example, illness, accident, or an unhealthy environment. As a result, if they are reasonably prudent, even negotiators with favorable personal characteristics will see definite advantages to themselves in incorporating certain significant social insurance measures into the social contract. And given that the likely alternative is either no agreement and a return to the state of nature, or the establishment of a commonwealth that is unstable because the needs of the least advantaged are not met, one would expect that almost all those possessing favorable personal features could be persuaded to accept provisions concerning such measures as part of the founding agreement.

Still *some* parties who are especially favored in all the personal

---

[28] Those who initially doubt this should ask themselves whether, e.g., ambition and drive are likely to produce success, under laissez-faire, for an uneducated ghetto-dweller as well as for a well-educated member of a middle-class family. Even if true, the adage that "anyone *can* succeed" (in free competition) does not imply that anyone (i.e., an individual from any socioeconomic background) is at all *likely* to succeed.

characteristics most associated with social and economic success might be so confident of success in any competitive system (including the state of nature) that they might rationally refuse to accept any proposal calling for (or allowing) social insurance that aids those badly off. Similarly, some parties may be quite free of risk aversion, so that even if they are not confident of success in a competitive social environment without social insurance, they would be willing to accept the risks of failing in an uninsured social environment (or of reaching no agreement) in preference to agreeing to pay their share of the "premiums" required to support an insurance scheme. Also, some dominators (as defined in section 3-5) may love conquest *so much* as to prefer the opportunities of the state of nature to the security of the State.[29] These possibilities pose potentially serious difficulties for theories that require unanimous consent to the hypothetical social contract. By not requiring unanimous consent, our Hobbesian theory avoids these difficulties. So long as the percentages of (1) those possessing extremely favorable personal features, (2) those who are extremely non-risk-averse regarding their vital interests, and (3) dominators who prefer conquest opportunities to security are quite small, the fact that they might not reach agreement with the other parties does not preclude the possibility of a social contract. In fact, the main advantage of jettisoning the unanimity requirement is that it prevents a reasonable agreement by the vast majority from being scuttled by the intransigent demands of a relative few with extremely atypical personal characteristics, attitudes toward risk, or aversions to peace and compromise. At the same time, it prevents such "extremists," or other clever bargainers, from tailoring the agreement to their own personal advantage, by threatening to veto it if it is not formulated as they demand.

We may sum up our treatment of the negotiating parties' specific knowledge as follows. We disallow parties' knowledge of their

---

[29] In Chapter 3, the existence of a *significant minority* of dominators, who prefer anticipation to lying low in the state of nature, was postulated. This does *not* imply, however, that a significant number will prefer anticipation to the security offered by the State.

social positions, for possession of such knowledge would defeat the Hobbesian purpose of understanding the State as an artifact created and chosen by independent individuals and might eliminate the possibility of the parties' reaching agreement. On the other hand, Hobbesian theory assumes that the parties know their personal features. This increases the motivational force and persuasive potential of the resulting version of hypothetical contract theory, and given the parties' vital common interest in reaching some agreement, and the absence of a unanimity requirement, possession of such knowledge does not preclude their coming to an agreement. We must next consider what the content of that agreement might be.

5-3. *Choice and Disaster-Avoidance*

It would be gratifying if we could proceed by a neat deductive argument from our characterization of the negotiating parties and their situation to a single detailed set of principles for governing society on which the parties would inevitably agree, but we cannot begin to do so. From the appropriate bargaining situation as described, many different sets of principles might emerge as outcomes, depending upon the interaction of such variable factors as the parties' attitudes toward risk, their particular values, their bargaining tactics, the particular trade-offs suggested during negotiations, and so on. Admitting this potential variability of outcomes might well doom our efforts, if we aimed at a complete theory of the ideal society, or even of social justice. But our more modest aims of refuting anarchism and explicating the grounds and conditions of political obligation can still be accomplished. This requires that we focus our attention on the *intersection* of the various agreements that might reasonably emerge, the principles or arrangements (if any) contained in all of them. Suppose there were such principles or arrangements and that it could be argued that parties in all such negotiations would reasonably prefer agreements containing them to agreements containing their main competitors, and to reaching no agreement at all. We could then treat such principles and arrangements as the determinant

200

outcome of our abstractly described negotiating situation, as the *content of the social contract.* These principles or arrangements would likely be quite general and hardly complete enough to fully characterize a governmental system. But they would specify (some of) the limiting parameters that such a system and its officials would have to satisfy to be properly regarded as exercising a legitimate authority, with which citizens are obligated to comply.[30]

It may clarify matters to note the distinction, drawn by David Gauthier and by Jean Hampton,[31] between *bargain* and *choice* versions of social contract theory. In a bargain theory, distinct parties with somewhat divergent interests make trade-offs or compromises to reach agreement. In a choice theory, such as Rawls's, the parties are conceived as being in essentially identical situations, so that the same line of reasoning leads each to choose the same outcome.[32] Our account, in contrast to that of Rawls, allows individual parties knowledge of their individual characteristics; hence there is no supposition that they will all favor the same proposals for precisely the same reasons. Rather, we suppose that genuine bargaining would take place, leading to a variety of possible outcomes. Viewing the social contract in this way as an outcome of a bargain (rather than of shared preferences) fits better with Hobbes's idea that the State is a device created to ameliorate conflict and enable cooperation among rational individuals with differing goals, aims, and interests. The Hobbesian State should not be mistaken for a Kantian kingdom of ends.

Still, in focusing on the intersection of the various reasonable bargains that might emerge among state-of-nature negotiators, our argument comes to resemble those employed in choice theories, for the principles in the intersection are presumably those that enough parties would have a sufficient common interest in adopting that they are never likely to be traded off. And we shall

[30] There are alternative grounds of political obligation which, when present, could create obligations to systems not satisfying the substantive requirements laid down by our hypothetical consent theory. See section 10-4.

[31] Gauthier, "The Social Contract as Ideology"; and Jean Hampton, "Contracts and Choices: Does Rawls Have a Social Contract Theory?" *Journal of Philosophy* 77 (June 1980): 315–38.

[32] Rawls, *Theory of Justice*, p. 139.

argue for these principles by showing how almost all the parties could be expected to choose them in preference to relevant alternatives (including no agreement) and to resist trading them off for reciprocal concessions that other parties would be likely to offer. Even here, however, our procedure differs from that employed in a pure choice theory such as Rawls's. In assessing the acceptability of a principle, we shall often consider the perspective of *two* groups—usually those possessing more- and less-advantageous personal characteristics. And reasons for agreeing to the principles will in some cases be different for members of the two groups.

We shall consider in turn principles and arrangements concerning three aspects of social life: economic welfare, the powers and structure of government, and rights and liberties of individuals. In determining what principles in these areas negotiating parties would prefer to what others, and what matters the parties would generally refuse to compromise on, a characteristically Hobbesian conception of rational choice under uncertainty will be repeatedly employed. As a preliminary step, therefore, we must explicate this conception, referred to in section 4-3 as disaster-avoidance reasoning.

The disaster-avoidance principle is intended to guide choices rationally in a limited range of situations. Let us say that a course of action which has a nonnegligible probability of leading to some disastrous[33] outcome or other possesses *disaster potential,* and that the higher this probability the higher the degree of disaster potential. Imagine a choice between alternative courses of action, all (or all but one) of which have disaster potential. Suppose further that the choice must be made under *uncertainty,* that is, the chooser does not possess reliable estimates of the probabilities of the various possible outcomes following from the various alternative courses of action. Yet the chooser is not mired in complete uncertainty. He has enough information to be confident about which

---

[33] I.e., disastrous from the point of view of the choosing agent. It will not always be easy for decision-makers to classify all potential outcomes as disastrous or nondisastrous, but it will be easier than making the ordinal or quantitative utility judgments that it is normally assumed people can make.

alternatives are more or less likely to produce some disastrous outcome, that is, he possesses *ordinal* but not cardinal data about the disaster potentials of the available courses of action.[34] Further, the chooser is able at least to order (even if he cannot reliably estimate in quantitative terms) the possible disastrous outcomes in terms of how bad they are. In other words, he possesses at least ordinal data about the (dis)utilities of the disasters that could follow from the available courses of action. When all these conditions are satisfied, we say that the agent faces a *choice among potential disasters under uncertainty.*

The disaster-avoidance principle is designed to guide such choices. It recommends choosing the course of action that minimizes the probability of ending up with a disastrous outcome, the act with lowest disaster potential. The basic intuition underlying the principle is that under uncertainty, with much at risk (as there will be if disastrous outcomes are possible), it is rational to play it safe by doing one's best to avoid unacceptable outcomes. According to the principle, it is worth forgoing potential gains and running a risk of suffering worse disasters in order to maximize one's prospects of avoiding disaster altogether and obtaining an acceptable outcome. To clarify this, and to make clearer the fundamental nature and rationale of the disaster-avoidance principle, it will be helpful to contrast it with two other principles of rational choice in the context of a specific (hypothetical) example.[35]

A forty-year-old man is diagnosed as having a rare disease and consults the world's leading expert on the disease. He is informed that the disease is not fatal but that it often causes serious paralysis that leaves its victims bedridden for life (in the other cases it has no lasting effects). The disease is so rare that the expert can offer only a vague estimate of the probability of paralysis: 20 percent to 60 percent. There is an experimental drug that, if administered now, would definitely cure the disease. However, it kills a significant but not accurately known percentage of those who take it. The expert guesses that the probability of the drug's

---

[34] This will be possible if different methods for determining the relevant probabilities yield quite different numerical estimates but agree in their orderings.

[35] The example is borrowed from my "Deterrence, Utility, and Rational Choice."

being fatal is less than 20 percent, and the patient thus assumes that he is definitely less likely to die if he takes the drug than he is to be paralyzed if he lets the disease run its course. The patient would regard bedridden life as preferable to death, but he considers both outcomes as totally disastrous compared to continuing his life in good health. Should he take the drug?

This patient faces a choice among potential disasters under uncertainty: each course he may choose risks a disastrous outcome with unknown but nonnegligible probability. The choice would be easy if a single course of action minimized both the probability of disaster-occurrence and the magnitude of the disaster that might be suffered. But here one act, taking the drug, minimizes the probability of disaster, while its alternative, not taking it, minimizes the magnitude of potential disaster.

How would alternative principles of rational choice deal with this choice between a smaller risk of suffering a greater disaster (death) and a greater risk of suffering a lesser disaster (paralysis)? The expected utility principle recommends using one's best estimates of the relevant probabilities and utilities—even if these are unreliable—to calculate the expected utility of each course, and then choosing the one with largest expected utility. Following this recommendation, the uncertain patient might simply assign values of, say, 0, −7, and −10 to the status quo, paralysis, and death, respectively; and choose the midpoints of the relevant probability limits as his estimates, thus taking 1/10 as the probability of the drug being fatal and 4/10 as the probability of paralysis if the drug is not taken. Comparing the resulting expected utilities of −1 for taking the drug and −2.8 for not taking it, he would choose to take the drug.

Critics of this approach would appeal to the old adage "Garbage in, garbage out." If the probability (and utility) estimates are unreliable (in effect, merely guesses), then the expected utilities calculated from them do not mean much and are not a secure basis on which to base an important decision. This criticism is buttressed by the observation that the selection of different probability estimates within the assumed limits may produce different favored actions. If, for example, 15/100 and 2/10 are taken as the probabilities of fatality with the drug and paralysis without it, respectively, and utilities are as assigned above, expected value maximization would then recommend *not* taking the drug.

The maximin and disaster-avoidance principles offer alternative approaches for those unwilling to simply maximize expected utility when they have little confidence in the value of the available numerical probability and utility estimates. The maximin principle, remember, recommends choosing the alternative with the best worst outcome. It prescribes playing it safe, under uncertainty, in the sense of choosing so as to assure yourself of the best outcome that can be assured ahead of time. This seems perfectly reasonable if that outcome is an acceptable one, but in choices among potential disasters under uncertainty, this will not generally be the case. If our patient followed the maximin principle, for example, he would forgo the drug, insuring that at worst he would be paralyzed. But is this reasonable? By so acting, the patient avoids death for sure, but at the cost of maximizing the probability of his suffering some disaster or other (in this case, paralysis).

Would it not be equally, or more, reasonable to undergo some risk of the graver disaster in order to give oneself the greater chance of obtaining an acceptable outcome? The supporter of the disaster-avoidance principle says it is. Like the maximiner, he believes in playing it safe when choosing among potentially disastrous courses of action under uncertainty. But while the maximiner interprets "playing it safe" as avoiding the worst surely avoidable outcomes, the disaster-avoider interprets it as maximizing one's chances of avoiding all disastrous outcomes. When some alternative offers sure disaster-avoidance, the two principles agree, but they part company when, as in the patient's problem, all alternatives have disaster potential and the alternative with smallest disaster potential risks a disaster of greater magnitude than does some other alternative. In such cases, it seems at least as reasonable to maximize one's prospects of disaster-avoidance as to insure against the occurrence of the worse disaster. If you were the patient, wouldn't you take the drug in hopes of being able to continue a normal life?

Suppose, as has been suggested, that the disaster-avoidence principle is at least as reasonable a rule for making choices among potential disasters under uncertainty as are the more familiar expected utility and maximin principles. In seeking to determine the content of a Hobbesian social contract, there are two further reasons for ascribing use of this principle to the negotiating parties. It reflects a mode of reasoning that Hobbes himself employs or suggests others do and should employ in making important decisions. And it is most plausibly applied in situations having many of the special features of the problem faced by our Hobbesian social contractors.

Consider first Hobbes's own uses of disaster-avoidance reasoning. As noted in section 4–3, any of the three principles discussed above—disaster-avoidance, maximin, or expected utility—may be used to explicate Hobbes's important reply to the Fool. But when it comes to the social contract, Hobbes appeals specifically to disaster-avoidance reasoning to defend what he takes to be the central feature of that agreement—its authorization of unlimited sovereignty. He writes:

> But a man may here object, that the condition of subjects is very miserable; as being obnoxious to the lusts, and other irregular passions of him, or them that have so unlimited a power in their hands. . . . [I answer] that the state of man can never be without some incommodity or other; and that the greatest, that in any form of government can possibly happen to the people in general, is scarce sensible, in respect of the miseries, and horrible calamities, that accompany a civil war, or that dissolute condition of masterless men, without subjection to laws, and a coercive power.[36]

This passage presupposes Hobbes's false doctrine that limitations on sovereign power inevitably lead to civil war and a return to the state of nature. But what is of present interest is the form of reasoning it employs to justify rational contractors' supposed preference for unlimited sovereign authority. Instead of weighing

[36] *Leviathan*, chap. 18, pp. 169–70.

206

off risks, gains, and probabilities as an expected utility maximizer would, Hobbes focuses solely on the disastrous outcomes that might arise from either choosing or forgoing unlimited sovereign authority. Further, his acknowledgment of the incommodities of all forms of government and subjects' vulnerability to the irregular passions of an unlimited sovereign indicates that he is aware that an individual (e.g., one persecuted and killed by the government) can suffer as badly in civil society as in the state of nature. Hence, his argument is not of the form "The worst that could happen to you under unlimited sovereignty is better than the worst that could happen under the alternatives," which would be a maximin argument.[37] It is rather of the form "Very bad things could happen to you under anarchy or any system of governance, but they are least frequent and hence least likely under unlimited sovereignty, which is therefore the choiceworthy alternative." This is straightforward disaster-avoidance reasoning.

Such reasoning is attributed to revolutionaries when Hobbes observes, "Needy men, and hardy, not contented with their present condition; . . . are inclined . . . to stir up trouble and sedition: for there is no . . . such hope to mend an ill game, as by causing a new shuffle."[38] Considering their present condition unacceptable ("not contented"), and seeing violence as maximizing their prospects of attaining a decent living situation ("there is no . . . such hope"), they are willing to risk a worse fate, death,[39] in hopes of achieving an acceptable outcome. Thus, in revolting, they act as rational disaster-avoiders, and though a primary message of *Leviathan* is the irrationality of rebellion,[40] Hobbes does not condemn them for it.[41] This is clear evidence that he accepts the rationality of their disaster-avoidance reasoning.

[37] The argument could be read as a maximin one only if addressed to "the people" as a single collective entity. Such collectivization is alien to the general individualist themes of Hobbes's philosophy.

[38] Ibid., chap. 11, pp. 86–87.

[39] In the sentence preceding the quoted one (ibid., p. 86), Hobbes observes that fear of death and wounds generally disposes people to peace.

[40] See section 6-4.

[41] See also Hobbes's discussion of the fifth law of nature (ibid., chap. 15, pp. 138–39), where the rebellion of the truly needy is blamed on those who do not provide for them.

There are textual reasons, then, for regarding the disaster-avoidance principle as congenial to Hobbes and incorporating it into the deliberations of Hobbesian social contractors. Given our practice of departing from Hobbes when he is clearly in error, however, this does not settle the question of whether to attribute disaster-avoidance reasoning to our contractors. We may do so only if the disaster-avoidance principle is a reasonable or plausible one to apply in the specific sort of situation faced by our Hobbesian contractors.[42] In suggesting that it is, we again have in mind a comparison to the expected utility and maximin principles. It shall be assumed that if the disaster-avoidance principle is superior to them in the described circumstances, it is appropriate to use.

Consider first the features of the contractors' situation that make it attractive to use the disaster-avoidance principle rather than the expected utility principle in comparing alternative proposals, or parts thereof. The contractors do not know enough to estimate reliably the probabilities of their ending up at various levels of well-being under various proposals, for an individual's personal characteristics are only weak evidence of how he would fare under a proposed social system, given that neither the individual's social position nor the particular characteristics of the society in question are known. But when probability estimates are quite unreliable, use of the expected-utility principle—which relies so heavily on them—is less attractive than in other contexts. This is especially so when much is at stake, in the sense of disastrous or unacceptable outcomes being possible if the wrong choice is made. Maximizing expected utility as calculated from unreliable probability estimates is of doubtful rationality when it entails running greater-than-necessary risks of obtaining outcomes with which one cannot live. But our contractors are playing for very high stakes: their life prospects and their places in the social order. And a disastrous outcome—agreement on a social system in which the individual will end up living a less than decent life—is

[42] Note Rawls's similar defense of the maximin principle in *Theory of Justice*, p. 153.

possible for anyone, regardless of personal characteristics, if the wrong choices are made during negotiations. Given this, playing it safe, in the sense of forgoing possible (or expected) gains in favor of likely security against unacceptable outcomes, seems eminently reasonable in the circumstances described.

The matter would be otherwise, perhaps, if our contractors faced a *series* of like choices (e.g., if a new social contract were to be negotiated each year, starting from scratch), for averaging principles, like the expected utility principle, are especially plausible when applied to sequences of similar choices. But our Hobbesian parties face a unique, binding, once-and-for-all choice that will strongly and permanently affect their prospects of happiness and well-being. This too suggests the wisdom of playing it safe and hedging against unacceptable outcomes, for each contractor has but one life to live and must live it under the terms first agreed to, if any are.

In claiming that the uniqueness and importance of the social contractors' choice, and their lack of reliable probability data as to outcomes, tell against the use of the expected utility principle by the contractors, we follow the lead of Rawls.[43] However, Hobbesian theory rejects Rawls's proposal that the contracting parties would guide their choices by the maximin principle (rather than the disaster-avoidance principle). Rawls himself imagines the maximin principle applied to representative members of major social groups, yielding a prescription to maximize the prospects of the representative of the least-advantaged group. But the most cogent reason he suggests for using the maximin principle—that it avoids the risk of unacceptable outcomes—is more a reason for applying the disaster-avoidance principle and accepting a guaranteed economic minimum. As noted in section 5–2, maximizing the prospects of the least-advantaged representative person does not assure *individuals* of a decent minimum, since some individuals will be worse off than this representative. (An additional reason that many Hobbesian contractors would prefer a guaran-

[43] Ibid., pp. 154, 176.

teed minimum to maximizing the prospects of the least-advantaged representative is that it is likely to be less costly.)

Would the parties opt for applying the maximin principle to individuals, maximizing the prospects of the least-advantaged *person* in society? No, because the expense involved in providing economic resources to maximize the prospects of the very most disadvantaged individuals (e.g., the severely physically and psychologically handicapped) would be enormous. (Imagine, as an analogy, the cost of maximizing the lowest level of educational competence among all the students in a large school district.) Those with advantageous personal characteristics (and many with less-advantageous characteristics) would not be willing to shoulder such expenses to maximize their prospects in the unlikely event of their being at, or ending up at, the absolute bottom of the social heap. Thus, Hobbesian parties would reject "representative maximining" because it offers too little insurance against unacceptable outcomes, and "individual maximining" because it exacts too high a premium for a chance of higher payoffs if the very worst contingencies ensue.

5-4. Terms of Agreement: Economic Welfare

We shall discuss in turn three substantive aspects of the social contract: economic measures, government powers, and individual liberties. The primary economic proposal that our Hobbesian parties could reasonably be expected to agree to is, as suggested in section 5-2, some sort of guaranteed economic minimum for all citizens, a social insurance program that provides the very needy with at least enough economic resources to support a minimally decent life in the society. We shall elaborate on the meaning of, and rationale for, the guaranteed economic minimum, but first it is worth demonstrating that such a proposal is in the spirit of Hobbes.

Though it is rarely noticed, Hobbes is a bit of an economic liberal, that is, he believes in some form of the welfare state and in the redistributive taxation needed to support it. In his discussion of the fifth law of nature requiring mutual accommodation, he exhibits his attitude toward those who would not aid the desperately needy:

> [A] man that by asperity of nature, will strive to retain those things which to himself are superfluous, and to others necessary; and for the stubbornness of his passions, cannot be corrected, is to be left, or cast out of society, as cumbersome thereunto. For seeing every man, not only by right, but also by necessity of nature, is supposed to endeavor all he can, to obtain that which is necessary for his conservation; he that shall oppose himself against it, for things superfluous, is guilty of the war that thereupon is to follow.[44]

And he clearly states that it is the duty of the *State* to insure that those in need are cared for: "Whereas many men, by accident inevitable, become unable to maintain themselves by their labour; they ought not to be left to the charity of private persons; but to be provided for, as far forth as the necessities of nature require, by the laws of the commonwealth."[45] These passages indicate that the idea of a guaranteed economic minimum is not inimical to Hobbes's own views.

But what is a "guaranteed economic minimum"? A variety of problems arise when trying to understand this concept, four of which shall concern us here. In what form is economic aid provided, when needed? Is the guarantee absolute, or is it conditional on recipients' being willing to work, if able? How is the appropriate minimum level defined in principle? Finally, is such a concept applicable to very poor societies or to the worst-off individuals, for example, the severely handicapped?

The first question is the easiest to answer. A guaranteed economic minimum could take many concrete forms—a negative income tax, direct cash payments, in-kind aid (e.g., food, medical services), government serving as an employer of last resort (or subsidizing enough private-sector jobs to ensure full employment), or some combination of these. Hobbesian theory does not claim that a particular way of providing a guaranteed minimum

---

[44] *Leviathan*, chap. 15, p. 139.
[45] Ibid., chap. 30, p. 334.

will be agreed on by the state-of-nature negotiators, only that the concept will be agreed to, along with a general understanding of the sorts of aid that could constitute satisfying the requirement, if supplied by government to the right people in the right quantities.

The fact that the economic minimum is guaranteed is important for Hobbesian theory. Remember that as forwardlooking agents, occupants of the Hobbesian state of nature are interested in securing their lives, and sufficient goods to sustain them, for the indefinite future. The State is created to obtain such security, thereby dissipating both painful anxiety about the future and normal citizens' reasons for defensively violating the laws of nature. Since economic ruin without aid can destroy life and well-being as surely as physical attack, it is entirely within the spirit of Hobbes's rationale for the State to regard economic as well as physical insurance as a necessary element of the commonwealth.

But the guarantee in question need not be unconditional. In particular, Hobbes himself—in the continuation of the last-quoted passage—supposes that the able-bodied will be required to work to receive aid.[46] And there are some reasons for thinking that Hobbesian parties might adopt such a requirement. Guarantees without a work requirement might provide a disincentive to work for some, thus lowering economic production. Also, considerations of equity suggest that it is unfair to the person who works hard to earn a minimally decent living to have others live as well (partly supported by taxes on his earnings) without having to work when they are able to do so. Nor could especially lazy people be expected to successfully veto work requirements during the negotiations, since they are likely to be in a small minority, will be against working harder to support the able-bodied needy if they turn out not to be needy themselves, and will be more fearful (on average) of not reaching agreement than are others (since the lazy do not fare well in the state of nature). On the other hand, the disincentive effect of minimal guaranteed government

[46]Ibid., pp. 334–35. For purposes of our discussion, caring for young, dependent children may count as work in the relevant sense.

212

support without work may be small in many societies, and the costs of distinguishing the able-bodied from others and providing the former with jobs may be quite large. Hence, it is not obvious that the negotiators would agree on explicitly tying the guaranteed economic minimum to work requirements. And we must leave this as an open question, noting, however, that if the parties do opt for work requirements it would be with the stipulation that the government, if necessary, directly or indirectly[47] provide jobs for the able-bodied—or else there would be no genuine guarantee of individuals' being able to receive the minimum.

Where is the minimum level of support to be set? It is well known that people's conception of a decent minimum material standard of living varies with their social surroundings; those in wealthier societies tend to set the minimum standard higher than those in poorer societies. One might try to avoid this problem of relativity by focusing on an apparently absolute standard—the bare amount of economic resources that satisfy physiological necessities and allow the individual to survive—but even this standard is variable and ill-defined, because individuals vary in their physiological needs and because survival (or life-expectancy) is positively correlated with greater expenditures on nutrition and health care. Further, as we shall see, one major motive for the parties' adopting a guaranteed minimum is to best insure against social disruption and rebellion by the disadvantaged—and people are likely to be prone to rebel if they view their share of social goods falling below what *they perceive* to be a decent minimum for *their society*, irrespective of "objective" cross-societal minimums.[48] As a result, it appears that we both must and should adopt some culturally relative standard for the guaranteed minimum.

Our proposed interpretation identifies the minimum for a given society (at a given time) with that level of economic support which would allow most all individuals (1) to live out their normal

[47] Hobbes (ibid.) suggests that it do this by stimulating the economy (and by exporting the excess poor to uninhabited foreign territories).

[48] See Ted Robert Gurr, *Why Men Rebel* (Princeton: Princeton University Press, 1970), p. 24.

physiological life spans, save for the effects of accident, homocide, and unpreventable or incurable disease, and (2) to participate in the normal economic and social activities of members of the society. Clause 1 attempts to capture the idea of supplying the physiological necessities of existence, while including the prevention and cure of treatable diseases within the denotation of "physiological necessities." Clause 2 reflects the notion that possessing economic resources beyond those needed for survival is necessary if one is to be a full participant in many societies. For example, in modern industrial soceieties one's job opportunities may be severly limited if one lacks the money to use public transportation systems, to attend a good educational institution, or to buy newspapers, a telephone, a car, or a clean and varied wardrobe.[49] Without money for many of these same things, one may be unable to be a full participant in the social, cultural, and political life of one's community or society.

The cross-cultural variability of our standard comes across in two ways. The wealthier the society, the more resource investment will be required, on average, for participation in its normal social activities. Wealthier societies will also tend to have a greater potential for health-care delivery, a higher standard of education, and so forth, so that more diseases are preventable or curable within it. This entails a higher support level for satisfaction of clause 1.

Even with this interpretation made explicit, the guaranteed economic minimum remains both variable and vague, but this is as it should be. It is variable because it is agreed to by parties not knowing the specific nature or circumstances of their society and because the concept it interprets is culturally relative. It is vague in the sense of being compatible with various specific programs, even within a given society. This is because we could not reasonably expect a consensus on more specific details to emerge among the negotiating parties in the state of nature. Nearly all, for reasons we give below, will agree on the guaranteed minimum idea,

[49] See the discussion of functional needs in S. I. Benn and R. S. Peters, *Social Principles and the Democratic State* (London: George Allen & Unwin, 1959), pp. 146–47.

generally formulated. But agreement on details is too much to hope for. We would therefore expect the parties to agree to enshrining the idea in the form of a binding general principle, then leave it to the agreed-upon governmental and political institutions to work out the details and apply the principle. This is analagous to deciding on having *some* sovereign and choosing a *procedure* for his selection, without at this stage selecting the sovereign himself.[50]

Our stated interpretation of the economic minimum refers to support sufficient for *most all* individuals to live a normal life span and participate in economic and social life. Why the "most"? One reason is this: some diseases may be treatable, but at such enormous expense per capita that it would be unreasonable for society to guarantee to pay treatment costs out of public resources. Rational contractors may well be willing to risk having such diseases while being too poor to pay for best treatment, rather than committing themselves to helping support others who suffer from the disease without being able to pay. They would opt for an economic insurance scheme that pays those needy individuals who come down with this treatable disease less than they need to live out their normal life spans.

The term "most" is also an acknowledgment that some people suffering from severe physical and/or psychological handicaps cannot be brought to normal participation in social life, and others of them can be brought to such participation only by the investment of enormous resources. The economic minimum guarantee is to be interpreted to require neither the former (which is impossible) nor the latter (which is unreasonable). To secure the agreement of the handicapped, their families, and their friends, to hedge against their later becoming handicapped themselves due to accident or disease, and perhaps out of a measure of general altruism and sympathy, nonhandicapped parties might well agree to special supplements to the guaranteed minimum for the handicapped, or other special programs to aid persons thus afflicted.

[50] See section 5-1.

But the exceptional needs of the severely handicapped are not to be the criterion that establishes the level of the basic minimum.

Handicapped persons are a specially disadvantaged minority in any society. In interpreting the economic-minimum principle, we must treat them as a special case. But what if a whole society is extremely disadvantaged, in the sense of being so poor (even when aid from other countries is taken into account) that it cannot provide resources allowing nearly all to live out their normal physiological life spans and participate in normal social interactions? That is, what if provision of a social minimum, in the sense indicated, is impossible? The best way of dealing with this problem within the context of Hobbesian social contract theory is to say that such situations fall outside the scope of the theory. As Hobbes indicates, if population is so great relative to available resources that many will starve no matter what and emigration is not possible, no social system will preserve order in the long run, and war will be the likely outcome.[51] So we restrict our theory by supposing that the negotiating parties know that resources in their society are abundant enough that a guaranteed economic minimum of the kind described above is feasible.[52] This allows us to preserve the guaranteed-minimum principle, but at the cost of acknowledging that an account of political obligation in the starving "fifth world" nations must be found elsewhere, if at all.[53]

Having provided a general interpretation of what a guaranteed economic minimum is, we may turn to the argument that our Hobbesian negotiating parties would agree to it as an element of the social contract. Remembering that our parties reason as disaster-avoiders, consider the perspectives of the members of two subgroups—those with personal characteristics favorable to success in a purely competitive socioeconomic system ("the en-

[51] *Leviathan*, chap. 30, p. 335. Note, however, that our discussion of the Ik in section 3-6 suggests that the "war" in question will not always be a violent one.
[52] Rawls does likewise in his assumption of "moderate scarcity." See *Theory of Justice*, pp. 126–28.
[53] See, however, my "Deterrence, Utility, and Rational Choice" (pp. 46–8), where the disaster-avoidance principle is tentatively applied to this problem to yield an outcome that may be viewed as a natural extension of the guaranteed minimum idea to conditions of extreme scarcity.

dowed") and those without such characteristics ("the unendowed"). The unendowed would reason to a guaranteed minimum
by straightforward application of the disaster-avoidance principle.
The adoption of a guaranteed minimum would virtually[54] assure
each of them of economic resources sufficient to support a long
and decent life involving participation in the normal activities of
their society. Alternative economic arrangements would involve
greater risks of suffering the disaster of abject poverty, having
too little wealth or income to survive and/or function as an active
member of society. For some alternatives, such as laissez-faire,
the risk might be very great. Other alternatives would be safer
than laissez-faire but would run greater risk of personal economic
disaster for an unendowed person than would a guaranteed minimum. A requirement that income be distributed so as to maximize per capita utility might well leave many people below the
abject poverty line, with additional utilities accruing to those above
this line offsetting the suffering of those below in the calculation
of social utility. A requirement of pure economic egalitarianism
could be expected, in many societies, to so destroy or erode incentives as to decrease production to the point where the equal
share of each is too little to support a decent life.[55] A Rawlsian
principle that maximizes the prospects of a representative member of the worst-off economic class may, as noted in section 5-2,
leave those toward the bottom of the worst-off economic class
below the abject poverty line. Only the guaranteed-minimum
principle minimizes one's chances of encountering economic disaster.[56] In this sense, it is the direct economic manifestation,
within a social system, of the disaster-avoidance principle.

[54] This qualification is necessary both because of the special case of the handicapped and because there can be no absolute protection against domestic violence,
civil war, or foreign conquest.
[55] This possibility is not ruled out by our above stipulation that the parties
know that their own society has enough resources to support its people at a decent
level. Resources may be adequate but not fully utilized because pure egalitarianism saps incentives.
[56] Special principles rigged to provide advantages to those possessing (some of)
one's own personal characteristics might also do the job. But one could not reasonably hope to get those lacking these characteristics to agree to such principles.

FOUNDING THE STATE

Of course, there are potential costs to the individual of following the disaster-avoidance principle and supporting a guaranteed minimum as part of the social contract. Under an alternative system, especially one that invests fewer resources in helping the poor, one might have fared better. This potential cost would not weigh too heavily in the minds of the unendowed, since—knowing their own personal characteristics—they would not reasonably expect to be successful in a competitive system with higher rewards for the successful and less (or no) protection for the unsuccessful. But such costs would be highly salient to the endowed. Why then would they agree to a guaranteed economic minimum when they possess some evidence of their own likely success in a more competitive system?

There are two reasons. The first is the same reason the unendowed have: to avoid personal economic disaster. While each of the endowed has *some* evidence of likely personal success in a competitive system, we noted in section 5-2 that the evidence will not be strongly predictive of success, except in a few extreme cases. That is, even the endowed individual has a substantial chance of ending up toward the bottom of the social heap, and hence has a personal security interest in a guaranteed minimum. Further, there is the additional possibility that someone else whom the individual cares much about (a close relative or friend) will be threatened by abject poverty at some time. This disaster (from the individual's perspective) is also insured against by the guaranteed minimum. The second reason for which we would expect the endowed to agree to a guaranteed minimum is insurance against rebellion, social disorder, and the disintegration of the State. Hobbes urges, in passages quoted above,[57] that people deprived of necessities are especially likely to foment rebellion,[58] as, we may reasonably hypothesize, are those exluded for economic reasons from the mainstream of social life.[59] If this is so, the endowed also

[57] See notes 38 and 44 and attached text, this chapter.
[58] For evidence providing some support for this, see Gurr, *Why Men Rebel*, pp. 62–64.
[59] See, e.g., Gurr's use of what he calls *participation values, interpersonal values,* and *societal opportunities,* in his explanatory theory of revolution (*Why Men Rebel*, chap. 2, esp. pp. 26–28).

218

minimize the probability of a second sort of disaster—disintegration of the social system into civil war or anarchy—by agreeing to a guaranteed economic minimum in the sense defined above. They cannot safely guard against this possible disaster more cheaply by choosing, as Hobbesian contractors, a repressive government system that suppresses disorder by overwhelming and ruthless use of force, for as noted above, endowed individuals cannot safely assume that they will not be among the economic and social outsiders upon whom this repression is exercised. Thus, as disaster-avoidance reasoners, the endowed too can be expected to agree to a guaranteed economic minimum, though this costs them more and benefits them less (on average) than the unendowed.

There will be dissenters, of course. Some of those most endowed may demand to exercise their talents in completely unfettered economic competition. Some extreme dominators may love power over others so much that they prefer the mere possibility of conquest to a high likelihood of safety. Some committed to egalitarian ideals may refuse to agree to any but a purely egalitarian economic system. Some of the severely handicapped might hold out for a guaranteed minimum interpreted in terms of overall well-being rather than level of economic support, with them receiving economic compensation for their physical and psychic disabilities. And so on. But in our Hobbesian theory, unanimity is not required. So long as the arguments for a given provision are compelling enough to command *nearly* unanimous (e.g., 95 percent) consent among the parties as characterized, the possible or probable existence of a small, stubborn minority of extremist refusers is no bar to adoption of the provision. Given the characterization of the parties as rational disaster-avoiders, and the powerful considerations which support the guaranteed economic minimum from a disaster-avoidance perspective, we may safely include the guaranteed minimum as an element of the Hobbesian social contract.

Adoption of a guaranteed economic minimum assures at least a minimally acceptable economic outcome for most everyone. It thus largely exhausts what we can reliably infer about the economic content of the social contract directly from the assumption

219

that our Hobbesian parties are disaster-avoiders. But once economic disaster avoidance is assured, our parties will not simply stop reasoning about economic measures. They may well adopt certain measures on the grounds that they provide expected net benefits to all, from the perspective of the negotiating situation. Two sorts of general economic measures would likely emerge in this way. The first would require that the economic system be such as to provide incentives for individual productivity and innovation and to generally assign positions according to qualifications and merit.[60] The second measure would provide for equal opportunity and social mobility, in the sense of prohibiting discrimination against racial, ethnic, religious, or gender groups and providing access to education and training (if necessary at public expense) to members of socially and economically disadvantaged groups.

Why would the parties agree on having incentive and merit elements in the economic system? Mainly to increase productivity and output. If jobs are filled by the best-qualified people, and workers and managers are rewarded for hard, good, and innovative work, the society's economy will function more effectively and efficiently and produce a higher general standard of living for citizens. Those with advantageous personal characteristics would obviously favor this requirement, as they would expect to be likely to fill desirable slots assigned by merit and collect the incentives provided to the dedicated and the innovative. But even the unendowed could expect to gain—relative to a system without incentives or merit hiring—because of the indirect benefits of increased efficiency and production (e.g., more jobs, a higher guaranteed economic minimum) and because the reward system would cement and insure the future cooperation of the endowed.

The last reason is worth elaborating upon. We argued above that endowed negotiators want a system that will provide society's poor with enough benefits to insure their continued loyalty to the chosen system. Similarly, unendowed negotiators will want

[60] Following Rawls, this requirement is deliberately formulated to be compatible, in principle, with either a capitalist, a socialist, or a mixed economic system. See Rawls, *Theory of Justice*, pp. 273–74.

a system that can insure they will have an economic minimum and that will last; hence they want those better off to also feel benefited enough to wish to maintain the system. Since talented but relatively unrewarded people may seek to withdraw into a separate system of their own, or forcibly revamp the entire present system in hope of gaining greater advantages within it, the incentive-merit proposal can serve to protect the poor (which the unendowed expect for the most part to be) against social revolution in somewhat the same way as the guaranteed minimum protects the rich (which the endowed for the most part expect to be) against it. When we add this consideration to the productivity spawned by an incentive-merit system (compared to, say, a pure egalitarian system, with jobs assigned by lot when they cannot be matched to personal preference), it seems that even unendowed negotiators could be expected to agree to having such a system.

The argument for agreement on equal opportunity and social mobility is equally persuasive. Lacking knowledge of their social positions, the negotiating parties will not know whether they are members of groups that are subject to past deprivation and potential discrimination.[61] Not wanting to be held back by uncontrollable characteristics unrelated to one's performance capabilities, all parties would have a strong motive for agreeing to some equal-opportunity principle. Equal opportunity and social mobility provide two other general benefits to society. They increase long-run efficiency and productivity by making the talents of members of all groups available for proper use in the economy, and they reduce social tensions and tendencies to rebellion by providing channels (and hopes) of advancement to members of groups currently low in the socioeconomic order.

It is worth noting, however, that the form of equal opportunity agreed to by Hobbesian contractors is different from that which emerges in Rawls's theory of justice. Rawls advocates a very strong

[61] If we allow religious affiliation, ethnic backgrounds, etc., as known individual characteristics, we assume that the parties know nothing of the minority-majority status or social standing of different such groups in their society. Otherwise, parties would have indirect knowledge of their likely current social standing.

form of equal opportunity in which the fruits of the talents of the naturally able are used to compensate the less able for their lack of *natural* advantages.[62] Robert Nozick and others have rightly objected to this on the grounds that it fails to respect the individuality, and entitlement to their natural powers and talents, of the naturally more able.[63] Hobbesian theory is not subject to this difficulty. Since the parties are aware of their personal characteristics, the naturally advantaged would not agree to a principle of equal opportunity (or one of social justice) that treats their individual features as social resources on which others have equal claim.

Are there other economic provisions that can be included in our account of the Hobbesian social contract because (nearly) all could be expected to agree to them independent of trade-offs? Though none come immediately to mind, Hobbesian theory leaves open the possibility that there are others, or will come to be others, as our general empirical knowledge increases. Consider, for example, the argument that the parties must agree on an unfettered[64] free market system (rather than a socialist or mixed system) because its greater productivity and efficiency provides net benefits to all. There is also the opposed argument that the parties would impose absolute limits on the degree of wealth inequalities in society, because people are inevitably miserable (and inclined to revolt) if they live in proximity to others many times wealthier than they. These arguments rest on unestablished empirical claims within the domains of economics and psychology respectively. It is conceivable (though unlikely) that either might, in the future, be sufficiently supported by evidence to count as a piece of general knowledge—in which case the resulting principle could be added to the content of the Hobbesian social contract. In this sense, that agreement is potentially open-ended.

Before turning to other matters, let us briefly consider an objection to the idea that a Hobbesian contract would contain any

[62] Rawls, *Theory of Justice*, pp. 65–75, 100–104.
[63] Nozick, *Anarchy, State, and Utopia*, pp. 189–204, 213–31.
[64] Save perhaps by the guaranteed minimum and equal opportunity requirements argued for above.

economic provisions at all. This objection is pressed by Michael Levin, who contends that Hobbesian contractors would agree only on a minimalist State whose sole functions are to enforce agreements and protect us from agression by our fellows or outsiders.[65] Hobbesian contractors will turn their swords over to a sovereign, Levin contends, because their all doing so obviates their need to use the swords (against their fellows). But they will not agree to turn over their plows, because others' doing so does not obviate each party's need to use his plow to produce food. In other words, they will not agree to government interference in their economic affairs, and in particular would not agree to redistributive measures, such as a guaranteed economic minimum.

The difference Levin notes between surrendering our swords and our plows to the sovereign really exists, but it does not have the implications for Hobbesian contract theory that Levin thinks it does. Levin errs in two ways. He mistakes the aims of the Hobbesian contractors, and he ignores, as Hobbes does not, the empirical connection between one's own physical security and others' economic security. Hobbesian contractors aim at obtaining, and securing, a decent life. Living a decent life requires both protection from assault and possessing the economic resources to support oneself. (We saw in Chapter 3 that Hobbes's criticism of anarchy emphasizes its *economic* as well as physical insecurities.) By recognizing only the former requirement—protection from assault[66]—Levin wrongly narrows the primary aims of Hobbesian parties. Further, as Hobbes points out in passages quoted above,[67] the sovereign can reliably provide one with protection against others in the long run only if others have access to a decent minimum of economic resources. Otherwise, needy and hardy men will seek a violent reshuffling of the social deck.

Once we realize that the primary aim of Hobbesian contractors

[65] Michael Levin, "A Hobbesian Minimal State," *Philosophy and Public Affairs* 11 (Fall 1982): 338–53.

[66] Levin ("Hobbesian State," p. 341) writes: "The sovereign's fundamental right is to secure us all against attack—primarily each other's attacks—and we give him our swords for this security. It is no part of the Hobbesian bargain to gain security against hunger, cold, ignorance, or poverty."

[67] See notes 38 and 44 and attached text, this chapter.

is physical *and economic* security (rather than physical security and unfettered oppportunity for wealth maximization), and that one's physical security is likely to *depend on* others' economic security, we see why they would agree on measures like a guaranteed economic minimum. They prefer to swap some of their plow's output for a guaranteed share of the output of their fellows' plows, if and when needed, and stronger assurances (than under a minimalist State) that others will not put down their plows and take up their swords again.

5-5. Terms of Agreement: Government and Liberty

Beyond the economic principles expounded in the last section, to what would Hobbesian social contractors agree? Certain principles concerning the powers and structure of government, and others protecting individual rights and liberties. Let us begin with government, noting first an apparent problem for Hobbesian social contract theory.

To perform its functions, a government must possess a sufficient concentration of power to awe citizens into obedience to its directives. But after the making of a social contract, and the initial selection of government officials by a designated procedure, how do these officials come to possess this awesome power? After all, they are not any stronger after contracting and selecting than they were previously, for, as Hobbes points out,[68] the other contractors cannot literally transfer their strength to the officials. This is an especially acute problem for Hobbes, who allows that the selected officialdom may consist of a single individual, who could hardly be capable himself of ganging up on his subjects.

The general way out of this problem rests on our earlier distinction (in section 3-3) between natural and social powers. The contracting parties cannot transfer their natural powers to the government simply by contracting, but they can transfer to it their social powers, or means of influencing one another. For "reputation of power, is power,"[69] and the contract does bestow

[68] *Elements of Laws*, part 1, chap. 6, sec. 10, p. 123.
[69] *Leviathan*, chap. 10, p. 74.

the reputation of power on the selected officials, by creating among the citizenry a mutually reinforcing network of expectations concerning one another's likely obedience to those officials. We shall elaborate on this point in the next section and the next chapter.[70] For now, we shall take the possible creation of government powers by contract as established and proceed to consider the nature and limits of those powers from the perspective of our contractors.

Hobbes himself considers roughly eight powers to be essential to the existence and continued functioning of a government.[71] Five of these we need not quarrel with, and we shall assume that— for the obvious reasons—Hobbesian parties would agree to their selected government's possessing and exercising these powers in some form or other. The five powers are (1) legislative or *lawmaking* (including the making of laws assigning, regulating, and redistributing property), (2) *law enforcement* (judicial and police functions), (3) formulation and execution of *foreign and military policy*, (4) *taxation* to support government functions, and (5) *appointment* of subordinate officials to aid in carrying out government policy and functions. A sixth power that Hobbes emphasizes—the bestowing of official honor and titles reflecting the public worth of individuals—is a bit antiquated and will be set aside, especially because it conflicts with the principle of equal status to be discussed below. The seventh suggested power, censorship, will also be considered below, in the context of the rights and liberties of individual citizens. What remains is the power of the government to decide, for itself, what means are necessary to the peace and defense of the commonwealth. By ascribing this power to the sovereign, Hobbes stakes out an extremist position on the key issue of limiting and dividing government power. To see why we should *not* incorporate this position into Hobbesian theory, it will be useful to contrast Hobbes's views on government power with those of Locke.

Let us say that government power is *divided* if and only if

[70] See also the discussion in section 5-1 of going along with the agreement once a specific sovereign is selected.
[71] See *Leviathan*, chap. 18.

there are distinct government bodies or institutions that must agree and concur before certain government functions (e.g., imposing a new tax) are performed, *or* have final control and authority over different government functions. Thus, there is a government with divided powers if a king (or president) and an independent legislature must agree to pass new laws, and also if an independent judiciary has final authority to interpret, apply, and enforce laws made by other bodies or agencies. A government is *limited* if there are understood to be things it is not permitted to do, certain ways that it cannot conduct itself, certain procedures it cannot follow in carrying out its functions, or certain procedures it *must* follow in carrying out those same functions. (The understanding in question may be embodied in a written constitution, in unwritten traditions in the political system, or—in the case of pure theory—in a State-founding social contract.) Governments can be limited without being divided, for example, if a single sovereign body is constrained by a written constitution from infringing certain well-defined rights of individual citizens. Similarly, division without limitation is possible—there might be no limitations on what a government as a whole might do, but its functions might be divided among independent bodies, or those bodies might have to concur to exercise certain powers.

Hobbes is against both limited and divided government.[72] His own social contract theory imagines, in effect, state-of-nature contractors choosing among three social alternatives: absolute (i.e., unlimited and undivided) government, limited or[73] divided government, or the state of nature. He argues that the parties would rank absolute government above the other two. Locke, in his social contract theory, considers the same alternatives but favors this very different ranking: limited (or divided[74]) government, the state of nature, absolute government. The ranking disagree-

[72] Though, as noted in section 4-4, he allows for the limitation or division of the powers of subordinate (i.e., nonsovereign) government officials.

[73] This is the inclusive "or," equivalent to the awkward "and/or."

[74] Locke emphasizes limitation rather than division of government power. But see *Second Treatise*, chap. 8, sec. 107, p. 382, and chap. 12, secs. 143–44, pp. 409–10, for passages in which some division of powers is recognized.

ment stems from divergent views on two largely factual matters: the degrees of harm and danger to individuals under absolute government and in the state of nature, and the stability of systems of limited or divided government.

Locke's main argument is that the individual's plight is less grave in the state of nature than under absolute government:

> It cannot be supposed that [the social contractors would] . . . put a force into the Magistrates hand to execute his unlimited Will arbitrarily upon them: This were to put themselves into a worse condition than the state of Nature, wherein they had a Liberty to defend their Right against the Injuries of others, and were upon equal terms of force to maintain it. . . . He being in a much worse condition who is exposed to the Arbitrary power of one Man, who has the Command of 100000. than he that is expos'd to the Arbitrary Power of 100000. single Men.[75]

But this argument is inconclusive. Surely, as Locke indicates, you are safer being attacked by one man than by than 100,000, but you are more likely to be attacked if you live in an ungoverned mob of 100,000 than if you live under an absolute government. Even if that government decides to kill some people to intimidate the populace, you are but one of many and are therefore unlikely to be victimized. Since it may be better to face a small chance of persecution by an overwhelming force, rather than a large chance of deadly attack by an equal, Locke's argument fails to convince. Whether you are safer under absolute government or anarchy would seem to depend upon the nature of the particular absolute governments and anarchical situations in question. No reliable basis for preferring one condition to the other, in general, has been provided.

Hobbes tries to provide one. Having established that life in the state of nature is insecure and undesirable, he attempts to show that absolute governments are unlikely to treat their citizens badly. He claims that a sovereign's interests coincide with those of the

---

[75] Locke, *Second Treatise*, sec. 137, p. 405; see also sec. 93, p. 372.

people, since his (or their[76]) wealth, power, and glory are dependent on the prosperity and strength of the people. But this claim, in the sense in which it is true, does not support Hobbes's conclusion that absolute governments are unlikely to rob and persecute segments of their citizenry.[77] It is correct that a government cannot reliably stay in power if its people are too impoverished, and that leaders of more prosperous nations tend to have more status and influence in world affairs—but so do leaders of nations with greater military forces and larger foreign aid budgets. And spending in these latter areas may increase the status, power, prestige, and wealth of the government and its members, while reducing aggregate domestic consumption (and lowering the standard of living). Further, even if we supposed that there is a perfectly monotonic relation between the *aggregate* level of wealth of the people and the wealth and power of the government, we still must consider matters of *distribution*. A government's survival and wealth may depend on the support of certain groups in the population, for example, party members, the military, and landowners. It may well be in the government's interest, then, to favor those groups and persecute and overtax their opponents, to the opponents' immense disadvantage. Finally, even if it were in governments' interests always to promote their people's wellbeing, absolute governments might irrationally fail to do what is in their and the people's best interests. Absolute governments consisting of a single sovereign or small sovereign body may be especially prone to shortsightedness and irrationality—because exercise of great power over time creates illusions of omnipotence, because subordinates may inhibit learning or analysis by concealing problems or bad consequences resulting from earlier actions, or because the dynamics of small, insulated groups inter-

---

[76] Twice the claim is made about sovereigns in general, and once about monarchs, or sovereign individuals, in particular. See *Leviathan*, chap. 18, p. 170; chap. 30, p. 336; chap. 19, p. 174.

[77] In developing my arguments against Hobbes on this point, I have benefited from seeing some unpublished notes by David Braybrooke on the subject, from a lecture he gave at Purdue in 1975.

feres with proper decision-making.[78] In other words, absolute power tends to blind as well as corrupt, so that even complete actual coincidence of interest between an absolute government and its people would not make protection of the latter's interests by the former secure.

So there are failed general arguments going each way. Locke is wrong that the immense power of absolute government, by itself, makes it more dangerous than anarchy. Hobbes, in turn, is wrong that the actual degree of correlation between sovereign and citizen interests suffices to insure that absolute government creates a better life than can be found in the state of nature. No general ordering seems possible here, but there remains a third alternative: limited or divided government.

Hobbes rejects both limited and divided government as inherently unstable. A division of powers leaves no group with sufficient power to insure peace and defense and creates ready-made competing factions that will eventually be at war with one another, as in the civil wars of Hobbes's time.[79] Limited government also invites rebellion and civil war, since there is no judge but the sword to appeal to should some citizens think the government has violated the prescribed limits of its powers.[80] Hobbes is right to this extent: limitations on, or divisions of, government power *can* lead to rebellion and civil war in any of the ways he indicates. But they need not do so, for a number of reasons. Officials or bodies that share power in a system of divided governance will be strongly motivated to compromise differences among themselves and to coordinate their actions to promote peace and defense, for they have much to lose—their present power, status,

---

[78] On this last point, see Irving Janis, *Victims of Groupthink* (Boston: Houghton Mifflin, 1972).

[79] *Leviathan*, chap. 18, pp. 167–68.

[80] Ibid., pp. 161–62. One passage in *Leviathan* (chap. 17, pp. 157–58) suggests that Hobbes may limit legitimate government acts to those done to promote "the common peace and safety." Other nearby passages, however, indicate that this limiting phrase falls outside the scope of the sovereign's authorization and merely names the contractors' aim in making an unlimited authorization of the sovereign. See ibid., chap. 18, p. 158; chap. 19, p. 159.

wealth, and life—in a civil war or a collapse of the State through paralysis. And while they might hope to gain undivided power through victory, power-sharing officials would place a higher priority on the avoidance of collapse or war, at least if they reasoned as Hobbesian disaster-avoiders. As to limited government, the limitations themselves may serve to keep the government in check and to preserve the rights of the people so that there seldom are critical disputes between citizens and their government. In addition, if we *combine* the limitation and division of power, there may now be available effective referees for disputes between citizens and government. A person or group in conflict with one government body or branch over the existence or nature of a limit on government power may seek arbitration or protection from another government body or branch.

Though Hobbes fails to show that systems of limited or divided government are maximally unstable, the key question is whether they tend to be *more* or *less* stable than systems of absolute government. In acknowledging that the "needy and hardy" will revolt,[81] Hobbes implicitly acknowledges that even absolute governments are not perfectly stable.[82] So he could not simply claim that any potential instability renders limited or divided governments more unstable than absolute governments. There are good reasons for expecting people to be more satisfied, on average, under limited and divided government than under absolute government. The limits will directly protect people, the division will allow for effective refereeing of the limits in the manner indicated above, and, by bringing more actors into the policy-making process, the division will tend to encourage moderate and reasoned, rather than extreme and rash, government conduct. So people will generally be more satisfied under limited and divided governments. Since more satisfied people are less inclined to rebel, we would in fact expect less instability for governments with limited and divided power. Locke expresses the same point from another direction: "When the *People* are made *miserable*, and find

[81] See passages quoted in text accompanying notes 38 and 44, this chapter.
[82] See also sections 6-2 through 6-4.

themselves *exposed to the ill usage of Arbitrary Power* . . . [they] will be ready upon any occasion to ease themselves of a burden that sits heavy upon them.''[83] Modern history lends a degree of support to this point. Absolutist governments have not tended to be long-lived in recent centuries, certainly not longer-lived than less-absolutist forms. The main advantage that Hobbes thought he saw in unlimited and undivided government was, in all likelihood, an illusion.

The upshot is that Hobbesian social contractors, unlike Hobbes, would opt for divisions of and limitations on government powers. They would agree on some form of division of powers, to minimize the risks of tyranny and rash government behavior. They would also agree to limit government behavior to protect individual liberty and well-being. Some of these limits are implicit in the economic terms of agreement discussed above. For example, because of the equal-opportunity clause, the government cannot practice or promote discrimination in hiring, education, or provision of benefits. And because of the guaranteed minimum, the government may not tax people living on the edge of abject poverty unless compensating economic resources are provided. Other general limits on government conduct will be discussed below.

A prior question about government power and organization must be settled first. How are government officials or personnel, other than appointed subordinate officials, to be selected? Hobbes's idea of a two-stage social contract, discussed in section 5-1, can here be adapted into the suggestion that the parties first agree on the terms of the social contract and the procedures for electing officials, with the selection of officials (by application of those procedures) coming later. Further, we may, as also noted in section 5-1, interpret Hobbes's proposal that the soveriegn be elected by majority election as aiming at a selection procedure designed to minimize citizen dissatisfaction and preserve some degree of uncertainty as to the outcome. Of course, our parties, having decided upon a division of powers, are choosing selection procedures for more than one government body. A general principle that

[83] Locke, *Second Treatise*, sec. 224, p. 463.

they could reasonably be expected to agree on is that high-level government officials be elected by, or otherwise held accountable to, the general citizenry. This could mean that officials are periodically subject to election, are continually subject to recall, are selected by representatives themselves freely selected by the people, or are appointed by officials who are themselves subject to election or recall. Different groups of contractors might converge on different specific procedures. All groups, however, would presumably opt for some such accountability mechanism as a protection against facing a future choice between accepting ill-governance and revolting, and to create a relationship that Hobbes falsely supposed to be automatic: a positive correlation between the interests of officials and of citizens. This procedural limitation on the powers of government officials—their inability to remain in office indefinitely without confirmation by the citizenry—serves to enforce other specified limits on government action by deterring potential usurpations by officials.

We turn finally to substantive limits on government action designed to protect the personal liberty and well-being of subjects. Here there are four points that we can accept, or adapt, from what Hobbes says.[84] First, it is a responsibility of the government to enforce the laws of nature—moral laws protecting individuals from murder, assault, robbery, cheating on contracts, and so on.[85] Second, there is a requirement of equal status among citizens; each possesses the same fundamental rights, including equal treatment under the law.[86] Third, individuals possess freedom of action in matters permitted by the government because they do not infringe on the interests of the community. Hobbes lists as examples the freedoms to contract, to choose a profession, diet, and place to live, and to raise one's children as one sees fit.[87] Exaggerating a good bit, we shall interpret this in a Millian spirit

[84] Discussion of a further issue of personal liberty that might be addressed in the social contract—the right of self defense—is deferred until Chapter 8.
[85] *Leviathan*, chaps. 14–15; chap. 26, p. 253; chap. 30, pp. 322–23.
[86] This is implied by the second and eleventh laws of nature (ibid., chap. 14, p. 118; chap. 15, p. 142) being incorporated into civil law (ibid., chap. 26, p. 253).
[87] Ibid., chap. 21, p. 199.

as a general warrant for individuals to engage in conduct apparently not harmful to others and as a restriction on government interference with such conduct in the absence of evidence that it is harmful to the community. Finally, though he sanctions freedom of trade and contract, Hobbes does not recognize unrestricted economic freedom or property rights. Property rights for him are *conventional*, begin only with the establishment of the State, and are within the authority of the government to assign or regulate.[88] In particular, as we have seen, Hobbes believes in taxation to support the activites of the State, including providing aid to the needy.

It is easy to see why Hobbesian contractors, not knowing their own social positions, would agree to these requirements and limits concerning government activities. One is protected by the enforcement of fundamental moral laws, insured against ending up a second-class citizen by virtue of one's social position, allowed to practice harmless liberties without having to suffer harm as a result of one's neighbors' similar liberties, and guaranteed enough economic resources to support a decent life. But Hobbesian contractors would also agree to the protection of certain other liberties that Hobbes opposes on the grounds that they tend to provoke civil war[89]—political participation (voting, petition, organization, and candidacy rights) and freedom of speech, thought, press, and religion.

It is true that publicly expressed religious, ideological, and political differences can spark rebellion and civil war, but so too can their suppression. People's ideas and beliefs are highly valued, often as much or even more than material well-being and physical liberties such as the freedoms to travel, to choose an occupation, and so on, so when certain ideas or beliefs (or related prac-

---

[88] See ibid., chap. 13, p. 115; chap. 18, p. 165. Though the fourteenth law of nature allows first seizure as a means of distributing "those things that cannot be enjoyed in common, nor divided" (ibid., chap. 15, p. 142), there is no Lockean (or Nozickean) initial acquisition theory of property rights in Hobbes. For property, arguably, can be used commonly or divided, and any natural property rights are surrendered in the original social contract (as are all rights save for the right of self-defense).

[89] Ibid., chap. 18, pp. 164–65.

tices such as forms of religious worship) are prohibited, and their expression is banned, a high level of dissatisfaction will be experienced among many holding those ideas and beliefs. These people will form a core of political revolutionaries. In the political shpere especially, freedom of expression has a triply beneficial function. It provides a nonviolent outlet for people's discontents, it increases government accountability by opening the activities of officials to public scrutiny, and it paves the way for an educational clash of ideas. Rights of political participation serve the same functions in essentially the same ways, as well as being virtual prerequisites of maintaining government accountability to the citizenry in the long run.

Thus, on balance, we would expect rights of political participation and the freedoms of expression to decrease the likelihood of the following outcomes that a Hobbesian contractor might well view as disastrous: suppression of expression of his own strongly held beliefs, tyrannical government (due to a lack of effective accountability), and revolution or civil war (sparked either by the suppression or expression of political, religious, or ideological beliefs). As rational disaster-avoiders, our Hobbesian parties would opt for rights of individual political participation and the freedoms of expression and forbid (or strictly limit) government interference with the practice of these rights and freedoms.[90]

We may now summarize the content of the social contract that, we have argued, would be agreed to by Hobbesian contractors in the state of nature. Economic provisions would guarantee an economic minimum and would provide for a form of equal opportunity within a system containing incentives for work and initiative, and hiring according to merit. Government powers would be divided among, or shared by, independent bodies, and officials would be accountable to the public through a system of elections or potential recalls. Government would be responsible for inter-

---

[90] This is not to say that the parties would require that the individual rights in question be absolute. E.g., reasonable restrictions on public speech, such as temporary bans on particular speeches or demonstrations because of the evident likelihood of violence being precipitated, would presumably be consistent with the right of free speech as understood by the contractors.

nal and external security and the enforcement of core moral laws. Citizens would have rights of political participation, freedom of expression, all personal liberties harmless to others, and equal status—all of which would have to be respected by the government. For ease of reference, let us say that a State satisfying all these conditions is *satisfactory*. The conditions in question are all general and familiar ones, and this should be no surprise, since they represent the *consensus* of most all state-of-nature contractors. Taken together, the conditions are the minimal conditions a State must satisfy to be legitimized via hypothetical contract theory. Political obligations owed to other than satisfactory States must be explained by some other theory or theories.

Before considering, in the next section, some objections to our version of Hobbesian social contract theory, let us briefly tie up two loose ends. In our discussion of the content of the social contract, we have generally viewed the parties as reasoning solely in terms of their own interests. But as predominant egoists, many might be quite concerned with the interests of some others, for example, loved ones and friends. It has been an implicit assumption that each individual negotiator knows no more about others than he knows about himself, that is, personal characteristics but not social position. Further, proxy knowledge of the social position of oneself or one's associates, based on knowledge of the associates' personal characteristics, is—as in the case of knowledge of one's own characteristics—ruled out. The result is that the same safeguards the parties would adopt to promote their own interests would be adopted to promote the interests of those they cared about as well, for as rational disaster-avoiders, our Hobbesian parties will want to minimize the risks of their loved ones, as well as themselves, suffering disaster. Wanting to secure their loved ones against abject poverty, tyranny, civil war, and a return to the state of nature, predominantly egoistic parties will agree on a guaranteed minimum, a divided and accountable government, and so on. Actually, the case for some of our proposals, like the guaranteed economic minimum, is *strengthened* by allowing for some altruism among the parties, for while an endowed pure egoist might gamble on laissez-faire, a similarly endowed predominant egoist is likely to have some loved ones who are unendowed and will face a bigger risk in any case that someone he loves (endowed or not) will sometime face economic disaster and require government assistance.[91]

The formulation of the Hobbesian social contract finally completes the multipart argument against anarchy. The first stage of that argument establishes the miseries and problems of pure anarchy—the war of all individuals. In the argument's second stage, we saw how groupings short of the State fail to solve individuals' security problems. The third stage demonstrates that and how the State can solve this problem. This chapter outlines the form of a realizable[92] State—the satisfactory State—that state-of-nature parties would voluntarily agree to because it solves their security problems *without imposing on them harms or risks worse than they could expect to suffer under anarchy.* The terms of the founding agreement insure this by providing the parties with physical security, economic security and opportunity, personal and civil liberties, safeguards against tyranny, and minimal risks of revolution. This demonstration that a realizable State is rationally preferred to the state of nature completes the Hobbesian argument against anarchy.

5-6. Remaining Problems

We now turn to some remaining problems concerning the Hobbesian social contract. The first involves the security of the bargainers. How is it possible, it may be asked, for state-of-nature parties to come together to negotiate a social contract when they distrust and fear one another? Will not the same logic of

---

[91] This is a consequence of the statistical fact that the occurrence of the disjunction of a number of unlikely independent events is much more likely than the occurrence of any particular one of them. (It is assumed that this more than outweighs the possibility that, among the parties one cares for, some will always be willing and able to help the others if need be.)

[92] If the satisfactory State were unrealizable, its clear superiority to anarchy would not constitute much of an argument against anarchy. However, the conditions defining the satisfactory State are weak and general enough as to be obviously realizable—quite arguably some contemporary States actually realize them.

anticipation which leads to the war of all individuals or all groups operate to preclude the possibility of peaceful assembly and discussion?

Solutions to the security problem are readily available. In the social contract negotiating setting, the parties have an obvious special motive, which is not present in other state-of-nature situations, for avoiding anticipation and conducting themselves peacefully—awareness that they have a realistic opportunity, if they conduct themselves properly, to trade in the insecurities of the state of nature for the lasting security of civil society. Hence, each party is likely to apply, and expect others to apply, to the contracting situation the fifteenth law of nature, which requires *"that all men that mediate peace, be allowed safe conduct."*[93] With these mutual expectations, normal security precautions, such as turning away anyone attempting to bring arms to the negotiating site, would likely provide enough safety for the parties to make negotiations possible.

Furthermore, we must remember that the social contract is, within Hobbesian theory, a hypothetical one. Its content is what such-and-such parties so situated would agree to, where the characteristics of the parties and situation are not all intended to be realistic. In particular, we can simply *stipulate* that the contractors have nothing to fear from one another during negotiations, unless so stipulating might inappropriately affect the content of the agreement. Since there seems to be no reason to think that it would, we may unobjectionably stipulate the security problem out of existence.[94]

A second, more serious problem involves *insufficiency* of social resources. It is costly, in terms of social resources, to support the social, economic, and procedural arrangements required by the terms of the Hobbesian social contract. The economic minimum requires funding, as do the educational institutions required to

[93] Ibid., chap. 15, p. 143.
[94] Perhaps if assured of physical security during negotiations the parties would never end them. To deal with this problem, we need only imagine a generous but definite time limit on negotiations, or a rising economic cost function for time spent in negotiations (and away from normal economic activities).

ground equal opportunity and social mobility, the legal apparatus needed to protect harmless liberties, the elections required for accountability, and so on. But won't many societies simply lack the economic and social resources to comply with the terms of the social contract? If so, Hobbesian contract theory would appear to fail, both as an account of what state-of-nature parties would agree to and as a basis for a normative theory of political obligation.

One possible approach to dealing with this sort of problem is to strictly order or prioritize the principles that make up the content of the social contract, so it is clear which must be satisfied when not all can be. This is the general strategy followed by Rawls.[95] The fundamental difficulty with this approach is that it is difficult to believe that consensus could be reached among the state-of-nature parties about the relative priority of the various elements of the social contract. Perhaps Hobbesian contractors could agree on giving first priority to the guaranteed economic minimum, on the grounds that individual survival and social stability are prerequisites of enjoying the other social goods expected under the terms of agreement.[96] But beyond this, it seems highly likely that parties would assign different intrinsic and extrinsic values to religious freedom, equal opportunity, the practice of harmless personal liberties, political participation, and so on, disagreeing in their judgments of which are more important than the others.

It must therefore be conceded that Hobbesian political theory applies only to nations or societies in which there are enough resources to support *all* the elements of the satisfactory State.[97] This admission is not, however, as damaging as might initially be supposed, for most all the elements of the social contract are stated in quite general terms and may be interpreted in more or less

[95] Rawls, *Theory of Justice*, secs. 8, 11, 46.

[96] Even Rawls, who assigns liberty priority over economic welfare, hints that this priority may apply only after a basic economic minimum is attained. See ibid., pp. 542–43.

[97] This extends a point in section 5-4 about the guaranteed economic minimum. See text accompanying note 52, this chapter.

strict ways, with less-strict interpretations generally requiring fewer resources for their satisfaction. This has already been seen to be the case as regards the level of the economic minimum: it is higher in wealthier societies. The same is true of the education required for equal opportunity, the enforcement of nondiscrimination, the degree of participation open to each citizen in the political process, and so on. These are not, in general, matters of all or nothing, but rather matters of more or less, with more of the good in question costing more. Universal elementary and secondary education costs more than universal elementary education. Universal higher education would be more costly still. Nondiscrimination in hiring laws can be enforced with greater vigor, at greater cost. Political participation can be made easier and more common if government partially finances campaigns or ensures access to media. And so forth.

Since the principles contained in the social contract have various and more and less costly interpretations or modes of implementation, we can partly solve the insufficiency-of-resources problem without ordering the principles once and for all. We simply assume that the parties adopt the principles with the understanding that they will be interpreted and put into practice in accordance with the actual economic and social resources of their society, whatever these turn out to be. So if their society is very rich, so that all the principles can be fully satisfied under quite strict interpretations, they will be. But if resources do not allow this, some or all of them will be satisfied less strictly or fully, for example, with a lower guaranteed minimum and a lower level of government-supported education. The decisions about marginal trade-offs between the principles, that is, whether to use available resources to better satisfy one principle rather than the other, will be left to the selected (and accountable) government institutions and officials to wrestle with in the context of fuller specific information and the hurly-burly of political life. This is not an ideal solution, but it is surely preferable to forcing the state-of-nature contractors, without knowledge of specific social circumstances, to establish a nearly absolute once-and-for-all priority order among the elements of the social contract.

It is still possible that some countries or societies would be so lacking in resources as to be unable to satisfy all the requirements of the social contract even at the most minimal level. Under these circumstances, Hobbesian theory cannot be applied, and promises no solution to the problem of political obligation. But once we have recognized that the elements of the social contract can be satisfied to varying degrees, we no longer need fear that this will be a widespread or general condition. The insufficiency-of-resources problem remains, but it has been shrunk to manageable dimensions.

The third problem for Hobbesian social contract theory concerns the scope of the contract—who is included under it. We offered reasons earlier (section 4-4) for supposing that state-of-nature parties would group themselves into defense groups smaller than the entire world community. And we could simply stipulate that the negotiators can be thought of as all the citizens or members of whatever actual State it is to which we wish to apply Hobbesian theory at a given time. There is, though, a difficulty concerning whether a theory making use of this stipulation can really represent the satisfactory State we have described as the outcome of a rational state-of-nature agreement.

This difficulty—the problem of *secession* as we shall call it—is brought out clearly in Gauthier's claim that "it is . . . a necessary condition of rational agreement that there is no sub-group, each of whom prefers agreement only with other members of the sub-group, to agreement with all."[98] This raises the specter of more-favored negotiators seceding from the negotiations to form a commonwealth with fewer, but on average more productive, members. Thus, for example, the endowed negotiators might break away and form their own State, leaving the unendowed behind, or the nonhandicapped negotiators might reach an agreement among themselves that excludes the handicapped. Allowing individuals knowledge of their own personal characteristics, as we have, opens the door to this possibility that certain subgroups

[98]Gauthier, "The Social Contract," p. 62.

240

would view it as in their interests to secede from the larger group and found a State among themselves.

To solve the secession problem, we must explain why the endowed, the nonhandicapped, and so on would probably not prefer to secede from the negotiations. Part of the explanation is our restriction on the formation of coalitions during the negotiations (see section 5-2). This restriction does not absolutely preclude secession of a subgroup intending to set up its own commonwealth, but it does inhibit the formation of such groups during the negotiating process by forbidding the coalitions from which secession groups would be most likely to arise. By thus interfering with possible agreement by a subgroup on an alternative social contract prior to withdrawal from the full-group negotiations, our restriction introduces a substantial element of risk into secession. The individual who secedes sacrifices his hopes of inclusion in a full-group commonwealth, without knowing precisely who will join him in secession and whether and on what terms agreement might be reached among those who secede. Hobbesian disaster-avoiders could be expected to accept such risks only if agreement among all seemed quite unlikely. But we have argued above that agreement on at least the elements of the satisfactory State could reasonably be expected.

Beside the risks of being left without any satisfactory agreement, there are other reasons why the endowed, for example, would not secede. As noted in section 4-4, it is desirable to have a larger State for more effective external defense, other things being equal. Further, it is a priori unlikely that the endowed and unendowed negotiators occupy distinct territories. They are most likely highly interspersed within a single geographic region. Hence, secession and agreement by the endowed alone would still leave them with the problem of dealing with the unendowed in their midst. In all likelihood, this could be done most stably and effectively by including the unendowed in the social contract in the first place, rather than by dealing with them as a mass of "independents" residing in the territory of the endowed State. The latter approach would seem very likely to eventually produce violence and civil war.

But what of the handicapped? They are a small and fairly help-less minority. Rather than agreeing to help support them even to the degree required by our interpretation of the guaranteed min-imum, might not the nonhandicapped form a State without them, leaving the handicapped to fend for themselves as independents? Here we must make use of our assumption that people are pre-dominantly, rather than purely, egoistic. The handicapped have nonhandicapped relatives and friends who would not join a seces-sion movement aimed at leaving the handicapped to their own devices. And some of *their* friends and relatives, in turn, would refuse to join without them. Further, the handicapped—who are generally both needy and unthreatening—are likely targets of whatever general altruism or sympathy is possessed by the par-ties. Given these factors, and the knowledge that some of their own children or grandchildren could be handicapped, the parties could be expected to prefer to help support the handicapped (when necessary), rather than deal with them (and their supporters) as independents living in their midst.

Our mention of independents—those residing in the territory of a State without being members of it (or any other State[99])—raises yet another problem for Hobbesian social contract theory. In allowing for nonunanimous ratification of the social contract, we leave open the possibility that even the contractually founded State will contain within its boundaries some who did not, or would not, agree to its fundamental principles. What should be the attitude of the State and its citizens toward these indepen-dents?[100]

Hobbes suggests that they may be regarded and treated as ene-mies,[101] but this seems harsh, unless they declare themselves to be enemies of the State or its citizens and act accordingly. A more reasonable view, which will be developed in section 10-5, is

[99] Foreigners residing in a State do not constitute independents in the relevant sense. Their treatment, unlike that of independents, falls under the theory of international relations.

[100] Nozick discusses a related problem in *Anarchy, State, and Utopia*, pp. 54–56.

[101] *Leviathan*, chap. 18, pp. 162–63.

that independents may rightly be compelled to respect the persons, property, and liberty of others and to contribute to the functions of the State from which they benefit. If this view can be suitably elaborated and defended, the existence of nonconsenters, which is allowed for by our Hobbesian social contract theory, need constitute no embarrassment to that theory.

A final problem for Hobbesian social contract theory has been thought by some to be the most serious of all.[102] It centers on the question of why the parties should comply with the social contract once it is made, why they should obey the orders of the government created by it. After all, the social contract is a state-of-nature agreement, and Hobbes says you should not keep these (as a first party) since the other party or parties may not follow suit. Consider especially the very first person commanded to act by the newly created and selected government. If he obeys at some cost or danger to himself, he risks being a harmed unilateral complier with the social contract. If he does not obey, the government may command someone else to punish him, but this latter command apparently faces the same problem. Why should the person it is addressed to obey? We may call this the problem of *first compliance*, as it concerns the apparent irrationality of being the first to obey a newly founded government's orders.

The general nature of our solution to the first compliance problem has been hinted at above.[103] The social contract is different from other state-of-nature agreements in that it promises, if successful, to remove the parties from the state of nature. Thus, each has a tremendous amount to gain by its success. This means that the risk of being a unilateral complier is worth running if it attaches to a reasonable chance of mutual compliance. Further, since others also obviously have much to gain by the effectiveness of the government, one runs little risk of being a lone complier—others will be only too glad to make the arrangement work once you have set the example. Nor must one expect universal

[102] See, e.g., David Braybrooke, "The Insoluble Problem of the Social Contract," *Dialogue* 15 (March 1976): 3–37.

[103] See the discussion of the security problem at the beginning of this section, and the discussion in section 5-1 of the election of a particular sovereign.

compliance to make one's own first compliance worthwhile. So long as many are willing to comply with the government's orders, you are almost certainly better off under its protection than you would be returning to the state of nature by refusing to comply.

We may see this solution as an extension of Hobbes's reply to the Fool. There it was suggested that compliance with a state-of-nature contract is rational if it increases your chances of later membership in a viable commonwealth. But surely first compliance with the orders of a government newly founded by agreement increases your chances of membership in a viable commonwealth. All the problems of commonwealth formation have been solved at this point, save possibly one: firmly establishing general expectations of obedience to the government. But your act of obedience will itself help solve this problem and will increase your chances of escaping the state of nature far more than second-party compliance with an ordinary state-of-nature contract does. If, as we argued in section 4-3, the latter is rational and reasonable, surely the former is.

Nonetheless, the problem of first compliance contains a valid and important insight that Hobbes largely ignores. The security problem that infects the state of nature cannot ever be completely eliminated and carries over into civil society. Danger is the constant fate of mortal men; absolute security for individuals or their State is but a pipe dream. Explaining why this is so is the final task of the descriptive part of Hobbesian theory.

S I X

POWER AND ORDER
IN THE STATE

6-1. Crime and Punishment

According to our characterization of the State in section 4-4, its government must possess enough power to enforce its rulings with sufficient regularity to discourage self-help among citizens. The enforceable rules of Hobbes's (and the Hobbesian) State include the laws of nature and other laws made known to the citizenry by the government. As explained in the first part of section 4-3, by credibly threatening substantial punishments for violations of natural and civil laws, a government prevents both offensive and defensive violations of these laws. Danger of punishment directly deters offensive violations, and successful deterrence of offensive violations renders defensive violations largely unnecessary (as well as risky, by virtue of their own liability to draw punishment). Thus, the prisoner's dilemma structure of the problem of compliance with natural laws can be eliminated in the State by sufficient threats of government-imposed sanctions.[1]

The enforcement power of government facilitates internal security in a further way that Hobbes recognizes. Even if individuals sincerely try to follow the laws of nature, and other laws laid down by government, disagreements and disputes may arise because of different interpretations of what the laws in question mean or what they imply in a particular case. The government, as the author of civil laws and the one body in the State with sufficient power to physically enforce its rulings when necessary

[1] See esp. Figures 4 and 5 and the accompanying text in section 4-3.

against any domestic party, is in a position to settle disputes by providing umpires (i.e., judges) who can offer (and have enforced) authoritative interpretations, and applications to specific cases, of natural and civil laws.[2] Thus, private disputes can generally be settled by hearings and rulings backed by the *threat* of force, rather than by actual fighting, as might well occur in the state of nature.

We should also mention, in passing, two further general functions of government that Hobbes recognizes only in specific instances. As is now widely acknowledged, governments facilitate the provision of desirable levels of *public goods*—goods such as national defense, clean air, and an efficient system of public thoroughfares. For our purposes, a public good is one whose consumption individuals cannot (or cannot without excessive expense) be excluded from, if they fail to contribute (their share of) resources to support the provision of the good.[3] Without provision of public goods by government, they will generally be undersupplied. Most any individual faces a situation similar to multiparty prisoner's dilemma regarding contributing to the provision of such goods: the marginal cost of contribution must be borne by him alone, so it will nearly always exceed his share of the marginal benefit, since that benefit will be spread over the entire group. Because contributing is not necessary for receiving the benefit, relatively few will contribute relatively little, and the good in question will be undersupplied. However, financing of the good by enforced taxation can eliminate the prisoner's dilemma aspects of the situation and produce the socially desirable outcome. Hobbes realized this as regards the public goods of national defense and safety from attack by one's fellows, but he did not generalize the point, as have modern public goods theorists.

Hobbes notes an instance of an important general function of

---

[2] *Leviathan*, chap. 18, pp. 165–66; chap. 23, pp. 228–30; chap. 26, pp. 262–63.

[3] Nonexcludability, rather than jointness of supply, is chosen as the key defining feature of public goods, since this is what produces the prisoner's dilemma type of problem. A good selection from the vast public goods literature is in *Rational Man*, ed. Barry and Hardin.

governments: the efficient establishment, preservation, and modification of socially useful conventions. Conventions are essentially solutions to social coordination problems. Often it matters less what is done, among a limited range of alternatives, than that all do the same (or at least know what others will do). The most familiar example concerns the side of the road on which people drive. Left or right will do about equally well—what must be avoided is some people driving on each. Roughly speaking, conventions are mutually expected regularities of behavior in situations of this kind (e.g., I expect you and others to drive on the right and to expect me and others to do the same, so I drive on the right; you similarly expect me and others. . . .[4])

Conventions are mutually beneficial and largely self-enforcing, but because they involve choices between behaviors that are intrinsically equal in rationality, they may be slow and difficult to start. Also, there may be conflicting local conventions that neither locality wishes to abandon. And once established, conventions may be difficult to modify when this would be useful, because unilateral modifiers lose out or because many fear that the modifications may escalate into elimination of the convention. Finally, the coordination-related rewards of following an established convention may not be sufficiently large or salient to deter individual deviations. (Think of the likely scale of violations of conventions on automobile traffic movements if there were no traffic police.) Government can contribute to (partial) solutions to all these problems of convention. By public pronouncement and promises of enforcement, government can (1) create useful conventions where they might otherwise be unable (or slow) to form, (2) arbitrate among competing local conventions and enforce national uniformity, (3) modify existing conventions when desirable, while clearly defining where the modifications stop, and (4) increase the size and salience of penalties for deviance from conventions. Hobbes does not explicitly discuss these convention-enhancing capacities of government, but in his discussion of the

[4]See David Lewis, *Convention* (Cambridge, Mass.: Harvard University Press, 1969).

paradigm conventional good—money—he implies that governments possess the capacities to create and modify some conventions.[5]

Though government has a number of functions, the remainder of this chapter is about the function that Hobbes is most concerned with: the provision of domestic security. It shall be argued that some fundamental problems concerning security in the state of nature *carry over into the State* in ways that Hobbes does not sufficiently emphasize. Hence, there are more and deeper difficulties involved in government's performing its central function than Hobbes acknowledges. Ironically, in presenting this argument we shall sometimes rely on insights of Hobbes himself that should have led him to note the relevant difficulties. The main problems to be dealt with concern the protection of individuals by enforcement of criminal law, and the protection of the government itself (i.e., the power that protects individuals) against revolution and rebellion. The protection of individuals will be discussed in the present section, and revolution in the following three sections.

Individuals are protected in civil society by the enforcement of civil laws by means of penalties for breach. Civil laws are rules of behavior publicly commanded by the sovereign.[6] Civil law thus contrasts with natural law, which is a body of moral rules discoverable by reason that exists already in the state of nature and is independent of any proclamations, conventions, agreements, or contracts.[7] Despite this contrast, Hobbes claims that civil and natural law "contain each other."[8] This *mutual containment thesis*, as we shall call it, requires comment before we turn to the problems of enforcing civil law.[9]

The meaning of half the thesis, that the civil law is contained in the natural law, is reasonably clear: obedience to civil law is

[5] *Leviathan*, chap. 24, pp. 238–39. Here Hobbes notes the power of governments to create and devalue national currencies.

[6] Ibid., chap. 26, p. 251.

[7] Natural law will be discussed in Chapter 9, below.

[8] *Leviathan*, chap. 26, p. 253.

[9] For further discussion of this thesis, see Warrender, *Political Philosophy of Hobbes*, chap. 7.

required by the laws of nature. The supporting argument Hobbes offers is that, by virtue of the social contract,[10] the third law of nature—"Perform [thy] convenants"—binds subjects to obey the civil law.[11] Since, however, the social contract is merely hypothetical, this is a very insecure grounding for the containment of civil law within natural law. After all, the third law of nature does *not* say "Keep the convenants you would make if. . . ." Hobbesian philosophy would therefore substitute for this argument a direct appeal to the first law of nature, "Seek peace," for once a satisfactory government is established with sufficient power to enforce laws and protect its citizens, disobeying its commands amounts to leaving a relatively secure condition of peace and risking starting a violent conflict between oneself and the government or between different factions within the State. Thus, we may say that obedience to the civil laws of a satisfactory State, at least, is required by natural law.

The other half of the mutual-containment thesis is more difficult to understand. Read at face value, Hobbes's claim that civil law contains natural law faces the objection that a sovereign could explicitly disavow a natural law or enunciate civil laws that contradict it. Given Hobbes's legal positivism, and his firm doctrine that the sovereign, not lawyers or philosophers, is the final authority on what the civil law says,[12] it would be difficult for him to answer this objection. Perhaps this half of the mutual-containment thesis really makes only some weaker claim: that natural law must be interpreted by the sovereign or his agents and hence is not fully developed until embodied in civil law,[13] or that natural laws (unlike others) are to be presumptively regarded as part of the civil law of any State even without explicit enunciation or enactment.[14] Once again, however, Hobbesian philosophy is in a better position to support a strong containment claim than is

---

[10] An obligation of obedience to a conqueror based on a direct promise to him also is legitimized, for Hobbes, by the third law of nature. But see section 10-2.

[11] *Leviathan*, chap. 15, p. 130; chap. 26, p. 254.

[12] Ibid., chap. 26, pp. 263, 266.

[13] See ibid., pp. 253, 260–63.

[14] See ibid., pp. 257–58.

Hobbes himself. Natural law, it would say, is contained in the civil law of all *satisfactory* States, for the parties to the social contract would agree to including the laws of nature in the civil laws of their State, because these laws promote both individual well-being and social peace.[15]

Having somewhat clarified the mutual-containment thesis, we may proceed to the problems of enforcing domestic law within the State. Hobbes's general theory of criminal punishment is a plausible two-level theory that has many modern exponents.[16] The general justification for applying punishments for law violations is a purely forwardlooking one: to prevent crime, primarily by deterrence.[17] But decisions about guilt or innocence, and sentences, in particular cases are to be decided by applying known rules of law to the facts of the case.[18] Utilitarian calculations by judges are excluded, and, in particular, punishment of the innocent is forbidden.[19] Within this generally plausible framework, however, there are significant problems about law enforcement, involving trade-offs among important values, which Hobbes does not face up to.

Hobbes seems to rely on a simple rational actor model of deterrence: make the punishment for violation of a law exceed the value of the violation to the violator, and save for some irrational violations due to strong passions, the law in question will be followed.[20] But this ignores the problem of identifying and apprehending lawbreakers. Since not all lawbreakers will be identified and apprehended, a predominantly self-interested rational agent

---

[15] See section 5-5.

[16] See, e.g., John Rawls, "Two Concepts of Rules," *Philosophical Review* 64 (January 1955): 3–32; and H. L. A. Hart, "Murder and the Principles of Punishment," in his *Punishment and Responsibility* (New York: Oxford University Press, 1968), pp. 40–50.

[17] *Leviathan*, chap. 15, p. 140; chap. 28, pp. 298–99.

[18] Ibid., chap. 26, pp. 268–69; chap. 27, p. 281; chap. 28, p. 299.

[19] Ibid., chap. 28, p. 304.

[20] See ibid., chap. 27, p. 281, and chap. 28, p. 299, where he asserts that lesser punishments than this will not deter and thereby suggests such punishments will. The rational actor model can be applied to predominant egoists (or nonegoists) as well as pure egoists, once we recognize that what an agent *values* and what he expects to *benefit himself* need not coincide.

considering a possible violation will take into account the *probability* of being apprehended and punished for a violation as well as the severity of the penalty (discounting the latter by the former if he is an expected utility maximizer). This may render law violations "rational" in a large number of cases. Very highly effective detection of violations and violators could ameliorate this problem, but with the exception of very small societies this would require something approaching a police state, with corresponding loss of personal liberty and privacy, danger of police agencies seizing or exercising political power, and damage to personal relations brought on by the use of massive networks of undercover agents and informers. Aside from these problems, the purely economic costs of law enforcement will grow with the percentage of malefactors identified, and a point of rapidly diminishing returns will likely be reached where the criminal's probability of being apprehended is far short of one.

Given the large economic and social costs of identifying a very high percentage of violators, the State might increase the harshness of penalties well beyond the minimum necessary to make the punishment (when applied) exceed the value derived from the violation. This alternate way of increasing the expected costs of crime is not without its own difficulties. Two sorts of apparent inequities may be created or exacerbated: those between nonapprehended criminals and their unlucky fellows who now are paying, in effect, the costs of the formers' crimes as well as their own, and those between the harm caused by the offense and the harm inflicted on its perpetrator.[21] These "inequities" might not bother us so much, since violators have been warned ahead of time of the punishments they are risking.[22] Nonetheless, disproportionate punishments are likely to produce antagonism in the criminal, his family and friends, and others who identify with

[21] For discussion of the latter "inequity," see Alan Goldman, "The Paradox of Punishment," *Philosophy & Public Affairs* 9 (Spring 1979): 42–58.

[22] See *Leviathan*, chap. 27, pp. 280–81. A similar view is developed in Lawrence Alexander, "The Doomsday Machine: Proportionality, Punishment, and Prevention," *The Monist* 63 (April 1980): 199–227.

him, thus interfering with the criminal's rehabilitation and the cohesion and stability of the society.[23]

Two other difficulties with improving deterrence by increasing penalties involve recently observed deviations from the expected value maximizing model of the potential criminal. Criminologists generally agree that the probability of punishment is more important for deterrence than its magnitude.[24] Hence, increasing penalties rather than detection rates may be easier, but less effective. Also, criminal sentencing would seem to be an instance of the statistical lives phenomenon: our psychological and social tendency to overdiscount probabilistic harms or benefits to unknown persons relative to sure harms to particular known persons.[25] This tendency may lead to underexpenditure on the prevention of disease, accidents, and so on, relative to expenditures for care of victims. Since the prisoner in the dock is an identifiable individual who will surely suffer if sentenced, while those who might benefit from the marginal increase in deterrence resulting from the sentence are unidentifiable (even in retrospect), the tendency to undervalue merely statistical lives could be expected to interfere with the actual imposition of severe sentences. In particular, judges with sentencing discretion could be expected to withhold harsh and "disproportionate" sentences, while juries might convict only on lesser charges if such sentences are mandated.[26] To the extent that this occurs, the intended gains to deterrence via the establishment of harsh penalties will be diminished.

[23] Concern for rehabilitation is implied by the sixth law of nature's call "to pardon the offences past of them that repenting, desire it" (*Leviathan*, chap. 15, p. 139). The potential tension between this advice, and the "direction [deterrence] of others" (ibid., p. 140) by example, goes unnoted by Hobbes.

[24] See, e.g., Andrew von Hirsch, *Doing Justice* (New York: Hill & Wang, 1976), pp. 60–64.

[25] See, e.g., Charles Fried, *An Anatomy of Values* (Cambridge, Mass.: Harvard University Press, 1960), chap. 12.

[26] See Mr. Gilpin's suggestion that some juries find guilty defendants innocent rather than subject them to capital punishment ("Speech Against Capital Punishment, 1868," in *Punishment: Selected Readings*, ed. Joel Feinberg and Hyman Gross [Encino, Calif.: Dickenson, p. 1975], p. 118). See also Susan Jacoby, *Wild Justice* (New York: Harper & Row, 1983), p. 325.

The problems concerning the levels of detection and punishment to pursue in a legal system are complicated by the problem of discriminating between the innocent and guilty at trials or similar proceedings. Different questioning and trial procedures, and different rules governing conviction, will yield different likelihoods that accused persons will be convicted of and punished for violations. If it is easier to obtain convictions, guilty persons are more likely to be punished, and there will be greater deterrence. At the same time, however, more innocent people are likely to be punished for crimes they did not commit. Here again there is a trade-off between security and liberty: the law-abiding citizen obtains greater protection against other citizens, but at the cost of greater risk of being wrongfully deprived of his own liberty. This trade-off can to some extent be ameliorated by improving trial procedures so that they are more *accurate*—convicting fewer innocent parties and more guilty ones—but it is likely to be quite expensive to reach reasonably high levels of accuracy, and at some point diminishing returns will set in.

In sum, there are many more difficulties involved in law enforcement than suggested by Hobbes's simple formula that the punishment be made to exceed the value to the agent of the violation. There are trade-offs to be endured between security assured by deterrence of violations, on the one hand, and liberty, privacy, rehabilitation, social cohesion, minimizing the costs of goverment, and equity, on the other hand. Unless we are willing to completely subordinate all these latter values to the search for security, we cannot—even in a politically stable State—escape a reduced version of the threat to our security posed by our fellows in the state of nature. We will still be liable to attacks on our person and property by other private citizens acting out of both rational and irrational motives, and undeterred (or insufficiently deterred) by the law enforcement apparatus of the State. Though Hobbes fails to acknowledge this sufficiently, his argument against anarchy does suggest a general criterion for making the trade-off between security and competing values. At a minimum, law enforcement must provide most citizens with enough security of person and property to (1) make cooperative social life and pro-

ductive labor worthwhile for most everyone and (2) make anticipation an irrational strategy for individuals to follow.[27] Other
wise we will either lose the advantages of civilization, degenerate
into an active war of individuals or small groups, or both. Therefore, in Hobbesian philosophy, other values—liberty, equity, and
so on—must give way if necessary to maintain security above
this vital threshold level. Once this threshold is passed, however,
the exact trade-off between these values is left as an open question to be settled by political procedures and arguments, within
the framework of the satisfactory State established by the
Hobbesian social contract.

6-2. The Paradox of Perfect Tyranny

We have seen that establishment of a government with sufficient
power to make and enforce laws does not guarantee that a citizen
will not be victimized by other citizens. Governments and their
agents cannot reliably identify, apprehend, and punish enough
law violators to deter all substantial crimes against individuals.
Nonetheless, sufficient protection and deterrence can be furnished
in the State to allow individuals to pursue normal social and economic activities with risk levels much lower than could be expected in a state of nature. Thus, while government cannot provide us with absolute security against our fellows, it certainly can
provide us with a considerable amount of security.

But this security will last only as long as the government itself
(or some suitable replacement) lasts. If it collapses or is unable to
enforce the laws at certain times and places because of disorder,
organized opposition, or out-and-out rebellion, citizens will suf-

---

[27] At *Leviathan*, chap. 17, p. 154, Hobbes writes: "If there be no power erected,
or not great enough for our security; every man will . . . rely on his own strength
and art" (emphasis supplied).

Kurt Baier suggests (in "Rationality, Reason, and the Good," in *Morality,
Reason, and Truth*, ed. Copp and Zimmerman, p. 206) that if individuals are
rational egoists, adequate security can be provided only by absolutist government.
By "rational egoists" he seems to mean pure act egoists. Thus, even if true, his
charge will not directly challenge our Hobbesian theory, which regards individuals
as predominant egoists (section 2-5) and treats rule egoism as more rational than
act egoism (sections 9-3 and 9-5). For further discussion, see section 9-5.

fer substantial decreases in their security levels, at least temporarily.[28] They will be subject to violence and coercion at the hands of criminals, frightened people, and groups competing to seize power. And since one may suffer grievous and irreparable losses (e.g., of life and limb) during even temporary suspensions of law enforcement, a threat to the government constitutes a significant danger to citizens of the State.

So, in addition to the danger posed by ineffective or incomplete crime deterrence, citizens of established States face the potential dangers of revolution. Why this latter danger is present, and how it might be ameliorated, is the subject of the remainder of this chapter. First, we shall consider two paradoxes concerning revolution that point to opposite conclusions about revolt against tyranny. One says that it is virtually inevitable, the other that it is virtually impossible. Discussion of these opposed paradoxes will uncover a fundamental insight concerning political power, order, and stability within a State. This will be followed by analysis of Hobbes's argument that rational citizens will not support or participate in rebellion against an established government.

Our first paradox emerges from consideration of one version of Hobbes's social contract. Imagine that state-of-nature contractors covenant with one another to authorize all the actions of a single sovereign and transfer to him their right to rule themselves, and then elect S sovereign by majority vote. S then issues his first command, requiring of citizen X a costly or dangerous action directed at furthering some end of which X does not approve. Setting aside the possible moral motive of wanting to keep his word,[29] is it rational for X to obey? In section 5-6 we noted that it may be, because obedience promises X his best hope of escaping the state of nature. But suppose that, in the initial election of a sovereign, X voted against S and regards him as so iniquitous or incompetent that living under his rule would be

---

[28] Members of groups that are persecuted or left unprotected by a government may enjoy a net *gain* in security as that government loses its effectiveness. This qualification presumably does not come into play in satisfactory States.

[29] Whether and how the social contract morally obligates the contractors is discussed in sections 10-1 and 10-3.

more dangerous than living under anarchy. This presents us with an especially troubling version of the problem of first compliance.

Presumably, rational X will obey S under these circumstances only if he fears punishment for not doing so. But since S's own direct physical powers have not been altered by the social contract, X need fear punishment by S alone no more than he did in the state of nature. But others may join S, now their sovereign, in punishing X if he disobeys.[30] Which others? Presumably not those who share X's opinion of S, for analysis of *their* reasons for obeying an order to (help) punish X would raise the same motivational problem one step removed and would threaten us with vicious regress. But those who approve of S as ruler, and even those who simply consider his rule better than the alternative of dissolution of the social contract and a return to the state of nature, might well join in punishing X for disobeying S. So X has reason to obey.

We should especially note two features of this analysis of our special version of the problem of first compliance. First, the problem itself extends to *later* commands of the sovereign, for no matter how long S has ruled, the question of the rationality of obedience by X—who disapproves of both S and the particular command at issue—can be raised. Past obedience by X and others does not, *in itself*, give rational X any reason to obey S now, though it may provide evidence about the likely reactions of others to disobedience. Second, the above solution to the problem depends upon there existing contractors (citizens) who approve of the ruler (at least compared to the risk of return to the state of nature) or his policies. Putting these points together, we might be tempted to conclude that no ruler will ever by obeyed unless some of his subjects approve of him or his policies. If we define a *perfect tyranny* as a regime in which the ruler is never obeyed execpt out of fear of punishment, this can be put simply by saying that perfect tyranny is impossible. Hume expressed the idea this way:

[30] Hobbes holds that citizens are obligated to help the sovereign punish, if needed. See *Leviathan*, chap. 28, p. 297.

No man would have any reason to *fear* the fury of a tyrant if he had no authority over any but from fear, since, as a single man, his bodily force can reach but a small way, and all the farther power he possesses must be founded either on our own opinion or on the presumed opinion of others.[31]

Hume's view has been endorsed by a number of modern writers,[32] but it is mistaken. Suppose our ruler is the physically frailest individual in the State and that his rational subjects all dislike him and disapprove of his policies even to the extent of preferring the state of nature to his rule. Still, it is theoretically possible for him to rule over them purely by fear, to exercise power as a perfect tyrant. Because of its implausibility, to Hume and others, let us label this claim the *paradox of perfect tyranny*.

How is perfect tyranny—obedience by a citizenry that unanimously opposes a ruler—possible, even in principle? The solution to the paradox is this: Rational citizens may obey a frail and universally disliked ruler out of fear of one another. That is, each citizen is obedient out of fear that some of his fellow citizens would answer the ruler's call to punish him if he were not. So citizen A obeys out of fear of citizens B, C, et al., B obeys out of fear of A, C, et al., and so on. In this situation, the beliefs of rational citizens that their fellows will punish them for not following the ruler's orders constitute a network of interlocking mutual expectations, a "net of fear," that provides each citizen with a sufficient motive of obedience.

As suggested above, it may be doubted that such a network of expectations can exist unless *some* citizens are loyal to the ruler independent of fear generated by the network, for it might appear that unless some are known to be independently motivated to obey the ruler, each will have no reason to expect his fellows to

---

[31] David Hume, "Of the First Principles of Government," in *Hume's Moral and Political Philosophy*, ed. Henry Aiken (Darien, Conn.: Hafner, 1970), p. 309. "Opinion" refers to the specific belief that the ruler promotes the public good or has a right to rule. See ibid., pp. 307–8.

[32] See, e.g., J. R. Lucas, *The Principles of Politics* (Oxford: Clarendon Press, 1966), pp. 75–76; H. L. A. Hart, *The Concept of Law* (Oxford: Clarendon Press, 1961), pp. 23, 89, 196, 198; John Plamenatz, *Man and Society* (London: Longmans, 1963), vol. 1, p. 127; and Gauthier, *The Logic of Leviathan*, p. 168.

punish disobedience. In other words, there must be a "first punisher," himself moved to punish other than by fear of punishment, if a sequence of threatened punishments (and fears thereof)
is to be generated. That such a first punisher is not required is
suggested by consideration of an analogous network of expectations involving the value of money. For it to be rational for each
member of a community to value the medium of exchange (e.g.,
dollar bills), it is not necessary that any of them attach intrinsic
value to the bills or have any use for them other than for exchange. Each may quite rationally value dollar bills only because
he expects that others will accept them in exchange for useful
items, because they in turn will expect others to accept them in
exchange for useful items. No "first valuer" who values dollar
bills for their own sake is necessary to generate, support, or justify the expectations of the members of this economic community. Each party's expectations about his fellows' exchange behavior, and his corresponding attachment of *extrinsic* value to
dollar bills, is fully justified by his fellows' similarly justified expectations about *their* fellows' exchange behavior. Similarly, a
community-wide net of rational fear of being punished for disobedience does not presuppose the existence of a punisher motivated other than by fear.

But does not the existence of the net of fear require, if not a
first punisher, the suspicion among the populace that he may exist? If all dislike the ruler (i.e., none is a potential first punisher),
and all know this, it seems that they need not fear punishment
at each other's hands. If so, the rule of a perfect tyrant can rest
only on the ignorance of his subjects concerning each other's attitudes. In fact, given certain reasonable assumptions about rational fear, it does turn out that citizen ignorance of a sort is a
prerequisite for perfect tyranny. To see what sort of ignorance is
required, and why, we must describe the net of fear more precisely.

Consider a four-person society, a ruler and citizens A, B, and
C. To simplify matters, assume that the ruler is too frail to punish by himself but that the citizens are equal enough in strength

that any citizen plus the ruler can punish any other citizen (and all know this). Also, all know that if the ruler and one citizen join to punish a second citizen, the third will stand aside.

Why might A obey an order from the ruler to do something he otherwise would not do? He might be bribed by the ruler, he might fear anarchy if the ruler is disobeyed, or he might possess a positive attitude toward the ruler or his policies. Suppose he does not. He might obey anyway out of fear of punishment. First, he may fear that B or C, or both, will join with the ruler to punish him if he disobeys, for if B and/or C approved of the ruler, they might want the ruler's orders enforced.

But suppose A believes that B and C, like himself, disapprove of the ruler, and that each would obey the ruler's order to punish A only if he (B or C) feared punishment for disobeying this order. Can A then be confident that B, for example, would not punish him? No, for B might punish anyway, out of fear that if he does not obey the ruler's order to punish he will himself be punished by the ruler and another citizen. Which other citizen? B could reasonably assume that A would not punish him (B) for failing to punish A. And presumably A can count on B's making this assumption. But B might punish A out of fear that C and the ruler will punish him if he does not.

Of course, if B believes that C dislikes the ruler, he will not punish A out of fear of C.[33] And if A believes B believes C dislikes the ruler, he will not fear B punishing him out of fear. Similarly, if A believes that C believes that B dislikes the ruler, he will not fear C punishing him out of fear of B. Thus, in our three-citizen society, the following condition seems to preclude rational A fearing punishment for disobeying the ruler:

---

[33] "Belief," in this and similar contexts, means belief of a degree or strength sufficient to insure that the agent's possible awareness that he might be mistaken does not generate fear. Thus, if B thought that C probably disliked the ruler, but was sufficiently uncertain that he was motivated to obey the ruler by his awareness of the *possibility* that C might otherwise punish him, then he would not, in the relevant sense, "believe" that C disliked the ruler.

(1) A believes that all citizens believe that all citizens do not approve of the ruler.[34]

If, however, A lacks this belief, it may be rational for him to obey the ruler's orders, out of fear that he will suffer punishment by either B or C, motivated either by approval of the ruler or by fear. In particular, obedience may be the rational course for A even if all three dislike the ruler, and each believes the others do, provided A is not *aware* that all have this belief. So long as A lacks the belief, for example, that B believes C dislikes the ruler, A may rationally obey the ruler out of fear of B punishing him out of fear of C.

Our analysis of the three-citizen example can be completed by bringing one of our background assumptions to the surface. Only if A is aware that he, B, and C are the only citizens does his lack of fear of their punishing him for disobeying the ruler imply that he is free of all fear of such punishment. If he believes (or believes that others believe or that others believe that others believe) that there is a fourth citizen, D, he may obey out of fear of being punished by D or by others motivated by fear of D, and so on. To rule out this possibility of fear of a nonexistent fourth party, we must assume that

(2) A believes that all citizens believe that all citizens believe that there are at most three citizens.

Together assumptions (1) and (2) preclude rational A fearing punishment for disobeying the ruler.

If one is willing to postulate the existence of higher-order beliefs of any finite order, this result can readily be generalized to apply to a community of any finite population size n.[35] All that is required is that we generalize the assumption that people know A would not punish B for failing to punish A, so it covers similar knowledge that A would not punish B for failing to punish C for failing to punish A, and so on. Given this assumption, it follows

[34] We assume that if A believes that he believes X, then A believes X; and that if A believes he does not approve of the ruler, he does not so approve. Thus, (1) implies, among other things, that A disapproves of the ruler.

[35] For details, see my "Rule by Fear," *Nous* 17 (November 1983): 601–20, sec. IV.

by reasoning like that employed in the three-citizen example that the ruler will not be obeyed whenever the appropriate generalizations of conditions (1) and (2) are satisfied.[36] This result, which may be called our *restriction on perfect tyranny*, may be restated as follows: If all citizens are rational and are sufficiently mutually aware of one another's universal disapproval of the ruler and knowledge of the size of the population, then perfect tyranny over them is impossible. ("Mutual awareness" here refers to all knowing that all know that all know, and so on.)

This restriction says that the rule of a perfect tyrant must ultimately be based on ignorance of some sort. It informs us that if rational citizens' knowledge about each other's numbers and disapproval of the ruler is extensive enough (i.e., extends to sufficiently high orders), rule purely by fear is impossible. However, the amount and kind of knowledge required to bring the restriction into play—involving as it does high-order beliefs about the beliefs of others—is nearly certain not to be possessed by the citizens of any community of more than a few members.

Of these two general conclusions—that perfect tyranny presupposes citizen ignorance and that it presupposes only high-order ignorance—the latter is of greater practical import. In general, citizens lack beliefs about each other's beliefs of higher than second or third order. Even if it makes sense to speak of the much higher orders of belief required for satisfaction of the generalizations of conditions (1) and (2), it is doubtful that members of a population of any significant size would possess such beliefs. Further, many citizens may lack even lowest-order true beliefs about the groups's size. Hence, it is virtually inconceivable that our restriction on perfect tyranny could have application to an actual community of significant size.

It seems fair to conclude that rational obedience to and universal disapproval of a ruler are compatible under all *plausible* conditions of citizen knowledge. The practical limits on the complexity of citizens' beliefs about one another, and the vulnerability of

---

[36] These generalizations are just like (1) and (2) save that the phrase "all citizens believe that" is iterated so it occurs a total of $n - 2$ times.

each citizen to a greater number of his fellows, are such as to render rule by fear eminently possible—possible, but certainly not necessary. Our restriction states a condition on citizen knowledge that precludes perfect tyranny over rational citizens. If citizen knowledge of each other's numbers, beliefs, and attitudes toward the ruler falls short of this, a perfect tyrant may reign, or he may not. Which of these is the case will depend on a variety of factors, including how much citizens do know about one another's beliefs and attitudes. In particular, it is plausible to conjecture that, in general, the more widespread and the higher the order citizens' knowledge of each other's nonapproval of the ruler is, the less likely it is that they will obey him and that he will remain in power.[37]

A final source of skepticism about the possibility of perfect tyranny can now be put to rest. While it may be rational to obey a disliked ruler once a system of mutual expectations of obedience has formed around him, one might question whether such a system could arise in the first place if the ruler is universally disliked. One may wonder, that is, whether or how a tyrant's net of fear can be woven in the first place.

There are at least three ways this could happen. First, the ruler or his policies may initially be approved by many, and a network of mutual expectations of obedience may thereby be created. (Perhaps it will be solidified by a social contract, a public investiture, or something of the sort.) As citizens' attitudes change over time, until eventually none approve of the ruler, their knowledge of one another's changed attitudes does not keep pace, and mutual expectations of obedience to the ruler remain intact. Second, except in the special case considered so far, in which the ruler is too frail to conquer anyone, a universally disliked person could, with sufficient courage and good fortune, create a net of fear around himself by successive conquests—first overpowing A, then overpowering B with A's help, then using A and B to overpower C, and so on. Third, and finally, if unlike our citizen X, people disapprove of an individual as ruler but *prefer him to an-*

[37] For the sketch of an argument supporting this conjecture, see ibid., sec. V.

archy, that individual might initially become generally obeyed because people perceive his rule as the only alternative to anarchy. This might occur, for example, if negotiations between rival groups inhabiting the same territory agree on this individual as a compromise candidate for ruler. Given these possibilities, we may say that, in principle, rule purely by fear could be created as well as sustained once it exists.

But will rule by fear be stable? Is it likely to last? Clearly not, for two reasons. First, it requires that citizens remain *ignorant* of matters about which people, unless severely inhibited, are likely to communicate with one another: their attitudes toward the ruler. Therefore a perfect tyrant's power may disintegrate as a result of the normal exchange of political information that accompanies social interactions. Second, since perfect tyranny rests solely on a system of mutual expectations, it is subject to *tipping*. That is, any public event that casts doubt on the depth and range of the ruler's support could set off an escalating spiral of expectations of nonobedience to the ruler, thus quickly unraveling the net of fear.[38]

That real-world tyrants have recognized these sources of instability is reflected in some of the tactics employed by unpopular regimes to stay in power. Secret police and informers fulfill a double function. They identify and isolate potential rebels before they can "infect" others with their opinions or form effective conspiracies among themselves. And general knowledge of the existence of such a network of spies and informers inhibits citizens from frankly communicating to others their attitudes toward the regime. Government control of the media serves to limit public knowledge of events that might make citizens wonder whether the regime will survive. And immediate massive shows of force against public protesters serve to convince any doubters that the regime remains in control and to deter future protests that might be destabilizing.

While such repressive measures may be quite effective for a time, they tend to breed stronger dislike of the ruler that em-

[38] See section 6-3. On tipping, see, e.g., Mark Granovetter, "Threshold Models of Collective Behavior," *American Journal of Sociology* 83 (1978): 1420–43.

to be serious conflicts among groups within the State, and events like wars, the loss of allies, and economic crises, which could produce strong opposition to the government and lead people to wonder if it will maintain its popular support. Such doubts are likely to be less destabilizing under a predominantly popular regime than under a predominantly fear-based regime, for citizens are less likely to abandon a government whose policies they support and are less likely to expect others to desert a popular government. Nonetheless, once a substantial number of people begin to wonder about a popular regime's continuation in power, many might abandon it because they underestimate the extent to which others are loyal to it or because they are afraid of the consequences of continuing their support should the present government's rivals come to power. Under these circumstances, the regime might well collapse if it were unable to inspire fear among the citizens. Hence, a completely unfeared regime, like a purely fear-based one, is likely to be unstable, and one would expect motives of both approbation and fear to be operative among the citizenry in any regime that is long-lasting.

The importance of viewing political power as substantially a function of mutual expectations is that this allows us to see that any State is *potentially* unstable. Since systems of mutual expectation are highly vulnerable to tipping, any such system that contains many elements disposed to disturb the status quo is susceptible to serious instability. This should lead us to doubt Hobbes's suggestion that establishing the right sort of State would assure the avoidance of rebellion[42]—unless, of course, we believe that practically no rational person would ever be inclined to start, or join in, a rebellion. Arguments in support of this belief are the subject of the next two sections.

6-3. The Paradox of Revolution

In recent years, it has been observed that members of an oppressed or exploited citizenry are apparently in an multiparty

---

[42] *Leviathan*, chap. 29, p. 308.

prisoner's dilemma situation with respect to participating in a mass revolt. Collectively they have the power to overthrow their oppressors, and would probably be better off if they did so. But an individual's participation in a revolt is dangerous and will have only a minute effect on the prospects of the revolt succeeding, while the individual can expect to reap most of the benefits of a successful revolt (should one occur) without participating. Hence, rational individuals will not participate, and mass revolts of rational citizens will never occur even against tyrannical, repressive, or exploitive regimes. This odd conclusion—that the rationality of the members of a society prevents them from overthrowing a despised government—is called the *paradox of revolution*.[43]

This argument is, to a certain degree, in the spirit of Hobbes. He recognizes multiparty prisoner's dilemmas, as in his analysis of the state-of-nature security problem, and he endorses the present paradox's central claim that nonparticipation in revolution is the rational course for individuals. But Hobbes does not derive this latter claim from the prisoner's dilemma structure of the revolutionary situation. That is, he does not hold that nonparticipation is irrational because one can make only a marginal contribution to revolutionary success and can hope to ride free on the revolutionary acts of others. Perhaps he bypassed this argument simply because he failed to recognize the prisoner's dilemma structure of the potential revolutionary's situation. But there were good reasons for not relying on this argument, even if he were aware of it. Hobbes did not *need* it to support his antirevolutionary stance, since, as we shall see in section 6-4, he had an argument that revolution is both individually and *collectively* irrational. Also, the free-rider aspect of the present argument would presumably imply the rationality of *promoting others' participation* in revolution (when one could do so without the authorities

[43] See discussions in Mancur Olson, Jr., *The Logic of Collective Action* (New York: Schocken Books, 1965), pp. 105–6; Gordon Tullock, "The Paradox of Revolution," *Public Choice* 11 (Fall 1971): 89–99; and Allen Buchanan, "Revolutionary Motivation and Rationality," *Philosophy & Public Affairs* 9 (Fall 1979): 59–82.

knowing), and this Hobbes would not accept. Finally, the argument itself is not fully persuasive, as we now proceed to show by considering some possible solutions to the paradox of revolution.

The main steps of the paradox may be stated as follows:

(1) Rational individuals act to maximize expected payoffs.

(2) In a potentially revolutionary situation, the expected costs of participation are higher than the expected costs of nonparticipation, and there are no sufficiently compensating expected benefits of participation.

(3) Therefore, rational individuals in a potentially revolutionary situation will not participate in a revolution.

On the surface, this appears to be a valid argument. So to find a solution to the paradox that allows us to reject (3), we must either give reasons for rejecting one of the premises or discover an equivocation in the meaning of key terms of the argument.

Before proceeding to this task, we may observe that one could, as Hobbes does, accept conclusion (3) and still acknowledge that mass revolts sometimes occur. One need only ascribe *irrational* behavior in revolutionary settings to enough members of the population. Thus, for example, Hobbes attributes much religiously motivated revolutionary action to irrational and ill-founded fears of ghosts and supernatural punishments.[44] More generally, it is plausible to suppose that in times of social turmoil and distress many people can get carried away with anger and frustration or get caught up in group hysteria, so that they act without even considering costs and benefits. This is worth noting, because the possibility of others irrationally joining a revolt may influence the cost-benefit analyses of *rational* potential revolutionaries.

With this in mind, let us consider three potential solutions to the paradox of revolution that challenge the claim that rational individuals must be expected utility maximizers in the sense that

---

[44] *Leviathan*, chap. 29, pp. 316–18. Note that if we do not treat belief in divine punishments for nonparticipation (or divine rewards for participation) in revolution as irrational, we have a theological solution to the paradox of revolution in some cases. When God is on the rebels' side, participation maximizes one's expected payoffs over this life and the next.

allows us to derive (3) from (2). The first of these is the *utilitarian* solution. According to it, the paradox arises only if the payoffs discussed in (1) and (2) are taken to be costs and benefits to the individual in question. But if instead agents act as rational utilitarians, maximizing net expected benefits of their actions *for all concerned*, they will participate, for the potential benefit *to all* of a successful revolt may be huge and dwarf the costs to the individual (and his dependents) of his participation.

However, the utilitarian approach does not get us very far. The problem is that the probability that a given individual's participation will make the difference between success and failure of a revolution is tiny, so tiny that even the huge benefit to all from a successful revolution, *when discounted by this minute probability*, will likely be exceeded by the substantial expected costs to the individual of participation. Perhaps in a few cases of quite beneficial revolutions in small countries (where each individual's stance has more effect), the typical individual's participation will produce greater expected benefits than costs to himself. But because one's contribution will be only a drop in the bucket, this will very seldom be so, even if we count benefits to all, as the utilitarian urges.

Furthermore, it is a tenet of Hobbesian philosophy, argued for in section 2-5, that people are predominantly egoistic. Thus, while anger at prevailing injustices and the charged political atmosphere of a potential revolutionary situation may temporarily raise many people's tendencies toward self-sacrifice, it is highly unlikely that enough altruism will be created or stirred up in the typical individual so that, in planning his acts, he counts his own interests for no more than those of any other individual. If this is so, and most people remain predominantly egoistically motivated, even in a revolutionary context, the above-noted weakness of the utilitarian solution is compounded. A rational predominant egoist will further discount his "drop in the bucket" contribution to revolutionary success relative to his personal costs of participation, in accordance with the degree to which he favors promotion of his own welfare over that of fellow citizens. This will likely render participation in a revolution "nonmaximizing" from the individual's perspective, even in those few cases in which his participation might yield expected benefits for the population as a whole. Thus, the utilitarian solution to the paradox of revolution fails because it is subject to the "drop in the bucket" problem and because it presupposes an unrealistic level of altruistic motivation or impartiality among members of the potentially revolutionary population.

A second possible solution to the paradox of revolution rests on the *disaster-avoidance* principle. This solution is suggested by Hobbes's observation that "needy and hardy men" will be inclined to foment rebellion in hopes of improving their own social position.[45] If we interpret their being needy as being in an unacceptable or disastrous life-situation, and their being hardy as providing them with grounds for believing they might fare better in an atmosphere of social turmoil (or its aftermath), these men seem to be acting as rational disaster-avoiders in stirring revolt. It is reasonable to suppose that, like these men, many or most people living under a repressive government regard the status quo as unacceptable. Might we not then solve the paradox of revolution by replacing (1) with the following assumption, which states that rational individuals are disaster-avoiders?

(1') Rational individuals act to maximize the probability of avoiding all disastrous outcomes.

Unfortunately, this solution too falls prey to the "drop in the bucket" problem. By participating in a rebellion, the average dissatisfied or desperate citizen raises the probability of being liberated from his unacceptable condition through successful revolution by only a miniscule amount. It is highly unlikely that he could not raise his prospects of moving to an acceptable condition *somewhat* more than this by alternative actions within the present system—for example, working harder at his current livelihood, pursuing education or training, or moving to a region with more opportunities. Further, participation in a revolution significantly raises the probability of suffering another presumably disastrous outcome: violent death. Hence, even if the downtrodden

[45] Ibid., chap. 11, pp. 86–87.

act as rational disaster-avoiders instead of expected utility maximizers, most apparently would not participate in a revolt.[46]

One way of avoiding the "drop in the bucket" problem is to suppose that individuals act to maximize the payoffs that would be produced by them, *and everyone like them*, acting in a certain way. Thus, according to the *collective-reasoning* solution to the paradox, a rational potential revolutionary reasons that if all those in his circumstances participated the revolt would very likely succeed, to his own (and their) great benefit, while if they did not participate the revolt would fail and he (and they) would remain in their present unsatisfactory condition. The "drop in the bucket" problem does not arise here, because—in effect—rational agents are supposed to take into account the results of all the individual "drops" taken together. When the expected benefits of participation are calculated in this way (whether by an egoist, a utilitarian, or something between), the last clause of (2) is likely false, and the paradox of revolution collapses.

Now there is no doubt that some people sometimes reason collectively, in the above sense, that is, they choose acts according to what would happen, or be the case, if everyone (similarly situated) did the same. In fact, criteria like this for selecting among alternatives are embodied in Kant's first form of the categorical imperative, and in various versions of the principle of utilitarian generalization.[47] Yet it is, to say the least, *controversial* whether so acting is rational.[48] In prisoner's dilemma situations, for ex-

[46] This somewhat modifies the analysis offered in my "Two Solutions to the Paradox of Revolution," *Midwest Studies in Philosophy* 7 (1982): 455–72, sec. 5. It is noted below, however, that Hobbes's "hardy" men may constitute a special group, like revolutionary leaders, who face different payoff structures than the typical citizen.

[47] Two well-known books on utilitarian generalization are David Lyons, *Forms and Limits of Utilitarianism* (Oxford: Clarendon Press, 1965); and Marcus Singer, *Generalization in Ethics* (New York: Alfred A. Knopf, 1961).

[48] In my "Two Solutions to the Paradox of Revolution," collective reasoning is given a sympathetic treatment, including consideration of an especially promising version of collective reasoning derived from ideas in Donald H. Regan's *Utilitarianism and Co-operation* (Oxford: Clarendon Press, 1980). The problem concerning *control* that is mentioned below in this paragraph is not sufficiently noted in "Two Solutions."

ample, reasoning collectively involves each player bypassing a dominant choice in favor of a strictly dominated one, on the grounds that all will benefit if all do this. But since each player controls only his own act, by reasoning collectively, the individual risks being played for a sucker and ending up a unilateral cooperator.

There are further difficulties with adopting collective reasoning as a solution to the paradox of revolution to be incorporated into *Hobbesian* theory. Hobbes himself frequently stresses the unreasonableness of risking unilateral cooperation. More important, if we posit that rational agents will reason collectively, then rational agents should comply with the laws of nature without the need for enforcement, and our central Hobbesian argument against anarchy, and for the State, may collapse.[49]

We are left, finally, with the option of directly challenging the claim, in (2), that the expected costs to individuals of participating in a revolt exceed the expected benefits. This approach leads to what we may call the *dynamic-maximizing* solution. It begins by noting that the paradox rests on the twin observations that individuals do not make significant contributions to the success of revolutions and that the benefits flowing to individuals from successful revolutions are public goods. But there will be circumstances in which neither of these observations holds true with respect to some individuals. Key leaders who, by virtue of their official positions and/or the personal loyalty of their subordinates, have substantial control over large groups can significantly increase the chances of a revolt succeeding by joining (or starting) it and can reasonably hope to attain a high position in the new government if the revolt succeeds.[50] This explains, perhaps, the behavior of government officials who institute coups and of revolutionary leaders who try to exhort and organize the masses to revolt.

[49] We can only say *may* collapse because the activities of, and difficulties of identifying, irrational individuals in the state of nature might be sufficient to generate a high degree of violent conflict and insecurity, even if all rational individuals reasoned collectively.

[50] See Tullock, "The Paradox of Revolution," p. 98.

But what of those ordinary citizens who must participate in large numbers if a true revolution of the masses is to occur and succeed? Even for them the benefits of a successful revolution will not always be a *pure* public good. Participants in revolutionary organizations (especially early participants), and not just leaders, are often assigned better jobs than others and various public honors and privileges, when the revolutionary government is installed. Furthermore, it is not uncommon for revolutionary leaders and their followers to attach costs to nonparticipation during a revolt or during preparation for one. Thus, we have the revolutionary slogan "If you are not with us, you are against us," which is used not only to attract converts but also to justify punishing nonconverts. Nor is it always irrational for revolutionary leaders, especially those who perceive themselves as taking part in a long-range worldwide movement, to thus punish neutrals during a revolution and reward participants after, for in view of the paradox of revolution, these practices might be thought necessary as a device for recruiting participants in current and future revolutions.

There are, however, substantial drawbacks to using some of these methods to tilt individuals' expected utility calculations in favor of taking part in a revolution. Punishing nonparticipants can seriously undermine popular support for the revolution and its leaders, and in any case the revolutionaries may lack the power to apply such punishment in a systematic way. Further, if the existing government is not already using, to the maximal extent, the same tactics of promising rewards for collaborators and punishing the opposition, it may be goaded into doing so by the use of such tactics by the revolutionists.

In view of these difficulties, the manipulation of costs and benefits by revolutionary leaders does not by itself provide a very plausible account of how mass revolution can arise from individual utility-maximizing behavior on the part of the general populace. We can provide such an account, however, by introducing dynamic considerations into our analysis. The underlying idea of this account is that rational agents' expected utility calculations about participation in revolution will *change* as they observe others joining the revolutionary struggle. In particular, as a first approximation we would expect agents' estimates of the probability of the revolution succeeding to go up, and their estimates of the probability of being punished for taking part in the revolt to go down, as the number of people they observe taking part in the revolt increases. These changes in probability will in turn raise the expected benefits associated with participation (since the receipt of many such benefits is contingent upon the revolt succeeding) and decrease the expected costs (e.g., the risk of being punished for participating). It is also possible that the instrinsic payoffs of participation, such as the pleasure of taking part in a mass enterprise, and the intrinsic costs of nonparticipation, such as the guilt one may feel over being a free-rider, will increase as the number of others participating increases.

Now it may be that the initial expected utility calculations of all citizens, at time t_0, lead only a small minority to engage in revolutionary or prerevolutionary activities. But the participation of this minority may alter, in the manner suggested above, the expected utility calculations of others at time t_1, so that it now maximizes expected utility for some of the latter to join the movement. And their recruitment into the movement may, in turn, affect the calculations of others at t_2 and bring them into the fray, and so forth.

Whether this process ever gets started, and whether, if it does, it continues to escalate until a sufficient active revolutionary group is formed, cannot be determined a priori. Suppose we call the number of persons that must be engaged in revolutionary activities before it seems to an individual to maximize expected utility to join them that individual's *revolution-participation threshold*. Whether a revolution will occur will depend upon the distribution of revolution-participation thresholds among the members of the population.[51] If the distribution is right—for example, if many

[51] This is an oversimplification. It treats participation as all-or-nothing, while in fact it can exist in various forms and degrees. Also, for some agents, their effective threshold will depend on the rate of increase of participation or on a number of situational variables, rather than simply on the number of participants. Note the parallel between revolution-participation thresholds, as defined here, and anticipation thresholds (for anticipation in the state of nature), as defined in section 3-5.

have very low thresholds or if the thresholds are evenly distributed and relatively "connected" so that the crossing of one subgroup's threshold adds enough participants to breach the threshold of the next group—a revolution may be virtually inevitable. On the other hand, if there are too few people with low thresholds, or too many with high ones, or if there is a "gap" in the distribution of thresholds at a level below the critical mass needed for revolutionary success, a winning revolution may be virtually impossible.

We have so far ignored the regime's likely response to revolutionary activity. This factor requires modifying our analysis in one important respect. Regimes may tend to ignore revolutionary activity so long as it remains below some safe level, but increase enforcement and punishment once this level is surpassed. Hence, the individual's expected costs of participating in a revolt may be low when there are few other participants and when there are very many other participants (as the regime's forces will be greatly outnumbered), but relatively high at some *intermediate* level of revolutionary activity.

Could a budding revolution by expected utility maximizers escalate right through this peak in the expected-costs curve? It very well could, for the curve of expected benefits for participants is, for two reasons, also likely to rise steeply at the point at which the regime "cracks down." First, the crackdown is likely to be based on evidence, perceived by the citizens as well as by the regime, that a successful revolt is a real possibility and will itself signal to the citizens that the regime is in trouble. Second, one of the main components of the expected *benefits* of participation in a revolt—status and job preference if the revolt succeeds—is not a simple increasing function of the number of participants. Because there are so many of them, and because earlier participants may resent them, those who join a revolt in the late stages, when there is little danger and victory is all but assured, are much less likely to obtain special benefits from the victory. Thus, there is a strong incentive for those who have not already joined the revolt to join during the dangerous, but promising, intermediate period.

No doubt it is likely that increased police activities by a regime would stop many (or even most) potential revolts by expected utility maximizers. But for the reasons just cited it is not implausible to suppose that, even taking regime responses into account, in *some* cases the revolution-participation thresholds of dissatisfied utility maximizing citizens are distributed in a way that could lead to mass revolt, by the escalatory process described earlier. If so, it is safe to endorse the general insight underlying our dynamic analysis, namely, that it is not required that participation in revolutionary activities be expected utility maximizing for a large revolutionary mass during the early stages of a revolution in order for that revolution to be successful. Hence, even if it is implausible, given the potential costs and benefits, that many dissatisfied citizens would regard being a first (or early) participant in a revolt as expected utility maximizing for them, mass revolts of expected utility maximizers can occur.

So we have a solution to the paradox of revolution that fits within our general Hobbesian framework. It retains the standard assumption that a rational person acts so as to maximize the expected utility of the consequences of his acts, but it avoids the paradoxical conclusion by noting that the benefits of revolution are not a *pure* public good and by introducing dynamic considerations into what has heretofore been a static analysis.[52]

This version of the dynamic maximizing solution represents all individuals as independent rational agents who act to maximize their own utilities. Three realistic modifications in that assumption increase the power of the solution by allowing for factors that enhance any tendency toward escalating participation in revolution. First, Predominant Egoism allows that most individuals are not purely self-interested and that a small percentage may genuinely act as purely impartial utilitarians, or self-sacrificers serving a cause like revolution.[53] The latter may form an initial participation group in a revolt (or the planning of a revolt) against a repressive regime, even if the prospects of success seem slim.[54]

[52] For static analyses along these general lines, see the references in note 43, this chapter.

[53] See section 2-5.

[54] See David Braybrooke, "Self-interest in Times of Revolution and Repression," in *Revolutions, Systems, and Theories*, ed. H. J. Johnson et al. (Dordrecht: Reidel, 1979), pp. 61–74.

The former will perceive greater relevant benefits flowing from revolutionary success (i.e., better lives for those they care about, as well as for themselves) than if they were pure egoists, and hence will have lower revolution-participation thresholds, other things being equal. Second, it is fairly realistic to picture a potentially revolutionary society as made up of a large number of multimember subgroups (e.g., families, villages, local organizations) in which rational members save information-gathering and decision-making costs by following the political lead of a single subgroup leader (or a few subgroup leaders). Members of these subgroups are very likely to participate in a revolution if their leader participates or recommends (or orders) their participation. Subgroup leaders can therefore make greater contributions to revolutionary success than individuals, and they have greater likelihood of attaining postrevolution rewards—in return for these contributions. Thus, the expected benefit-to-cost ratio for participation will generally be higher for subgroup leaders than for individuals, and escalation to mass revolt can therefore occur more easily because of the subgroup structure. Third, and finally, we noted above that individuals may often participate in revolutions for nonrational or irrational reasons—they are merely expressing rage, or like fighting, or are striking out at symbols of their frustration, or are caught up in mob frenzy. This means that, in gauging whether one's own revolution-participation threshold will be passed, a rational potential revolutionary will estimate and count on the participation of some nonrational revolters as well as that of his rational colleagues. In many cases, this will lead to earlier passing of more participation thresholds and quicker escalation.[55]

What if we regard some or all of our rational agents as disaster-avoiders rather than standard expected utility maximizers? Will this have an effect on the dynamic-maximizing solution to the paradox of revolution? At first, it may seem to threaten this solution, for we observed earlier that, for the average individual, revolutionary participation would not seem to minimize the pros-

[55] Of course, some people who would personally benefit from participation might *refrain* for irrational reasons, e.g., neurotic inhibitions against challenging authorities. Too much irrationality of this sort can counteract the described effect and prevent escalation.

pects of disaster-avoidance. But revolutionary leaders or initiators may well view the absence of a revolt, or the absence of their own best efforts to promote a revolt, as a personally disastrous or unacceptable outcome. And *some* ordinary people may find the status quo unacceptable, may see no hope of changing their personal position unless the social deck is reshuffled, and may expect because of their special skills (e.g., military hardiness) to fare relatively well during a revolutionary period. The efforts of these two groups (conjoined perhaps with the nonrational actions of some angry people) may be enough to get a revolt going. Once it is in progress, many others may find their own nonparticipation "unacceptable" for a number of reasons—danger of punishment by the rebels, guilt about free-riding on comrades' efforts,[56] fear of missing the chance to get ahead by being an active participant in a revolt that might well succeed, and so on. And once there are enough participants to make success seem very likely, joining the apparent winners may yield the best chance of disaster-avoidance for nearly everyone. So even among rational disaster-avoiders, escalation to successful revolution is *possible*. The revolution-participation thresholds of disaster-avoiders may be distributed differently from those of utility-maximizers, but they need not be distributed in a way that precludes revolution. Thus, the dynamic-maximizing solution extends its scope to cover the "dynamic disaster-avoiding" case as well.

Our earlier solution to the paradox of perfect tyranny and the dynamic-maximizing solution to the paradox of revolution represent different sides of the same coin. They trace extreme, but opposite, potential effects of the key role that mutual expectations play in the establishment of political power. The former shows that if mutual expectations of power are extensive enough, they can in principle support political power that has no other foundation. The latter reminds us that to the extent that power depends on mutual expectations, it is subject to destabilization and tipping effects. In the playrooms of politics, as in those of

[56] See Braybrooke, "Self-Interest in Times of Revolution and Repression," pp. 69–70.

children, houses may be built of cards, but they are all too liable, then, to come tumbling down.

6-4. An Argument Against Revolution

The paradox of revolution discussed in the last section arises only in situations in which the overthrow of the present government could be expected to produce a large net gain in utility for most all citizens. Hobbes denies that this will ever be the case when there is a functioning government that has the capacity to protect its citizens.[57] He believes that most all individuals, and therefore society as a whole, will suffer net expected losses as a result of a revolution against an established government. Accordingly, he attributes most revolutionary behavior to irrational beliefs or attitudes—expectations of rewards in heaven, unrealistic utopian conceptions of postrevolutionary society, excitement caused by clever but deceptive oratory, or a misreading of the lessons of history.[58] And his recommended policies for preventing revolt are aimed primarily at limiting the force and scope of such beliefs among the populace. Therefore, he urges education of the populace about the foundations of their duties to the State and the personal and social costs of rebellion, and subordination of the church to the State.[59]

Hobbes does not offer much explicit argument for the claim that revolution has negative expected social utility. He suggests that revolution returns society's members to a war of all against all,[60] but this is implausible if it is meant to imply that citizens in a country torn by revolt suffer all the disadvantages of pure individualist anarchy[61] and suffer them to a comparable degree. Even during civil war, a considerable amount of ordinary law enforcement and cooperative economic activity is likely to con-

---

[57] *Leviathan*, chap. 18, p. 170; chap. 21, p. 208.
[58] Ibid., chap. 15, pp. 134–35; chap. 29, pp. 308, 314–18, 320–21.
[59] Ibid., chap. 30, pp. 323–27; chap. 31, pp. 355–56; chap. 43, pp. 584–602, esp. 600–602.
[60] Ibid., chap. 13, pp. 114–15; chap. 18, p. 170.
[61] See section 3-2 for discussion of these disadvantages.

tinue—though perhaps separately in government and rebel strongholds.

Nonetheless, it is possible to construct a quasi-utilitarian argument against revolution that relies heavily on the consideration that Hobbes stresses: the heavy costs and dangers of the revolt itself. The argument begins by noting the immediate costs to society's members of revolution. Except in the case of mere palace coups, where little changes but the leaders' names, a revolution with any chance of success is likely to involve sustained violence on a significant scale. Thus, there will very likely be substantial loss of life and limb, separation of families, destruction of economic and natural resources, disruption of productive economic activity and economic growth, and an at least temporary weakening of the society compared to its neighbors and foreign foes—rendering it more vulnerable to outside pressures, threats, or even conquests. On the other side of the ledger, the benefits of a revolution are both uncertain and likely to be small—*uncertain* because overthrow of an established government may result in foreign conquest, long-term civil war, or the installation of a *worse* regime; *small* because even if the new regime makes life better for the people it is unlikely to make it much better.

On what grounds is it claimed that the new regime is unlikely to improve things much if at all? Historical observation suggests that while some revolutions do lead rather quickly to significantly beneficial changes, equally many others make things no better or worse.[62] In this century, for example, the success—in much improving the lives of most of society's members—of frequent violent rebellions in the third world is doubtful. And there are good theoretical reasons for not being surprised at this. New revolutionary governments are often faced with social divisions and hostility left over from the revolution and with a weakened or

---

[62] See, e.g., Gordon Tullock, *The Social Dilemma* (Blacksburg, Va.: University Publications, 1974), chap. 4, pp. 26–30, 33–35. One well-known writer on revolution says: "I estimate some revolutions as worth it. But at present no one has enough systematic knowledge about the probable structural consequences of one variety of revolution or another to make such estimates with confidence. Except, perhaps, in retrospect." (Charles Tilly, *From Mobilization to Revolution* [Reading, Mass.: Addison-Wesley, 1978]; p. 222).

wrecked economy. It has often been observed that power corrupts and that even revolutionary governments tend to become bureaucratized over time as ideologically inspired revolutionary leaders are replaced by officials bred within the new system. Further, successful revolutionary leaders are likely to have used violence, or even terrorism, to come to power and may therefore be more prone than others to apply similar measures against any domestic opposition, real or imagined.[63] Hence, revolutionary leaders and governments are likely to face the same or worse social and economic problems as the governments they have overthrown, and are likely to display some of the same harmful tendencies in response—corruption, bureaucratic indifference, and repressive use of coercive violence.

If this is correct, revolution in countries with established governments would appear not to be aggregate expected utility maximizing. There are likely to be very substantial short-run costs, and the benefits are too uncertain and too likely to be small to offset these large costs. This is especially clear when we note that those who bear the short-term physical, economic, and social costs of revolution may not be around long enough to collect many of the long-term benefits,[64] for many will die in the struggle, and—in any case—the period of revolt plus recovery could easily cover an entire generation or more. So from the collective perspective of the present generation, revolution would seem to be a bad bargain.

This argument against revolution is subject to three major objections. First, it may be suggested that the interests of future generations must be treated on a par with the interests of the present generation. Remember, however, that we are here concerned with the *descriptive* theory of rational action by predominantly egoistic beings, not with *moral* theory.[65] This *quasi-util-*

---

[63] See Crane Brinton, *The Anatomy of Revolution*, rev. and exp. ed. (New York: Vintage Books, 1965), chaps. 6–7.

[64] See *Leviathan*, chap. 27, p. 284, where Hobbes applies this argument to the special case of those that start revolutions.

[65] On the protection of future generations viewed as a moral issue, see section 12-1.

itarian antirevolutionary argument concerns what it is collectively rational for the present generation to do. And if its members are predominantly egoistic, the determination of this will involve a substantial discounting of the long-run benefits of revolution relative to its short-run costs.

A second objection rests on the claim that citizens may know that a particular revolution would improve their lives because of the quality of the leaders of that revolution. This objection has some force. It might be replied, however, that many of the negative features of revolution—for example, economic devastation and the tendency toward bureaucratization—are essentially beyond the control of revolutionary leaders. Also, even initially admirable leaders may be corrupted by power, especially when they must rule over a divided and economically devastated country. And most important of all, ordinary citizens face a serious information problem in assessing the features of revolutionary leaders, since the latter have obvious motives to deceive the former about their own character and beliefs, the nature of postrevolutionary society, and so on. If citizens have no reliable way of distinguishing wise and moral revolutionary leaders from clever power-seekers, it is not rational for them to assume that a particular revolution will be atypically good in its effects because of its quality of leadership. Or, at least, they will discount this assumption in proportion to their rational uncertainty about the characteristics of the leadership.

There is, however, a more reliable basis for expecting a revolution to improve things. If the current regime is abnormally repressive or exploitive or inept, citizens could rationally expect, on statistical grounds, that what followed a revolution would likely be better. This third objection to the argument against revolution is strengthened if combined with the second: if the present government is extremely bad, and the revolutionary leaders seem exceptionally good, revolution might well be a good rational gamble for the citizenry.

It is interesting to note that, despite his unflinching opposition to revolution, Hobbes twice indirectly acknowledges the force of our third objection. He writes that our obligation of obedience to the State lapses when the State lacks the power to protect us, for "the end of obedience is protection."[66] By the same logic, it would appear to follow that our obligation lapses if the State has the power to protect us but patently does not do so. Then a repressive (or hopelessly ineffective) State that clearly fails to protect the citizenry, or identifiable groups within it, from the depredations of its own agents or other groups is owed no obedience by the nonprotected, who may rightly establish a rival revolutionary government to secure protection. Also, as we have previously noted, Hobbes allows that it is rational for needy and hardy men to seek a violent reshuffle of the social deck. But a repressed citizenry, or subgroup thereof, is likely to be needy and perhaps collectively hardy enough to bring off a reshuffle that will take care of their needs. If it is rational for needy and hardy individuals to rebel under these circumstances, would it not be equally rational for such *groups* to rebel under them?

Our third objection (implicitly acknowledged by Hobbes) implies that revolution is sometimes rational and that the scope of the above antirevolutionary argument must therefore be restricted. The natural restriction to impose, from the point of view of Hobbesian theory, limits the argument to revolts against the governments of *satisfactory* States. For a variety of reasons, revolts against the governments of satisfactory States are much more likely to be destructive of social utility than revolts against other States. People are likely to be better off in a satisfactory State, and hence there is more to lose and less likelihood of gain if the replacement State's features can be expected to be average. A satisfactory State is sure to have many ardent defenders; hence a successful revolt against it will likely have to be long and bloody. The motives of revolutionary leaders who seek to overthrow a satisfactory State are suspect; there is a greater risk that they will turn out to be either mere power-seekers or dangerous ideological fanatics. Finally, given citizen political liberties and government accountability within the satisfactory State, there are hopes for achieving needed or desired changes without violent revolution.

[66] *Leviathan,* chap. 21, p. 208.

When these considerations are added together, it appears most unlikely that citizen revolts against satisfactory States will often be expected utility maximizing.

Thus, there is a valid Hobbesian lesson to be drawn from the quasi-utilitarian argument against revolution. There is a *presumption* that a given revolution against an established State is irrational from the citizens' point of view, because of the likely heavy costs and highly uncertain gains. This presumption is especially strong, perhaps nearly nonoverridable, in the case of satisfactory States. But in the general case the presumption can be overridden: contra Hobbes, there can be collectively rational revolutions (and if the arguments of the last section are correct, individually rational revolutions as well).

This completes our discussion of security within the State. It may be, as Hobbes suggests—quoting the Book of Job—that this man-made leviathan *"is made so as not to be afraid. [It] seeth every high thing below [it]; and is king of all the children of pride."*[67] Yet we have seen that the State does not completely solve the security problems of individuals that Hobbes so perceptively revealed in his discussion of the state of nature. Even within the State, people remain somewhat vulnerable because of the military capacities of other States, the criminal activities of their fellows, the State's own capacity for repression, and the State's instability—its susceptibility to "intestine discord."[68] Nor can we agree with Hobbes that this last susceptibility can be fully removed by the use of reason.[69] Since political power rests substantially on mutual expectations, it is inherently vulnerable, to some degree, to escalating dissolution and collapse.

Despite these shortcomings of the State, it cannot be dispensed with. Our study of the interactions of rational predominantly self-interested agents has indicated that they would be physically and economically insecure without a State. And in a state of nature they would see it to be in their interests to establish a satisfactory State, since this would provide them with much greater—though

---

[67] Ibid., chap. 28, p. 307.
[68] Ibid., chap. 21, p. 208.
[69] Ibid., chap. 29, p. 308.

far from absolute—security. These are the most general conclusions of our descriptive account of rational interactions within and outside of the State. The normative structure that hangs on the skeleton provided by this descriptive account is the subject of Part II.

II

NORMATIVE THEORY

S E V E N

MORAL CONCEPTS

7-1. Facts and Values

Part I of this book consists of an exposition of the *descriptive* part
of Hobbesian theory. It proposes a general descriptive theory of
human nature and characterizes certain general background conditions of human life and interaction. From these, and certain
canons of rationality, a theoretical account of the origins and nature of conflict and cooperation among rational human beings—
both within and outside the State—is developed. The basic theme
of Part I is that certain tendencies toward conflict, and interfer-
ences with cooperation, are present in anarchical situations and
in non-State social groupings. These tendencies are greatly ameliorated, though not fully eliminated, by the founding of a State,
especially a satisfactory State.

A Hobbesian *normative* theory concerning how people ought
to act within and outside the State will be developed in this second part of the book. The basic theme of Part II is that the requirements of morality and the claims of self-interest can be generally reconciled. This theme has a venerable history, being clearly
discernible in Western moral thought at least as far back as Plato.
Recently, however, it has fallen into philosophical disrepute. We
shall show how it can be resurrected within the context of a general Hobbesian theory.

The two parts of Hobbesian theory are intimately connected.
Hobbesian descriptive theory poses the central problem which
Hobbesian normative theory must solve: given mutual vulnerability, predominant self-interest, and the dangers of unilateralism, how can cooperative moral behavior be expected or required

of rational individuals? At the same time, it provides the basic tools needed for the solution to that problem: the idea of present cooperation pursued partly as a means to future mutually beneficial cooperation, and the notion that the State is both a cause and an effect of such cooperation. But the influence between the parts of Hobbesian theory is not completely one-sided. Some features of the descriptive theory (e.g., the characteristics and circumstances of the social contractors) were selected with the normative applications of the theory in mind. And the normative account of political obligation worked out in Chapter 10, below, in effect completes the hypothetical contract theory that constitutes an important element of Hobbesian descriptive theory. Hence, the two parts of Hobbesian theory are somewhat mutually dependent, and to the extent that they fit together we may hope that they are mutually reinforcing and lend plausibility to one another.

It would be remiss, however, in the light of the themes of modern philosophical ethics, to attempt to base a normative moral and political theory on a purely descriptive theory without explaining how the problem posed by the so-called fact-value gap is to be treated. If we assume a sharp demarcation between, on the one hand, descriptive or factual concepts, and, on the other hand, normative or value concepts, it may seem problematic—as it apparently did to David Hume[1]—how a conclusion containing normative concepts (e.g., an "ought-judgment") could be derived from premises containing only descriptive concepts (i.e., "is-statements"). This transition from factual premises to normative conclusions clearly could be made if the relevant normative concepts were analyzable as logical combinations of purely descriptive concepts. But supporters of the notion of a fact-value gap assert, on various grounds, that such analysis is impossible. For example, G. E. Moore claims that it is an "open question" whether the referents of a given value term and the factual terms making up its purported analysis coincide; he concluded that the two cannot

---

[1] David Hume, *A Treatise of Human Nature*, ed. L. A. Selby-Bigge (Clarendon Press: Oxford, 1965), book III, part 1, chap. 1, pp. 469–70.

possibly mean the same thing.[2] And R. M. Hare contends that normative terms have a prescriptive, or action-guiding, force as part of their meaning, so that no logical combination of purely factual terms could mean the same as such terms.[3]

Fortunately, for our purposes, we need not evaluate these and other arguments for and against the existence of a fact-value gap. It will suffice instead to note the nature and plausibility of Hobbes's general strategy for bridging—or sidestepping—the purported gap. As its main tools, this strategy employs a plausible descriptive theory of human nature and a weak and noncontroversial conception of practical rationality. The theory of human nature posits that, as a matter of fact, human beings share certain dominant common ends, aims, or goals: security, continuation of life, and the avoidance of material deprivation. The weak conception of practical rationality says it is rational to pursue the necessary means to your ends. It follows that it is rational for each and all of us to pursue the necessary means to our dominant shared ends. If we now picture moral rules as action-guiding principles recommending pursuit of specific necessary means to these shared, or common, ends, we have grounded such rules in the requirements of practical reason and our natures. And if establishment of, and obedience to, the State is one of the specific necessary means of achieving these common ends, a rational justification of political obligation has been provided.

Of course, if there is a genuine fact-value gap, this strategy does not noncontroversially bridge it, for it assumes, as John Stuart Mill apparently did,[4] that universally shared ends are morally worthy ends, and this might be denied or be pictured as itself a controversial value judgment. There is, however, another way of looking at the matter that is more in line with Hobbes's own thinking. Suppose we accept the "ought implies can" principle as

[2] G. E. Moore, *Principia Ethica* (Cambridge: Cambridge University Press, 1903), chap. 1.

[3] R. M. Hare, *The Language of Morals* (New York: Oxford University Press, 1952), chap. 5.

[4] John Stuart Mill, *Utilitarianism* (Indianapolis: Bobbs-Merrill, 1957), chap. 4, pp. 44–45.

a logical or metaethical principle. That is, setting aside a compli-
cation to be discussed in section 7-5, we treat it as part of the
meaning of a moral ought-judgment that the agent is assumed to
be capable of doing what it is judged he ought to do. Then if
some of our dominant shared ends, like survival, are unavoidable
givens of our nature, rational beings with such natures will be
unable to avoid pursuing what they perceive to be the necessary
means to those ends. It follows that the requirements of any moral
system capable of effectively guiding human action must be compatible with undertaking these means, that is, these means must
be at least morally *permissible*. Here is a derivation of moral
permissions, if not ought-judgments, from facts (about our natures) and the logic of the moral concept "ought."

This general strategy of grounding moral principles on the shared
ends inherent in our human natures is carried out by Hobbes
using a variety of intertwined moral concepts: good, evil, rights,
obligation, justice, contract, covenant, and natural law. The task
of this preliminary chapter is to explain, and occasionally correct
and modify, Hobbes's analysis and use of many of these concepts. Only then may we turn to the main substantive issues of
morals and politics addressed by Hobbesian normative theory.

7-2. Good and Evil

In chapter 6 of *Leviathan*, Hobbes writes:

> But whatsoever is the object of any man's appetite or desire,
> that is it which he for his part calleth *good*: and the object
> of his hate and aversion *evil*. . . . For these words of good,
> evil, . . . are ever used with relation to the person that useth
> them: there being nothing simply and absolutely so; nor
> any common rule of good and evil, to be taken from the
> nature of the objects themselves; but from the person of the
> man, where there is no commonwealth; or, in a common-
> wealth, from the person that representeth it; or from an ar-

bitrator or judge, whom men disagreeing shall by consent set up, and make his sentence the rule thereof.[5]

For simplicity, let us focus on Hobbes's analysis of "good," assuming that the analysis of "evil" contains similar ambiguities and carries like implications. One thing is abundantly clear from this passage: Goodness is a *relational* concept; it applies not to objects and states of affairs in themselves, but to them as they stand in certain relations to people and their desires. However, the specific relational analysis implied by this passage is not so clear, and two major alternatives must be considered.

According to what we may call the *straightforward interpretation* of this passage, the first sentence offers an analysis of the concept of goodness and expressions making use of that concept. On the first variant of this interpretation, statements of the form "X is good" mean roughly "I, the speaker, desire (that) X." On the second variant, inspired by ethical emotivism, we capture the meaning of such statements by noting that they express the speaker's desire for, or approval of, X. The difficulties with each of these analyses of goodness are well known, having been noted by the emotivists,[6] and their critics,[7] respectively. But it is doubtful that Hobbes really intended to offer either analysis, for each conflicts with his clear view—stated in the second sentence of the above paragraph and elsewhere[8]—that what is good in *civil society* is determined by the sovereign, not by the various conflicting desires and opinions of private citizens. But the meaning of the concept of goodness must cohere with its primary use, which is, as Hobbes realized, as a tool of interpersonal discourse within civil society. Hence, if consistent, Hobbes could not have in-

[5] Hobbes, *Leviathan*, chap. 6, p. 41. Hobbes's references to contempt are deleted, as they are not germane to our purposes.

[6] See, e.g., Charles Stevenson, *Facts and Values* (New Haven: Yale University Press, 1964), p. 13. Stevenson takes the first variant of the straightforward interpretation to be Hobbes's view.

[7] See J. O. Urmson, *The Emotive Theory of Ethics* (New York: Oxford University Press, 1968).

[8] E.g., *Leviathan*, chap. 29, pp. 310–11.

tended to relativize the concept of goodness to individual persons *by its very meaning.*[9]

Attempting to reconcile the apparent personal relativism of Hobbes's analysis of good with his beliefs about goodness within the commonwealth leads to the *subtle interpretation* of the above-quoted paragraph. The key to this interpretation is the notion of a "common rule" or interpersonal standard of evaluation. Judgments of goodness explicitly or implicitly appeal to, or presuppose, such standards. To say that something is good of a kind (or for a purpose, or from a point of view) is to say, roughly, that it satisfies to a reasonable degree the standards of evaluation appropriate to things of that kind (or given that purpose or point of view). Such standards may be established in a variety of ways: by tradition, convention, explicit agreement, agreement on a party who shall set the standards followed by his enunciation of what the standards are, common acceptance of a purpose or objective or point of view that implies a particular standard, and so on.

Since judgments of goodness involve at least implicit appeals to purported common standards, several distinct sorts of disagreements can lead to conflicting judgments of goodness. There may be disagreement about application of a commonly accepted standard, as when one person asserts that Cadillacs are stylish while another denies it. Disagreements about what the appropriate standards are is also common. Some may treat safety and economy as evaluative standards for automobiles, while others regard them as irrelevant. Even when standards are agreed upon, people may differ over their relative weights and importance, either in general or in the specific case at hand. Thus, we might agree that Edsels are both rare and funny-looking but disagree on whether they are good cars because of differing views on the relative importance, in cars, of good looks and rarity.

The subtle interpretation, incorporating this picture of the

---

[9] In view of this difficulty, the straightforward interpretation can be saved only by assuming that, for Hobbes, (1) "good" has a different meaning in the state of nature and in civil society or (2) citizens not only should, but necessarily do, desire whatever the sovereign desires. I know of no textual support for either assumption.

meaning of judgments of goodness, fits all parts of the key paragraph under consideration. Goodness is not a feature of objects or states of affairs in themselves, but of their relations to standards of evaluation created and employed by people for human purposes. The standards or common rules of evaluation in civil society are those laid down by custom, tacit agreement, referees agreed to by the relevant parties, authorized public officials, or private arbitrators. (In this case, the term "good" is still used "with relation to" the user; the relation is the complex one of satisfying standards of evaluation embodied in customs accepted by the user or laid down and interpreted by an authority agreed to by the user.) Outside civil society—and presumably within civil society in matters wherein public standards have not been laid down or agreed to—an individual is free to choose his own standards of evaluation and to treat objects or states of affairs as good or evil according to his desires or preferences. But it is understood that the individual here labels things good "for his part," that is, from his own point of view. There is still a "common rule" of evaluation operating, but in this case it is a second-order rule: in the absence of common substantive or procedural standards of evaluation set down by public authorities, or explicitly or implicitly agreed to by the individuals involved, each is free to employ standards of evaluation reflecting his own personal preferences, desires, and point of view. This opens the way for disagreements about good and evil of all three types discussed in the last paragraph.

A somewhat different perspective on disagreement emerges if we remind ourselves of a point raised in section 1-2. Hobbes speaks as if it were only objects that we describe as good or evil, but more generally and more accurately it is states of affairs (including actions and states of persons) to which we apply these appellations. This is important in the present context, because it bears on the question as to whether opposed judgments about good and evil are prone to produce conflictual behavior. Imagine two persons, A and B, outside of civil society or dealing with a matter within civil society that has been left to their discretion by authorities. Suppose that they disagree over whether X is good. Is this likely to produce conflict? Not if we think of "X" literally as an object, for then such disagreement implies that one desires X while the other does not. Hence both will be satisfied if the former gets X and the latter does not. Conflicting judgments of good and evil here produce harmony of action rather than conflict.

It is by treating *states of affairs* as objects of desire and aversion, and as the referents of the terms "good" and "evil," that we see how conflicting judgments about what is good lead to practical conflicts. Suppose that our two parties A and B are situated as before and disagree about whether X is good or evil, where "X" now stands for some state of affairs, for example, "A having object O" or "institution of a progressive income tax in our civil society." This implies, on Hobbes's analysis, that one of them desires the existence of the state of affairs and is disposed to act to promote it, while the other is averse to the existence of that state of affairs and is disposed to act to prevent it. From conflicting judgements of good and evil, we are able to infer practical conflict (i.e., incompatible objectives) among the judgers.

The danger of such conflict between public authorities and private individuals is also present, should the latter presume the right to "judge of good and evil"[10] within the commonwealth, on matters decided by the authorities. In fact, Hobbes identifies such "private judgment of good and evil"[11] as one of the main causes of dissolution of States. Whether we agree with Hobbes about this, and its implications as regards freedom of speech and expression (see section 5-5), we can at least understand—given the subtle interpretation—what he means. He is saying that if individuals apply their own private standards of evaluation to social states of affairs, and act on these, rather than the standards and rulings laid down by public authorities, the activities of those authorities will tend to be thwarted. If, for example, some citizens judge as "evil" a foreign war called "good" by their sovereign, and act accordingly by withholding their physical and financial support, the war effort may fail.

[10] Ibid., p. 311.
[11] Ibid., p. 310, marginal heading.

The subtle interpretation of our key paragraph provides us with a not implausible account of judgments of goodness of states of affairs. According to that interpretation, Hobbes is telling us several things of interest in his remarks on good and evil. People's preferences and values differ, and, as a result, so do the standards of evaluation they apply to states of affairs in arriving at judgments of goodness. These differing standards and judgments tend to produce practical conflicts, which can be ameliorated by agreement on common standards or on authorities to enunciate and apply such standards. But unless individuals reach wide-ranging agreement on standards of evaluation or completely subordinate their judgments of goodness to those of public authorities, substantial sources of practical conflict will remain in the form of differing private values and standards of evaluation. As shall be seen later, we may view natural and civil laws as common public standards that limit and contain such conflict.

7-3. Rights

The concepts of good and evil, which were discussed in the last section, play only a limited role in Hobbes's moral and political philosophy. Of much greater importance is the concept of a right, and the various moral concepts that Hobbes defines in terms of rights.

We may distinguish three different, though closely related, concepts of rights that Hobbes employs. The weakest form of a right is a *permission right*. A party has a permission right to do something if and only if it is permissible for him to do it. A *noninterference right* consists in a permission right conjoined with an obligation on the part of others not to interfere with the agent's performance of the act in question. The strongest right is an *aid right*, which an agent possesses if and only if he has a noninterference right to do something and others are obligated to actively aid him in doing that thing.[12] The sovereign's rights to raise rev-

---

[12] To the extent that the distinction between aid and noninterference is fuzzy in particular contexts, the distinction between noninterference rights and aid rights will be similarly fuzzy in those contexts.

enue from citizens[13] and to conscript able-bodied persons into the armed forces "when the defence of the commonwealth, requireth at once the help of all that are able to bear arms"[14] are aid rights, for they require the active cooperation of citizens: handing over portions of their wealth and fighting for the commonwealth. An example of a noninterference right is the sovereign's right to punish lawbreakers, which consists in the permissibility of his punishing, together with the obligation of citizens "not to assist him who is to be punished."[15] The most important permission rights are the right of nature and its corollaries, which we discuss below.

Before turning to that discussion, a few points should be noted about the three concepts of rights we have distinguished. First, we have analyzed rights as rights to perform actions rather than as rights to objects. Hobbes himself uses both modes of analysis on occasion.[16] The action analysis is superior because it is more general and allows us to conveniently encompass rights to objects. Thus, a permission right to an object can be interpreted as the moral permission to *use* it, a noninterference right to an object can be interpreted as a permission to use it conjoined with an obligation of others not to use it (without one's approval), and so forth. Second, these analyses may, in principle, apply to rights that are either moral, legal, or both, depending upon whether the relevant permissions and obligations are moral, legal, or both. Finally, noninterference and aid rights will vary in scope according to how many others (e.g., everyone or some particular person) have the relevant obligations to not interfere or to aid. As a result, a noninterference right to perform a given action, if of broad enough scope, may be more valuable than an aid right, of narrower scope, to perform the same action.

Modern theorists distinguish conventional or legal rights, whose existence depends on social rules, from human or natural rights,

[13] *Leviathan*, chap. 18, pp. 166, 167–68.
[14] Ibid., chap. 21, p. 205.
[15] *Philosophical Rudiments*, chap. 6, sec. 5, p. 75. The same view is expressed at *Leviathan*, chap. 21, p. 205, but at chap. 28, p. 297, Hobbes suggests that the sovereign's right to punish is an aid right.
[16] Cf., e.g., *Leviathan*, chap. 14, p. 116 (quoted below) and p. 117.

which all human persons possess simply by virtue of being human.[17] The foundational right of Hobbes's moral and political system is, in this sense, a natural human right. This *right of nature* he defines as "the liberty each man hath, to use his own power, as he will himself, for the preservation of his own nature; that is to say, of his own life; and consequently, of doing any thing, which in his own judgment, and reason, he shall conceive to be the aptest means thereunto."[18] Given Hobbes's official definition of liberty as "absence of external impediments,"[19] ascribing to us a right of nature amounts to asserting that there are no external impediments to our using our power to preserve our lives. But depending upon how we interpret this claim, it is either false or tautological and useless, for mountains, storms, floods, plagues, deserts, and wolves—to say nothing of the actions of other people—sometimes are external obstacles to our using our power to preserve our lives, if "preserve" is taken as a success verb. That is, people not infrequently succumb to these life-threatening objects and events, despite their own best efforts to survive. But, one might respond, such external objects never prevent us from using our powers to *try* to survive, for our powers are internal to us, and therefore no purely external impediment can preclude their use. This maneuver preserves the right of nature, however, only by rendering it empty and useless. What would be the point of ascribing to us a right that amounts to no more than the observation that no purely external impediments can prevent the exercise of a purely internal faculty?

Hobbes is surely after more than this. In ascribing to us a right of nature, he means to attribute to us only a certain *kind* of liberty, or—in negative terms—the absence of only certain kinds of external constraints or impediments. The sort of impediments he has in mind are normative ones—legal rules, moral principles, obligations, and so on. In saying that we have a right of nature, he is saying that as human beings we are under no natural *nor-*

---

[17] See, e.g., H. L. A. Hart, "Are There Any Natural Rights?" in *Human Rights*, ed. A. I. Melden (Belmont, Calif.: Wadsworth, 1970).

[18] *Leviathan*, chap. 14, p. 116.

[19] Ibid.

mative restrictions on our pursuit of self-preservation. Physical obstacles to our survival there may be; moral or legal ones there are not—at least until we consent to or create them. This is a controversial claim that we shall discuss in section 8-1, but at least it is understandable and makes sense, unlike the claim that there are no external impediments to our pursuit of survival.

Our account of the meaning of the right of nature is confirmed by the main corollary that Hobbes attempts to derive from the existence of that right. He claims that in the state of nature everyone has a right to all things. But let us say that two parties have *competitive rights* if each party's exercising his right would constitute an external impediment to the other's use of his power to exercise his right. For example, my right and your right to consume this particular piece of cake are competitive in this sense. Hobbes recognizes that there are competitive rights. He says, "The effect which redoundeth to one man, by another man's defect of right, is but so much diminution of impediments to the use of his own right"[20] or, in other words, "One man's right is another's impediment." But if any competitive right were ever exercised in the state of nature, as surely some would be, all cannot have rights to all things, if this implies absence of all external impediments. Such an exercise, by definition, would constitute an external impediment to another's use of his power to exercise his right. Thus, we have further reason to shy away from Hobbes's stated definition of liberty and to define the right of nature in terms of the absence of external *normative* constraints on action.

How does Hobbes attempt to derive the right to all things from the right of nature? Schematized and adapted to our interpretation of rights as action rights, the argument goes as follows.[21]

(1) For any action X, if one believes that doing X is necessary for one's preservation, one has a right to do X.

(2) Since a state of nature is a war of all against all, *any* action may be (and hence may be believed to be) necessary for one's preservation in a state of nature.

[20] Ibid., p. 118.
[21] Ibid., p. 117.

(3) Therefore, in a state of nature, for all actions X, one has a right to do X.[22]

Premise (1) is simple a statement of the right of nature. Given the arguments of Chapter 2 about life in the state of nature, premise (2) is not implausible, if tacitly restricted to exclude suicidal actions. But the inference to conclusion (3) from the premises exhibits a clear modal fallacy.[23] One might just as well argue that since whoever marries Jack will be his wife, and any woman might possibly marry Jack, therefore every woman is Jack's wife. From universal possible possession of a property (e.g., being necessary for defense, or marrying Jack) and universal implication of another property by that one (e.g., being necessary for defense implying being rightful, marrying Jack implying being Jack's wife), one can only infer universal *possible* possession of the latter property (e.g., any act may be rightful, any woman may be Jack's wife), not its universal *actual* possession (e.g., all acts are rightful, all women are Jack's wives). Therefore, from (1) and (2) we may not infer (3), but only such weaker conclusions as:

(3')   Therefore, for all acts X, in a state of nature, one may have a right to do X.

(3'') Therefore, for all acts X, there exist circumstances that could arise in any state of nature (namely, X being believed necessary for self-preservation), such that, *in those circumstances*, one would have a right to do X.

These conclusions express two points that Hobbes would surely have accepted. No (nonsuicidal) act is such that we can a priori rule out its being done with right. And there are specifiable circumstances which would render any nonsuicidal act rightful in the state of nature. Hobbes might wish to add that, in the warlike

---

[22] In *Elements of Law* (part 1, chap. 1. secs. 10–11, pp. 84–85) and *Philosophical Rudiments* (chap. 1, secs. 10–12, pp. 9–11), the war of all is treated as a corollary of the right to all things. This is reversed in *Leviathan*. The exposition of this book, which treats the descriptive war-of-all argument as independent and the normative right-to-all-things argument as derivative, follows *Leviathan*.

[23] The (invalid) argument form it exhibits is:

(x) (A(x) ⊃ B(x))

(x) (◊ A(x))

_____

(x) B(x)

conditions of the state of nature, there can be no other judge of whether those circumstances are present than the individual or his own conscience.[24] But beyond this, his premises do not allow him to go. Still, we have already arrived on contentious moral ground, for (3') and (3'') imply that deadly attacks, even against innocent parties, may be permissible under certain circumstances. Whether this is so is a difficult issue, to which we shall return in section 8-1.

The concept of a right is central to Hobbes's entire scheme of moral concepts in that he defines many of these other concepts—obligation, contract, covenant, justice—in terms of rights. The basic notion that he employs is the idea of *laying down* a right, and the kinds of rights he has in mind in characterizing this notion are permission rights derived from the right of nature. To lay down a right, for Hobbes, is to give up the liberty of interfering with another's exercise of what we earlier labeled a competitive right. It is to place oneself under a normative constraint not to interfere with certain of his possible actions. Rights can be laid down in either of two ways. One *transfers* a right when one accepts a constraint for the benefit of a certain party, and one *renounces* a right in taking on the constraint when one "cares not to whom the benefit thereof redoundeth."[25] Note that this account works fairly well if we imagine everyone starting from a state-of-nature position with permission rights to all things. To lay down a right is to surrender the permission to interfere with some possible acts of others, thereby giving these others the benefit of freer, less costly, or more effective action. If you give up the permission to interfere with certain classes of action (e.g., using a piece of land) by anyone, you have renounced your right, and the benefit of your noninterference may fall on anyone. If you only surrender your permission to interfere with certain particular parties, but retain it with respect to others, you have transferred your right to the former, and they in particular will benefit.

This reasonably neat picture falls apart when we consider one

[24] *Philosophical Rudiments*, chap. 1, secs. 9–10, pp. 9–10.
[25] *Leviathan*, chap. 14, pp. 118–19.

frequent consequence of the laying down of a permission right: creation of a right of noninterference. By renouncing a natural permission right, I create a noninterference right (with respect to me) for all those who have retained their own permission rights with respect to the matter in question. By transferring such a right, I create a noninterference right (with respect to me) for the specific party to whom I transfer the right, assuming that this party has retained his permission. At this point, complex noninterference rights consisting of conjunctions of permissions and obligations of noninterference exist. But transfer and renunciation of *such* rights do not fit Hobbes's definitions at all. Your renouncing such a right may consist in (1) releasing me from my obligation of noninterference or (2) surrendering your permission to do the act in question or (3) both of these. Different parties benefit to different degrees and in different ways, depending upon the sort of renunciation in question. Similarly, your transferring a noninterference right against me can amount to a number of different things. You may transfer my obligation not to interfere to a third party—now I may interfere with you but not him. You may yourself undertake an obligation not to interfere with a third party, or you may do both—rendering him the double treasure of my noninterference and yours. Or you may pledge your noninterference to one party and transfer my obligation to another. As these transactions multiply, so do the complexities of the rights involved and the possible senses of renunciation and transfer. The simple distinction between these two notions offered by Hobbes will not do once noninterference rights have entered the picture.

Be that as it may, the central insight of Hobbes's account of laying down a right remains intact. Surrendering a moral permission amounts to placing oneself under a moral constraint. This insight leads from rights to the definitions of a number of significant moral concepts.

7-4. Obligations

To lay down a right, Hobbes tells us, is to place oneself under an *obligation*.[26] If, for example, you perform the voluntary act of

[26] Ibid.

transferring your right to do X to party Y, you (the obligor) are then under an obligation *to* Y (the obligee) not to do X. This account emphasizes three key features of obligation that are frequently noted by contemporary theorists.[27] (1) Obligations are created by *voluntary actions* of the obligor. (2) Obligations have a *specific content* (e.g., to perform or not perform certain actions), which is determined at least partly by the obligation-creating act. (3) Obligations are owned *to specific other parties*.[28]

The assumption of obligations or—what amounts to the same thing—the laying down of rights may be either mutual and reciprocal, or not. In the latter case, the obligor has rendered a *free gift* to his obligee.[29] In the former case, we have a *contract* between the parties, in which each owes performance of his part to the other. Contracts in which one or more parties are called on to perform their parts as some time after the contract is made are *covenants*; in particular, if both are to perform later and in sequence, we have a *covenant of mutual trust*.[30]

Hobbes offers two accounts of unjust actions, assuming that just acts can be simply characterized as those that are not unjust.[31] The narrower account of injustice defines it as failing to perform one's part of a covenant.[32] The wider account defines injustice as any breach of obligation.[33] Hobbes apparently finds the narrower account tempting because he feels that incentives for injustice are greatest in the case of covenants—first performers may be unwilling to accept the danger of unilateral compli-

---

[27]See, e.g., Rawls, *A Theory of Justice*, p. 113; A. John Simmons, *Moral Principles and Political Obligations* (Princeton: Princeton University Press, 1979), chap. 1; and Richard Brandt, "The Concepts of Obligation and Duty," *Mind* 73 (July 1964): 374–93.

[28]An obligation undertaken by complete renunciation of a natural right produces the atypical limiting case of an obligation owed to each and every person.

[29]*Leviathan*, chap. 14, p. 121. As noted in section 2-3, Hobbes (in *Leviathan*) actually defines free gifts as surrenders of right in hopes of receiving future benefits. In line with our rejection of Psychological Egoism, we here offer a repaired definition that does not presuppose egoism.

[30]Ibid., pp. 120–21, 124.

[31]Ibid., chap. 15, p. 131.

[32]Ibid.

[33]Ibid., chap. 14, p. 119.

ance, while second performers may seek the advantages of unilateral noncompliance. Still, the wider account seems to be preferable. It encompasses the narrower definition of injustice as a special case, since to break a covenant is to violate an obligation, and it allows that violations of noncovenantal obligations—those created by free gifts and contracts in which both parties perform at the time of agreement—are injustices. Hobbes clearly implies that this is so as regards free gifts. He says that recipients of free gifts are *due*, or merit, performance, just as are first performers of covenants.[34] Further, as we shall note in section 10-1, he claims that citizens do injustice to a sovereign if they take from him the rights of sovereignty, which he receives from them through free gift rather than contract. It would be silly not to extend this point to cover violations of noncovenantal contracts, for example, the surreptitious switching of what you hand over at the time of an agreement to trade immediately. Hobbes would have no reason to deny that such violations of contract are injustices; hence, the wider definition encompassing free gifts and all contracts shall be taken as his favored account.

To summarize all this, we may say that an obligation is created by the voluntary act of laying down a right, which may take the form of a free gift or a contract, some of the latter of which are covenants. A person has due to him what another is under an obligation to provide him, and injustice is done when an obligation is not fulfilled, and never otherwise. The main idea that filters through this set of definitions is that the moral relations among people described by such terms as "obligation," "due," "free gift," "contract," "covenant," "justice," and "injustice" are created by those people's actions. As Hobbes puts it, "There [is] no obligation on any man, which ariseth not from some act of his own."[35] Thus, Hobbes (and Hobbesian theory to the extent that it follows him) adopts a purely *voluntarist* account of moral obligation and justice—one's moral obligations and duties of justice are limited to those things to which one has, in some sense,

[34] Ibid., p. 123.
[35] Ibid., chap. 21, p. 203.

305

agreed or consented. This idea will seem less outrageous when we come to see that the relevant sort of agreement may be purely hypothetical (section 10-3), and that duties of justice (in this narrow sense) and moral obligations are not the only kinds of moral requirements that constrain our behavior (sections 7-5 and 9-1 through 10-1).

For the moment, however, let us focus on straightforward obligations created by an agent voluntarily transferring a right to another. We believe, as Hobbes did, that morally speaking one should fulfill such obligations unless released from them by the party to whom they are owed (or perhaps by other overriding considerations). But how is this belief to be justified? Hobbes offers two justificatory arguments, one applying specifically to obligations, the other applying to a wider class of requirements that includes obligations. The latter argument is most conveniently considered later,[36] but the former, since it applies only to obligations, may be dealt with here. Hobbes suggests that injustice (in the wide sense of violating obligations) is "somewhat like" absurdity, which involves contradicting what one earlier maintained, for injustice involves voluntarily undoing what one has earlier voluntarily done.[37]

There is a germ of an interesting idea here. The basic purpose of linguistic assertion is to communicate information by expressing one's beliefs about the world. If one asserts "P" and then, without explicitly or implicitly withdrawing this assertion, asserts "not P," one necessarily leaves one's listeners baffled concerning one's beliefs about the state of the world (is it "P" or "not P"?) and thus fails to carry out the very purpose of assertion. The basic purpose of people undertaking obligations to others is to coordinate actions by allowing the obligee to rely firmly on the obligor to act as he has obligated himself to act. Suppose, however, that one obligates oneself to another to perform some act and then does not perform. Then the basic purpose of coordination via reliance will not be achieved. If the other party has ra-

---

[36] See Chapter 9 in this book. See also the discussion of Hobbes's reply to the Fool in section 4-3.

[37] *Leviathan*, chap. 14, p. 119.

tionally conditioned his actions on the assumption that you will act as obligated to, there will necessarily be a failure of coordination, in the sense that the combination of your actions and his will fail (except perhaps by accident) to achieve his purposes. So injustice is like absurdity in this respect: instances of each necessarily fail to fulfill the fundamental purposes of the general speech-act types that respectively make them possible, undertaking obligations and making assertions. However, whether this observation even shows that just action is *as morally important* as truth-telling, depends on the relative importance of the purposes of the two relevant speech-act types: coordination and communication. Hence, Hobbes's suggestion of likeness between absurdity and injustice provides, at best, a fragment of a moral justification for fulfilling one's obligations. Achieving more than this requires viewing the fulfillment of obligations within the general moral framework provided by the Hobbesian theory of natural law.

Before leaving the subject of obligation, it will be useful to briefly consider the skeptical objection that Hobbes has no genuine concept or theory of obligation. This objection, which has several variants, is ultimately answered by the overall account of Hobbesian normative theory developed in the remaining chapters. Since, however, the objection is important, and the material which comprises an answer to it is not concentrated in a single section or chapter, an explanation of why the objection fails will be provided here.

The most radical version of the objection says that Hobbes has no genuine concept of being obligated to do something, as opposed to being obliged to do it by threat of punishment. This radical objection derives from certain passages in which Hobbes indicates that fear—not the inherent bindingness of obligations—is what primarily motivates people to live up to their obligations.[38] But that Hobbes believes there are problems concerning motivating people to live up to their obligations does not imply

---

[38] See, e.g., ibid., chap. 14, pp. 119, 128–29. I thank Russell Hardin for suggesting that the skeptical objection about obligation be explicitly addressed and for drawing my attention to one of these passages.

that he is using something other than our standard normative concept of obligation. As noted above, his account of obligation fits with that of modern writers, and he attempts to provide a normative justification for performing one's obligations in his argument about the absurdity of injustice. This argument cannot sensibly be extended to cover cases of being obliged by force or threat. Hence, in offering it, Hobbes clearly had in mind a concept of obligation distinct from being obliged to act by force or threat.

As we shall see in section 9-1, Hobbes also justifies fulfilling obligations by treating the keeping of agreements as a "law of nature" or rule of his rule-egoistic moral theory. This observation might lead to a second version of the skeptical objection: Hobbes has no theory of *moral* obligation, because his laws of nature are not binding in the state of nature and because genuine moral obligations cannot be grounded in egoistic considerations. This objection is answered in sections 9-2 and 9-3, where it is argued that the laws of nature are binding in the state of nature and that a *rule*-egoistic system of the Hobbesian type satisfies all the appropriate criteria for being a moral system.

One might, however, acknowledge that Hobbes has a concept (and theory) or moral obligation, but still doubt that he has an account of *political* obligation which is distinct from the notion of obedience to the overwhelming power of the State. As will be discussed in section 10-2, Hobbes sometimes grounds political duty on forced promises of obedience to a conqueror. Fortunately, however, Hobbes also has a hypothetical consent theory (see sections 1-3, 5-1, and 10-3) which provides a normative justification for obedience to the State. The presence of this hypothetical consent theory, together with Hobbes's rule-egoistic moral system, refutes the claim that accounts of political and moral obligation are lacking in *Leviathan*.[39]

[39] The term "political obligation" usually refers to any valid moral requirement of obedience to the State, not just those grounded in actual consent. In other words, political obligations need not be "obligations" in the sense used by Hobbes and characterized earlier in this section.

7-5. *Ought-Principles*

Most moral systems contain general action-guiding (i.e., prescriptive) rules concerning how people ought to behave and ought not to behave. These may be very few in number and highly general—such as the utilitarian prescription to maximize utility or the Kantian imperative to treat people as ends rather than as means only—or more numerous and somewhat more specific, such as the Ten Commandments of traditional Judeo-Christian morality. Even in the latter case, however, the rules cover general classes of actions, are thought to apply to all irrespective of whether they have agreed to them, and state requirements for action that (usually) are not owed to particular other parties. Such rules are thus clearly distinct from obligations, as we have characterized them. Because they state how one ought to and ought not to act, we shall call them (moral) *ought-principles*.[40]

The ought-principles of Hobbes's moral system, and Hobbesian theory, are the *laws of nature*.[41] Hobbes defines these, roughly, as general rules, discovered by reason, that prescribe adopting the necessary means of self-preservation and avoiding those things which tend toward loss of one's life.[42] Hence, the laws of nature are grounded in self-interest and may be considered rules of rational prudence.[43] The fundamental law of nature tells us to seek peace as the necessary means of preservation in a world of mutual vulnerability, rough equality, and potential conflict. The other laws of nature prescribe other modes of behavior (e.g., justice, gratitude, mutual accommodation) as means to, or parts of, peace.

---

[40] Hobbes does not use the term "ought" frequently, and when he does it is not used as here suggested. Hence the distinction drawn in this section between obligations and ought-principles is usually described in the secondary literature as a distinction between two concepts of obligation in Hobbes's work. See, e.g., D. D. Raphael, *Hobbes: Morals and Politics* (London: George Allen & Unwin, 1977), pp. 32–34.

[41] The laws of nature will be discussed in more detail in Chapter 9.

[42] *Leviathan*, chap. 14, pp. 116–17.

[43] See section 9-1 for elaboration. In describing the means of peace, the laws of nature characterize the means of living decently or well, not the means of bare survival. See sections 2-6 and 3-2.

But the laws of nature have a conditional form: "Do X, provided that others are doing so." They require reciprocal, but not unilateral, forbearance.[44] Obligations, the sort of specific moral requirements discussed in the last section, derive their moral backing from the third law of nature, which says we must fulfill our covenants (obligations). And as suggested in section 7-2, the laws of nature provide (the only possible) interpersonal standards of good and evil in the state of nature, by identifying and prescribing common necessary means to the satisfaction of each person's basic desire to survive. Thus, the ought-principles expressed in the laws of nature are the fundamental, as well as most general, moral requirements within Hobbes's theory.

Why are these fundamental principles grounded in considerations of prudence and reciprocal in form? The answer, for Hobbes and Hobbesian theory, is that if moral systems are to be *practical* their requirements must link up in appropriate ways with people's motivational capacities. Rules of conduct grounded in prudence, and reciprocal in form, connect with two of the most ubiquitous and reliable of human motivations: rational self-interest and a sense of reciprocity or fair play. They are therefore much less likely to enmesh moral theory in problems concerning motivation than are principles requiring unilateral action or impartial concern for the welfare of all.

Much the same point can be approached from a different direction. As has been extensively documented by Howard Warrender,[45] Hobbes, though he does not often speak directly on the matter, is committed to the "ought implies can" doctrine—that is, he holds, as do many contemporary philosophers, that it is the case that a person ought to perform an act only if he is *capable* of performing it, where this includes being capable of being motivated to perform it.[46] When conjoined with Psychological Egoism—at least in the form that says we are, by nature, purely self-interested creatures—this doctrine implies that moral ought-prin-

[44]See section 9-1. See also my "Right Reason and Natural Law in Hobbes's Ethics," *The Monist* 66 (January 1983): 120–33.
[45]Warrender, *Political Philosophy of Hobbes*, pp. 23–26, 32–33, 87–97.
[46]Ibid., pp. 23–26.

ciples can require of an individual only conduct consistent with his self-interest (or believed by him to be so consistent). For the individual would be motivationally incapable of performing acts known to be against his interests. This strict implication does not hold in Hobbesian philosophy, wherein Psychological Egoism has been replaced by Predominant Egoism. Even here, however, compliance with the theory's ought-principles must generally be compatible with the agent's interests, or else these principles will often be impossible to follow and hence be nonapplicable.

We should not, however, endorse the "ought implies can" doctrine in unrestricted form. Though an ought-judgment is normally canceled by a true claim of incapacity, it may not be so canceled if the agent himself is culpable for the incapacity or has previously waived his right to claim the incapacity as a defense. We do not, for example, withdraw our judgment that the watchman ought to have stopped the midnight robbery when he points out he was unable to do so because he was sound asleep at the time. Culpable incapacity, like culpable ignorance, is no excuse.[47]

Hobbes apparently recognized this.[48] He generally held that one ought not and cannot be bound to act against one's own interests. And in at least one work he explicitly links this to one's incapacity to so act, thus relying on the "ought implies can" doctrine.[49] Yet he notes several special cases in which one ought or is bound to act in a way that is believed to be against one's interests. All involve situations created by previous voluntary acts of one's own that in effect waive the right to claim incapacity. If you are foolish enough, in the state of nature, to covenant to perform first, and no new reasonable cause of suspicion of the second party arises, you must perform despite the grave danger of being cheated and harmed.[50] Similarly, if you are so rash as to covenant with a heretic, or someone with a known past record of

---

[47] The relationship between culpable ignorance and culpable incapacity is briefly explored in Holly Smith, "Culpable Ignorance," *Philosophical Review* (October 1983): 543–71, sec. II.

[48] Warrender unfortunately overlooks this point in his otherwise excellent discussion of the "ought implies can" doctrine.

[49] *Philosophical Rudiments*, chap. 2, secs. 14 and 18, pp. 23, 25–26.

[50] *Leviathan*, chap. 14, pp. 124–25.

cheating, you are not freed of your obligation by the other party's presumed untrustworthiness.[51] The same applies to the special Hobbesian covenant by which the State is formed. In joining in it, you tacitly consent to the rule of whatever sovereign is then elected by the majority, and you are bound to obey him even if you regard him as foolish and dangerous.[52] Other voluntary acts (e.g., accepting pay as a soldier or office as a Christian pastor) may even obligate you to risk or accept death.[53] Finally, Hobbes directly implies that culpable inability is no excuse in two cases involving the obligation to obey the civil law. He says that a person's obligation to obey is canceled by his ignorance of the law "not proceeding from his own default" or by his capture by the enemy "if it be without his own fault."[54] This clearly indicates that the obligation remains in cases in which the agent *is* culpable for his own ignorance or capture, and the resulting inability to obey the law.

Is the restriction which Hobbes imposes on the "ought implies can" doctrine a reasonable and correct one? It might be thought not, on the grounds that it does not cohere with the most plausible justification of the doctrine itself. This justification says that ought-judgments are by their nature action-guiding and tell agents how to act in the case at hand and relevantly similar cases. But this function cannot be served by an ought-judgment that directs performance of an act the agent cannot perform.[55] Hence, ought-judgments must presuppose relevant abilities to act on the part of agents, that is, "ought implies can."

We may, however, accept this sort of justification of the "ought implies can" doctrine and still endorse Hobbes's restriction on that doctrine, for an ought-judgment requiring an act of which the agent is incapable can still perform an important function in special circumstances, that is, when the agent gets in an undesirable situation of incapacity due to his own prior acts. The ought-

[51] Ibid., chap. 15, p. 135.
[52] Ibid., chap. 18, pp. 162–63.
[53] Ibid., chap. 21, p. 205; chap. 45, pp. 655–56.
[54] Ibid., chap. 26, p. 257; chap. 27, p. 288.
[55] See, e.g., Hare, *Freedom and Reason*, chap. 4.

judgment, in this case, in effect directs people to avoid the prior act and acts of its kind. In particular, ought-judgments sustained by Hobbes's restriction guide people away from acquiring incapacities they should not have (e.g., the guard's inability to stop the robbery) or from agreeing to actions, commitments, or responsibilities that they may not be able to carry out because of motivational incapacities (e.g., a timorous man volunteering for the infantry). Of course, once the prior faulty act is done and the fatal incapacity is acquired or others come to rely on promises of performance the agent cannot live up to, the agent cannot be guided by an ought-judgment into doing what he cannot do. But such judgments rendered earlier may motivate the agent to avoid the commitment or incapacity (e.g., the guard either resigns or drinks coffee to stay awake), and those rendered at the time of action or later may usefully instruct the agent and others as regards similar future situations. So ought-judgments may be action-guiding, in a broad but genuine sense, when they fall under Hobbes's restriction of the "ought implies can" doctrine.

One might still worry that the action-guiding force of such ought-judgments is *superfluous*, and hence that the judgments themselves are pointless. In such cases, there will always be a prior wrongful act on which blame, and an action-guiding ought-judgment, can be focused. We can, for example, simply blame guards for falling asleep on duty, rather than for allowing the robberies that result.

This is true. But there are some reasons for blaming the sleeping guards for allowing the robberies as well and for asserting that they ought to have prevented them. As a matter of psychological fact, it seems easier to blame and judge (and accept blame and judgment) when a significant harm has actually occurred than when a self-imposed incapacity merely risks harm. Also, it may be difficult or costly to monitor and identify wrongful incapacitating acts (e.g., guards sleeping on duty) and relatively easy and cheap to determine that harms (e.g., robberies) have occurred that certain parties were responsible for preventing. Similar considerations apply to those (like the timorous volunteer) who waive their right to use incapacity as an excuse. Hence, there are good

313

practical reasons for applying ought-judgments and rejecting incapacity as an excuse, when there is prior waiver of the excuse or the agent is culpable with respect to the incapacity. Hobbes's restriction on the "ought implies can" doctrine is vindicated.

These observations are important for Hobbesian theory, because Hobbes uses the "ought implies can" doctrine (in conjunction with the right of nature) to support certain significant but controversial claims about the right of self-defense. His arguments on this matter are problematic and unclear, though, and do not take sufficient account of his own restriction of the "ought implies can" doctrine. In the next chapter, we attempt to clear up, and clean up, these arguments, which involve Hobbes's key moral concept of laying down a right.

EIGHT

THE RIGHT OF
SELF-PRESERVATION

8-1. The Right of Nature

The foundational right of Hobbes's normative system is an un-limited and inalienable right of self-preservation that he calls the *right of nature*. However, Hobbes's discussions of this right and its implications are full of errors. This chapter attempts to clarify and correct Hobbes's position on self-defense and self-preserva-tion. It does so by accepting (with some qualms) the unlimited right of nature but rejecting the poorly argued claim that this right is inalienable. We begin in this section by clarifying the main features of Hobbes's right of nature and the problems its postulation presents for Hobbesian theory.

As noted earlier, Hobbes defines the right of nature as "the liberty each man hath, to use his own power, as he will himself, for the preservation of his own nature; that is to say, of his own life; and consequently, of doing any thing, which in his own judgment, and reason, he shall conceive to be the aptest means thereunto."[1] No argument is ever offered for ascribing this nat-ural right to us, and all other rights are derived, by Hobbes, from it. Hence, it functions as a normative *postulate* of Hobbes's moral theory.

The right of nature is only a permission right—its possession does not imply that others have any obligation to stand out of your way as you pursue your own preservation. But it does as-cribe a genuine moral permission, and thus characterizes self-

[1] *Leviathan*, chap. 14, p. 116.

315

preservation as a sufficient justification for action, not merely as an excuse or mitigating circumstance. Further, it is an *unlimited* right—any sort of act, no matter how harmful to others, would be sanctioned by it, provided this act was reasonably believed by the agent to be necessary to his preservation.[2] Nor is the right one of self-defense in some narrow sense, for example, fending off actual attacks on one's person. It is a broad right of self-preservation that includes the right to the physical means of existence and can sanction conquest and preemptive attack in the state of nature.[3]

Should we incorporate Hobbes's right of nature into our Hobbesian philosophy? Since it is the foundational postulate of his moral theory, we have strong reason to do so. On the other hand, there is an apparent clash between our intuitions about certain hypothetical cases and Hobbes's claim that the right of self-preservation is unlimited. The hypothetical cases in which our right of self-preservation seems to be limited fall into roughly three classes: those involving prior acts of our own that surrender or forfeit parts of our right, cases involving property rights, and cases involving the preservation and bodily integrity of other innocent parties.

Consider cases of surrender or forfeiture first. One may explicitly or tacitly commit oneself to not doing all one can to preserve oneself if certain contingencies arise. Thus, it may be wrong for a hired bodyguard to flee to save his life when his employer is attacked, or for a participant in a lifeboat lottery to refuse to jump overboard once he has lost. One may also be limited in one's rightful self-preserving actions if the threatening situation has been created by one's own intentional misconduct, recklessness, or negligence. For example, if you have maliciously, recklessly, or negligently spilled much of the lifeboat's limited supply of food overboard, you hardly have a claim to an equal share of

---

[2] See the discussion of the right to all things in section 7-3. Perhaps charitably, the phrase "and reason" in Hobbes's definition of the right of nature is interpreted as implying that the agent's belief in the necessity of the act must be reasonable.

[3] *Leviathan*, chap. 21, p. 204, chap. 13, pp. 110–11; chap. 14, p. 117.

what is left, and certainly are not permitted to take for yourself whatever you need.

It also seems that property rights of others sometimes limit one's own right of self-preservation. If we each need the one dose of medicine to live and you legitimately own the dose, it would be wrong for me to take it from you. Similarly, when others are not responsible for the danger we are in (i.e., when they are "innocent" in the relevant sense), their rights of self-preservation and bodily integrity may limit what one may permissibly do to preserve oneself. If a powerful gang credibly threatens to kill you unless you murder some innocent person (who would otherwise survive), you may not do so. If you need a kidney transplant from a particular person to survive, it would be wrong for you to have him kidnapped and the kidney transplanted against his will.[4]

Our intuitions about limits on the right of self-preservation seem firm and wide-ranging enough to pose a serious challenge to Hobbes's claim that the right of nature is unlimited. Within Hobbes's own philosophy, one might construct a three-part response to this challenge. First, there is the observation that we may sometimes sacrifice the lives of other innocents to save our own—if, for example, an innocent person is falling toward you from a great height so that standing still would save him but kill you, it is perfectly permissible for you to step aside. If we may sacrifice the innocent here, why not in other cases? Second, lifeboat lottery cases may be regarded as involving invalid covenants of mutual trust in the state of nature. Thus, you can reasonably refuse to abide by the results of a lifeboat lottery that you lose, on the grounds that you have no assurance that the other party or parties would have complied had he or they lost. Third, and finally, it may be argued that it would be *unfair* to punish anyone for harming others as a necessary means of preserving himself, for it is probable that many or most in the group doing the punishment, or the group in whose name the punishment is ap-

[4] For discussion of a similar case, see Judith J. Thomson, "A Defense of Abortion," *Philosophy & Public Affairs* 1 (Fall 1971): 47–66.

plied, would have done the same had they been in similar circumstances.

But this piecemeal response is too weak and too narrow. The third argument, even if accepted, would at most show that self-preservation can *excuse* anything, not that it justifies anything or renders it permissible. The supposed lesson of the first argument—that the innocent may be sacrificed to our preservation—cannot be generalized without ignoring certain potentially significant moral distinctions (e.g., between killing and letting die) and running afoul of intuitions about cases that are just as firm as the intuition upon which the "lesson" is based. Finally, the second argument, if sound, covers only one type of case (lifeboat lotteries) among the several in which it initially seems that the right of self-preservation is circumscribed by the rights of others.

A more systematic defense of an unlimited right of nature might be based on the "ought implies can" principle. According to this argument, if we are psychologically *incapable* of refraining from acts we reasonably think necessary for our preservation, then it cannot be the case that we ought to so refrain. However, as will emerge in our discussion of the inalienability of the right of self-defense in the next two sections, there are significant flaws in this argument. These flaws undercut both the above defense of an unlimited right of nature and Hobbes's claim that this right is inalienable.

Jettisoning this latter claim, however, leaves Hobbesian philosophy in a position to reconcile an unlimited right of nature with the fact that our intuitions imply limits on the right of self-preservation, for we may hold that the right of self-preservation is initially unlimited in a pure state-of-nature situation but can be limited by one's own actions and commitments, and is so limited—by explicit or tacit consent—upon entering civil society. This idea fits well with the three specific kinds of limits on the right of self-preservation, mentioned above, that have intuitive force. Limits arising directly from forfeiture or surrender of one's rights by consent or misconduct are precisely what is allowed for on the present account. Limits arising from other parties' property rights (which are noninterference rights) are ultimately based on consent, for in Hobbesian theory, property rights themselves are conventional rather than natural.[5] Finally, limits on the right to attack, carve up, or actively endanger other innocents to protect oneself are plausible elements of the Hobbesian social contract, for it is arguable that mutually vulnerable Hobbesian contractors would agree to such limits to protect themselves from dangerous self-protective activities of their fellows within civil society.

This compromise position, which may be incorporated into Hobbesian philosophy, faces criticism from two different directions. Hobbes himself argues that the natural right of self-preservation can in no way be surrendered. These arguments are analyzed and criticized in the next two sections. On the other hand, it may be contended on the basis of our intuitions about hypothetical cases that the rights of others impose limits on one's own right of self-preservation *even in a pure state of nature*. Several points may be made in response to this. Our intuitions about limits on the right of self-preservation are developed in a social and civilized context and are therefore not a wholly reliable guide concerning pure state-of-nature situations. Even so, when considering direct conflicts between individual or collective self-defense and the rights of innocent others, philosophers as divergent as utilitarians, nonutilitarian rights theorists, and libertarians are reluctant to come down unambiguously on the side of restraint.[6] (Hume, in fact, comes down clearly on the Hobbesian side on this question.[7]) Most important, postulating an unlimited natural right of self-defense allows us to construct an illuminating Hobbesian account of the rational foundations of morality without carrying over any potentially objectionable claims about self-preservation into civil society. (No such claims are carried over, because on

[5] See section 9-4, and *Leviathan*, chap. 18, p. 165.

[6] See Richard Brandt, "Utilitarianism and the Rules of War," 1 (Winter 1972): 145–65, esp. 152–54; Michael Walzer, *Just and Unjust Wars* (New York: Basic Books, 1977), chaps. 16–17, esp. pp. 254, 274; Nozick, *Anarchy, State, and Utopia*, pp. 34–35; and John Hospers, "Some Problems About Punishment and the Retaliatory Use of Force, Part 2," *Reason* (January 1973): 19–26.

[7] David Hume, *An Enquiry Concerning the Principles of Morals*, chap. 3, in *Hume's Ethical Writings*, ed. Alisdair MacIntyre (New York: Collier Books, 1965), pp. 37–39.

our account the right of self-preservation is not fully inalienable and is partially surrendered upon entering civil society.) Hence, there is much to be gained, and apparently little to be lost, by accepting Hobbes's postulate of an unlimited right of nature and seeing where it takes us.

But, before proceeding, there is an important problem to be faced here. It may be claimed that the existence of an unlimited right of nature is an implicit presupposition of Hobbesian *descriptive*, as well as normative, theory, for if it were morally wrong to attack innocent people in the state of nature, even out of defense motives, many parties in the state of nature would refrain from such attacks because they were wrong. And this might well be sufficient to prevent the escalating cycle of violence upon which the Hobbesian argument against anarchy depends.

Strictly speaking, the moral permissibility of anticipation against the innocent in the state of nature is not presupposed by our Hobbesian argument against anarchy. Our key assumption of Predominant Egoism implies either that such anticipation is permissible *or* that it would be generally practiced even though not permissible. All the Hobbesian argument against anarchy requires is a general willingness to anticipate if this seems necessary for self-defense. Whether this willingness is consistent with moral norms is irrelevant to the arguments as stated.

Still, there is a problem here. Suppose we assume (1) that attacks on the innocent which are necessary for defense are wrong, even in the state of nature, and (2) that most people are aware of this, and (3) that people are very strongly motivated to avoid doing what they believe is wrong, even when it would protect them from danger. Then the state-of-nature parties would have very strong moral motivation against anticipation, which, when combined with recognition of the dangers of anticipation discussed in section 3-6, would lead them not to anticipate, and the Hobbesian argument that the state of nature is a state of war collapses. This combination of assumptions does conflict with Predominant Egoism, but the supporter of these assumptions will claim that the combination has greater plausibility than Predominant Egoism and that the inconsistency between them should lead us to reject it rather than them.

Fortunately, Hobbesian theory can reply to this line of objection in any of three ways. The *nonconcessionary* reply involves simply rejecting moral restrictions on defensively necessary state-of-nature conduct (assumption (1)) and/or the overriding motivational efficacy of moral motivations when these are in conflict with defensive motivation (assumption (3)). The *moderate* reply allows that moral beliefs could, in some state-of-nature situations,[8] produce enough additional constraint on behavior to prevent an intolerable escalation of violence. But since this would not generally be the case, the Hobbesian argument against anarchy would still retain much of its force.

Finally, the *concessionary* reply claims that the main structure and conclusions of Hobbesian theory should remain in place *even if the above objection is accepted.* This is so because if we accept the objection we can simply replace our Hobbesian argument against anarchy with a Lockean argument against anarchy. Locke, after all, accepted state-of-nature prohibitions on attacking the innocent and allowed considerable motivational efficacy for moral beliefs (e.g., beliefs about rights). Nonetheless, he held that there was danger of a state of nature becoming a "State of War (wherein there is no appeal but to Heaven [i.e., fighting], and wherein every the least difference is apt to end, where there is no Authority to decide between the Contenders)."[9] And in his view this danger was sufficient to justify submission to a limited, though not absolute, government. Since Hobbesian theory, like Locke and unlike Hobbes, seeks only to establish the rational preferability of some forms of limited government (i.e., the satisfactory State) over anarchy, its main political elements could survive substitution of the Lockean antianarchy argument for the Hobbesian one.

In the sequel, the nonconcessionary stance is adopted. In particular, Hobbes's postulate of an initially unlimited right of nature is provisionally accepted, and its consequences are developed.

[8] E.g., if an occupying power withdrew from, and left without government, a country with strong moral traditions against violence.
[9] John Locke, *Second Treatise*, sec. 21, p. 323.

Readers who find this postualte implausible and the above objection persuasive are invited to proceed as follows. They may imagine a Lockean argument against anarchy substituted for the Hobbesian one in our descriptive theory, and they may follow a conditionalization strategy, like that proposed at the end of section 2-5, with regard to Hobbesian normative theory. That is, they may read our subsequent arguments and conclusions as having this form: "If the postualte of an unlimited (permission) right of nature were true, then. . . ." This will perhaps allow them to learn from the arguments, despite disagreeing with some of them. And it frees us to pass on to the issue of whether the postulated right of nature is inalienable.

8-2. The First Argument for Inalienability

Two distinct arguments to the conclusion that the right of nature is inalienable are found in chapter 14 of *Leviathan*. Each presupposes a different version of Psychological Egoism, yet neither succeeds even if the truth of the relevant version is granted. Nonetheless, there are some insights contained in or hinted at by each of the arguments.

To begin, three points about the wide scope of the arguments should be clarified. The arguments themselves all involve situations of self-*defense*, in the narrow sense of resisting attack; hence, in analyzing them we shall speak of the right of self-defense. Still, it is clear from certain applications of the arguments that they are meant to cover acts of self-preservation in general.[10] Also, while the arguments merely deny the possibility of surrendering the right of nature as part of a contract, they can easily be generalized to rule out surrendering it as a free gift. (This is important because, as noted in sections 5-1 and 10-1, Hobbes's own version of the social contract is, from the sovereign's perspective, a free gift.) Finally, Hobbes argues that the right to resist wounds and imprisonment, as well as the right to resist death, is inalienable. While focusing mainly on the status of the

[10] See *Leviathan*, chap. 21, p. 204.

latter right, we shall note some further problems concerning resistance to wounds and imprisonment.

Hobbes's first argument that the right to defend oneself is inalienable is contained in the following passage:

> Of the voluntary acts of every man, the object is some *good to himself*. And therefore there be some rights, which no man can be understood by any words, or other signs, to have abandoned, or transferred. As first a man cannot lay down the right of resisting them, that assault him by force, to take away his life; because he cannot be understood to aim thereby, at any good to himself. . . . And lastly the motive, and end for which this renouncing, and transferring of right is introduced, is nothing else but the security of a man's person, in his life, and in the means of so preserving life, as not to be weary of it. And therefore if a man by words, or other signs, seem to despoil himself of the end, for which those signs were intended; he is not to be understood as if he meant it, or that it was his will; but that he was ignorant of how such words and actions were to be interpreted.[11]

The argument that Hobbes presents here may be schematized in four steps.

(1) The object of any voluntary act is some personal benefit to the agent.

(2) The object of an apparent voluntary act of laying down the right of self-defense is an obligation on the part of the agent not to resist attack on himself.

(3) An obligation not to resist attack on oneself is not a personal benefit.

(4) Therefore, an apparent act of laying down the right of self-defense cannot be a genuine and binding voluntary act that places the agent under an obligation.

One might object to this argument by questioning the truth of one of its premises. Indeed, the first premise, which asserts Nonmaximizing Egoism, has been challenged in section 2-4. But this

[11] Ibid., chap. 14, p. 120.

approach is unnecessary. Contrary to first appearances, the argument is *invalid* because of an equivocation involving the term "object" in steps (1) and (2). The "object" of an act in the sense of step (1) is the agent's objective in performing the act—what he expects to get as a result of doing the act (the "perlocutionary" object, we might say, adapting J. L. Austin's terminology).[12] In the case of laying down a right, it is what others give him (or he expects them to give him) in return for laying down that right. On the other hand, the "object" of an act in the sense of step (2) is what the performance of the act inherently brings about in virtue of being the kind of act it is (in Austinian terminology, the "illocutionary" object). In the case of laying down a right, it is the obligation that is created for the agent by the surrender of the right. The difference between the two sorts of objects is made clear by noting that the connection between the later sort of object and its act is logical, while that between the former sort and the corresponding act is merely contingent. To lay down a right *is* to assume an obligation; it may or may not result in one's receiving some benefit. But the chance that it will do so makes it an action eligible for performance by a nonmaximizing egoist.

That there is a fallacy in the argument can be demonstrated also by *reductio*. If we substitute the phrase "to do X" for all occurrences of the phrases "to resist attack on oneself" and "of self-defense" in steps (2) through (4), we obtain an equally valid argument to the effect that *no right can be laid down*. Hobbes is committed to this absurd argument by his endorsement of the earlier one, if any obligation is presumed to be a burden, so that obligations are undertaken only in trade for, or in hope of obtaining, compensating benefits.

Things are even worse for Hobbes than this, for he attempts to derive from this first argument a corollary establishing the inalienability of the right to resist wounds and imprisonment.[13] His main argument for this conclusion—that one cannot tell that

[12] J. L. Austin, *How to Do Things with Words* (New York: Oxford University Press, 1962).
[13] *Leviathan*, chap. 14, p. 120.

324

one's assailants do not intend one's death—has several weaknesses. It depends on the above faulty argument that the right to resist death is inalienable. It ignores the fact that in many contexts (e.g., arrest by the police in modern countries for noncapital offenses, first beatings by the enforcer for the local extortion ring), one *can* know that one's "assailants" do not intend one's death. Further, the corollaries' derivation seems to rest on the general principle that if one has a right to avoid X, one has an equal right to avoid things that may—or are fairly likely to—lead to X. But no argument is offered for this principle, and it seems to be a questionable one. One may have a right to avoid contact with persons whom one does not like, but one does not have a right to avoid carrying out the duties of one's job because they are likely to bring one into contact with some such persons. Similarly, the right to prevent others from tramping over your beloved family estate does not imply a right to avoid the tax payments that are likely to lead to such an eventuality by forcing you to sell or to open the estate to paying visitors. These and similar cases indicate that we should reject the principle Hobbes uses to derive his corollary concerning the right to resist imprisonment and wounds.

A different argument for extending the inalienable right to resist to cover wounds and imprisonment is hinted at by Hobbes's use in the last-quoted passage of the phrase "in the means of so preserving [his] life, as not to be weary of it."[14] The suggestion here is that what people value is not the continuation of life per se, but the continuation of an at least minimally decent life. Since, for many, life in prison or with the handicaps brought on by severe wounds may not be minimally decent, one would sometimes have as much reason to resist these fates as to resist death itself. This argument is worth noting, because it fits with and confirms our earlier observations that, for Hobbes, death is not always the greatest evil (section 2-6), and the state of nature is undesirable because its inhabitants are poor as well as insecure (section 3-2). Nonetheless, the argument fails because wounds

---

[14] Ibid.

and imprisonment are often temporary, or bearable, and because it rests on the invalid first argument for the inalienability of the right to resist deadly attack.

Though Hobbes's first argument for inalienability is clearly fallacious, a somewhat different (though ultimately unsuccessful) argument is lurking in the background. Consider the status of the "cannot" in (4), the conclusion that the right of self-defense cannot be laid down. What kind of impossibility is involved here? Hobbes does not claim it is impossible to utter the words "I hereby voluntarily lay down my right of self-defense," but he does hold that such speech acts as contracting and making free gifts are performatives which can, as a matter of logic, be brought off only if certain preconditions are satisfied. In particular, Hobbes seems to think that for a valid contract (or free gift) to exist between X and Y which involves X surrendering right R, it must be the case that (a) X has given signs that express X's will to surrender R and that (b) Y has taken these signs as signs of X's will to surrender and has accepted this surrender.[15] Hobbes's fallacious first argument may be read as saying that since the object of the will must be a personal benefit, and the loss of the right to self-defense is not a personal benefit, condition (a) cannot be satisfied with respect to it. Since no one can have the will to surrender that right, nothing one says can express that will.

We have seen why this argument fails, but a more promising argument can be developed based on logical preconditions (a) and (b) of successfully laying down a right. If a party, under otherwise appropriate circumstances, says "I lay down right R," let us say that the laying down of that right constitutes his *express will*. Suppose that it is common knowledge (or an appropriate presumption) that this party possesses overriding end E, and that it is a fact that doing act A is necessary for the attainment of E. Then, this party's *tacit will* is that he retain the right to do A. But there may well be a conflict between one's express will and one's tacit will. One may be unaware of or not attentive to the

[15] *Elements of Law*, part 1, chap. 2, sec. 4, p. 88; *Philosophical Rudiments*, chap. 2, sec. 5, p. 18; *Leviathan*, chap. 14, p. 119.

fact that laying down right R entails surrendering the right to do A. Or one may be unaware that doing A is necessary to attain E. Under these circumstances, one may say "I lay down right R," even though the loss of that right might or would prevent attainment of one's overriding end E. In such a case, which of the two wills—express or tacit—is to count as the agent's *real* will, for purposes of determining whether conditions (a) and (b) are satisfied?

Hobbes's views on this question changed over time. In *Human Nature*, he implies that express will must take precedence, but later, in *Leviathan*, he favors tacit will (in the sense just defined) over express will.[16] This latter doctrine allows us to construct the following argument against the possibility of a party to the social contract, who pledges to "*authorize* all the actions . . . of*" and to "*give up my right of governing myself, to*" the sovereign,[17] thereby surrendering his right to resist death at the hands of the State. (This is, of course, the potential surrender of the right of self-defense that most interests Hobbes.)

(1′) A party to the social contract expressly wills the surrender of the right to resist any act of the sovereign.

(2′) It is common knowledge that avoiding death is an overriding end of any party.

(3′) Resisting when subject to deadly attacks is a necessary means of avoiding death.

(4′) A party's tacit will is to retain the right to resist deadly attacks. (From (2′) and (3′).)

(5′) In cases of conflict between express will and tacit will, tacit will takes precedence.

(6′) Therefore, despite the express content of the social contract, as expressed in (1′), parties to that contract retain the right to resist deadly attacks, even those authorized by the sovereign. (From (4′) and (5′).)

The key question regarding this valid argument is whether Hobbes's doctrine of the precedence of tacit will over express will

---

[16] *Human Nature*, chap. 13, sec. 9, pp. 75–76. *Leviathan*, chap. 18, p. 168; chap. 21, pp. 207–8; chap. 22, p. 211.

[17] *Leviathan*, chap. 18, p. 159; chap. 17, p. 158.

is acceptable. This doctrine amounts to a normative claim about when people should be held to their expressed word. And this claim has some basis. Sometimes a party should not be held to his express agreement, if it was so demonstrably against his interests at the time of entry into it that we must presume him to have been ignorant of the implications of the agreement and must presume the other party to have been deliberately taking advantage of this ignorance. But mere apparent ignorance of implications, *without disproportion* in terms of burdens undertaken and benefits received, does not normally oblige the other party to enlighten one or incline us to regard the agreement as void. Hence, Hobbes's general principle about tacit will taking precedence over express will would seem to apply only in the case of disproportionate express bargains. But to trade, via social contract, one's right to resist deadly attack by agents of the State for the security and benefits provided by the State, is not—at least in the case of the satisfactory State—a bad or disproportionate bargain. Rational parties aware of all the relevant facts might well make such a trade, preferring the small risks of execution to the larger risks of the state of nature. Therefore we may not presume the parties' real wills to be otherwise than as expressed in the terms of the social contract, and premise (5') in the above argument cannot be accepted, insofar as it is interpreted to apply to the previous steps to yield (6').[18]

In the end, then, all versions of Hobbes's first argument for the inalienability of the right of self-defense fail. A different approach, one not based solely on the agent's will, intention, or objectives at the time of commitment, is needed. Just such an approach is adopted in Hobbes's second argument for inalienability.

---

[18] There may be other grounds than disproportion for giving tacit will precedence over express will in particular cases, e.g., if there is special evidence that the agent is unaware of the implications of his commitment and would not have made it were he so aware. But there is no reason to think that these grounds must always be present if the right of resistance is given up in a social contract.

8-3. *The Second Argument for Inalienability*

Hobbes's second argument for the inalienability of the natural right of self-defense focuses on an agent's psychological states at the time he is attacked as well as at the time he is imagined to lay down that right. This argument, of which versions appear in both *Philosophical Rudiments* and *Leviathan*, presupposes Maximizing Egoism and, on one interpretation, the "ought implies can" principle.[19] The best statement of the argument is in this passage from *Leviathan*:

> To promise that which is known to be impossible, is no covenant. . . . The promise of not resisting force, in no covenant transferreth any right; nor is obliging. For though a man may covenant thus, *unless I do so, or so, kill me*; he cannot covenant thus, *unless I do so, or so, I will not resist you, when you come to kill me*. For man by nature chooseth the lesser evil, which is danger of death in resisting, rather than the greater, which is certain and present death in not resisting. And this is granted to be true by all men, in that they lead criminals to execution, and prison, with armed men.[20]

The argument may be set out in seven steps.
(1) When facing a choice between two courses of action which one realizes may result in personal harm, it is psychologically impossible not to pursue the course of action that seems at the time to be the lesser personal evil.
(2) At the time one is attacked (i.e., when physical force that threatens death is used against one), resistance will always seem to be a lesser personal evil than nonresistance.

---

[19] *Philosophical Rudiments*, chap. 2, sec. 18, pp. 25–26; *Leviathan*, chap. 14, pp. 126–28. While the *Philosophical Rudiments* version of the argument is more explicit in some respects, it is inferior in that it does not clearly imply premise (4) of the argument as given in the text below.

[20] *Leviathan*, ibid.

(3) It is psychologically impossible not to resist when attacked. (From (1) and (2).)

(4) It is believed by all potential contractors to be psychologically impossible not to resist when attacked.

(5) It is known (truly believed) by all potential contractors to be psychologically impossible not to resist when attacked. (From (3) and (4).)

(6) A contract to do what is known (truly believed) by both parties to be impossible is invalid and not binding.

(7) A contract not to resist attack is invalid and not binding. (From (5) and (6).)

It will be convenient to discuss this argument in three parts consisting, respectively, of steps (1)–(3), (4)–(5), and (6)–(7). Starting with the first part, note that (1) is an immediate corollary of Maximizing Egoism as defined in section 2-2. More particularly, it is a statement of Maximizing Egoism confined to a limited domain of choices—those between two courses of action each potentially leading to personal harm. Premise (1) would thus seem subject to the main objection to Maximizing Egoism: the phenomenon of weakness of will and its implication that even if people are egoists they are not maximizers. However, because of the limited domain of (1) (and the even more limited domain to which it need be applied to imply (3)), a fairly plausible defense of it *as used here* can be imagined. One may reasonably claim that when an agent fails to maximize, it is because the best, or least bad, alternative was *less salient* to him than the alternative chosen. Joining this claim with the contention that the prospect of immediate death is never less salient, when one is attacked, than other alternatives leads to the conclusion that weakness of will cannot lead one to choose nonresistance in an attack situation. For if the prospect of immediate death as the result of nonresistance is never exceeded in salience and is perceived as the greatest evil (as implied by (2)), and if people always maximize, save for distortions introduced by salience differences, it follows that people always will resist deadly attack (as stated in (3)).

But is immediate death always perceived as the greatest evil, as asserted in (2)? As noted in section 2-6, even Hobbes admits that it is not. People may prefer death to dishonor, or being hated by all, or other tragedies. Further, even if death is the worst evil, actively resisting an attack could risk death *plus* some other great evil, for example, torture first or the death of one's loved ones.[21] In that case, even if nonresistance meant certain death, and resistance offered some prospect of survival, nonresistance might be the lesser personal evil on balance.

To this it may be replied that whatever the real balance of risks and harms, instinctual fear of death will take over when one is attacked, and either make resistance seem the best course or trigger resistance automatically. This is doubtless true in some cases. Humans, like other animals, are subject to a "fight-or-flight" response when endangered. But Hobbes concedes that this response is not invariable. He implies that some are "stout enough to bear" death, wounds, or torture and suggests that only the naturally "timorous" tend to flee battle.[22] So premise (2) fails, and with it the subconclusion (3) that it is psychologically impossible not to resist death imposed by others. The falsity of (3) is confirmed by historical knowledge of those who have chosen martyrdom. The case of Socrates, who drank the hemlock rather than flee (as he easily could have) the sentence of the State, is one of a number of familiar examples.

Though the failure of the first part of Hobbes's second argument for inalienability dooms the argument, it is worth briefly considering the other parts to show how seriously flawed the argument is and to prepare the way for a weakened version of it to be presented in the next section. The second part of Hobbes's argument—steps (4) and (5)—is needed because mere impossibility of fulfillment does not generally void an agreement. As Hobbes notes,[23] if the parties do not *know* one party's part cannot be fulfilled, that party owes the other party something of equivalent

---

[21] We can imagine a State seeking to deter resistance to capital arrests by torturing, or killing the families of, those who resist.

[22] *Philosophical Rudiments*, chap. 2, sec. 18, p. 25. (There is some ambiguity about whether the quoted term is meant to apply to death as well as to wounds and torture.) *Leviathan*, chap. 22, p. 205.

[23] *Leviathan*, chap. 14, p. 126.

value, or at least his best attempt to carry out his part. Otherwise, the other party is treated unfairly. But if parties A and B both know that the agreement cannot be carried out by A (and know that they both know, etc.), perhaps they will not take the agreement seriously; and perhaps if B relies on the agreement being fulfilled, he has only himself to blame. If this were always so, we might agree with Hobbes that when it is common knowledge among all potential contractors ("granted to be true by all men") that compliance with a certain sort of agreement is impossible, any agreement of that sort would be void *ab initio*.[24]

But is there such common knowledge about agreements of nonresistance to deadly attack? Even setting aside our earlier claims that compliance with such agreements *is* possible, Hobbes fails to make the required common-knowledge claim plausible. He infers it from the universal practice of leading men to execution with armed guards, but this practice is rational provided only that there is a significant *risk* that the condemned person may flee. One cannot infer general knowledge of the certainty of resistance from the universality of a practice that can be justified by the mere possibility of resistance. (The same point applies to the modern practice of not allowing bail in capital punishment cases.)

The key issue of the third part of the argument is whether (6)—which claims the invalidity of covenants known by the parties to be impossible—is an acceptable principle. Step (6) might be derived in either of two ways. From the "ought implies can" principle, one may infer that there is no obligation to do the impossible. But valid contracts create obligations, and hence there can be no valid contract here. To defeat this derivation, it suffices to remember from section 7-5 that Hobbes (rightly) restricts the "ought implies can" principle so that it does not apply where the agent has voluntarily surrendered his excuse of not being able to do the thing in question, for an agreement to do the thing would surely be such a voluntary surrender.

The possible second derivation of (6) was mentioned above. Since the promisee will or should place no reliance on a promise

---

[24] But see three paragraphs below in the text.

to do what is commonly known to be impossible, the promisor is not bound to carry out the promise. But might not the promisee desire the promisor's endeavor, or something of equivalent value to what is promised? And might not he be owed this, as in the case of a promise not originally known to be impossible? Imagine, for example, that in order to get you to practice harder and strain to your absolute limits, your track coach exacts a promise from you to run a four-minute mile this year, though both of you know this is beyond your physical capabilities. Would you not be obligated to him to try your best to do the impossible? (Even if we say that the real content of this promise is merely to try your best to achieve or approach a four-minute mile, still you end up with some positive obligation.) Analogously, it would seem that those who promise that they will not resist deadly attack are obligated to try their best not to, contrary to the meaning of (7) and Hobbes's apparent intentions.

In summary, then, Hobbes's second argument for the inalienability of the right of self-defense contains several fatal errors. Unfortunately, among the evils one may face, death is not always the greatest, nor is nonresistance to death always the lesser. So even if people were maximizing egoists (which they are not), nonresistance to deadly attack would sometimes be possible. Further, even if nonresistance were impossible, Hobbes gives us no good reason to believe that this fact would be common knowledge. And if it were, a promise to do this known impossible thing might still bind one to the utmost endeavor not to resist deadly attack. Thus, in the end, Hobbes's second argument for inalienability is no more persuasive than his first.

8-4. An Acceptable Argument

As we shall see in Chapter 11, most all of Hobbes's applications of the idea that the right of nature is inalienable concern citizen's rights to resist attacks by the State and its agents. Hence, much of the work that Hobbes performs with his general inalienability doctrine could still be accomplished with an argument of much narrower scope than those he presents. What must be established is simply that in agreeing to the original social contract, parties do not lay down their right to resist death at the hands of the State.

A fairly plausible argument to this limited conclusion can be constructed, based largely on ideas contained in Hobbes's faulty second argument for inalienability. We start with the idea that, in general, whatever commitments they may have made, people are quite *likely* to resist deadly attacks—acting either from instinctual fear or calculation of lesser risks or evils. Further, there is wide common knowledge of this probabilistic fact. To this may be added the observation that those subject to deadly attack or capital punishment by the State will almost always know whether they are guilty or innocent of having committed the acts for which the State seeks to punish them. If innocent, they are likely to resist fiercely what they perceive as an unjustified attack on them, even if it is carried out by honest law enforcement personnel who are "only doing their duty."[25] But those who have committed capital offenses (at least in the satisfactory State where such offenses may be presumed to involve very serious misdeeds) have already shown their unwillingness to abide by law and to bow to authority, so they are unlikely to surrender their lives simply because they have promised to do so. Given all this, we may raise again a question suggested by our reinterpretation of Hobbes's second argument. Would the social contractors see any *point* in including the surrender of the right to resist death at the hands of the State in their agreement? Knowing that resistance would occur anyway in most all cases, and knowing that the State would have the authority and power to generally overcome it and to punish it if it so chose, it seems highly doubtful that the contractors would agree on such a surrender. If this is so, it is appropriate within the context of Hobbesian theory to view the original social contract as not including surrender of the right to resist death at the hands of the State.

This argument succeeds where Hobbes's arguments failed, be-

---

[25] A fictional illustration is provided in Stephen Becker's *A Covenant with Death* (New York: Atheneum, 1965), a novel about an innocent condemned man who kills his hangman.

cause of its less ambitious conclusion. There is no claim that it is logically impossible to surrender portions of one's right of nature. Rather, it is said to be *unlikely* that a *specific portion* of that right (i.e., resistance to deadly attacks by the State) would be surrendered as part of a *particular agreement* (i.e., the original social contract). This is consistent with holding, as we do, that portions of one's right of nature can be surrendered and that some might be surrendered as part of particular agreements, including the social contract. In fact, it was suggested in section 8-3 that the parties to the social contract would agree not to preserve themselves by attacking their innocent fellows who were not attacking them.

Is such a suggestion consistent with the argument just advanced? Wouldn't the surrender of this right be seen to be pointless also, and hence not included in the social contract? It probably would not be, for the following reason. We do seem to make two important intuitive distinctions involving self-defense that, within civil society, have substantial motivational force. One is between repelling actual attack ("defense" in the narrow sense) and preventing other dangers to our lives ("self-preservation"). The second is between active and passive self-preservation. Other things being equal, we are more likely to regard as justified, and to engage in, acts of self-*defense* that harm others than other acts of self-preservation that harm them equally. (Defense against actual attack is more likely, and easier to justify, than preventive attack.) Similarly, all else being equal, we are more likely to regard as justified, and to engage in, *omissions* that preserve ourselves at the expense of others than positive actions that have like effects. (Killing to preserve oneself is less likely, and more difficult to justify, than "letting die" as a means of self-preservation.) When these two distinctions reinforce one another in a particular case, they have potentially great motivational force. Thus, even a committed pacifist could be expected to allow a deadly attacker on himself to step off a cliff, without saving him by a warning. (The pacifist *defends* against an actual attack by *letting the attacker die*.) And many of us would, within civil society, refrain from murdering, or stealing kidneys from, innocent others even to save our own lives. (We will not *preserve* ourselves by an *active* attack on someone who is not attacking us.) If this is so, potential complaince with a social contract provision that surrenders or limits the individual's natural right to preserve himself by attacks on other citizens (who are not attacking him) might well be great enough that it would not be pointless to enact such a provision. Thus, the above argument does not rule out restrictions on the right of self-preservation, in civil society, to protect the vital rights and interests of others.

Can the argument for social contractors retaining rights to resist the State be extended to cover "wounds and imprisonment" as well as death? This seems impossible to answer, in general. For roughly the same reasons given above, both innocent and guilty people could be expected to usually resist wounds and imprisonment at the hands of the State. But since the evils suffered are not as great, and since resistance may well risk the greater evil of death, one would expect more cases of nonresistance here than when death is the expected punishment. Whether enough social contractors would think there to be sufficient potential for compliance, so as to give a point to including a surrender of the right to resist arrest in noncapital cases, would seem to be incapable of general determination.

It is time to summarize our Hobbesian position on the right of self-preservation. Hobbes's postulate of an unlimited natural right of self-preservation is accepted, though with some reluctance. But his arguments that this right is inalienable are seen to fail. Parts of that right can, in principle, be surrendered in specific contracts. In fact, the right to attack innocent others within civil society to preserve oneself would probably be surrendered as part of the original Hobbesian social contract. But it is doubtful whether the right to resist deadly attacks by the State would be laid down in the social contract. (Those who suspect that this leaves the individual with too much right to resist authorized punishment should remember two things: Only necessary force is sanctioned by the right of nature, and this right is only a permission right, whose exercise the State has a right to prevent and to punish.) In any case, any limits on surrenders of the right of nature by means of

336

the social contract are empirical, not logical. Whether such surrenders are included in that agreement, and if so just which ones, would depend on the advantages and disadvantages perceived by the parties, given their view of the possibilities of compliance. There is undoubtedly considerable indeterminacy concerning these matters, enough to render it uncertain whether a general Hobbesian social contract theory could ever hope to fix precisely all the boundaries of the right of self-preservation within civil society.

Why then have we paid so much attention to these issues, and so carefully dissected Hobbes's arguments concerning them? For three reasons. First, our analysis confirms the observation of section 2-3 that Hobbes uses two distinct versions of Psychological Egoism in his arguments about self-defense. Second, Hobbes applies his doctrine of the inalienability of the right of nature to certain important questions of political theory. To prepare for our discussion of these questions in Chapter 11, it has been necessary to examine closely the nature and grounds of that doctrine. Finally, our departure from Hobbes on the inalienability issue signals an important general difference between Hobbes's philosophy and our Hobbesian theory on the question of the individual's relationship to the State. For Hobbes, social contractors surrender all they can and retain as rights against the State only what they cannot surrender—the right of individual self-preservation and its corollaries. Our Hobbesian account is less individualistic than this in that it allows parts of the right of self-preservation to be lost in making the social contract. But it more than compensates, as regards individual liberty, by supposing that not all that could be surrendered in the social contract is surrendered. Hobbesian social contractors retain certain liberties and safeguards on liberty, including a right to resist, and in extreme cases overthrow, the State when it acts improperly. We shall return to these matters in Chapters 10 and 11, but first we must outline a general Hobbesian moral theory.

NINE

RULE EGOISM

9-1. Right Reason and Natural Law

We now turn to a sketch and defense of Hobbes's distinctive theory of morality. Hobbes's account of morality has two primary purposes. First, like Hume after him,[1] Hobbes seeks to explain *why* we regard as virtuous the particular kinds of actions (and dispositions to act) that we do so regard. Second, Hobbes's moral theory takes on the age-old task of reconciling the requirements of morality with those of rational prudence, with the hope of thereby motivating predominantly egoistic individuals to live in accordance with moral rules. The two purposes are achieved together by the construction of a *rule-egoistic* moral theory that treats familiar principles of moral conduct as rational guides to the promotion of individual interests in a multiparty environment.

We have seen that, for Hobbes, individuals have powerful moral rights flowing from the right of nature. They are also subject to certain moral constraints, the moral ought-principles expressed in the laws of nature. Hobbes's reconciliation of morality and prudence is carried out by interpreting the laws of nature so as to encompass, reflect, and express the right of nature. The complex linkage between natural rights and natural law is mediated by the concept of *right reason*. Looking briefly at Hobbes's use of this concept will enable us to understand better the nature and status of Hobbes's laws of nature.

Hobbes's uses the term "right reason" (sometimes "natural

---

[1] See, e.g., David Hume, *Treatise of Human Nature*, book III, part III, sec. I, pp. 574–91.

reason" or simply "reason") to refer to a certain kind of reasoning process, or its conclusions, or the mental faculty that enables us to engage in such a process. Right reason(ing) viewed as a process has three defining characteristics: it is sound, it is about kinds of acts that affect others' interests, and it concerns such acts insofar as they secure and advance the agent's own preservation. In short, it is correct prudential reasoning about interpersonal conduct.[2]

Hobbes claims that if right reasoning prescribes an act we have a (permission) *right* to perform it. His express arguments for this claim, based on general consensus or linguistic usage, are weak,[3] but he hints at a better argument: under the right of nature, one has the right to perform acts that are needed to secure one's preservation. This would immediately establish the universal right to act in accordance with right reason, if the right of nature were inalienable, as Hobbes claims. But in the last chapter we rejected that claim, arguing that parts of the right of nature would be surrendered in the social contract. If this is so, the right to act in accordance with right reason might not survive the creation of civil society.

In fact, however, there is no serious problem here, for the conclusions of right reasoning are principles of conduct—the laws of nature—that promote the well-being of others as well as the agent.[4] Hence there can be no valid objection to agents pursuing their survival by following these principles. Further, Hobbes holds that the laws of nature are contained in the civil law (see section 6-1) and that the State is the authoritative interpreter of that law, that is, the civil arbiter of what the conclusions of right reason are.[5] So the right to act in accordance with right reason carries over into the State, but in an attenuated form that requires obedience to the civil law. This restriction renders the right to follow right

[2] See my "Right Reason and Natural Law in Hobbes's Ethics," *The Monist* 66 (January 1983): 120–33, sec. 1.
[3] See *Philosophical Rudiments*, chap. 2, sec. 1, pp. 15–16; *Elements of Law*, part 1, chap. 1, sec. 6, p. 83.
[4] Except when the qualifying clauses of these principles apply. See the discussion below in this section of the logical form of the laws of nature.
[5] See *Leviathan*, chap. 5, pp. 30–31; chap. 18, p. 165.

reason in civil society fully consistent with parts of one's right of nature having been surrendered in the original contract.

If one is permitted to follow the conclusions of right reason, is one also *required* to do so? The answer, for Hobbes, is yes, since the dictates of right reason are the laws of nature,[6] and "A LAW OF NATURE, *lex naturalis*, is a precept or general rule, found out by reason, by which a man is forbidden to do that, which is destructive of his life, or taketh away the means of preserving the same; and to omit that, by which he thinketh it may be best preserved."[7] From this definition we learn that natural laws are general rules, discoverable by reason, which prescribe pursuing certain means of self-preservation. Certain of these features are expanded upon later in the text. Hobbes tells us that a specific use of reason suffices to uncover these rules—application of the Golden Rule.[8] And from Hobbes's claim that these general rules are eternal and immutable,[9] we may infer that the rules are intended to apply at all times and places. But there are important ambiguities in the definition concerning the standards of conduct prescribed by the laws of nature and the sense in which following such standards is required of us.

Consider first an ambiguity concerning the standards themselves. A law of nature forbids an agent's doing "that which *is* destructive of his life" and his omitting "that by which *he thinketh* it may be best preserved" (emphasis supplied). There is an apparent waffling here on whether it is objective or subjective means-ends relations that determine the content of the laws of nature. The former phrase suggests that the laws of nature prescribe certain specific kinds of acts that *in fact* tend to promote preservation, whether or not the agent is aware of this. But the

---

[6] See *Philosophical Rudiments*, chap. 2, sec. 1, p. 16. Some laws of nature are not dictates of right reason in the sense we have defined, since they do not concern interpersonal conduct. But Hobbes dismisses them as unimportant for the purposes of moral and political theory. See *Leviathan*, chap. 15, p. 144.

[7] *Leviathan*, chap. 14, pp. 116–17.

[8] Ibid., chap. 15, pp. 144–45.

[9] Ibid., p. 145. Presumably immutability does not imply that the laws of nature are necessary truths, but only that they must hold if human nature and the human condition are as described in Hobbesian theory.

latter phrase indicates that they prescribe doing whatever the agent believes to be supportive of his preservation, even if he is wrong. This second "subjective" interpretation of the content of the laws of nature must be rejected, because it is incompatible with the claim that the laws of nature are general prescriptions having the specific content that Hobbes says they have. Hobbes simply does not treat the laws of nature he lists as mere rules of thumb that may be disregarded if the individual does not accept them as promoting his own preservation either in general or in specific cases. We shall see below that Hobbes's laws of nature each contain two clauses. Perhaps Hobbes inserted the subjective wording in the final part of his definition of a law of nature to indicate that an agent must judge which clause of the relevant law of nature applies in the particular case. Whatever his motivation, we shall adopt the objectivist view of the content of the laws of nature, because this is essential for construction of a rule-egoistic Hobbesian moral theory.

A further problem with Hobbes's definition of a law of nature concerns the sense in which such laws are moral requirements. Hobbes's definition follows immediately after his characterization of the right of nature, and he suggests that the right of nature and laws of nature differ not in their content (both concern promoting self-preservation) but in their status as requirements. The right of nature implies liberties or permissions to act as we choose, while the laws of nature bind us to act in particular ways.[10] But to what does the binding status of the laws of nature amount? We are not in general *obligated* to follow them, for as indicated in section 7-4, obligations are specific moral requirements undertaken by consent which derive their moral force from the third law of nature. Nor, as we shall argue against Howard Warrender in section 9-3, are the laws of nature really laws, in Hobbes's sense of being commands of a rightful authority. Rather, as suggested in section 7-5, it is better to think of the laws of nature as moral ought-principles, general moral prescriptions created neither by command nor by consent. But why, then, are they re-

[10] Ibid., chap. 14, pp. 116–17.

quirements, when the right of nature does not involve requirements? Because of the manner they operate as means of self-preservation. The laws of nature, as dictates of right reason, concern interpersonal behavior. They prescribe pursuing self-preservation by cooperation with others (when such cooperation is possible) and thus require acts that promote the well-being of others as well as oneself. But cooperation requires mutual reliance, and often the performance of acts that are not in one's immediate interests. Hence, to operate effectively as means of mutual (and individual) preservation and benefit, the laws of nature must be binding prescriptions, which the agent does not have the option of following or not as he chooses, as he would if these laws constituted mere permissions or advice.

We shall return to the relationship between the right of nature and the laws of nature, but first we must consider the contents and logical form of the latter. The first and fundamental law of nature tells us to "seek peace, and follow it,"[11] that is, try to establish peace with others when it does not exist and maintain it when it does. Hobbes treats this law as a straightforward corollary of his previous observations about the horrible conditions in a state-of-nature war of all individuals or small groups, as described above in sections 3-2 and 4-4. But other arguments are needed here as a supplement, since the first law of nature also requires us to seek and maintain peace within civil society and the State. In particular, the Hobbesian arguments against the rationality of revolution (section 6-4), agreement-breaking (section 4-3), and crime (section 6-1) together constitute a strong case for regarding "seek and maintain peace" as a general rule of prudence within civil society.

Hobbes proceeds to derive eighteen other general theorems of prudence from the fundamental law of nature. The kinds of acts or dispositions prescribed in each of these laws are recommended as necessary, or generally effective, means to peace. The following list concisely summarizes the contents of all nineteen of Hobbes's laws of nature by indicating what each is for or against.

[11] Ibid., p. 117.

1. For peace
2. For mutual and reciprocal surrender of natural rights
3. Against injustice, i.e., against violating obligations (see section 7-4)
4. For gratitude
5. For accommodating others (including giving up one's luxuries for their necessities; see section 5-4)
6. For pardoning offenses of those who repent and guarantee future good conduct
7. Against punishing for revenge
8. Against declaring contempt or hatred for others
9. For acknowledging others as one's natural equals
10. Against claiming for oneself rights that one denies to others
11. For equity by judges
12. For common use of resources that cannot be divided
13. For alternating use, or assignment by lot, of what cannot be used in common
14. For primogeniture or first seizure as a form of natural lottery in distributing goods
15. For safe conduct for mediators
16. For submitting controversies to an arbitrator
17. Against being a judge in one's own case
18. Against using arbitrators who are partial
19. For using witnesses to settle controversies of fact

All these laws of nature, save for law 14 (see section 9-4), seem quite acceptable as general principles of rational prudence. Why this is so becomes apparent when we note that the laws can be sorted into five (nonexclusive) categories: seeking peace with others who seek it (1, 5–7, 16); practicing reciprocity and cooperation (2–4); according others respect and equal rights (2, 7–10); dividing material goods equally or fairly (12–13); and settling disputes by fair arbitration (11, 15–19). To suppose that such conduct tends to promote peace is to suppose that people are often inclined to fight when their efforts at peace are ignored or rebuffed, when they are cheated, when they are denied respect and equal rights, when they receive less than equal or fair shares of material goods, and when there is no opportunity to achieve impartial hearings and fair settlements of their disputes. Experience suggests that these are accurate suppositions. Further, Hobbes does seem to be right that rational agents could, in principle, derive these laws of nature from suitable applications of the Golden Rule,[12] for such agents presumably would not want to be cheated, to have their own sincere peace efforts rebuffed, to receive less than their fair share of material goods, and so on. However, Hobbes fails to explicitly note an interesting point about the content of the laws of nature that emerges from the above categorization of those laws. The causes of quarrel that compliance with the laws of nature is designed to prevent are nearly all *injustices* in a broad sense of that term which contrast with Hobbes's narrow usage (as described in section 7-4). They are denials of respect, equal rights, and fair treatment in the settlement of disputes and the distribution of goods. We shall delve into the significance of this point in section 9-4.

Though the above categorization is novel, the general content of Hobbes's natural laws is well known and easy to read off from the text of *Leviathan*. What has often escaped attention, however, is the logical form of these laws. They possess a common two-part structure. First, there is a main clause which requires behavior of a traditionally moral kind. Second, there is a qualifying clause which indicates that the agent is released from the requirement of the main clause if others are not satisfying that requirement (or other requirements of the laws of nature). Thus, a simple approximation of the logical form of each of Hobbes's laws of nature is "Do X, provided others are doing so as well." Hobbes's plausible rationale for including the qualifying clause is that no one is required to make himself prey to others by unilaterally accepting constraints that others do not accept.[13]

We may illustrate the two-part structure of Hobbes's laws of nature by looking briefly at the first three laws as stated in *Leviathan*. The first and fundamental law says, "That every man, ought to endeavour peace, as far as he has hope of obtaining it;

[12] Ibid., chap. 15, pp. 144–45.
[13] See *Philosophical Rudiments*, chap. 3, sec. 27, pp. 45–46; and *Leviathan*, chap. 14, p. 118; chap. 15, p. 145 (quoted below).

and when he cannot obtain it, that he may seek, and use, all helps, and advantages of war."[14] On the reasonable assumption that one can obtain peace if and only if others are endeavoring to promote peace, this statement of the fundamental law fits our proposed analysis. It is worth noting here, as well, that when the condition laid down in the qualifying clause is not satisfied, one is free, according to Hobbes, to pursue one's own interests without moral restrictions. The second law of nature displays its two-part structure even more clearly than does the first. It concerns mutual surrender of the right to all things—the permission right that Hobbes ascribes to each person in the state of nature to do whatever he judges most conducive to his preservation, including attack others. The second law requires, "That a man be willing, when others are so too, . . . to lay down this right to all things; and be contented with so much liberty against other men, as he would allow other men against himself."[15]

On the surface, the third law of nature, which requires keeping your covenants (i.e., agreements), does not contain a qualifying clause, but investigation of Hobbes's theory of covenants reveals that such a clause is in fact operative. According to the broad outlines of that theory, covenants are morally binding in civil society where there is a civil authority to ensure their enforcement. But in the state of nature, covenants are generally void and not binding, for the party called on to perform first does not have sufficient assurance that if he does his part the second party will follow suit.[16] If, however, the first party for some reason performs his part, the covenant is then binding on the second party.[17] Thus, the implicit two-part structure of the third law of nature is revealed. You are obligated to keep an agreement, provided the relevant "other" has done the same (i.e., has already performed) or you have reasonable assurance that he will do the same (as one has in civil society). If, on the other hand, there is

---

[14] *Leviathan*, chap. 14, p. 117.

[15] Ibid., p. 118.

[16] Ibid., chap. 14, pp. 124–25; chap. 15, p. 131. On complications in the theory of covenants, see section 9-2.

[17] Ibid., chap. 15, p. 133.

no assurance that the other has done, is doing, or will do his part, the qualifying clause is not satisfied and one is not obligated to perform.

Like the third law and unlike the first two, the subsequent laws of nature do not have an explicit two-part structure. But immediately after setting out the laws of nature, Hobbes inserts this famous passage:

> The laws of nature oblige *in foro interno*; that is to say, they bind to a desire they should take place: but *in foro externo*; that is, to the putting them in act, not always. For he that should be modest, and tractable, and perform all he promises, in such time, and place, where no man else should do so, should but make himself a prey to others, and procure his own certain ruin, contrary to the ground of all laws of nature, which tend to nature's preservation. And again, he that having sufficient security, that others shall observe the same laws towards him, observes them not himself, seeketh not peace, but war.[18]

This lays bare the two-part structure of all the laws of nature. An agent is required to act as the main clauses of these laws require (i.e., is obliged *in foro externo*) when and only when others are doing the same. "If no man else" is following the laws of nature, the qualifying clauses are not satisfied and the main clauses do not apply to the agent. But if "others shall observe the same laws toward him," the qualifying clauses are satisfied and the agent is required to obey the main clauses.

Here is a fruitful way of looking at the structure of Hobbes's laws of nature. Think of the rules of traditional morality as summarized in the main clauses of the laws of nature. Hobbes wishes to draw a crucial distinction between two different sorts of violations of these rules, based on a difference in the motives of the violating agents. Imagine that one agent violates a moral rule in hopes of gaining an advantage over others who he believes are following the rules (a lone thief in a group of law-abiding citizens

[18] Ibid., p. 145.

346

would be an example). In section 4-3, we suggested calling such a violation *offensive*. Another agent may violate a moral rule because he believes that others are generally violating it and that he will suffer an unfair disadvantage if he complies while they are not (e.g., an individual in a society of inveterate tax-cheaters may underestimate his income with the aim of paying only his fair share). In the terminology introduced in section 4-3, his violation is *defensive*. Then we may express Hobbes's point by saying that defensive violations of traditional moral rules (e.g., the main clauses of the laws of nature) are morally permissible, while offensive violations are not.

On this interpretation, we must modify Hobbes's claim that the Golden Rule summarizes his laws of nature. It in fact summarizes only their main clauses, for in telling us to treat others as we *wish* them to treat us, it is a principle of unilateralism. It requires us to treat others well whether they are reciprocating or not. A principle that does summarize Hobbes's laws of nature, given their two-part structure, would read roughly as follows: Do unto others as they do unto you. Because it glitters less brightly as an inspiring ideal of moral conduct than does the Golden Rule, we shall call it the Copper Rule.

The Copper Rule, like the qualifying clauses of the laws of nature, is imprecise in two respects that concern matching our violations to the violations of others. First, with respect to a given law of nature, am I allowed to violate it only in my relations with specific individuals who are violating it in their relations with me? Or if enough others violate it, am I completely freed of any requirement to comply? If so, how many others must violate in order to trigger the lapse of my own obligation? Second, am I released from obligations law by law, according to whether (a sufficient number of) others are complying with that particular law? Or is it only a breakdown in compliance with the main clauses of the laws of nature in general that releases me from my obligations to comply with these clauses? Hobbes does not address these questions explicitly. In the last-quoted passage, he indicates that violation of several laws of nature by all others is a sufficient condition of my release from any obligation to follow those laws.

347

And in his discussion of covenants, he implies that lack of assurance that the single other party will comply with this particular covenant releases me from my duty to comply with it. But these two fragmentary statements are compatible with many different views about one's obligations under a system of rules with which some others are partly complying. In the absence of specification of such a view, Hobbes's laws of nature and the Copper Rule do not provide detailed practical guidance for action in the real world. We shall take up this point again in our discussion of justice and fairness in section 9-4.

Viewing all laws of nature as complexes of main and qualifying clauses helps us understand and clarify a potentially confusing remark that Hobbes makes right after the above-quoted statement of the first law of nature. He identifies the first clause of the rule ("seek peace") as the fundamental law of nature, and the second clause ("use all means . . . to defend ourselves") as the "sum of the right of nature."[19] This is confusing because it suggests that the qualifying clause is not really part of the relevant law of nature. On our interpretation, what Hobbes is trying to get across is expressed more clearly as follows: The first and fundamental law of nature consists of a conjunction of a requirement and a permission, each based on self-preservation. The requirement involves seeking peace as a necessary means of preservation, but applies only when there is reasonable hope of peace. This rule derives from right reason, or rational prudence, and is a moral *requirement* because its status as such is necessary if it is to enable agents to rely sufficiently on one another so as to obtain peace. (A mere *permission* to seek peace, even if everyone fully expected everyone else to act in accordance with it, would not insure peace, for such a permission is consistent with a like permission to seek war and conquest.) The permission to use any means necessary for defense expresses our right of nature and limits the application of the requirement to seek peace to those occasions where peace can reasonably be expected. (When peace can be expected, seeking it is the best means of self-preservation,

---

[19] Ibid., chap. 14, p. 117.

and the relevant permission permits just what the relevant requirement requires.) This two-part structure—a main-clause requirement limited by a qualifying-clause permission—carries over into the other laws of nature which derive from the first. The sorts of conduct listed in the main clauses are required as means to peace, when one can reasonably hope for peace. And the right-of-nature-based permission to use all necessary means of defense is represented by qualifying clauses covering circumstances of nonreciprocation.

But when do the main clauses of the laws of nature apply? When do the qualifying clauses come into play? And who is to decide this? As noted above, the wording of Hobbes's very definition of a law of nature hints that the agent himself is the appropriate decision-maker, at least in the state of nature where there are no authoritative interpreters of natural law. But if agents themselves decide whether moral requirements apply to them, are these still "requirements" in any reasonable sense? This raises a difficult issue, both for the interpretation of Hobbes and for the development of Hobbesian philosophy. Is there morality outside civil society, in the state of nature? Answering this question will lay the groundwork for our rule-egoistic interpretation of Hobbes's moral theory.

9-2. Morality in the State of Nature

Are there such things as principles of natural morality which exist independent of and prior to social arrangements established by consent or convention? In particular, are Hobbes's laws of nature such principles? Hobbes's own position on this issue is ambiguous. There is some evidence that he held morality, and justice in particular, to be purely conventional. This skepticism about morality existing outside civil society and its social conventions is clearly expressed in the following two passages from chapters 13 and 15 of *Leviathan*, which for convenience are labeled P1 and P2.

(P1) To this war of every man, against every man, this also is consequent; that nothing can be unjust. The notions of right and wrong, justice and injustice have there no place. Where there is no common power, there is no law: where no law, no injustice. Force, and fraud, are in war the two cardinal virtues. Justice, and injustice . . . are qualities, that relate to men in society, not in solitude.[20]

(P2) But because covenants of mutual trust, where there is a fear of not performance on either part, as hath been said in the former chapter [chapter 14], are invalid; though the original of justice be the making of covenants; yet injustice actually there can be none, till the cause of such fear be taken away; which while men are in the natural condition of war, cannot be done. Therefore before the names of just, and unjust can have place, there must be some coercive power, to compel men equally to the performance of their covenants.[21]

Passage P1 follows shortly after Hobbes's description of the nature of an (active) war of all against all, while passage P2 is the immediate sequel to his definition of injustice as the violation of a covenant. In these two passages, Hobbes seems to be making the very strong claim that terms such as "right," "wrong," and most especially "just" and "unjust" are *meaningless* outside of civil society. That is, certain logical prerequisites of their having meaning are not satisfied in the state of nature. Thus, "justice" without civil society is like "touchdown" without the game of football—a meaningless term cut loose from the contextual background that could give it a sense.

We should not, however, accept this skeptical view as Hobbes's considered position, for a contrasting and more plausible view can be derived from what he says about the validity of covenants of mutual trust in the state of nature. As noted in section 9-1, his *general* view is that such covenants are invalid because the first party called on to perform has no assurance that if he does his

[20] Ibid., chap. 13, p. 115.
[21] Ibid., chap. 15, p. 131.

part the second party will follow suit. In skeptical passage P2, Hobbes speaks as if this general view were his complete view on covenants of mutual trust in the state of nature, but it is not.[22] As pointed out in section 4-3, in his discussion of the Fool (which immediately follows passage P2), Hobbes clearly indicates that the *second* party to a state-of-nature covenant of mutual trust is bound to do his part if the first party does his. In this special case, the fear of "not performance" by the other side is absent; hence, an injustice is done if the party in question, that is, the second party, fails to reciprocate. Furthermore, Hobbes qualifies his claim that the first party is never required to perform his part of a state-of-nature covenant. This is so only if the first party's fear of being cheated derives from something that occurs *after* the covenant has been made (e.g., he then hears of past cheating by the second party), for in entering into a covenant one accepts an obligation under the known conditions and in effect waives the right to withdraw unless those conditions change in some relevant way.[23] This qualification is not only plausible in its own right, it fits with Hobbes's general view, discussed in section 7-5, that we can, by particular voluntary acts waive our rights to later use fear or self-defense as either excuses or justifications for certain actions (e.g., fleeing in battle).

Note also that the loopholes in Hobbes's claim that state-of-nature covenants of mutual trust are invalid are enormous ones. All second parties, and any first parties without new evidence about the untrustworthiness of their second parties, are obligated to perform their parts of state-of-nature covenants, and they act unjustly if they do not. Only the first party who learns something relevant and new between agreement and time for performance is not obligated to perform. It is therefore totally wrong for Hobbes, in passage P2, to summarize his stated doctrines as implying the invalidity of covenants of mutual trust in the state

[22] For generally fine discussions of covenants in Hobbes's state of nature, see Warrender, chap. 3; and Brian Barry, "Warrender and His Critics," in *Hobbes and Rousseau*, ed. Maurice Cranston and Richard Peters (Garden City, N.Y.: Doubleday, 1972), pp. 37–65.

[23] *Leviathan*, chap. 14, p. 125.

of nature. They instead imply the validity of many such covenants, and they entail—at a minimum—that the concept of a state-of-nature injustice makes sense. This concept is instantiated, for example, by any second-party violation of a state-of-nature covenant in which the first party has done his part. In addition, the qualifications to Hobbes's claim about the invalidity of state-of-nature covenants would seem, in principle, to carry over to the other laws of nature. If other parties are complying with the main clauses of these laws, or if one voluntarily waives one's right to treat others' noncompliance with these clauses as a justification for one's own noncompliance, one acts wrongly or unjustly if one fails to comply with the clauses.

What is the source of Hobbes's evident ambivalence about the status of morality and moral principles in the state of nature? A useful clue can be garnered from the context in which two of Hobbes's conflicting assertions occur. Passage P1 follows the argument that the state of nature is a war of all against all, and it emphasizes the absence of morality and justice when a condition of war exists. By contrast, the reply to the Fool, in which it is indicated that second parties are morally bound to complete state-of-nature covenants, emphasizes that the state of nature can be a prelude to the formation of a civil society. This suggests that Hobbes's claims about morality in the state of nature may vary according to the aspect of that condition which he is emphasizing (or thinking of)—its warlike present or its potential for transformation by agreement into a peaceful future. To be more precise, let us say that two or more parties are in an *unadulterated* state of nature (with respect to one another) if there is no common power over them and if they have no hopes, plans, or expectations of establishing one. Such parties are in an *attenuated* state of nature if, despite presently lacking a common power, they hope, plan, or expect to establish one in the future.[24] Our arguments

---

[24] These definitions are imprecise in the same ways as our original definitions of groups being in a state of nature. See section 3-2. Also, the parties' hopes or expectations of peace may be stronger or weaker. So the distinction between unadulterated and attenuated states of nature is really one of degree along several dimensions.

of sections 3-3 through 4-4 suggest that it is the unadulterated state of nature in which anticipation is likely to be the most rational strategy (for individuals and small groups), in which a war of all will likely ensue and in which morality (as described in the main clauses of the laws of nature) will have no place. In an attenuated state of nature, on the other hand, following the main clauses of the laws of nature is the most rational strategy, agreement on a common power may be forthcoming, and the precepts expressed in the main clauses of the laws of nature (including "keep your covenants") are both rules of rational prudence (right reason) and moral requirements.

What is important to realize, however, is that laws of nature, with their two-part structure, are appropriate for the state of nature in *either* form. If the state of nature in question is (predominantly) attenuated, the main clauses of the laws generally apply. If one is in a (predominantly) unadulterated state of nature, the qualifying clauses generally apply, and one is permitted to defend oneself by any means necessary. In either case, the laws of nature are operative: their main clauses hold as moral requirements in the former case, and their qualifying clauses function as moral permissions in the latter case. Thus, whatever Hobbes's ambivalences, his views about the laws of nature and the details of his theory of covenants point to the conclusion that there can be, and are, moral permissions and requirements (including requirements of justice) outside civil society. Hobbesian morality is social, that is, it concerns human interaction. But it is not purely conventional. It is partly natural, with its natural content expressed in the laws of nature.

Two major objections could be raised against our claim that there is morality—consisting of genuine moral ought-principles expressed in the laws of nature—in Hobbes's state of nature. First, it may be suggested that there are no real moral restrictions on agents' state-of-nature conduct, on the account we have given, for so long as each agent decides whether conditions are such as to release him from the requirements of the main clauses of the laws of nature, he is free to do as he pleases. As Hobbes says,

"He is free, that can be free when he will."[25] Second, in certain passages, Hobbes seems to endorse the view that might makes right, implying a skeptical attitude toward natural morality.

The first objection may be interpreted in various ways. In its *logical* version, it holds that by the logic of the concept of a (moral) *requirement*, any rule or principle whose application an agent is able to escape at will is not a requirement. But this logical claim, even though plausible, does not imply that the laws of nature are not requirements. According to Hobbes, one escapes applications of the main clause of a law of nature only if one *sincerely believes* that the qualifying clause is operative.[26] But belief is not directly subject to the will; we cannot simply believe whatever we want to believe. Hence, the laws of nature do restrict our freedom—they require us to follow their main clauses unless we really believe that others are unwilling to reciprocate.

Answering the logical version of the first objection this way leads naturally to an *epistemological* version of it. According to this version, only the agent himself can tell what he sincerely believes about others' likely compliance; hence he is free to invoke the qualifying clauses of the laws of nature at will. This is wrong for two reasons. As Hobbes admits, we can sometimes infer others' probable beliefs from their behavior and demeanor.[27] Therefore, other parties will sometimes be able to discern when a natural law violator's claim of acting in self-defense is insincere. Further, because the laws of nature prescribe individually and mutually beneficial means to peace, it is appropriate for rational agents to adopt what H. L. A. Hart calls an "internal" attitude toward them—that is, to regard them as valid standards of conduct for oneself and others, criticize deviations from them (including by oneself), and so on.[28] But one who has such an internal attitude toward the laws of nature will not be free to

---

[25] *Leviathan*, chap. 26, p. 252.
[26] *Philosophical Rudiments*, chap. 1, sec. 10, pp. 9–10 (note); chap. 3, secs. 27–28, pp. 45–46 (note).
[27] *Leviathan*, Introduction, pp. xi–xii.
[28] H. L. A. Hart, *The Concept of Law* (Oxford: Clarendon Press, 1961), pp. 55–56.

insincerely invoke their qualifying clauses at will. Powerful psychological constraints will inhibit or prevent this.[29]

However, if parties in the state of nature do insincerely invoke the qualifying clauses, there is no common power to punish them. According to the *enforcement* version of our objection, then, the laws of nature are not requirements in the state of nature, because anyone is free to violate them at will (by falsely invoking their qualifying clauses), in the sense of not being subject to punishment for doing so. But this is no real objection at all. Moral, as opposed to legal, requirements are not necessarily backed by any coercive enforcement mechanism. Lack of enforcement of the laws of nature is a serious problem in the state of nature. Together with the presence of dominators, it makes the state of nature tend toward a war of all against all. But this is, as Hobbes saw, a reason for establishing institutions to enforce the moral requirements embodied in the laws of nature, not a reason for doubting that they really are moral requirements until those institutions exist.

What of the second objection—that Hobbes, instead of acknowledging natural moral requirements, holds that might makes right? As we have seen, Hobbes does describe force as one of the cardinal virtues of war, and he emphasizes the obligation of citizens to obey their sovereign, to whom he ascribes "the greatest of human powers."[30] And he attributes God's authority to his omnipotence, writing, "The right of nature, whereby God reigneth over men, and punisheth those that break his laws, is to be derived, not from his creating them, . . . but from his *irresistible power*."[31] This may lead to the supposition that, for Hobbes, might makes right.

And there is a relationship between might and right for Hobbes, but it is an indirect relationship that is entirely consistent with viewing the laws of nature as moral requirements binding even

[29] This is not the same point we made when considering the logical version of the objection. The former concerned psychological constraints on belief; this one concerns psychological constraints on misrepresenting one's beliefs.
[30] *Leviathan*, chap. 10, p. 74.
[31] Ibid., chap. 31, p. 345.

TABLE 1

Who is bound by what moral requirements

	Laws of Nature (Prudentially Grounded)	Obligations (Created by Consent)
God	No	No
Sovereign	Yes	No
Citizen	Yes	Yes

in a state of nature. The key to understanding this relationship rests on our earlier (section 7-5) distinction between two sorts of moral requirements in Hobbes's theory: obligations and ought-principles. The latter are the laws of nature and are grounded in rational prudence. The former are created by consent and derive their binding force from the third law of nature. The rights of God and the sovereign consist in their not being subject to moral requirements of one or both of these kinds, to which ordinary citizens are subject, as indicated in Table 1.

Consider first the sovereign. He owes no contractual obligations to his subjects because he is not (qua sovereign) a party to the original social contract; and he is free to abrogate commitments to his subjects because the law at any time is what he wills it to be.[32] The sovereign thus fully retains his right of nature,[33] but he is—because of his potential vulnerability to foreign powers and his subjects' concerted actions—bound by the laws of nature. In particular, he is required by a special law of nature to procure the safety and well-being of his people.[34] Given Hobbes's assumption, discussed in section 5-5, that the sovereign's interests coincide with those of his people, this special law of nature has the same prudential basis as the other natural laws.

Citizens, being vulnerable to one another, are also bound by the laws of nature, but since they must surrender portions of the right of nature to achieve security through the original contract, they are also bound by *obligations*, most particularly the obliga-

[32] Ibid., chap. 18, pp. 161–62; chap. 26, p. 252.
[33] Ibid., chap. 28, pp. 297–98.
[34] Ibid., chap. 30, p. 322.

tion to obey the civil law. God, by contrast, being all powerful, has no need of prudent conduct and no need to consent to any obligations.[35] He retains his full right of nature and is subject to neither sort of moral requirement. His omnipotence accounts for his moral freedom, removing the grounds that—in the case of other beings—justify moral requirements and motivate compliance with them.

Thus, there is a sense in which might does make right for Hobbes. Unlimited might obviates the need to follow the laws of nature and to surrender parts of the right of nature. Lesser might, that of the civil sovereign, obviates the latter need but not the former. In neither case does might create right; it merely creates propitious circumstances for retention of natural moral permission rights. Further, save for the limiting case of God, the requirements laid down in the laws of nature apply to the mighty as well as to the meek. In the end, then, the might-makes-right doctrine, in the form that Hobbes may be said to endorse it, presupposes—rather than contradicts—the view that there are natural moral requirements which apply to all mortals. There *is* morality in Hobbes's state of nature, embodied in the laws of nature. It remains to consider what sort of moral system these laws constitute.

9-3. Rule Egoism

Consequentialist moral theories evaluate acts or kinds of acts according to the value of the outcomes (i.e., actual or expected effects) of such acts. Utilitarian and egoistic variants of consequentialism differ in terms of how specified outcomes are valued. Egoistic theories evaluate outcomes in terms of the well-being or preferences of the acting agent. Utilitarian theories evaluate them in terms of the well-being or preferences of all affected individuals, with each person's well-being or preferences being given equal weight. Thus, utilitarian and egoistic versions of conse-

---

[35] Though Hobbes allows, following the biblical story, that there is a special covenantal relationship between God and the people of Abraham. See, e.g., ibid., chap. 40.

quentialism differ in their answers to the question "Consequences for *whom?*" Act and rule variants of consequentialism differ in terms of what outcomes (consequences) are evaluated. Act-consequentialist theories evaluate *particular acts* in terms of the value of their (actual or expected) outcomes. Rule-consequentialist theories evaluate types of actions (or rules requiring them) in terms of the (actual or expected) outcomes of certain agents performing, or trying to perform, acts of that type as a rule (i.e., the outcomes of the relevant agents following, or trying to follow, rules requiring acts of that type). Act and rule consequentialists differ in their answers to the question "Consequences of *what?*"

While there is a large literature on the variety of utilitarian systems and the relative merits of act and rule utilitarianism,[36] until very recently most discussions of egoism have assumed that egoistic moral theories must be versions of act egoism.[37] But rule-egoistic moral theories are possible, and Hobbes's moral theory is of this sort.[38] In particular, Hobbes's laws of nature constitute a system of prescriptive moral rules, which are grounded or justified by a rule-egoistic principle (REP) of the following sort.[39]

(REP) Each agent should attempt always to follow that set of general rules of conduct whose acceptance (and sincere at-

[36] See, e.g., *Contemporary Utilitarianism,* ed. Michael Bayles (Garden City, N.Y.: Doubleday, 1968); and Dan Brock, "Recent Work on Utilitarianism," *American Philosophical Quarterly* 10 (1973): 241–76.

[37] See, e.g., Jesse Kalin, "In Defense of Egoism," in *Morality and Rational Self-Interest,* ed. David Gauthier (Englewood Cliffs, N.J.: Prentice-Hall, 1970), pp. 64–87. Cf., however, John Hospers, "Rule Egoism," *The Personalist* 54 (Autumn 1973): 391–95. Note that Hospers' characterization of rule egoism differs from that offered in this section.

[38] To the best of my knowledge, this was first observed in print by Stanley Moore, in "Hobbes on Obligation, Moral and Political," *Journal of the History of Philosophy* 9 (January 1971): 43–62; 10 (January 1972): 29–41. His reasons for ascribing rule egoism to Hobbes are, however, different from those emphasized here.

[39] This specific principle, as interpreted below, is not to be attributed to Hobbes in all its particulars. The claim is that a rule-egoistic grounding of some such sort is what he intends and that this is the most defensible form in which it can be put.

tempt to follow) by him on all occasions would produce the best (expected) outcomes for him.

Several points should be made in clarifying this principle. It is an *egoistic* principle in that it evaluates (sets of) rules in terms of the consequences *for the agent* of his attempting to follow those rules. It is a *rule*-egoistic principle, since it compares and evaluates (sets of) general rules, rather than particular actions, in terms of their consequences for the agent (i.e., the consequences for the agent of his always attempting to follow them). The principle evaluates (sets of) rules according to the consequences of the agent's *accepting* them (i.e., attempting to act on them), not according to the consequences of the agent's always succeeding in acting on them.[40] Rules, or sets of them, are evaluated in terms of the *expected* consequences of the agent's trying to act on them. This means that *prior expectations* of the consequences of general adherence to the rules, not their actual post hoc consequences, are what counts. It is not intended to imply that expected value maximization is necessarily the rational way to evaluate (sets of) rules, given such prior expectations.[41] Finally, it should be noted that the rules in question are *general* in two senses, but not in a third sense. They describe kinds or types of acts that the same agent might perform on different occasions and that different agents might perform (i.e., they do not involve time-specific or person-specific descriptions, such as "cheating-at-time-*t*" or "killing-by-Jones"). But the rules *need not* be general in the sense that the principle must pick out the same rules for everyone. Rather, principle (REP) provides a criterion for selecting a set of rules for each person. Whether or to what extent these sets of rules overlap is not decided or implied by the principle itself; it is to be determined by further considerations.

---

[40] The relevant notion of acceptance involves motivation to act, guilt at nonaction, and so on. See, e.g., Richard Brandt, "Some Merits of One Form of Rule-Utilitarianism," in *Utilitarianism: Text and Critical Essays*, ed. Samuel Gorovitz (Indianapolis: Bobbs-Merrill, 1971), sec. XIII. See also section 9-2 on Hart's notion of an "internal" attitude toward rules.

[41] In particular, we do not want to rule out the possibility that a rational egoist should follow a disaster-avoidance strategy (section 5-3) rather than a utility maximization strategy in choosing a set of rules to live by.

Having explained what a rule-egoistic moral theory is, we must now consider three distinct questions about such theories. Is Hobbes's own moral theory really rule-egoistic? What are the substantive advantages of and problems for rule-egoistic theories of the sort we attribute to Hobbes? Can a theory that is rule-egoistic genuinely qualify as a moral theory? The remainder of this section will be devoted to answering these questions in turn.

As regards the first question, the clearest evidence of the nature of Hobbes's moral theory is contained in his own description of the status of the laws of nature. It is obvious from Hobbes's definition of, descriptions of, and comments on the laws of nature that they are general prescriptive rules of conduct.[42] At the same time, his definitions of natural law in all three political works make it evident that these laws are fundamentally rules of *prudence*.[43] Further, in a key passage in *Leviathan*, Hobbes makes clear that the main aim of his moral theory is to reveal the consequentialist grounding or justification of traditional morality and its requirements. He writes:

> All men agree on this, that peace is good, and therefore also the way, or means of peace, which, as I have shewed before, are *justice, gratitude, modesty, equity, mercy*, and the rest of the laws of nature, are good: that is to say; *moral virtues*; and their contrary *vices*, evil. Now the science of virtue and vice, is moral philosophy; and therefore the true doctrine of the laws of nature, is the true moral philosophy. But the writers of moral philosophy, though they acknowledge the same virtues and vices; yet not seeing wherein consisted their goodness; nor that they come to be praised, as the means of peaceable, sociable, and comfortable living, place them in a mediocrity of passions.[44]

These observations would suffice to establish the general rule-egoistic interpretation of Hobbes's moral theory were it not for

[42] Nor are these mere rules of thumb of some act-consequentialist system. See the discussion below on the advantages of a rule-consequentialist system.

[43] See *Elements of Law*, part 1, chap. 2, sec. 1, pp. 86–87; *Philosophical Rudiments*, chap. 2, sec. 1, p. 16; *Leviathan*, chap. 14, pp. 116–17.

[44] *Leviathan*, chap. 15, pp. 146–47.

the prominent competing view—best represented by Warrender—that Hobbes's moral theory is a divine command theory.[45] This alternate view draws its inspiration from the passage in *Leviathan* immediately following that just quoted. There, after noting that the laws of nature are not "laws" in the proper sense, but rather theorems of prudence, Hobbes adds, "But yet if we consider the same theorems, as delivered in the word of God, that by right commandeth all things; then are they properly called laws."[46] Putting this passage together with the need to find a ground for moral requirements that exist independent of the State and sovereign, Warrender suggests that Hobbes intends his laws of nature to bind us because they are commands of God.

The divine-command interpretation of Hobbes's moral theory must be rejected.[47] In the first place, it is not implied by the last-quoted sentence. Read in the context of Hobbes's previous observation that the laws of nature are rules of prudence rather than laws (i.e., commands of an authority), that sentence most likely means "When (or if) these rules are viewed, in a religious context, as the commands of God, who has the right to rule all things, then they may be properly called or considered laws in that context." Read in this way, the sentence shows how religious people who make certain background assumptions may regard the laws of nature as laws and explains why they are generally called "laws." It also forwards Hobbes's project of reconciling various sorts of requirements placed on the individual by suggesting a way in which the requirements of two spheres—morality and religion—may be viewed as identical.[48] But it does not indicate that we should or must follow the laws of nature *because* they are God's commands.

[45] Warrender, *The Political Philosophy of Hobbes*. See also A. E. Taylor, "The Ethical Doctrine of Hobbes," *Philosophy* (1938), reprinted in *Hobbes Studies*, ed. Keith Brown (Oxford: Basil Blackwell, 1965), pp. 35–55; and F. C. Hood, *The Divine Politics of Thomas Hobbes* (Oxford: Oxford University Press, 1964).

[46] *Leviathan*, chap. 15, p. 147.

[47] For other discussions that concur on this point, see Barry, "Warrender and His Critics"; Watkins, *Hobbes's System of Ideas*, chap. 5; and Stuart M. Brown, Jr., "The Taylor Thesis: Some Objections," in *Hobbes Studies*, ed. Brown.

[48] For more on this reconciliation project, see section 9-5.

Second, and more important, God plays *no substantive role* in Hobbes's moral and political philosophy. In particular, God plays no role in the derivation of the actual contents of the laws of nature. Nor is this merely accidental, with Hobbes having simply neglected to mention how theological reasoning enters into the derivation of these laws. Rather, it is a necessary consequence of certain doctrines of Hobbes's "philosophical theology": that we lack knowledge of God and that we lack scientific-philosophical knowledge of what he commands. We lack knowledge of God, because while we can infer his existence by a first-cause argument, we can have no idea of him in our minds since he is infinite.[49] Thus, the descriptions we apply to him are either purely negative (e.g., he is not finite) or merely honorific.[50] We lack scientific-philosophical knowledge of what God commands because knowledge of this sort must be certain.[51] But the laws of nature could not be certain if grounded in salvational prudence, for we have no natural knowledge of man's estate after death,[52] nor can we rely with certainty on the Scripture's report of God's words, for these derive from the fallible testimony of other people.[53] In fact, relying on God's word as the ultimate standard of conduct leads to varying interpretations, conflict, and civil war.[54] The only appropriate standard of interpretation is not philosophical but political: the word of the sovereign.[55] In the end, we must infer the content of God's commands from our knowledge of the contents of the laws of nature, not vice versa.[56] The upshot of all this, as even Warrender seems to admit,[57] is that God plays no substantive role in Hobbes's derivation of the laws of nature or in his moral and political theory.

Therefore, the role of God in Hobbes's moral theory is at most

[49] *Leviathan*, chap. 11, pp. 92–93; chap. 31, p. 351.
[50] Ibid., chap. 31, pp. 350–54.
[51] See section 1-2.
[52] *Leviathan*, chap. 15, p. 135.
[53] Ibid., chap. 7, pp. 52–55.
[54] Ibid., chap. 29, pp. 311–12, 316–18.
[55] Ibid., chap. 42, pp. 537–47.
[56] *Philosophical Rudiments*, chap. 15, sec. 8, pp. 209–10.
[57] Warrender, *The Political Philosophy of Hobbes*, pp. 278, 309.

the purely formal one of grounding the laws of nature. Warrender suggests that this "grounding" operates either by reducing moral obligation to salvational prudence (via the supposition that we will suffer in the afterlife for violating God's laws) or by appealing to God as a self-evident source of obligation.[58] But if salvational prudence can be a genuine ground of moral requirements, then natural prudence can also—and we have no need to go beyond Hobbes's apparent rule egoism in interpreting his moral theory. Nor is it clear how God, *an unknowable first cause*, can be a self-evident source of moral obligation. Thus, putting God into the picture explains neither the content of the laws of nature nor their status as moral requirements. If we can supply a rule-egoistic account that does both these things, we need not be deterred by the existence of the implausible alternative account set forth by the divine-command interpreters.

Our second question concerns the substantive advantages of, and problems with, rule-egoistic moral theories of the type that Hobbes advances. Prior to discussing these, a specific feature of Hobbes's rule-egoistic theory must be noted. As indicated above, rule egoism, as represented, for example, by the REP, allows in principle that different agents may be bound by *different* moral requirements (ought-principles). But Hobbes's particular rule-egoistic theory holds that all individuals are governed by the *same* general requirements, the laws of nature. This claim is based on a key empirical assertion: for *everyone*, seeking peace (when it can be obtained) is the best long-run strategy for promoting one's interests, and the behaviors described in the laws of nature are means to peace. The most likely exceptions to this assertion would seem to involve those individuals in positions of great power or with the potential to seize such power,[59] for it might appear that these individuals do not need peace or that they can obtain a peaceful quiescence from their "inferiors" without treating the latter in the decent ways called for by the laws of nature. Hobbes

[58] Ibid., pp. 310–11.
[59] The case of needy and hardy troublemakers, discussed in section 5-3, might seem to be another exception. But Hobbes's discussion of the fourth law of nature (see section 5-4) suggests that they may be peace-seekers forced into war.

supports the universal applicability of the laws of nature by arguing, in effect, that even these extreme cases—that of the sovereign and the potential usurper of sovereign power—are not exceptions. Even the sovereign is subject to the laws of nature,
including the special requirement to promote the safety and well-
being of his people, for if he ignores natural law he risks loss of
domestic power (section 6-2) and/or the weakening of his position with respect to foreign nations.[60] Nor is it generally in the
interests of the potential revolutionary usurper to forsake peace
in the hope of seizing power. The risks of initial failure are too
great, and temporary success but encourages others to oust the
usurper in turn.[61] So even the most powerful, or potentially powerful, of mortals will generally best promote their interests by
pursuing peace—and the specific means to it enunciated in the
laws of nature—when peace is obtainable.

What are the merits of a rule-egoistic moral theory, which takes
Hobbes's laws of nature as general moral requirements applicable
to all? First, as an *egoistic* system it has great potential motivational force if, as Hobbesian theory suggests, people are predominantly egoistic. This is important, for if we want a moral theory
to be *practical*, in the sense that people can and will follow it if
they come to understand it, the theory must be capable of hook-
ing onto people's actual motivational capacities. Hobbes's theory,
with its two-part rules prescribing the means to peace and the
methods of war, *in that order*, is ideally suited in this regard. It
recommends the traditional principles of morality (with qualifying clauses) on grounds of long-run self-interest, thus achieving
a reconciliation of sorts between the demands of morality and
those of rational prudence.

As a *rule*-egoistic system, with the same rules of conduct applying to all, Hobbes's morality has many of the advantages over
act-consequentialist systems that have been noted by advocates of

[60] *Leviathan*, chap. 19, p. 174.
[61] Ibid., chap. 15, p. 134.

rule-utilitarian theories.[62] Decision-making is easier, less costly, and less time-consuming than under an act-consequentialist scheme. There is less room for self-deceptive shortsightedness. That is, actors cannot manipulate calculations of consequences to approve courses of action that are attractive in the short run but harmful over all, because conduct is determined by general rules rather than case-by-case empirical calculations. Interpersonal co-ordination, reliance, and cooperation, which promote mutual ben-efit, are facilitated by all individuals being required to act in ac-cordance with the same general rules of conduct. In particular, agents do not generally have to correctly estimate other agents' calculations of consequences in order to know how those agents will act in a given situation governed by moral rules.[63]

Along with these advantages, Hobbes's rule-egoistic morality faces certain problems and objections. It may be thought that an egoistic system cannot, for logical or metaethical reasons, prop-erly qualify or count as a *moral* system. Further, because of the qualifying clauses of the laws of nature, the substantive *content* of Hobbes's system may seem too far from the content of tradi-tional morality to be regarded as a reasonable interpretation or extension of the latter. Finally, like rule-utilitarian theories, rule-egoistic theories must deal with the charge that they require agents to act *irrationally* in cases in which those agents believe they could produce better consequences by violating the rules.[64] The remainder of this chapter is devoted to dealing with these diffi-culties, beginning with the metaethical problem.

A number of knowledgeable commentators on Hobbes have

---

[62] See, e.g., Richard Brandt, *A Theory of the Good and the Right* (Oxford: Clarendon Press, 1979), pp. 273–76.

[63] Still, strategic calculation may enter in concerning other parties' tendencies to invoke the qualifying clauses of laws of nature.

[64] See, e.g, J. J. C. Smart, "Extreme and Restricted Utilitarianism," in Bayles, *Contemporary Utilitarianism.* This may be viewed as an instance of the general charge that a moral theory or principle is unacceptable because it sometimes re-quires its own abandonment. For illuminating discussion of the general charge and related issues, see Derek Parfit, *Reasons and Persons* (Oxford: Oxford Uni-versity Press, 1983), chap. 1.

claimed that a system based on prudence cannot, despite Hobbes's assertions to the contrary, be regarded as a *moral* system in the proper sense.[65] Unfortunately, none of these writers describes Hobbes as a *rule* egoist or explicitly considers whether a rule-egoistic system of ought-principles could count as "moral." And it turns out that by the usual criteria offered for classifying principles or systems as "moral," Hobbes's rule egoism almost certainly qualifies as such.

Two sorts of criteria have been offered for distinguishing *moral* rules or principles from those of other sorts. *Material* criteria concern the content or ground of the principles. *Formal* criteria concern the relationship between the agent and the principle, or between society and the principle, without reference to the principle's content. Writers disagree over whether moral principles can be characterized by formal principles alone.[66] The best-known purely formal analysis is R. M. Hare's.[67] He holds that moral principles are prescriptive, universalizable, and overriding. Prescriptive principles are action-guiding; they involve or entail imperatives. Hobbes's laws of nature clearly possess this feature.[68] A universalizable principle contains no essential reference to individuals. It prescribes the same conduct to all unless there are relevant differences between them or their situations. There is no doubt that Hobbes's laws of nature are universalizable: they are eternal, unchangeable, and apply to all mortals, including the sovereign. Their main clauses are summarized in the Golden Rule, which is itself a kind of corollary of universalizability that requires acting on principles equally applicable to all.[69] The laws of nature also appear to be overriding, in that they take precedence

---

[65] Warrender, *The Political Philosophy of Hobbes*, pp. 3–5; Gauthier, *The Logic of Leviathan*, pp. 91–98; Watkins, *Hobbes's System of Ideas*, pp. 56–61; and Thomas Nagel, "Hobbes' Concept of Obligation," *Philosophical Review* 68 (1959): 74.

[66] Many of the best papers on this issue are collected in *The Definition of Morality*, ed. G. Wallace and A. D. M. Walker (London: Methuen, 1970).

[67] Hare, *Freedom and Reason*.

[68] See, e.g., the *Leviathan* definition of a law of nature quoted in section 9-1.

[69] On the relationship between universalizability and the Golden Rule, see Hare, *Freedom and Reason*, pp. 106–8.

over other principles in cases of conflict, or at least Hobbes never indicates that any other sort of principle overrides them. (The right of nature does not *override* the laws of nature when others will not reciprocate; it merely invokes the qualifying clauses of these laws.) Hence, if Hare's formalist position is accepted, Hobbes's rule-egoistic system clearly qualifies as "moral."

The other formal criterion most often appealed to is that the violation of *moral* principles brings on social sanctions like ostracism, criticism, and punishment.[70] Hobbes's laws of nature satisfy this criterion as well. As we saw in the reply to the Fool (section 4-3), state-of-nature violators of the laws of nature are ostracized and kept out of civil society. In the commonwealth, the laws of nature are incorporated into civil law (section 6-1), and violations of these laws are punished by the State.[71] We may conclude that, given the most prominent criteria in the literature, if a formalist account of "morality" is adequate, Hobbes's rule-egoistic laws of nature count as a system of moral principles.

Some, however, believe that a material criterion must be added to formal criteria to achieve an adequate analysis of what a moral principle or system is. The natural criterion usually cited is that the principle make reference to, or be designed to promote, social harmony, social utility, or the common good. Thus, for example, William Frankena writes: "This material condition, moreover, must reflect a concern for others or a consideration of social cohesiveness and the common good. . . . Some reference to the welfare of others, the security of social life, etc., is part of the meaning of words like 'moral' and 'morality.' "[72] It is arguable, however, that Hobbes's system satisfies even this material criterion. Because he assumes that social peace and harmony is a necessary condition for individual well-being, Hobbes views the laws of nature as instruments of both individual *and social* utility. When

---

[70] See the introduction to *The Definition of Morality,* ed. Wallace and Walker, pp. 14–16.

[71] *Leviathan,* chap. 26, p. 253.

[72] William Frankena, "Recent Conceptions of Morality," in Hector-Neri Castaneda and George Nakhnikian, *Morality and the Language of Conduct* (Detroit: Wayne State University Press, 1965), p. 9.

following these laws, agents promote their own utility *by promoting* the utility of all in certain specified ways. In fact, as we shall see in the next section, the ties between individual and social utility are so close here, for Hobbes, that he offers an essentially *rule-utilitarian* argument in support of at least one specific law of nature. Given all this, it would be difficult to deny that Hobbes's laws of nature give the required consideration to, in Frankena's words, "social cohesiveness and the common good . . . [and] the security of social life."

An alternative material criterion of "morality" that clearly rules out some egoistic systems is contained in a statement by Gauthier: "In no system of rational prudence, in which all reasons for acting must reduce to considerations of what, in each situation, is most advantageous for the agent, can moral obligation be introduced."[73] But this criterion does not disqualify Hobbes's *rule-egoistic* moral system, in which the laws of nature function as binding moral requirements that agents may not violate even if they believe such violation "most advantageous" in the particular situation.

We may conclude that Hobbes's rule-egoistic moral system qualifies as "moral" according to the usual metaethical criteria of morality. In spite of all this, one could still refuse to honor Hobbes's system with the appellation "moral" simply because of the role that egoistic considerations play in it. But this would be a rather arbitrary verbal move, serving only to obscure the many significant similarities between Hobbes's rule-egoistic system and other systems that are uncontroversially classifiable as "moral." It would also violate the spirit of a venerable philosophical tradition, going at least as far back as Plato, which emphasizes the intimate connections between morality and rational self-interest.

9-4. Egoism, Utility, and Justice

We have argued that the rule-egoistic theory of conduct embodied in Hobbes's laws of nature qualifies as "moral" according to

---

[73] Gauthier, *The Logic of Leviathan*, p. 97. A similar suggestion may be found in James Fishkin, *The Limits of Obligation* (New Haven: Yale University Press, 1982), p. 52.

the most prominent *metaethical* criteria in the literature. But is the actual content of Hobbes's moral system such as to allow us to view it as an interpretation or plausible extension of traditional morality, as Hobbes apparently intends? In this section, we shall undertake to answer this question by examining certain aspects of the relationship between Hobbes's moral system and the two central concepts of morality emphasized by modern philosophers: social utility and justice.

The main ground for skepticism concerning Hobbes's laws of nature representing traditional morality revolves around the qualifying clauses of those laws. Suppose traditional morality were unambiguously, and at all levels, a unilateralist Golden Rule morality. Then Hobbes's Copper Rule morality, with qualifying clauses that relax ordinary constraints when reciprocity cannot be expected, could not properly be considered a version (even a modified version) of traditional morality. However, Golden Rule unilateralism is best viewed as representing certain *ideals* of traditional Western ethics. Such unilateralism has not been required, in practice, nor has it been uniformly urged by theorists as a guide to practice. In book I of the *Republic*, the virtuous Polymarchus presents the then prevailing conception of justice— doing good to friends and evil to enemies. Later, Christian philosophers such as Thomas Aquinas acknowledge the existence of qualifying clauses in important moral rules by, for example, sanctioning killing in self-defense.[74] This Copper Rule conception of morality has survived to the present day, where it is represented by endorsements of various principles of fairness and reciprocity.[75] Thus, one might reasonably contend that Hobbes's laws of nature, with qualifying clauses, represent the actual practice morality of the Western moral tradition, as lived by ordinary people and described by a significant number of moral theorists.

To the extent that the qualifying clauses of Hobbes's laws of nature do represent a departure from more traditional moral theories, they may in some respects constitute an *improvement*. Consider a pair of now familiar objections against certain rule-

[74] See *Summa Theologica* II–II, Q64, art. 7.
[75] See, e.g., Herbert Morris, "Persons and Punishment," *The Monist* 52 (October 1968): 475–501; and Rawls, *A Theory of Justice*, sec. 18.

utilitarian systems.[76] Because they require people to follow the rules having best consequences if *all* followed (or tried to follow) them, these forms of rule-utilitarianism require individuals to act irrationally in two sorts of circumstances. They tell agents to follow the "best" rule even when this will have bad consequences because others are not following that rule or are following some alternative rule. And when enough others are following the "best" rule to produce its good effects without one's own compliance, they require one's compliance even if one could produce better consequences by acting otherwise. Following such a rule-utilitarianism system prevents one from *minimizing* the bad effects of others' noncompliance in the first sort of case and from *maximizing* the good effects made possible by others' compliance in the second sort of case.

Hobbes's laws of nature, with their qualifying clauses, may be viewed as avoiding the problem posed by minimizing cases, while still being subject to the problem with maximizing cases. The serious minimizing difficulty is avoided, because one is not required to comply with law-of-nature main clauses when others are not complying. The maximizing difficulty remains, but it is a much less serious one. The costs of inefficient "overcompliance" with a rule are generally less than the costs of wasted compliance when others do not comply. (For example, the likely cost to an individual of being an extra volunteer in a larger-than-needed volunteer army, wasted time, is much less than the likely cost of being another helpless member of a smaller-than-needed volunteer army—death, wounds, or imprisonment at the hands of an invader.) Further, when more than enough are willing to comply, a conventional or contractual scheme can usually be worked out by tacit or explicit agreement that allows some to noncomply efficiently. Various methods of parceling out the extra benefits reaped are possible—rotation of who need not comply, redistribution of some of the benefits of noncompliance, and so on. Such agreed upon arrangements of limited noncompliance are most likely to

---

[76]See David Lyons, *The Forms and Limits of Utilitarianism* (Oxford: Clarendon Press, 1965), pp. 128–32. The rule-utilitarian systems in question in this paragraph and the next are essentially systems of utilitarian generalization.

occur just when they are most important. That is, in ongoing or repeated situations where experience teaches how much compliance is needed, extra utility can be repeatedly reaped by limited noncompliance, and the benefits of noncompliance can readily be shared by regular patterns of rotation or redistribution. Thus, in practice, overcompliance, because it is a sign of general willingness to cooperate, is a much more tractable problem than undercompliance, which is often a sign of unwillingness to cooperate. It is this asymmetry which makes it rational to design moral rules, as Hobbes designs his laws of nature, so as to be sensitive to the minimizing problem but not the maximizing one.

Save for the qualifying clauses, which serve to deal with minimizing problems, the actual content of Hobbes's laws of nature do not differ much from the general substantive rules that one would expect in a rule-utilitarian system. The conduct recommended in the main clauses of the laws of nature—respect, equity, agreement-keeping, and so forth—is the sort of conduct that promotes the well-being of others and society, as well as that of the agent. Nor is this overlap between Hobbes's egoistic rules and utilitarian rules accidental. As noted in section 9-3, the main clauses of natural law are supposed to pick out precisely those kinds of conduct that tend to promote one's own interests, *because* they promote peace by also respecting and advancing the interests of others. On this view, which holds that peace is a prerequisite of well-being and that decent treatment of others is a prerequisite of peace, egoistic and utilitarian considerations tend to merge with one another. It is thus not too surprising that Hobbes, who held this view, occasionally supports his laws of nature with arguments that seem as much rule-*utilitarian* as rule-egoistic. Most notably, Hobbes argues for gratitude toward those who bestow free gifts as follows: "For no man giveth, but with intention of good to himself; . . . of which if men see they shall be frustrated, there will be no beginning of benevolence, or trust; nor consequently of mutual help; nor of reconciliation of one man to another."[77] This passage is utilitarian in that it appears to appeal

[77] *Leviathan*, chap. 15, p. 138. See also the argument for the seventh law of nature (ibid., p. 140).

to the general bad consequences of people's being ungrateful, rather than the bad consequences for an individual of his being ungrateful.

The close links between Hobbes's rule egoism and rule utilitarianism can be further illuminated by comparing Hobbes's position with one enunciated by John Stuart Mill. Early in chapter 4 of *Utilitarianism*, Mill argues that "each person's happiness is a good to that person, and the general happiness, therefore, a good to the aggregate of all persons."[78] This argument is puzzling, because it is difficult to understand what the conclusion means. What is it for something comprised of many parts (i.e., the general good) to be a good for an aggregate of persons? If it suffices that one of the parts (e.g., X's happiness) be a good for one of the aggregate (e.g., X), then the conclusion follows from Mill's highly plausible premise. But if more than this is meant—if, for example, it is implied that any or each member of the aggregate values any component of the general happiness other than his own individual happiness—it is difficult to see how the conclusion follows without auxiliary premises being introduced.

Hobbes, like Mill, holds that certain general social states or modes of conduct should be regarded as good by all and that this follows from each regarding his own welfare as good. But, unlike in Mill's case, the assumptions that underlie the inference are readily discernible. These assumptions posit the existence of certain specific causal relations. For Hobbes, *social peace* is a general good, something desired by everyone, because it is a causally necessary condition of the security and welfare of each individual. This idea is represented in Figure 13, with solid arrows standing for causation, broken arrows for desires, and X and Y for any

FIGURE 13

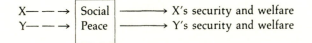

X— — → | Social | ———→ X's security and welfare
Y— — → | Peace | ———→ Y's security and welfare

[78] In *Utilitarianism*, ed. Gorovitz, p. 37.

distinct individuals. Conduct in accordance with the laws of nature, *lawful conduct*, is also a general good, something desired by everyone. Each individual values his *own* lawful conduct as a means to social peace and his own security, and each values *another's* lawful conduct as contributing to one's security in two ways— directly (i.e., he treats one decently) and indirectly by promoting peace (i.e., he does not promote escalating violence and a breakdown in the social order). This idea is represented in Figure 14, with the symbols having the same meaning as in Figure 13. Positing the causal relationships depicted in Figure 14, as Hobbes does, enables us to see how rational concern for one's own well-being can, in an interactive setting, lead each and all to value certain general goods: social peace and lawful conduct (by oneself and others).

Remember, however, that one's lawful conduct tends toward peace only when others are seeking peace; otherwise it tends toward one's victimization and ruin. This observation leads us back to a problem concerning the interpretation of the qualifying clauses of the laws of nature that was noted in section 9-1. Perfect compliance with the main clauses of all the laws of nature by all others clearly requires your own compliance even in a state of nature. And universal noncompliance with all main clauses by all others clearly invokes the qualifying clauses and frees you to do as you wish. But what of compliance by others that falls between these two extremes—*partial* compliance? What if, as would generally be the case, *some* others follow the main clauses of *some* laws of nature *some* of the time?

Though Hobbes does not specifically address this question, we can construct a plausible Hobbesian answer that is consistent with

FIGURE 14

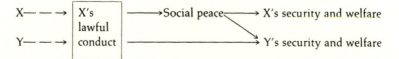

373

both the letter and the spirit of what he does say. First, there is some general threshold of lawlessness (i.e., violation of law-of-nature main clauses) which, if exceeded in the state of nature, frees individuals to use force, wiles, and anticipation *even against specific others who might be willing to cooperate with them.* This is because one cannot readily and reliably tell who the potential cooperators are and because one may need to efficiently subordinate (or steal from) even peaceful others to protect oneself against the many who are not peaceful. When lawlessness is below this threshold, things are more complicated. One certainly may use "any means" against those who consistently violate the laws of nature in their dealings with oneself and others. And presumably one is not required to obey the main clauses of the laws of nature in one's dealings with a party who consistently violates those clauses in response, even if that party acts lawfully toward others. This leaves two difficult cases for consideration: the party who acts lawfully toward you but not toward others, and the party who acts lawfully to some extent some of the time.

The first case is a problem because the general Hobbesian prescription to seek peace when (and where) it can be found has ambiguous implications in such situations. If one reciprocates the lawful conduct offered one by the generally lawless party, one risks being betrayed in the future by him and risks the enmity of those he has harmed. If, however, one fails to reciprocate, one has made an enemy out of a potential friend or ally. Perhaps the best strategy is to try to reform an unlawful friend by persuading him of the long-run benefits of lawful conduct. Aside from this, it is doubtful that there can be any generally applicable prescription for this kind of case derived from Hobbesian theory. Whether it is proper to cooperate reciprocally with a generally lawless person cannot be determined except by careful analysis of the specific features present in each case. Perhaps it is some comfort to the Hobbesian theorist that there is no generally recognized or common-sense solution to a parallel problem from everyday life: how should one respond to a friend or loved one who treats other people badly?

The second problem, concerning partial compliance toward oneself, or oneself and others, by particular individuals invites an obvious solution: proportionality. In bilateral dealings, one should act lawfully toward another roughly to the degree and extent that he acts lawfully toward you. The main difficulty here is developing suitable *substantive criteria* of proportionality which integrate information about the number, kind, and degree of violations and allow us to establish when there is an equitable balance between the two parties in their dealings with one another. These criteria must also take account of the fact that some violations are accidental, based on nonculpable ignorance, or performed by persons not fully responsible for their actions. These problems are further compounded in the multiparty case, where there are many and complex interactions, with unlawful conduct harming and benefiting various parties to various degrees and in various ways. In fact, the problem is so complex in the multiparty case that there seems to be no feasible way of solving it except by establishing, by tacit or explicit agreement, predetermined sanctions (and lists of excuses) for various kinds of violations of natural law. In civil society, these punishments are established by officials authorized by the members.[79] Presumably the same would be true within state-of-nature defense groups, unless the groups were small enough for their members to agree directly on the penalties for various violations of natural law.

Solving the problem of proportionality by appeal to consent or convention is clearly Hobbes's strategy for dealing with the issue of *distributive justice*, that is, the proper division of the material benefits and burdens of social cooperation. While contemporary theorists such as Rawls and Gauthier have suggested that decision or bargaining theory can be used to derive quite specific criteria of distributive justice, an older tradition, represented by Aristotle and Mill, notes that there are a variety of attractive but distinct and potentially conflicting principles of distribution.[80] Hobbes and Hobbesian theory are firmly within this older tradition.

[79] *Leviathan*, chap. 15, p. 138; chap. 26, p. 253.
[80] Aristotle, *Nicomachean Ethics*, trans. Martin Oswald (Indianapolis: Bobbs-Merrill, 1962), book 5, sec. 3, writes: "Everyone agrees that in distributions the just share must be given on the basis of what one deserves, though not everyone would name the same criterion of desert." See also Mill, *Utilitarianism*, chap. 5, pp. 44–45, 52–53.

Hobbes identifies justice in distribution with equity, which he characterizes as "distribut[ing] to every man his own" or "equal distribution to each man, of that which in reason belongeth to him."[81] Such distribution applies to things that can be divided. Those that cannot be divided are to be used in common if they can be, or if they cannot be, distributed by lot. Primogeniture and first seizure are, Hobbes says, forms of natural lottery and hence should be allowed as methods of distribution for things that cannot be divided or used in common. This last inference, as it stands, is fallacious, for there may be *other* forms of natural lottery—for example, by greatest need or greatest ability to use—whose outcomes conflict with the system of first seizure and primogeniture. If so, the use of one form of distribution by natural lottery rather than another can be properly established only by explicit or tacit agreement. This suggests that in drawing his conclusion that first seizure and primogeniture are proper methods of distribution, Hobbes implicitly relies on the assumption that these are the tacitly accepted methods of distribution by natural lottery.

Even given this assumption, however, it would be quite wrong, for a number of reasons, to view Hobbes as a natural property rights theorist in the mold of Locke (or Robert Nozick).[82] First, Hobbes holds that there are no property rights in the state of nature (or at least the unattenuated state of nature), where everyone has a right to everything. Second, first seizure and primogeniture are explicitly limited to apply to things that cannot be divided or used in common—while the most important material goods, such as land and capital, can be divided or used in common. Third, individual property rights to superfluous goods are, according to the fifth law of nature, circumscribed and limited by the needs of others (see section 5-4). Fourth, and most important, property rights in civil society are determined by the State, and hence indirectly by the agreement individuals do (or would) make in forming the State. This last point is what firmly

[81] *Leviathan*, chap. 15, pp. 138, 142.
[82] Locke, *Second Treatise*, chap. 5; and Nozick, *Anarchy, State, and Utopia*, chap. 7.

establishes Hobbes's account of distributive justice as *convention-alist*. Equity requires each receiving "that which in reason belongs to him," but in civil society it is the *State's* reason—expressed in the civil law—which determines what belongs to him. Hobbesian philosophy *partly* follows Hobbes in this regard. It denies that rational considerations alone can determine exact criteria of justice or adjudicate among various plausible rival conceptions of justice. But it does not assume that canons of justice are purely conventional—it allows that abstract reasoning may rule out certain possible principles of social distribution and that correct principles of distributive justice within a given society may be determined by the interplay of social conventions and various abstract rational arguments.

We have now observed the operation of three concepts of justice in Hobbes. Justice, in his own narrow sense, is doing what one has agreed to do. Justice in distribution, or equity, is proper distribution of goods. The criteria of such distribution are determined, directly or indirectly, by agreement, so that distributional justice is reducible, in a sense, to justice in Hobbes's narrow sense. As noted in section 9-1, there is also a broader notion of justice, more akin to our modern concept, operating in Hobbes's laws of nature. This broader concept encompasses agreement-keeping and distributive justice, together with other important moral notions such as equality of respect and rights, reciprocity, and fair settlement of disputes. As laws of nature in Hobbes's system, the components of this broad concept of justice are supported by considerations that are, as noted above, both rule-egoistic and rule-utilitarian. Mill has suggested that "justice" is the name we attach to the content of the most important rules of social utility, insofar as they affect the rights and interests of specific individuals.[83] Hobbes's account of the broad sense of justice may be similarly described. The rules of justice, in this sense, are among the most important rules for promoting individual and social utility. We submit that this account of justice, with its accompanying views about the close relations between individual and social

---

[83] Mill, *Utilitarianism*, chap. 5, p. 54.

utility, place Hobbes's substantive moral views close enough to those we find familiar to allow us to treat his moral theory as a reinterpretation of traditional moral theory.

9-5. Rule Worship

Suppose that you believe that in a particular case you can bring about best consequences by violating a moral rule that it generally maximizes utility to follow. Critics of rule utilitarianism charge that not violating the rule in such a case would constitute irrational *rule worship*.[84] It would be like following a map that is generally accurate but you have reason to believe will lead you astray in seeking the best route to your current destination. A like charge may be leveled against rule egoism. It is irrational and imprudent, according to this view, to follow moral rules that generally promote one's interests, in cases in which one believes one can do better by breaking these rules. Hobbesian theory must develop a plausible response to this charge, if Hobbes's rule-egoistic theory is to be regarded as a defensible reinterpretation of morality.

The outlines of Hobbes's own answer to the rule-worship charge are clear. His nonunilateralist Copper Rule interpretation of moral rules leaves the agent free to violate the main clauses of moral rules when others are violating them, thus minimizing his losses in what we have called *minimizing* cases. The real bite of the rule-worship charge against Hobbes comes in *maximizing* cases, where others are complying and one expects to gain most by cheating them or free-riding. Thus, the rule-worship objection is essentially a restatement of the argument of Hobbes's Fool, who urges the rationality of such offensive violations. Hobbes's reply, based on the grave risks of offensive violations both in the state of nature and in civil society, was discussed in sections 4-3 and 6-1. There it was allowed that Hobbes's reply succeeds generally, but fails in special cases in which the risks due to violation are both low (compared to the potential gains) and calculable. Fur-

[84] J. J. C. Smart, "Extreme and Restricted Utilitarianism," in *Contemporary Utilitarianism*, ed. Bayles.

thermore, Hobbes's argument presupposes a punitive social environment, in which society or potential coalition partners are sufficiently able and motivated to identify violations and to respond to them by withdrawing future cooperation or applying other significant sanctions.

This last point forms the basis of a recent objection to Hobbes's ethics by Kurt Baier. Baier notes the trade-off (discussed in section 6-1) between personal liberty and effective law enforcement and claims that it poses a "fatal dilemma" for Hobbes's philosophy. Egoistic citizens will find it most rational to subvert law enforcement with bribes and favors, and egoistic officials will find it most rational to go along. Only an absolutist State that subverts personal and economic freedom can prevent this.[85]

Hobbesian philosophy concedes the existence of a personal liberty/law enforcement trade-off in *any society*. But Baier offers us little reason to think that a satisfactory level of both could not be achieved in a society of rational egoists. If bribery and subversion of officials is a special danger here, then it will be in the mutual interest of citizens to establish especially harsh penalties for officials who abuse the public trust and to subject officials' conduct in office to scrutiny by press and public and to investigation by other branches of government. This may limit the privacy and personal liberty of officials, but becoming a public official is a voluntary act that generally carries with it material and psychic benefits. So long as individuals are willing to trade some privacy and liberty for these benefits, it is difficult to see what the moral objection would be to the society's accepting such a bargain for the benefit of all. Nor is it clear that a public policy of being especially hard on official corruption (and corrupters of officials) should devastate economic productivity, unless one supposes, contrary to ordinary beliefs about efficiency, that corruption and "sweetheart" deals are necessary to keep a modern economy rolling along smoothly. Of course, there would be some bribery and corruption by rational egoists even in the face of

[85] Kurt Baier, "Rationality, Reason, and the Good," in *Morality, Reason, and Truth*, ed. Copp and Zimmerman, p. 206.

harsh potential penalties, but Baier has given us no good reason to think that an unbearable amount would exist, especially if our egoists were rule egoists who reasoned on a general—rather than case-by-case—basis.

Perhaps Baier would be willing to concede this much, for he considers as an improvement on rational egoism a theory he calls Rational Conventionalism, which is defined by the following principle: "The requirements of the social order are to be regarded by its members as reasons for acting accordingly and, where they come into conflict with independent self-interested reasons, as overriding them."[86] If we interpret "the requirements of the social order" as Hobbes's prudentially grounded laws of nature, and "independent self-interested reasons" as those applying to the particular case under consideration, Baier's Rational Conventionalism looks very much like the Hobbesian rule egoism we have been discussing.

But Baier is not satisfied with this rule egoism that he calls Rational Conventionalism. He claims that people will have reason to accept it, and to regard reasons of social order (or, in Hobbesian terms, laws of nature) as overriding, only if the nature of the social order is such as to provide each with reasons for obedience that are "the best possible *everyone* [taken together] could have."[87] And he denies that Rational Conventionalism (i.e., rule egoism) satisfies this condition, since its social order is shown to be only better than the state of nature, not the best possible for everyone.

Hobbesian theory may respond to this last objection in either (or both) of two ways. First, if we accept the Hobbesian satisfactory State as the most that parties would agree to, if deprived of knowledge of their individual social positions which could unfairly bias them, then we may view that State as representing "the best possible *everyone* could have." If there were a demonstrable way of making the State better for everyone, this way would presumably have been agreed to by all and incorporated in the original social contract.

[86] Ibid., p. 207.
[87] Ibid., p. 208.

Second, one may question whether in order to have sufficient reason to obey a set of rules we must have the best possible reasons that could be available to everyone. There may be no "best possible reasons for everyone." Consider, as an analogy, a buyer-seller situation in which the buyer benefits if he pays B or less, and the seller profits if he gets S or more, where B > S. At any price in the closed interval between B and S, a sale is mutually beneficial, but there is no unique point in the interval at which each has the best possible reasons to trade. At any point X in the interval, the buyer has a "better reason" for a lower price and the seller has a "better reason" for a higher one. It hardly follows that, for any price in the interval, neither has sufficient reason to agree on that price. Both benefit by trading at price X and may think (with good reason) that they cannot do better, or that further bargaining is not worth the time and expense it would require. The same situation may apply with respect to rules of conduct. No particular set of rules may be supported by the best reasons for everyone, but some such sets may be *good enough* for everyone. Further, even when there *are* possible sets of rules that would be best for everyone, these sets may not be among the available alternatives because of information problems (we do not know they are best), huge transition costs, or irrational resistance to change on the part of others. Still, if the rules of social order which we have are good enough and better than readily available alternatives, we can have sufficient reasons to accept them. Hence, Baier's objections to rule egoism fail to be convincing.

Nonetheless, it will not be possible to defend Hobbes's moral theory if it is interpreted as requiring that it be most prudentially rational in every case, for every agent, in every possible (or even actual) social environment to follow the laws of nature and eschew offensive violations.[88] But at least for the purposes of Hobbesian theory we need not so interpret it. Instead, we observe that to be *motivationally adequate* it is only necessary that a moral scheme or set of moral rules be such that most everyone

[88] For elaboration of this point, see the introductory section of my "The Reconciliation Project," in ibid.

can be motivated to comply with it most all of the time and that present compliance with it tends to promote motivations compatible with future compliance with it, so that the scheme is stable.[89] Hobbes's reply to the Fool goes a good way toward assuring satisfaction of these conditions—it indicates why even pure egoists would have good reasons to generally follow the laws of nature and notes that present compliance tends to produce attitudes and actions on the part of others that reinforce cooperative tendencies on all sides.

Within the broader confines of Hobbesian theory, we can do even more to support the motivational adequacy of a moral system centered on Hobbes's laws of nature. The agents of Hobbesian theory are predominant, not pure, egoists. Typically, they care very much about the well-being of certain others, and care to some extent about the well-being of people in general. For most such persons, it will pay to adopt a generally *conscientious attitude* toward moral rules and to teach such attitudes to their children whom they love. To have a conscientious attitude toward moral rules is to have the tendency to feel guilty for violating moral rules and to value one's own compliance with them at least partly for its own sake. There are three sorts of reasons why it would, in general, be rational for predominant egoists initially to adopt (and teach to their children[90]) a conscientious attitude toward moral rules. Possession of such an attitude facilitates mutually beneficial relations with others, produces certain distinct and valuable psychic rewards and satisfactions,[91] and disposes one to acts that promote the well-being of others one cares about. Once adopted, however, such attitudes give one further reason to comply with moral rules: violation leads to painful guilt and the frustration of some of one's values. This means that offensive viola-

---

[89] The importance of stability in this sense is emphasized in Rawls, *A Theory of Justice*, pp. 454–55.

[90] Predominant egoists have an additional reason to encourage conscientiousness in their children. Conscientious children are likely to treat their parents better.

[91] Bishop Butler makes this point in his *Sermons*. An extreme version of this claim—that concern for and good treatment of others is a necessary condition of self-love and self-respect—is argued for in Richmond Campbell, *Self Love and Self Respect* (Ottawa: Canadian Library of Philosophy, 1979).

tions are much less likely to be rational, in the sense of best promoting the agent's ends (which now need not be supposed to be purely self-interested[92]), and it greatly strengthens the claim to motivational adequacy of a Hobbesian moral scheme that prohibits offensive violations.

Two loose ends of the rule-worship problem remain. First, Hobbes's reply to the Fool presupposes likely punishment by others for known violations of moral rules, but all too frequently such violations are not punished or discouraged when directed at outsiders. Therefore, are not offensive violations directed at weak outsiders rational? Second, what of the important special case in which compliance with moral rules risks death? Does not rationality require violation here, even if others are complying? These important issues are most conveniently discussed later, in sections 12-1 and 11-2 respectively. To the extent that they can be satisfactorily resolved, we may regard it as rational to follow the rules of Hobbesian morality.

Whatever ultimate verdict is rendered on rule egoism as a viable moral system, viewing Hobbes as a rule egoist is surely necessary to enable us to understand what he is up to in his moral philosophy. His primary aim is to make the traditional moral virtues—justice, equity, and so on—attractive to his fellows, whom he views as (at best) predominant egoists. He points out that long-term and short-term interests do not always coincide and that, when reciprocation can be hoped for, practicing the traditional virtues is the best and most reliable way to maximize one's long-term self-interest in an uncertain and perilous world of interpersonal interactions.

This attempted reconciliation of prudence and morality is the main element in a wider project of Hobbes's, which is designed to show the consistency of a whole series of seemingly conflicting demands on individual citizens. Morality and prudence are joined in the laws of nature. The first three of these laws recommend

[92] These claims about the rewards and consequences of conscientiousness may not apply to some people who lack both moral values and the capacity or inclination to acquire them. See section II of my "The Reconciliation Project" in *Morality, Reason, and Truth*, ed. Copp and Zimmerman.

founding, and submitting to the authority of, the State. This State, in turn, is the authoritative interpreter of the individual's religious duties, so that there is no significant conflict between religious and civil obedience.[93] Thus, the demands of four spheres—morality, prudence, politics, and religion—are joined in the imperative: seek peace by obeying the laws of the commonwealth or, if in a state of nature, cooperating in creating a commonwealth and then obeying its laws. This argument, if successful, could motivate and justify political obedience on the part of individuals whose primary commitment is to any of those four spheres, thereby promoting civil peace between moralists, clerics, ordinary citizens, and officials of the State. Having considered in this chapter the part of this project intended to reconcile the demands of morality and prudence, we must next consider the reconciliation of these demands with those imposed by the State.

[93] See *Philosophical Rudiments*, preface, p. xix.

T E N

POLITICAL OBLIGATION

10-1. Obligation and the Social Contract

What moral reasons, grounds, or considerations, if any, imply that individuals residing within the territory of a State (or a State of a certain kind) ought to obey the laws and directives of the officials of that State? This, in broad terms, is the problem of political obligation,[1] which concerns whether and when there is a moral justification for political obedience. Answering this question is a necessity for any successful nonanarchistic political theory, especially a theory such as Hobbes's, which takes individuals as its fundamental moral units and ascribes to them quite substantial natural rights to liberty. Among the most popular and enduring general approaches to the problem of political obligation is *consent theory*, according to which people should obey their governments because they somehow have (or would have) agreed, contracted, or promised to obey them. This approach has the initial attraction of seeming to reduce political obligation to a familiar and solid sort of moral obligation—that of keeping one's agreements, or "justice," in Hobbes's narrow use of that term.

Unfortunately matters are not that simple. Relatively few people, worldwide, expressly consent to their governments. Hence, consent theories of political obligation that seek wide scope and applicability must appeal to some notion of *tacit* (i.e., actual but nonexpress) consent or *hypothetical* (i.e., hypothesized under certain counterfactual circumstances) consent. But, as we shall

[1]Cf. the narrow definition of the problem in A. John Simmons, *Moral Principles and Political Obligations* (Princeton: Princeton University Press, 1979), pp. 11–16.

see in the next two sections, tacit and hypothetical consent theories face significant, though perhaps not insurmountable, difficulties of their own. Before turning to an examination of such theories in the context of Hobbesian philosophy, it will be useful to clarify certain normative aspects of Hobbes's own account of political obligation as flowing from an original agreement or social contract.

As observed in section 5-1, the original social contract agreed to by Hobbes's state-of-nature individuals consists of a set of bilateral agreements between each pair of participants to transfer their rights of self-rule to, and authorize all the acts of, whatever individual or assembly is later elected sovereign by the majority of the group. The sovereign is not, qua sovereign, a party to this original social contract, and he receives the sovereignty as, in effect, a free gift which the parties bestow on him (or them) in hopes of thereby obtaining for themselves domestic peace and prosperity and effective common defense against outsiders. As a result, the parties are bound to their sovereign by a double tie of obligation—by contract, each owes every other citizen obedience to the sovereign, and by the obligation to carry out the terms of a free gift (section 7-4), each directly owes the sovereign obedience.[2] The extent of the authority that the sovereign receives in the social contract—unlimited authorization and the unrestricted right to rule all the parties—is not a function of the structure of the contract, but rather its purpose. His stint has no limits because, according to Hobbes, this is necessary for lasting peace and defense (see, however, section 5-5). This unlimited stint, together with the double tie of obligation, implies that so long as the State holds together, the parties may not withdraw their allegiance to it and alter or replace it. The sovereign may not forfeit his authority by exceeding its limits, as there are no such limits, and the citizens cannot, without violating their obligations, withdraw

[2] *Leviathan*, chap. 11, p. 160; *Philosophical Rudiments*, chap. 6, sec. 20, pp. 90–92. For an analogue in modern contract law, see the discussion of third-party beneficiaries in Charles Fried, *Contract as Promise* (Cambridge, Mass.: Harvard University Press, 1981), pp. 44–45.

their allegiance so long as a single one of them, or the sovereign himself, objects.

But all this supposes that the sovereign can get established as an effective and legitimate authority by the original contract. One might, however, doubt this, given that the social contract is a covenant of mutual trust in the state of nature. Do not Hobbes's doubts about the validity and bindingness of such covenants apply to the social contract? In other words, is there not a normative problem of first compliance with the social contract, parallel to the descriptive problem discussed in section 5-6, which suggests that the first party called on to obey the newly elected sovereign is not obligated to do so? There is such a problem, but it is readily solvable. First parties are freed from their obligations to perform their parts of state-of-nature covenants only if they do not have sufficient grounds for expecting other parties to comply if they do. But, as noted in section 5-6, first compliers have good reason to expect (enough) others to obey the sovereign if they set the example, since others can also be expected to seize this available opportunity to leave the dreaded state of nature and find lasting security under a common power. Further, to be free, according to Hobbes, to not perform as first party in a state-of-nature covenant of mutual trust, one must have new grounds—arising *after* the making of the contract—to expect noncompliance by others (see section 9-2). But there is no reason, in general, to suppose that there will be such reasons in the case of the original social contract, and hence there is no reason for supposing that this agreement would not bind the contracting parties.[3]

One particular normative feature of Hobbes's social contract requires further elucidation, especially since Gauthier has identified it as the centerpiece of Hobbes's political theory.[4] This is the concept of *authorization*, which plays no role in *Elements of Law* or *Philosophical Rudiments* but is introduced into *Leviathan* in a

[3] The nonunanimous election of a sovereign would not constitute such a reason, for one could surely expect at least those supporting the winning candidate to comply. And one should foresee lack of unanimity and could therefore not reasonably count it as a new ground for fearing noncompliance.

[4] Gauthier, *Logic of Leviathan*, pp. vi, 120–21.

short chapter between those on the laws of nature and those on the social contract.[5] There Hobbes distinguishes between (acting as) a *natural person*, whose words and actions are considered as representing himself, and (acting as) an *artificial person*, whose words and actions are considered as representing another person or entity. (A lawyer representing an individual client or corporation would be a typical example of the latter.) When an artificial person represents another in his words and deeds, the former is called an *actor* and the latter is called the *author*, who may be said to "own" the relevant words and deeds of the former. Since *authority* is the right of doing an action, an actor is acting with authority when he is acting under commission from he who has the right to so act. When he so acts, the author—not the actor— is responsible for the action, in the sense of being bound by the obligations it entails, being committed not to criticize or punish it,[6] and so on. Hobbes allows that the authorization of a representative may be limited, but does not explicitly discuss whether an author retains the right to do what he has commissioned his representative to do or the right to interfere with the representative's commissioned actions.[7]

One interesting feature of Hobbes's account of authorization has been noted by Hanna Pitkin: it is entirely asymmetrical.[8] The actor gets only new rights, the author gets only new obligations and responsibilities. Hobbes does not even say that the actor is obligated to promote the author's interests as best he can within the limits of his commission. However, even if we leave such an obligation out and retain the radical asymmetry of Hobbes's account, we can imagine that rational agents would often have reasons for authorizing others to act for them: the act itself may be dangerous, arduous, time-consuming, or inconvenient, or the actor may possess special expertise that enables him to do it bet-

[5] *Leviathan*, chap. 16, pp. 147–52. For excellent discussions of Hobbes's account of authorization, see Gauthier, *Logic of Leviathan*, chap. 4; and Hanna Pitkin, *The Concept of Representation* (Berkeley: University of California Press, 1972), chap. 2.
[6] See *Leviathan*, chap. 18, p. 163.
[7] See Gauthier, *Logic of Leviathan*, pp. 128–29, 154–57, for discussion.
[8] Pitkin, *Concept of Representation*, pp. 19–20.

ter than the author himself could. Further, the author has some security, he can carefully limit the terms of the commission, and he can presumably withdraw it if dissatisfied with the actor's performance. Nonetheless, the asymmetry of the authorization relationship makes it resemble another of Hobbes's normative concepts, that of free gift.

It is therefore not surprising that authorization and free gift (or nonreciprocal transfer of right) are the two normative concepts Hobbes uses to characterize the transaction between contractors and sovereign embodied in the original contract.[9] In and through that agreement, each contractor transfers his right of governing himself to, and authorizes all the acts and judgments of, the sovereign. The critical question to ask in evaluating the role of authorization in Hobbes's political theory is whether its inclusion in the social contract adds anything of substance to the contract or its consequences that is *not already implied in the transfer of the right of self-government or self-rule.* To determine this, we must analyze both these elements of Hobbes's social contract.

Let us begin by summarizing what it means for one person to authorize another to do something, on Hobbes's account. To give the concept of authorization of the sovereign the greatest opportunity to do work in Hobbes's theory, we shall resolve ambiguities concerning the relative rights of the author and actor in favor of the latter. Thus, we shall say that "A authorizes B to do X" if and only if

(1) A has a (permission, noninterference, or aid) right to do X; and

(2) A (perhaps revokably[10]) transmits use of his right to do X to B; i.e.,

    (2a) A obligates himself to not interfere with B doing X, and

[9] Hobbes does not use the term "free gift" to describe this transaction, but his characterization of it falls under his definition of a free gift.

[10] It is part of our normal concept of commissions, authorizations, representations, etc., that they are revocable. Hobbes never discusses this question as regards authorization in general, so we leave it open here. As noted below, however, he believes that the authorization of the sovereign is irrevocable.

(2b) A transfers to B others' obligations to A to not interfere with or to aid in, the doing of X; and

(3) A (perhaps revokably) assumes responsibility for B's doing of X, as if he had done it himself; i.e.,

    (3a) A takes on himself any obligations entailed by the doing of X, if B does X; and

    (3b) A obligates himself not to blame or punish B for doing X.

The authorization of the *sovereign* has two special features. It is irrevocable, which it must be (according to Hobbes) in order to achieve its purpose of providing lasting security, and it arises out of a state-of-nature situation in which everyone has a right to do anything. Thus, "The parties authorize all of the sovereign's acts" comes to the following:

(1') The parties initially have the right to do anything.

(2a') The parties obligate themselves not to interfere with whatever the sovereign does.

(2b') The parties transfer to the sovereign any obligations of aid or noninterference owed them by others. (The noninterference part of this clause is superfluous because of (2a'), except insofar as people not party to the agreement owe some of the parties noninterference.)

(3a') The parties take on themselves any obligations entailed by the sovereign's acts.

(3b') The parties obligate themselves not to blame or punish anything the sovereign does.

To see whether this gives the sovereign any significant power or authority that he would otherwise lack, let us analyze the rights-transfer aspect of the social contract. We shall distinguish A's ruling or governing B, in the purely descriptive sense, from his having a right to rule or govern B. The former simply means that B will act as A wills him to. From Hobbes's definition of transferring a right, it follows that if A transfers to B his permission right to do X, A obligates himself not to interfere with B doing X. Substituting "rule A" for "doing X," we get that a party's original contract transfer to the sovereign of his right of self-rule implies that he is obligated not to interfere with the sovereign ruling him. But by the above account of the meaning of one party ruling another, this means that each party C obligates himself, by the social contract, not to interfere with C acting as the sovereign wills. But since C controls his own actions, this amounts to obligating himself to act as (i.e., howsoever) the sovereign wills (except when he is unable to so act).

Given this blanket obligation arising from the rights-transfer element of the social contract, it is easy to see that the authorization element is basically redundant. The normative relations spelled out in (2a′)–(3b′) are already entailed, given the very likely assumption that the sovereign wills them, for example, that he wills that his subjects not blame or punish his actions. Furthermore, if the sovereign does *not* desire the existence of any of these relations, he is free by his right of rule to abolish them (so long as such abolition is consistent with maintenance of the powers necessary to provide peace and security). We may also note that the lack of limitation of sovereign power follows as reliably from the rights-transfer element as from the authorization element. Unlimited right of rule is as strong a normative warrant for sovereign power as unlimited authorization. Thus, while the concept of authorization may be, as Gauthier suggests,[11] an illuminating political metaphor, it is one that plays no essential logical role in Hobbes's political theory, even in *Leviathan*.

10-2. Tacit Consent

A social contract transferring individuals' natural rights of self-rule to a State or sovereign would plausibly solve the problem of political obligation as regards the parties to that contract. But few States, if any, have been originated by such a contract, and even in those that may have been, there is a serious problem concerning later members of the polity who were not original contractors and for the most part have never expressly agreed to the terms of the social contract. It is for this reason that Hobbes, and Hobbesian theory following him, construe the original contract

[11] Gauthier, *Logic of Leviathan*, pp. 173–76.

as *hypothetical*. So doing, however, raises the question of how a merely hypothetical contract is supposed to bind, or motivate, agents who have never actually agreed to its terms. We shall take up this question in the next section. It is an especially troubling question for Hobbes, who never confronts it head on and instead hedges his bets by developing a second theory of political obligation based on the notion of *tacit consent*. Unlike Locke's more famous tacit consent theory,[12] Hobbes's version has been given little attention by commentators, but we shall explore it here to show that it does not provide a viable alternative to hypothetical consent theory as a solution to the problem of political obligation.

Tacit consent theories of political obligation, like express consent theories, rest on the moral principle requiring that we do as we have agreed to do. They assert the *actual* consent of the individual to the political structure, but allow that such consent need not be given explicitly, "in so many words." As actual consent theories, they share with express consent theory problems arising from the fact that consent, if it is to create a genuine moral obligation, must be voluntary. In addition, they face three special problems of their own because of the nature of tacit consent. What are to count as sufficient signs of tacit consent to political rule?[13] What precisely do tacit-consenters consent to? Can express-*non*consenters (e.g., declared anarchists or revolutionaries) be plausibly regarded as bound to the State by tacit consent? Two of these issues pose no special problems for Hobbes's tacit consent theory. Express-nonconsenters are not bound but may be treated as enemies,[14] and the *content* of political consent must be an unlimited transfer of right (save for the right of self-defense) to the State, as only this can promote lasting peace and security. But the problems of voluntariness and the signs of consent do, as

---

[12] Locke, *Second Treatise*, secs. 119–22, pp. 392–94.

[13] This problem is already implied in Hobbes's definition of tacit, or inferred, consent (*Leviathan*, chap. 14, pp. 121–22), where Hobbes makes clear that the possible signs of tacit consent are many and various.

[14] Ibid., chap. 18, pp. 162–63; chap. 28, pp. 300–301.

we shall see, pose serious—ultimately fatal—threats to Hobbes's theory as a plausible tacit consent theory of political obligation.

The core of Hobbes's tacit consent theory is his account of sovereignty by acquisition or conquest, which he views as the only possible source of sovereignty other than institution, that is social contract.[15] Hobbes's paradigm case of sovereignty by acquisition is a conqueror forcing a victim to promise future obedience in return for having his life spared and liberty allowed him (at least for the time being). He supposes a tacit agreement with this content being made between a conqueror and all those who live openly and at liberty in the conquered territory.[16] This enables him to contend that conquest is a genuine source of political obligation, while adhering to the principle that there is "no obligation on any man, which ariseth not from some act of his own."[17] It also allows deduction of the conclusion that sovereigns by conquest, like sovereigns by institution, are not effectively bound or limited by the agreements that create their sovereignty, for the conqueror agrees only to spare the life and allow the liberty of the subject *for a time*. By letting the subject live and go free initially, he completely fulfills his part of the bargain, leaving him with no remaining contractual obligation to the conquered subject, but with an unlimited right to the subject's obedience.[18]

To complete his tacit consent theory of political obligation based on conquest, Hobbes must deal with the passing of generations on the side of both subjects and sovereigns. On the subject side, the children born after the conquest are not themselves conquered, so how do they come to owe obedience to the sovereign? (Note that a parallel question may be asked about the children of those who create a sovereign by institution.) Hobbes has a double answer available here. First, children are presumed to tacitly promise obedience to their parents, because the latter have it in

[15] Ibid., chap. 17, pp. 158–59.

[16] Ibid., "A Review, and Conclusion," pp. 704–5. Those held captive by force are not presumed to have made such an agreement and are not obligated to obey.

[17] Ibid., chap. 21, p. 203. We suppose that whatever the signs of tacit consent to political rule are, e.g., even if they are omissions, they count as "acts" under this principle.

[18] Ibid., chap. 20, pp. 189–90.

their power to sustain or destroy them.[19] But dominion (i.e., the right of rule) is transitive—if A has dominion over B, and B has it over C, then A has it over C.[20] As a result, if the parents owe obedience to the conqueror, so do their children, who have tacitly consented to the parents' rule. Second, if the children live at liberty in the conquerors' territory, they may be directly presumed to have consented to his rule, as did their parents.

The problem of generations on the sovereign's side is as easily solved.[21] A sovereign assembly may sustain itself indefinitely by replacing old members by new as it wills and by designating a successor should all its members perish at once. Monarchs, though mortal, have the right to determine their successors by express proclamation or by tacit acceptance of the results implied by standing conventions of succession (e.g., that a firstborn son inherits the monarchy from his father). In either case, assuming only that the right to rule or command of a sovereign by acquisition (or institution) includes the right to thus transfer the sovereignty by expressly or tacitly designating a successor, it follows that subjects (and their descendants) owe the same obedience to successor sovereigns as their conquered (or contracting) ancestors owed to the original sovereign.

Sovereignty may change hands by conquest as well as by succession. This presents no problem for Hobbes. If your sovereign submits to a conqueror, then—by transitivity of dominion—you are now obligated to the conqueror.[22] And so, if we ignore immigration for the moment, the principles of succession, tacit consent to conquerors and parents, and transitivity of dominion are sufficient to insure that most everyone in the territory is bound to its present sovereign by a *chain of actual* (explicit or tacit) *consents*. This is illustrated in Figure 15, where broken arrows represent transmittals of sovereignty by succession or conquest, and solid arrows represent express or tacit promises of obedience. The obligations of immigrants can be handled via the principle of

---

[19] Ibid., pp. 186–88.
[20] Ibid., chap. 20, pp. 188–90; chap. 21, p. 209.
[21] Ibid., chap. 19, pp. 180–84.
[22] Ibid., chap. 21, p. 209.

FIGURE 15

Original sovereign— — —→Intermediate sovereigns — — —→Current

sovereign

Original subjects   Intermediate generations

(by contract or   ←——— of subjects   ←——— Current

conquest)   generation

of subjects

tacit consent of those who live openly in a sovereign's territory. Spies, by contrast, are simply enemies,[23] while the status and obligations of foreign visitors are presumably to be determined by explicit or tacit agreement among sovereigns.

This historical theory of political obligation has the obvious attraction for Hobbes of tying individuals to their present sovereigns by chains of actual (though often tacit) consent. Political obligations appear to be moral requirements arising from citizens' own actions and commitments, but this appearance is deceiving.

Consider first the issue of voluntariness. Promises made under threat or duress, such as the promise of obedience made by a party who has a conqueror's sword at his throat, are not morally binding, but it is such promises that Hobbes builds his tacit consent theory around. He presents three arguments in favor of such promises being binding after all. First, he claims that fear being one's motive for entering a contract cannot void that contract, or else contracts like the original social contract (which the parties enter out of fear of anarchy) would be nullified.[24] Second, promises made out of fear are voluntary in the sense of reflecting the agent's will.[25] Third, our nullification of certain promises made under threat arises not from the general invalidity of such promises, but from the fact that one cannot promise what one has no right to deliver (e.g., you are not bound by a promise to pay a ransom if released, if the civil law forbids such payments[26]).

[23] Ibid., "A Review, and Conclusion," p. 705.
[24] Ibid., chap. 20, p. 185.
[25] Ibid., chap. 21, pp. 196–98.
[26] Ibid., chap. 14, pp. 126–27; chap. 20, p. 185.

Unfortunately for Hobbes, these arguments fail. To see this, it suffices to distinguish between promises made under two sorts of duress. A promise is *coerced* when the promisee threatens the promisor with some evil should the promise not be made, with the purpose of obtaining the promise. A promise is *forced*, by contrast, when the promisor enters into it to avoid some evil or danger not created by the promisee, or at least not created by the promisee with the intention of producing the promise. Coerced promises are *not* morally binding. Many, though not all, forced promises *are* morally binding. And this moral difference makes good practical sense. We cannot hope to keep people out of the bad circumstances (e.g., anarchy, poverty, illness) that might lead them to make forced promises simply by declaring such promises void; we would just deprive them of one tool for making the best of a bad situation. But by treating coerced promises as null, we can deter potential coercers from threatening potential promisors. Thus, Hobbes is right that fear being the motive for making a promise does not in itself void it—everything depends on the nature and source of the fear. The promise of obedience elicited by a conqueror is void because it originates from fear created by him for that very purpose. The social contract stands because A contracts with B primarily out of fear of C, D, and so forth, and because any fear A has of B is a natural result of their mutual existence in a condition of anarchy and is not induced by B to coerce A into making the agreement. Though both the making of the social contract and the conquered party's promise of obedience are *willed* actions involving surrenders of rights that the parties in question do possess, only the former is "voluntary" *in the morally relevant sense of noncoerced*, and hence is morally binding.[27]

This problem concerning voluntariness indicates that the "chain of obligation" pictured above is broken by the invalidity of the promise of obedience to the original sovereign by acquisition. One might hope to salvage Hobbes's tacit consent theory by relying

[27] Thus, Hobbes's second and third arguments are seen to be irrelevant, once the distinction between coerced and forced promises is made and the appropriate sense of voluntariness is identified.

on his claim that "if [one] live under their protection openly, he is understood to submit himself to the government,"[28] thus taking residency as a sufficient sign of tacit consent to political rule. But whether "open residency" is such a sign of people's wills would be a contingent matter concerning conventions and motivations in various human societies, and it would not seem to be a *reasonable* convention, given that people must reside somewhere and will typically suffer substantial, even prohibitive, costs in moving from one political jurisdiction to another. Perhaps it could be argued that those who live openly in a polity owe it obedience because they receive various benefits thereby (e.g., protection of the laws) or because others will obey the State in the expectation that they will do so as well, but these are arguments based on considerations of gratitude, reciprocity, and fair play, not on consent.

Putting aside these issues concerning the signs of tacit consent and its voluntariness, there is yet a further crucial defect in Hobbes's theory. The necessary assumption that children tacitly pledge obedience to their parents and that residents of conquered territories tacitly pledge obedience to their conquerors is based on the claim that "every man is supposed to promise obedience, to him, in whose power it is to save, or destroy him."[29] But can being in another's power constitute a reliable sign of one's *actual* will or consent? That it cannot be is suggested by the fact that Hobbes applies this claim to children while elsewhere implying that they cannot give binding consent.[30] More telling, when it comes to arguing for the claim, Hobbes's emphasis is on the will of the promisee, not that of the promisor. He argues that if parents (the promisees) are to be motivated to raise children (the tacit promisors), they must be able to assume later obedience on the part of the latter.[31] The logic of the argument appears to be: if they were rational and understood their situation, children would

---

[28] Ibid., "A Review, and Conclusion," p. 705.

[29] Ibid., chap. 20, p. 188.

[30] Ibid., chap. 26, p. 257. This point is made by Warrender, *Political Philosophy of Hobbes*, pp. 123–24.

[31] *Philosophical Rudiments*, chap. 9, sec. 3, p. 116; *Leviathan*, chap. 30, p. 329.

promise obedience to their parents to insure that the latter would care for and protect them; therefore they are obligated to their parents *as if* they had so promised. There is no actual consent here, only *hypothetical* consent.[32]

In the end, then, Hobbes's tacit consent theory of political obligation is a dismal failure. It does not solve the voluntariness problem, and insofar as it has any plausibility or arguments behind it, the notion of tacit consent is merely a proxy for other moral notions, such as gratitude, fair play, and hypothetical consent. Therefore, we may reasonably lay aside tacit consent and turn to other approaches to the problem of political obligation.

10-3. Hypothetical Consent

The utter failure of Hobbes's tacit consent theory leaves hypothetical consent theory as the only device in Hobbes's philosophical repertoire which is capable of providing a plausible solution to the problem of political obligation. Unfortunately, though Hobbes uses the hypothetical consent method, he never really discusses the problems with it. This method is also employed by modern theorists such as John Rawls, David Gauthier, and Richard Brandt,[33] and it underlies our Chapter 5 sketch of a Hobbesian social contract, so we are committed to defending it.

As noted in section 1-3, hypothetical consent or contract theories rely on the following basic argument schema:

(1) If people were rational and in such-and-such circumstances, they would choose or agree to social arrangements of a certain kind.

(2) Therefore, people actually living under social arrangements of that kind ought to obey the rules of these arrangements and the officials designated to enforce them.

---

[32] Nor is this particular hypothetical consent argument persuasive, since most parents surely will raise children without assurances of future obedience.

[33] Rawls, *Theory of Justice*; Brandt, *A Theory of the Right and the Good*; Gauthier, "Justice as Social Choice" and "The Social Contract: Individual Decision or Collective Bargain."

Depending upon whether the "social arrangements" in question are conceived as rules for distributing the benefits and burdens of social cooperation, rules for interpersonal conduct, or the institutions of a political apparatus (or State), this same argument schema will yield a hypothetical consent theory of social justice, social ethics, or political obligation. We, of course, are interested in the schema as applied in the last of these three ways, though some of our remarks about methodology will apply to hypothetical consent theories in general.

To begin, it must be noted that a hypothetical consent theory of political obligation is not, strictly speaking, a theory of *obligation*, nor is it grounded in consent. Obligation, as Hobbes and others have understood it (see section 7-4), is created only by actual consent, and people's actual consents (with their corresponding obligations to act as they have consented to act) play no role in hypothetical consent theory. Instead, according to that theory, people have good moral reasons for obeying political authorities in certain sorts of States (e.g., satisfactory States), because they *would* in certain *counterfactual* (i.e., nonactual) circumstances consent to do so. But this raises the central problem of hypothetical consent theory. Why should parties act in accordance with mere *hypothetical* consents? Why should their moral duties, and their inclinations, be shaped by agreements they would make under nonactual circumstances?

Actually, there are two distinct problems here; one concerns justification, the other concerns motivation. The first concerns whether and why the fact that people would consent to something (e.g., a set of rules or institutions) under hypothetical conditions can constitute a *justification* for their going along with that something where and when it exists. The second revolves around the issue of whether people can be *motivated* by considerations of what they would consent to under counterfactual circumstances. Each of these problems confronts us twice, for they may be raised concerning hypothetical consent theories in general and again with respect to specific theories of this kind that we have employed in Hobbesian theory to deal with the issue of political obligation. Let us first consider the general and specific versions of the justification problem, then turn to the issue of motivation.

Suppose it is conceded that if we were rational, and in conditions of equality and freedom, and collectively reasoned, debated, and bargained about the terms of our future social arrangements, (nearly) all of us would agree on arrangements S. How is it supposed to follow that arrangements S are morally justified? One plausible answer is this.[34] The circumstances of agreement and the characteristics of the parties—rationality, reasoned agreement, freedom, and equality—represent fundamental moral values concerning the conditions and nature of human interactions. The results of "applying" these values to substantive issues concerning social arrangements, as in hypothetical consent arguments, should therefore yield appropriate moral answers about these arrangements.

This point about "applying" moral values may be spelled out more fully as follows. Rationality, freedom, and equality are fundamental moral values concerning human persons and their relations with one another. Reasoned agreement is a norm of rational and moral interaction among moral beings. But it is reasonable to suppose that the deliberate outcomes of rational and moral interactions among rational and moral beings *inherit* the moral and rational status of the parties and procedures that produce them. Hence, if rational moral (free and equal) beings interact in a rational and moral way (reasoned agreement), the planned results of these interactions—the arrangements agreed on—are morally justified.

This defense of the justificatory role of hypothetical consent theories rests on the principle that rational-moral relations among rational-moral beings are preserved by rational-moral interactions among those beings (i.e., the outcomes inherit the rationality-morality of the parties, their initial relationship, and the interaction process in question). There may be exceptions or counterexamples to this general principle. It should therefore be noted that hypothetical consent theories *of political obligation,*

[34] See also Rawls, *Theory of Justice*, sections 3 and 4.

such as our Hobbesian theory, presuppose only a weakened version of the principle. The Hobbesian argument against anarchy demonstrates that some form of State-establishing procedure or interaction would be required by reason for parties situated in a state of nature. Hence, the weaker principle that rational-moral relations among rational-moral beings are preserved by rational-moral interactions among them, *if these interactions (or interactions of their kind) are required by reason*, suffices to establish the morality (and rationality) of arrangements created by the original social contract. This is important, since one might doubt that the rational-moral status of inputs is transmitted to outputs, when the rational-moral interactions which (hypothetically) produce the latter are optional, as opposed to necessary, for the parties in question.

An alternative (though not incompatible) defense of the claim that hypothetical consent theories produce moral justifications is based on the idea that there can be no reasonable objections to arrangements that would be agreed to under appropriate conditions. Suppose we acknowledge that arrangements S would be agreed to by rational people, possessing (only and all) appropriate information, under conditions of freedom and equality. How could one reasonably object to S? One *might* object, of course, because S has (lacks) some feature F of which one disapproves (approves). But if it is acknowledged that free and equal rational people would agree on S, nonetheless, it would seem difficult or impossible to pass off one's opposed judgments as principled and justified. After all, if one's grounds for these judgments were good ones, they would have been acknowledged by the rational bargainers, who would therefore have chosen alternative arrangements S', which exclude (include) F.

But perhaps the bargainers would have chosen S', or at least would have rejected or not agreed on S, if they had possessed knowledge ruled out by the information constraints of the theory in question. Would this ground a reasonable objection to S being justified? Not if, as we have supposed, the information constraints are *appropriate* ones, for then any preference for S' over S can be attributed to the operation of morally prohibited biases, which the information constraints are properly designed to suppress.

The idea that the circumstances and characteristics of hypothetical bargainers represent, or are expressive of, basic moral values is an attractive one. So is the idea that there can be no reasonable objection to the outcome of a properly characterized hypothetical bargaining situation. But even if we allow that these ideas can justify the outcomes of hypothetical consent theories with the *proper circumstances of agreement,* it remains to consider whether our Hobbesian social contract theory contains such circumstances. We have already dealt with the main aspects of this issue in section 5-2, where it was explained why our characterization of the parties and their circumstances is appropriate for a hypothetical consent approach to the problem of political obligation. The rules of proposal, debate, bargaining, and agreement set out there are supposed to reflect the freedom, independence, equality, and individuality of the parties. The absence of a unanimity requirement reflects, among other things, the morally significant fact that human individuals are importantly, occasionally irreconcilably, different in their attitudes, goals, and values. Making the establishment of a State of a certain kind the target of negotiations, and the state of nature the alternative to agreement, is justified because the theory is about the minimal conditions of political obligation, not the principles of morality, social justice, or the ideal society.

Still, given the above general justification for hypothetical consent theories which emphasizes the *freedom* and *equality* of the parties, it is worth considering possible objections concerning whether the parties to our Hobbesian social contract theory are free and equal *enough.* As regards freedom, it could be suggested that the parties are *compelled* to reach agreement, since return to the state of nature is their alternative. And this is, in a sense, true. But remember our distinction between coerced and forced agreements (section 10-2). The parties are not unfree with respect to one another; none can coerce others to accept unfair or unreasonable terms of agreement. All are forced to compromise and accept less than they might wish because of the necessity to reach agreement. But this sort of pressure, when it applies equally (or approximately equally) to each, does not call the fairness or morality of the outcome into question; it simply reflects a Hobbesian fact about the human condition—that the State and (a high risk of) insecurity and poverty are exhaustive alternatives.

If Hobbesian social contractors are free enough so as not to undermine the moral force that their hypothetical agreement confers on its terms, are they *equal* enough? After all, unlike in Rawls's theory, they are aware of individual differences and inequalities among themselves. Does this not vitiate the moral force of their agreement? We claim, for reasons already stated in section 5-2, that it does not. Hobbesian theory does abstract from the morally irrelevant social differences among the contracting parties, rendering those parties equal save for their individual differences, but it does not treat the remaining differences, and knowledge of them, as undermining the moral equality of the parties. Hobbesian contractors are full individuals, with individual characteristics and knowledge thereof. Morality, we contend, involves interaction and accommodation among such distinct individuals. It does not require, as in Rawls's theory, abstracting from individual differences to the extent that the individuality and moral personality of the contracting parties is erased. That the parties should be absolutely equal, in this sense of eviscerating their individual differences, if results of their hypothetical deliberations are to have moral force, seems highly implausible.

Of course, if the differences between parties are so great that some are able to force disproportionate terms on others, then these terms can claim no special moral status. But such is not the case in Hobbesian contract theory. There, all need agreement, and all must compromise—the endowed as well as the unendowed. And given the uncertainties of how individual endowments will lead to social rewards, all are forced to take out "insurance" against adverse contingencies. This is evident from the arguments of sections 5-3 through 5-6, on the terms of the Hobbesian social contract and how they are reached. Here, there is no indication of the advantaged blackmailing the weak into accepting their terms. Instead we have a description of various considerations that would lead the endowed and the unendowed to agree on provisions that, for the most part, could be expected to benefit all. In terms of how the arguments actually proceed, then, the Hobbesian contractors operate essentially as equals, and the social arrangements they select may properly be regarded as reasonable and morally justified.

Be that as it may, one may raise the question as to whether real-world parties can be *motivated* by recognition of what they would consent to under admittedly counterfactual circumstances. Would we not expect those who know their actual social positions to be totally unmoved by the fact that they would agree to arrangements S, though they have not done so? In particular, would those benefiting from inequalities not allowed by S be motivated to give them up, or could those faring relatively poorly under actual arrangements S be motivated to accept those arrangements as legitimate nonetheless?

On this issue, Rawls's general approach seems to be correct. He suggests that hypothetical consent theories appeal to motives, beliefs, and commitments that many of us already have, such as a sense of justice or fair play.[35] David Zimmerman has recently extended Rawls's idea by suggesting that hypothetical consent theories may also appeal to second-order desires or motives, for example, the desire that our systems of first-order desires satisfy appropriate norms of epistemic rationality or impartiality.[36] Thus, someone might conceivably be moved by the results of a hypothetical contract theory to give up an illegitimate social advantage (or accept a previously resented social disadvantage) because of their first-order belief in fair play or their second-order commitment to living by the dictates of "neutral rationality" or "unbiased reason." It must be acknowledged, however, that this answer to the general motivation problem cannot hope to catch everyone in its net. Some will lack the requisite desires at both the first level and the second level. And in others these desires

[35] Ibid., pp. 18, 21, 120, 587. Rawls discusses the sense of justice in his chap. 8.

[36] David Zimmerman, "The Force of Hypothetical Commitment," *Ethics* 93 (April 1983): 467–83.

will not be strong enough to overcome contrary motives, such as the desire to retain present advantages. How many people can be motivated by a hypothetical consent theory, and to what extent, will depend on the particular features of the theory and the motives that it appeals to, and on the existing distribution of such motives among the population to whom the theory is addressed.

How, in this regard, might our Hobbesian hypothetical contract theory be expected to fare? We have already noted one motivational advantage that the theory has over Rawls's theory of justice. It does not require identification, by one's audience, with abstract parties lacking any individuating features. Instead, it incorporates the personal features of individuals into the theory, thus promoting identification and lessening the likelihood of "alienation" from the results of the theory by those regarding concrete individuals as the fundamental units of morality.

On the other hand, our commitment to Predominant Egoism might seem to rule out fair play as a motive that our Hobbesian theory might appeal to, but fortunately (since fair play seems to be a widespread and often effective motive) it does not. Our Hobbesian theory allows for fair play as a motive in at least three ways. First, Predominant Egoism places no limits on the scope and strength of motives such as fair play for people in an established position of well-being and security (see section 2-5). But Hobbesian theory grounds allegiance only to the *satisfactory* State on hypothetical consent, and it takes as its primary audience those living within such States. Most of these people will be in an established position of well-being and security. Second, even for those not in such a position, Predominant Egoism allows that many of them might be somewhat motivated by considerations of justice or fair play and some of them might be highly motivated. Third, and finally, Hobbes's reply to the Fool (section 4-3) and parts of our discussion of Hobbes's rule-egoistic moral system (sections 9-3 through 9-5) suggest that adopting or developing a sense of fair play or justice can be entirely consistent with promotion of one's long-term interests. To the extent that this is so, the Predominant Egoism hypothesis does not undermine the potential efficacy of appeals to the motive of fair play.

405

A closely related observation supports the special motivational efficacy of Hobbesian theory. As in the general case, one might wonder how *Hobbesian* hypothetical consent theory can hope to effectively motivate compliance with the rules and officials of the satisfactory State by those who might hope to gain by changing those rules (e.g., poor people seeking violent change, rich people seeking to establish less equitable and "nonsatisfactory" alternative arrangements). In addition to the appeal to first-order and second-order moral motivations (e.g., fair play, neutral rationality), Hobbesian theory, with its arguments about the dangers of revolution (section 6-4), the potential instability and fragility of the State (sections 6-2 and 6-3), and the greater stability of the satisfactory State (sections 5-2 through 5-5 and section 6-4), appeals to enlightened long-run *prudence* as a motive of obedience to the satisfactory State. This reinforcement of other motives by direct prudential motives widens and deepens the motivational power of Hobbesian hypothetical consent theory.

Still, some will escape the motivational pull that the theory exerts for obeying the directives of the satisfactory State. Revolutionary fanatics, advantaged and well-positioned immoralists, and others will be unmoved by the theory, even if they accept its claim that the described parties in the described position would agree on the arrangements characterizing the satisfactory State. But this need not bother us. The most ambitious practical aim that Hobbesian theory might aspire to is to solidify the beliefs and assuage the doubts of the faithful and to guide the beliefs of those of goodwill who are confused and uncertain. The conversion of the immoral, the unreasonable, and the unmovable is beyond the reach of this (and probably any other) philosophical theory. Thus, Hobbesian theory follows the Socrates of the *Republic*, who primarily aims his arguments not at Thrasymacus, the immoralist, but at Glaucon, the confused decent citizen.[37] And it probably follows Hobbes himself, who seems more concerned with persuading the uncommited not to follow the lead of com-

[37] See the introductory section in my "The Reconciliation Project," in *Morality, Reason, and Truth*, ed. Zimmerman and Copp.

mitted revolutionaries and other troublemakers than with converting the latter into obedient citizens.[38]

10-4. *Other Grounds of Political Obligation*

If we accept the arguments of the last section, two significant problems remain for the Hobbesian account of political obligation. First, there is the problem of *limited scope*. Hobbesian hypothetical consent theory grounds political obligation only within satisfactory States. Even within such States, there may be those who could plausibly and correctly argue that they, even if deprived of knowledge of their social position, would have been among the small minority not agreeing to the formation of the satisfactory State. What, if anything, explains or grounds the political obligations of these persons and of the residents of nonsatisfactory States? Second, there is A. John Simmons' *particularity* problem, concerning how a theory of political obligation accounts for a person's being obligated to one particular State rather than another.[39] This problem poses a key question for Hobbesian hypothetical contract theory: why should a citizen of a satisfactory State obey the directives of his government rather than the (possibly conflicting) directives of the officials of some other satisfactory State?

The key to solving these problems lies in admitting that hypothetical consent theory, at least *Hobbesian* hypothetical consent theory, is not intended to provide an exhaustive account of people's moral reasons for political obedience. It must be supplemented by noting *other grounds* of political obligations. These promise to solve the particularity problem, while considerably expanding the net of political obligation to encompass many of those who are not covered by Hobbesian hypothetical consent theory.

[38] His harangues against certain types of "popular, and ambitious men" (*Leviathan*, chap. 29, pp. 320–21), "pretenders to political prudence" (ibid., p. 321), and "unlearned divines" (ibid., pp. 311–12) suggest he has no hope or intention of converting them.

[39] Simmons, *Moral Principles and Political Obligations*, pp. 30–35. Several of the points made in this section are borrowed from my review of Simmons' book in *Topoi* 2 (December 1983): 227–30.

Let us therefore look briefly at some other valid moral grounds of political obedience.

The most obvious such ground is *actual consent*, whether given expressly or tacitly. The number of persons in the world who expressly consent to their States by taking loyalty oaths, becoming naturalized citizens, and so on, is by no means negligible. Further, there are some acts that often do constitute tacit consent to a State, such as voluntary immigration, running for public office, and acceptance of high-level public employment. There are problems, of course, concerning when consent, express or tacit, to political rule is voluntary and therefore binding. Consenting individuals must have reasonable alternatives, and there must not be so much manipulation of information as to deprive them of the chance to evaluate these alternatives rationally. Further, some important borderline cases of tacit consent (e.g., long-term voluntary residence or voting in elections) are difficult or impossible to definitively classify one way or the other. Nonetheless, there will be many clear cases of binding actual consent (express or tacit). This substantially (though selectively) expands the scope of political obligation beyond satisfactory States. And because actual consent specifically binds one to the State one has consented to, there is no significant particularity problem for those to whom this ground of political obligation applies.

Another familiar ground of political obedience is that emphasized by Hume—social utility.[40] In particular, given the considerations advanced in the Hobbesian arguments against anarchy (sections 3-3 through 3-5 and section 4-4) and revolution (section 6-4), it is likely that a rule requiring obedience to existing laws and authorities under most all circumstances would be incorporated in a complete rule-utilitarian moral system.[41] This much is

[40] David Hume, "Of the Original Contract," in *Hume's Ethical Writings*, ed. MacIntyre, pp. 255–73. On the affinities between Hobbes's rule egoism and rule utilitarianism, see section 9-4.

[41] The exceptional circumstances in which (violent) disobedience would be allowed (by the relevant rule of a rule-utilitarian moral system) would be when the present government is very harmful, when violent resistance would very likely lead to its replacement by a substantially better government, and when no alternative course of action is likely to lead to similar improvements.

familiar, but it is worth noting that rule utilitarianism also provides a plausible general solution to the particularity problem, for there are good reasons why it generally promotes utility better for citizens to obey their own governments rather than (equally worthy) foreign governments. Governments, and one's fellow citizens, tend to expect and count on the cooperation of their countrymen much more than on the cooperation of foreigners. The obedience of foreigners is not needed much except when they are residing in or visiting one's country, and obedience on these occasions can be sufficiently assured by international conventions and coercive law enforcement. Further, loyalty by citizens to foreign governments leads to such harmful results as mutual suspicion among citizens and domestic spying and repression. Finally, we shall argue below that citizen obedience is often required by principles of gratitude and fair play. One would expect such principles to be contained in a complete rule-utilitarian moral system, because of the well-known tendency of gratitude and fair play to promote future reciprocity and cooperation and of ingratitude and cheating to promote future discord and violence. From a utilitarian point of view, then, there is a strong presumption in favor of obedience to one's own State, rather than simply any State possessing similar, or desirable, characteristics.[42]

Besides utility and consent (actual or hypothetical), the most plausible ground of political obligation is the *receipt of benefits*. In particular, it may be argued that a citizen in a stable law-governed society receives from his fellow citizens numerous important benefits following from their general compliance with the civil law and therefore owes them similar compliance on his own part as a matter of fairness. The obligation of obedience, on this view, derives from some general *principle of fair play* requiring those benefiting from a social practice, whose maintenance requires the acceptance of restrictions on personal liberty (and pos-

[42] What counts as one's own State is decided by conventions of citizenship. There may be borderline cases under the conventions, but it is not such cases of divided or indeterminable citizenship that bother Simmons. See Simmons, *Moral Principles and Political Obligations*, pp. 32–33.

sibly other burdens) on the part of others, to accept like restrictions and burdens on themselves.[43]

There are some notorious problems associated with a fair-play account of political obligation. What is the *baseline of comparison* against which the citizen's position is to be judged in determining whether he really benefits from a system of mutual constraint and obedience to civil law? To generate obligations under the principle of fair play, must the political system in question be a *just* one that distributes benefits and burdens fairly? We shall not attempt to deal with these thorny issues here beyond making two brief observations. First, the state of nature constitutes a natural baseline of comparison, within Hobbesian theory, for determining whether one benefits from a generally effective regime of civil law and civil order. Second, Simmons seems right, against Rawls, that there can be obligations of fair play even under unjust social practices.[44] For example, one could hardly disavow one's assigned responsibilities under a beneficial social practice on the grounds that the assigned share of the benefits is *too large*— instead one should comply and redistribute the "surplus" and/or attempt to reform the pattern of distribution.

A different problem concerning the fair-play account of political obligation has emerged in the recent literature. Nozick observes that mere *receipt* of benefits cannot generally obligate us under a principle of fair play, or else others could "thrust" unwanted benefits upon us and obligate us against our will.[45] Simmons develops this idea, contending that receipt of *open* benefits—those that are difficult or costly to avoid—does not obligate us; only when we *accept* benefits, in the sense of trying to obtain them or knowingly and willingly receiving them, are we obligated. But the benefits we receive from the State, such as security against domestic and foreign violence, are open benefits. Generally, they are not accepted, according to Simmons, since few view

[43] See ibid., chap. 5; and Rawls, *Theory of Justice*, secs. 18 and 52.
[44] Simmons, *Moral Principles and Political Obligations*, pp. 109–14.
[45] Nozick, *Anarchy, State, and Utopia*, pp. 93–95.

them as deriving from social cooperation or as worth the price that is exacted for them, namely, obedience.[46]

These arguments are unconvincing. Surely many people in many countries do recognize that social benefits flow from social cooperation and obedience to law and regard these benefits as worth the price that must be paid for them. Further, if such benefits do flow from mutual obedience and are, by some appropriate objective standard, worth the price, the principle of fair play may apply even to those who do not recognize these facts. To hold otherwise would be to suggest that ignorance, even self-deceptive and self-serving ignorance, exempts one from contributing one's fair share to a mutually beneficial scheme of interaction. Finally, it does not seem that open benefits must always be accepted for their receipt to create obligations of reciprocation under the principle of fair play. One's receipt of open benefits may well be *overdetermined* in the following sense: one in fact takes them because they are difficult or costly to avoid, but if they were not so, one still would take them because one would (or would if appropriately knowledgeable) recognize they were worth having, even at the cost of doing one's share in producing them. When our receipt of open benefits is overdetermined in this way, fairness obligates us to do our part in assuring their continued provision, even though we may not "accept" them in Simmons' sense. But it is quite plausible to suppose that many citizens' receipt of the open benefits of national cooperation are overdetermined in this way. If so, these people have some moral obligation of political obedience grounded in considerations of fair play.

Simmons worries that if we reject acceptance of benefits as a necessary condition of acquiring obligations of reciprocation, we must treat receipt of benefits as a sufficient condition thereof and consequently be stuck with Nozick's problem about benefits thrust upon us.[47] But the above account of obligation due to overdetermination requires, in addition to receipt of benefits, satisfaction

[46] Simmons, *Moral Principles and Political Obligations*, pp. 125–39.
[47] Ibid., p. 139.

of a further condition about what would be accepted under certain counterfactual circumstances. Nor is this the only plausible account that finds a middle ground between receipt of benefits as a sufficient condition of obligation to comply with a practice, and acceptance of benefits as a necessary condition thereof. In fact, we can readily identify at least seven factors that seem to influence our judgments, in specific cases, about whether receipt of benefits, in the absence of explicit consent, obligates one to go along with the rules of the social practice generating those benefits.[48] Other things being equal, the more a social practice (or an individual's relationship to such a practice) possesses the following features, the more we are inclined to regard the individual receiving benefits from it as obligated to carry out his assigned part in the practice.

1. Fairness, i.e., proportional distribution of the benefits and burdens of the practice
2. Size, amount, or significance of the benefits
3. Degree of sacrifice by others required to produce the benefits
4. Precariousness of the practice, that is, the degree to which its success requires compliance by nearly all or is subject to destabilizing effects, etc.
5. Ease of avoiding or refusing the benefits
6. Absence of explicit nonconsent to the practice
7. The existence of conventions or traditions of expectation that people will comply with the practice

We shall propose no explicit theory about how these and other considerations should be combined to generate necessary and/or sufficient conditions for being obligated by fair play to comply with a practice. Any such theory would undoubtedly be highly complex and controversial. It should be clear, however, that there are plenty of relevant considerations and distinctions here, so that we need not face Simmons' bleak alternatives of treating benefit

---

[48] Some of these factors may influence our judgments about obligation partly by generating beliefs about tacit consent or acceptance. But since the criteria of the latter notions are far from crystal clear, it is useful in the light of Nozick's problem to simply ask what is needed, in addition to receipt of benefits, to generate obligations of fair play.

receipt or benefit acceptance *alone* as the generating conditions of obligations of fair play. Further, for various citizens of many nations, a number of our seven features are satisfied to a considerable degree by the social practice of civil obedience. This strongly suggests that a carefully developed fair-play account of political obligation might actually apply to a large number of people, including some citizens of nonsatisfactory States.[49]

Receipt of benefits can generate obligations of *gratitude* as well as fair play. The distinction between these two sources of obligation seems to depend on the aims or motives of the provider of the benefit. If the provider supplies the benefit out of altruism or goodwill, without expectation of reciprocation, any obligations generated fall under the principle of gratitude. If the benefits are provided as part of a trade or cooperative practice, with reciprocity intended, any obligations generated fall under principles of fair play (or consent, if consent to the practice is given). In the case of complex social practices (e.g., compliance with political authorities), there will be many providers of benefits, each motivated by a different mix of self-interested and altruistic motives. To the extent that some providers accept the burdens of the practice because it helps others, rather than simply because it helps themselves, those others may owe some duties of gratitude to these providers. This will especially be the case if altruism motivates some to assume an extra share of the burdens. Now if compliance with the practice in question is the only, or most appropriate or natural, way of fulfilling these duties of gratitude, recipients of benefits may be obligated by gratitude, as well as fair play, to comply with the rules of the practice in question.

Simmons claims that governments are not suitable objects for duties of gratitude, as they (as collectives) lack motives, in the proper sense, and their individual officials are primarily motivated by career interests.[50] Be this as it may, it does not disqualify gratitude as a ground of political obligations. Some past leaders and citizens have altruistically sacrificed to create and sustain

[49] This last point follows from the fact that the seven listed factors are different from the defining features of the satisfactory State.
[50] Simmons, *Moral Principles and Political Obligations*, pp. 187–90.

413

political institutions that benefit us now, and many current officials and citizens comply with and support these institutions at least partly out of altruistic and idealistic motives. Also, our own compliance with these political institutions is likely to be what these people want (or wanted) from us most, should we choose to "repay" their beneficence. Therefore, we may have reasons of gratitude, as well as fair play, owed to past as well as present officials and fellow citizens, for our political obedience. Nor are these two grounds of obligation totally foreign to Hobbes's own theories. He endorses fair play and gratitude, respectively, in his second and fourth laws of nature, and, as noted in section 10-2, his tacit consent theory of political obligation may indirectly appeal to these grounds of obligation.

We have, then, noted four grounds of political obligation in addition to hypothetical consent: actual consent, social utility, fair play, and gratitude. Taken together, these four grounds may substantially expand the scope of political obligation to encompass many individuals not covered by our Hobbesian hypothetical consent account. Doubtless, many individuals do not fall under any of these grounds of political obligation, but this is as it should be. Many people in many places may simply not have any good moral reasons for political obedience, given the nature of the regimes they live under and their relationship to those regimes.

Nonetheless, these additional grounds of political obligation provide the means of solving, for Hobbesian theory, Simmons' particularity problem. Citizens of a satisfactory State have good moral reasons for obeying the directives of their *own* government (rather than that of some other satisfactory State), because in the light of benefits received they are bound by fair play to do so and because it generally promotes social utility to do so. Further, in some cases, considerations of consent and gratitude will reinforce these particularized political obligations.[51] Fair play and gratitude

---

[51] In other cases, e.g., where one has consented to and accepted benefits from a foreign government, the multiplicity of grounds of obligation can produce conflicting (prima facie) obligations. A complete theory of political obligation would have to prioritize, or integrate, the various grounds of political obligation. No such theory is aspired to here.

may even bind residents who have not and *would not* give consent to a satisfactory State to nonetheless obey the officials of such a State. But this special case of nonconsenters to the (hypothetical) social contract raises some special difficulties, to which we must now attend.

10-5. Independents and Oppressed Minorities

Our account of the Hobbesian social contract allows that a small minority of individuals might not agree to its terms under the appropriate bargaining conditions (section 5-2). Such parties are likely to have extremely advantageous personal characteristics and/or very little aversion to risk. Actual persons possessing these, or other unusual characteristics, might argue persuasively that they would not have consented to the founding of a satisfactory State, even under the knowledge limitations assumed in Hobbesian theory, and hence that they are not bound to their actual satisfactory State of residence via hypothetical consent theory. Correspondingly, they might object to the various restrictions on their liberty imposed by the satisfactory State—redistributive taxation and other requirements of the civil law. For convenience, let us refer to such individuals as *independents*[52] (within the satisfactory State).

Hobbes himself would have given short shrift to independents: if they do not obey State officials and their laws, they may be treated as enemies within the body politic and rightly treated however it is convenient for the State, its officials, and its citizens to treat them.[53] But the preservation of domestic peace, as well as considerations of humanity, would suggest that independents be accorded roughly the same treatment as foreign visitors—that they be invited to leave (emigrate) if they wish, be protected un-

[52] This term is borrowed from Nozick, who uses it—in effect—to refer to individuals not bound by his favored ground of political obligation, actual consent. Independents initially pose a serious problem for Nozick, because he is disinclined to acknowledge other possible grounds of political obligation. See *Anarchy, State, and Utopia*, chaps. 4–5.

[53] *Leviathan* (chap. 18, pp. 162–63) ascribes the status of enemies to dissenters from the original contract.

der the law while they stay, and be expected to obey the laws of the State while they remain in it. Suppose, however, that some independents refuse to emigrate on the grounds that it is costly and that they have a right to stay. And suppose further that they refuse to acknowledge an obligation to obey the laws of and pay taxes to a State they do not, and would not under appropriate conditions, consent to. How may the satisfactory State treat such recalcitrant independents?

On grounds of peace and self-defense (if nothing else), the State and its citizens may justifiably enforce against recalcitrant independents those civil laws embodying the fundamental rules of conduct necessary for civil peace. Thus, independents can rightly be prevented and deterred from killing, assaulting, stealing, cheating on contracts, defrauding, and so forth,[54] so long as they are provided with similar protection from others (should they wish it). Further, on grounds of fair play they may be required to pay their full share of the costs of these fundamental protections and any other benefits that they receive from the State that could be easily avoided. And they must pay at least some portion of the costs of significant benefits they cannot avoid receiving, such as national defense, environmental protection, and other costly public goods. The other citizens of the satisfactory State cannot, in fairness, be required to support independents as expensive free-riders if the latter have been offered the opportunity to emigrate as an alternative. Perhaps recalcitrant independents can even be required to share the costs of providing the economic minimum guaranteed by the satisfactory State. This would be so if there were reliable empirical evidence that recalcitrant independents tend to shed their claims of independence and seek government help if and when they fall on hard times, for example, go bankrupt. In sum, because there are moral grounds of political obedience besides hypothetical consent, independents in the satisfactory State

---

[54] Using force or fraud to enforce their conceptions of rights or justice would be covered by these prohibitions. For related discussion, see Nozick, *Anarchy, State, and Utopia*, chap. 5; and Daniel Farrell, "Coercion, Consent, and the Justification of Political Power," *Archiv für Rechts und Sozialphilosophie* 65, no. 4 (1979): 521–43.

are not morally free to do as they please. At a minimum they may be required to follow the core provisions of the civil law and pay taxes roughly proportional to the benefits they receive from residing in the satisfactory State.[55]

This short discussion of independents ties up an important loose end in the Hobbesian account of political obligation. There is another loose end, which must be left dangling because of its complexity and difficulty but which is worth mentioning for the sake of completeness. In sections 4-4 and 6-4, it was implied that the members of an oppressed and unprotected minority[56] within an otherwise satisfactory State would not owe allegiance to that State. But what of the protected majority group members within such a "restricted-satisfactory" State? The State is satisfactory with respect to its treatment of them, and it provides them with many substantial benefits. The majority group members would therefore seem bound to the State by obligations based on hypothetical consent, fair play, and (possibly) gratitude. On the other hand, we may doubt whether they really can be obligated to go along with an unjust system that treats a minority in such an "unsatisfactory" manner.

There is no easy answer to this dilemma, but one thing seems quite clear. A member of the majority cannot simply receive the benefits provided him by the restricted-satisfactory State and then refuse to carry out all corresponding duties on the grounds that the system is unjust.[57] This would amount to free-riding on the efforts of the other majority group members and callously exploiting the unfortunate situation of the oppressed for private gain. Beyond this, definite conclusions are hard to come by. Often it will be permissible for a majority group member to openly renounce allegiance to the State and take up the revolutionary cause

[55] It might be entirely reasonable, in practice, for a satisfactory State not to allow people to claim any tax reductions on grounds of being independents, for allowing such reductions would provide an incentive for people to lie about (or deceive themselves about) their status as independents.

[56] The usual term "minority" is used here, even though the repressed group might constitute a majority of the population, as in contemporary South Africa.

[57] Though he may rightly refuse to comply with assigned duties that involve directly or actively repressing the minority.

of the oppressed group. But is it permissible to change allegiance in secret and to live off the benefits provided by the restricted-satisfactory State and one's fellow group members while working surreptitiously from within to destroy the system providing those benefits? Is it more than permissible—in fact, *obligatory*—for majority group members to work within the laws of the restricted-satisfactory State to extend its protections and benefits to all? If so, how much risk, sacrifice, and effort is required? Answering these questions seems harder, rather than easier, once we note the analogy between the restricted-satisfactory State and the imperialist State which oppresses, dominates, or exploits *foreigners* (rather than domestic minorities) in order to provide benefits for its citizens. Each of our questions about the restricted-satisfactory State corresponds to a parallel question about the imperialist State, suggesting that adequate systematic answers can be found only within a comprehensive theory of international, as well as domestic, political morality. No attempt will be made here to provide such a comprehensive theory.

E L E V E N

THE LIMITS OF OBLIGATION

11-1. Self-Incrimination

Any comprehensive political philosophy must define the limits, as well as the grounds, of individuals' obligations to the State. Doing so involves facing difficult normative questions about how to balance individual rights against the public interest in three contexts in which vital interests are typically at stake: those of law enforcement, war, and revolution. In his attempt to ground political absolutism on strong individualistic moral premises, Hobbes glosses over some of the key issues in this area with imprecise claims and weak arguments. To be plausible, Hobbesian theory must correct Hobbes's errors and expand upon his insights so as to ameliorate the conflicts between political obligations and the individual rights from which they ultimately derive.

For Hobbes, the boundaries on one's obligation to the State arise from the inherent limits on the act of authorization, or rights transfer, which creates the State—such limits being due to the inalienability of the right of self-defense. In line with this view, Hobbes portrays the liberties to refuse to testify against oneself in criminal proceedings, to switch allegiances if taken prisoner of war, and to keep rebelling if not offered a pardon, as corollaries of the inalienability doctrine. Though in Chapter 8 we rejected Hobbes's arguments for that doctrine, we shall here specifically examine certain rights of criminal defendants, prisoners of war and soldiers, and rebels, both to clarify Hobbes's position on these matters and to see which aspects of that position might be worth preserving. In this section, our subject will be a purported right

419

of those accused of criminal offenses—the right of non-self-in-crimination, or refusal to bear witness against oneself.

Hobbes presents two distinct arguments for the claim that cit-izens have a right to refuse to testify against themselves. His first argument is that, because of the inalienability of the right of self-defense, members of civil society retain the natural right to resist force by whatever means they choose. But punishment by the State is force, and refusal to testify is one means of resisting it; hence the latter is within the citizen's rights, that is, it is permis-sible.[1] This argument is, however, directly subject to some of the difficulties with the inalienability doctrine that were noted in Chapter 8. Testifying against oneself will not always seem to be the lesser personal evil to a defendant, especially if leniency is offered for confession (or an additional penalty is threatened for refusal to testify). Therefore, even if Maximizing Egoism is as-sumed to be true, it is not the case—as the relevant version of the inalienability claim would require—that self-incrimination is generally psychologically impossible. Further, even in many cases in which it *is* psychologically impossible for a defendant to con-fess, it would not follow that it is permissible for him not to confess, for according to Hobbes's considered version of the "ought implies can" principle, inability to carry out an action does not cancel one's obligation to do it, if the situation in question was created by the agent's prior misconduct (see section 7-5). But in the case of guilty parties who are unable to confess, it is precisely their lawbreaking that puts them in the position in which they should confess but cannot bring themselves to do it.

Hobbes's second argument is that a defendant's testimony, like the forced testimony of family and friends or testimony given under torture, is not credible (presumably because of the strong incentives for guilty defendants to lie). But "where a man's tes-timony is not to be credited, he is not bound to give it."[2] There are two ways of taking this argument. Hobbes may be applying a general moral principle about communication to the effect that

[1] *Leviathan*, chap. 14, p. 128; chap. 21, p. 204.
[2] Ibid., chap. 14, p. 128.

420

one is not obligated to speak when one is unlikely to be believed. But there are surely exceptions to this principle, such as the person who has promised to give a speech before the Liars' Club, and a defendant's testimony may be another exception, since there arguably are social benefits to be gained by forcing such testimony, for example, enabling judges and juries to reach better verdicts by allowing them to assess the manner and substance of defendants' testimony, and deterrence of possible crimes by those who do not think they could convincingly lie on the witness stand.

Alternately, we may interpret Hobbes as claiming that it is essentially *pointless* to force defendants to testify, in view of the likelihood that the guilty will lie and truth-telling innocents will not be believed. This is very similar to the argument offered in section 8-4 for the claim that the original social contractors might well allow each other to retain the right to resist death at the hands of the State. But the present argument is both wider and narrower than that earlier argument—wider because it encompasses resistance to lesser penalties as well as death, and narrower because it is restricted to one particular method of self-defense: the refusal to testify against oneself. It seems doubtful, though, that the argument as stated can succeed, for as noted in the last paragraph, there are potential social advantages to forcing defendants to testify (even if guilty ones are likely to lie) and hence it would not be pointless to do so. Whether we or our original social contractors should view these advantages as outweighing the costs of forced testimony is the question we must next consider.

Leaving Hobbes's flawed arguments behind, what are the pros and cons of a civil society recognizing a right of non-self-incrimination? Before answering this question, we must clarify three points about the nature of that right. First, while for Hobbes the right of non-self-incrimination is a mere permission right,[3] in Anglo-American law it is a claim right. That is, within the Anglo-American system, the State is obligated not to punish defend-

---

[3] This is most directly inferred from the marginal paragraph heading: "Subjects have liberty to defend their own bodies, even against them that lawfully invade them" (ibid., chap. 21, p. 204; see also chap. 21, p. 200; chap. 14, p. 127).

ants for refusing to testify against themselves, for example, by treating such refusal as a separate offense or as establishing a presumption of guilt. In subsequent discussion, we shall be concerned with the right of non-self-incrimination viewed as a claim right. Second, we must distinguish the right of non-self-incrimination from the narrower right of noncoercion—the right not to be pressured into testimony against oneself (or others) by torture, physical force, or the threat thereof. We may assume that original social contractors would adopt this narrower right as a means of self-protection, but this right can be protected without according citizens a full right of non-self-incrimination, for instance, by making coerced confessions not admissible as evidence. Thus, by assuming that there is a right of noncoercion in the defined sense, we leave open the question as to whether defendants may be pressured to testify by threats of imprisonment or presumption of guilt on the present charges. Third, and finally, the right of non-self-incrimination is the right to defend oneself against legal punishment by a specific means: refusal to testify. It does not entail the broader right, which Hobbes apparently favors, of defending oneself against legal punishment by any means necessary, including using force against peace officers who come to arrest you.

The case *against* a society according a right of non-self-incrimination to its members must rest on the likelihood that so doing will allow some lawbreakers, who would otherwise be convicted and punished, to escape legal punishment. Retributivists would think this bad because it is inherently right that the guilty be punished. Hobbesian theory, however, is more concerned with the negative effects this would have on deterrence of crime. If the conviction rate is lower with the right of non-self-incrimination, deterrence—to the extent that it is a monotonic function of the conviction rate—will also be lower. Also, some potential lawbreakers (e.g., those who are aware they are not convincing liars) may be directly deterred if they expect to have to testify against themselves if caught. Direct deterrence of this kind is lost if citizens have, and are aware they have, a right of non-self-incrimination.

On the other side of the ledger, a variety of considerations might be offered in support of a right of non-self-incrimination. Let us briefly consider four of the most important considerations: protection against bad laws, privacy, protection of innocent defendants, and symbolic reinforcement of the importance of the individual.

In any society, there are likely to be bad laws which prohibit conduct that should not be legally prohibited and punished. Certain typical laws of this kind, for example, laws against holding certain religious or ideological beliefs or against performing certain sexual acts in private, are such that violations of them rarely can be proven except by obtaining confessions from a defendant. A right of non-self-incrimination therefore protects people from being punished for violating these bad laws.[4] Note, however, that by the arguments of section 5-5, there are likely to be few such laws in a satisfactory State. Hence, our original social contractors would assign relatively little weight to this consideration.

The right of non-self-incrimination protects people's privacy in at least two ways. It allows them, if they have done something wrong, to keep any confessions private—between themselves, their gods, or other confessors they choose,[5] and it helps them avoid viewing themselves and their activities as under a form of constant self-surveillance on behalf of the State. One's sense of privacy is more secure, we may say, if one need not carry around everywhere a potential witness against oneself.

Innocent defendants are protected in two ways by the right of non-self-incrimination. Some would make such a bad impression, if forced to testify, that they would be wrongly convicted. Others could be forced to reveal embarrassing or damaging facts about themselves, for example, that they were gambling at the racetrack when they should have been at work. That this latter consideration is not of decisive importance is suggested by the fact

---

[4] Historically, this seems to be a major reason for the introduction of the right of non-self-incrimination into English law. See Leonard Levy, *Origins of the Fifth Amendment* (London: Oxford University Press, 1968).

[5] See Robert Gerstein, "Privacy and Self-Incrimination," *Ethics* 80 (January 1970): 87–100.

that, in our legal system, unwilling *witnesses* can (in principle) be compelled to testify, even if they may suffer embarrassment or damage as a result. It is much harder to determine the importance of protecting "poor testifiers" from wrongful conviction, because there seems to be no good way of knowing what percentage of innocent defendants fall in this category.

Finally, it may be suggested that the right of non-self-incrimination is an important symbol of the value of the individual and the fact that the State exists to protect and serve individuals, not the other way around. On the other hand, forcing defendants to testify may symbolize another important value, the accountability of individuals to other individuals who may be threatened or harmed by their conduct. This value is especially important in a Hobbesian framework, given our observations in section 6-1 about the difficulties involved in obtaining effective law enforcement within the State.

Given the complex value trade-offs involved and the great uncertainties about how much deterrence and how many innocent convictions would result from defendants' being forced to testify against themselves by threat of legal punishment, it seems unlikely that a near unanimous consensus on this matter could emerge among our original social contractors. Hence, in Hobbesian theory, unlike in Hobbes's theory, a right of non-self-incrimination does not emerge from the social contract and assumptions about natural rights. This does not preclude, however, the possibility that individual satisfactory States might rationally accord citizens a right of non-self-incrimination to protect their privacy, to minimize wrongful convictions, or for other reasons.

11-2. National Defense

Theories, such as that of Hobbes, which attempt to ascribe extensive authority to States and extensive rights of life and liberty to individuals face difficulties when the fundamental rights of States and individual citizens come into conflict. In the last section, we saw that Hobbes deals with one such situation—that of self-incrimination—by reaffirming the individual's (permission) right to refuse to testify. This doctrine does not seriously threaten the State, since the State has overwhelming power to deal with individual lawbreakers, and the permission right, on its own side, to compel a defendant's testimony. When it comes to issues of national defense, however, the conflicts are starker. More often than in criminal cases, individuals' very lives, and not just their liberty, are at stake. And the State's very existence may be threatened, as it faces a more equal foe, a foreign power. In such circumstances, how are we to reconcile the individual's right of self-preservation with the State's authority to control its citizens' conduct for its own protection and the promotion of common security?

Rather than provide a general answer to this question, Hobbes suggests that when the commonwealth is threatened from abroad, individuals' rights vary according to circumstances. In particular, he seems to hold that these rights are a function of the actual needs of the State and the specific commitments undertaken by individuals. Consider first the needs of the State. Hobbes claims, in effect, that an individual is obligated to risk his life fighting external enemies of the State if and only if the State needs, and would benefit from, his specific contribution. Thus, a landowner whose estates fall to the enemy may switch allegiance and pay taxes to the invader, since resistance would only lead to total confiscation of the property, with greater benefits accruing to the invader.[6] Similarly, a prisoner of war, who is not in a position to help his original sovereign much, may trade his allegiance for life and liberty,[7] and an individual commanded to fight may substitute another soldier in his place.[8] But "when the defence of the commonwealth, requireth at once the help of all that are able to bear arms, every one is obliged."[9]

The individual soldier's commitments also affect his rights. Those who flee battle from fear are guilty of injustice and act impermissibly only if they have volunteered for service or taken pay-

[6] *Leviathan*, "A Review, and Conclusion," pp. 703–4.
[7] Ibid., chap. 21, p. 208.
[8] Ibid., p. 205.
[9] Ibid.

ment and accordingly waived the right to use fear as an excuse.[10] Prisoners of war are bound to those who capture them only if they expressly or tacitly commit themselves. Mere captivity does not alter their original obligations.[11]

There are, though, a number of problems with this attempt to achieve a compromise between the rights of individual and collective self-defense. It hardly seems that genuine draftees waive any rights simply by accepting pay. Nor, in view of our remarks about coerced promises in section 10-2, is it plausible to view prisoners of war as being bound by promises of allegiance they make to escape captivity. More important, the requirement to serve when "all" are needed is essentially vacuous if interpreted literally. Except in unusual circumstances involving a key military commander or political leader, the loss or gain of any particular single defender will make no difference to the success of the common defense. Hence, it is never the case that "all" are needed to defend the commonwealth. So by Hobbes's criterion individuals are free to avoid military service.

Now perhaps this problem could be solved by replacing the term "all" in Hobbes's criterion by the term "a certain number" and adding that an individual is obligated to serve if he is selected to be among that certain number by a fair or reasonable procedure. But whatever the circumstances in which nonvolunteering individuals are obligated to fight to defend the State, Hobbes still must explain how it can be possible for predominant egoists, and obligatory for those retaining the right of self-preservation, to risk their lives in this way. Let us try to partially rescue Hobbes by outlining a Hobbesian position on these two issues, beginning with the question of how it is possible for predominant egoists to risk their lives on the battlefield.

Predominant Egoism says that most all people put their own self-interest ahead of other considerations most all of the time. Yet throughout history soldiers have fought and died for their tribes, cities, and countries. Since death is nearly always contrary

[10] Ibid.
[11] Ibid., p. 208.

to a person's interests, there is an apparent anomaly here. Hobbesian theory, committed to the truth of Predominant Egoism, must deal with this anomaly by explaining why predominant egoists will often risk their lives in battle. The explanation consists of a mixture of four elements, which we shall call, respectively, Progressively Limited Options, Fates Worse Than Death, Training-Habituation, and Nonegoistic Motives.

As we consider these elements in turn, three points should be kept in mind. First, society is well aware of the potential influence of rational and instinctual fear in preventing individuals from becoming or performing effectively as soldiers.[12] Hence, it brings enormous pressures to bear on individuals to fight, partly in the form of material and psychological rewards for military service, and punishments for refusal to serve, desertion, or disobedience to orders. Second, while these pressures and other factors are generally sufficient to overcome the effects of fear, they often are not. Many people avoid military service if they can and, as Hobbes notes, "when armies fight, there is on one side, or both, a running away."[13] Third, while soldiers entering battle generally face a significant risk of death, they rarely face certain death. Each of these three observations contributes to our four-part explanation of the willingness to risk one's life in combat.

PROGRESSIVELY LIMITED OPTIONS. Soldiers who die on the battlefield rarely meet their fates as the result of a single decision. More typically, the individual's loss of life, insofar as it is a function of his own choices, depends on a *series* of choices and actions. He enlists or allows himself to be drafted (rather than fleeing or being punished). He goes through training without desertion or refusal to cooperate. He travels to the combat zone without deserting, obeys the order to advance to the battlefield, and engages the enemy rather than fleeing or surrendering. At each progressive stage, the risks of death grow higher, but one's options are correspondingly more limited and less attractive. Joining the army may be, statistically, not very risky, so for many the

---

[12] On the two sorts of fear, see section 2-6.
[13] *Leviathan*, chap. 21, p. 205.

advantages of a military career outweigh its dangers. Once in the military, penalties for desertion or disobedience are stiff, while the dangers of obedience are small unless one enters combat. Once in combat, the dangers increase, but there are now no safe alternatives. One may be killed (by one's own officers[14] or by the enemy) if one tries to flee, if one tries to surrender, or if one disobeys orders. Fighting on in coordinated fashion with one's comrades will often be the safest course, or at least a course that is hardly more dangerous than the few available alternatives. Since one's options become progressively more limited and enormously less attractive from the point of view of self-interest, as one proceeds toward the riskier end of this sequence of decisions, each decision to proceed toward (or continue) combat may be in accordance with rational self-interest in many cases. Typically, at no point, when one still has a chance to choose, does one face certain death, and as the risks increase with each successive choice, so do the risks associated with available alternatives. So if penalties for disobedience and desertion are harsh, casualty rates are not too high, and rewards for military success—in terms of honor, power, or pay—are significant, even pure calculating rational egoists might fight in defense of their countries.

FATES WORSE THAN DEATH. As noted in section 2-6, Hobbes acknowledges that there are fates worse than death. For some people, living with the dishonor of having deserted one's country and comrades at arms, and the official punishment (e.g., long imprisonment) for such action may seem, and be, a fate worse than death. For such people, the risk of death in battle is a lesser personal evil. The same is true of religious believers who expect to receive enormous rewards in the afterlife for participating in what they take to be a holy war (or enormous punishments for not participating).[15] Such beliefs apparently motivated some of

---

[14] See, e.g., Geoffry Brennan and Gordon Tullock, "An Economic Theory of Military Tactics," Public Choice Center, Virginia Polytechnic Institute and State University, January 1981.

[15] For reasons noted in section 9-2, Hobbes would regard these beliefs as irrational.

the World War II Japanese kamikaze pilots, as well as contemporary Iranian youths who are said to have walked unprotected into enemy minefields.

Predominant Egoism, since it is a form of Nonmaximizing rather than Maximizing Egoism,[16] also allows that agents are sometimes moved, by certain self-interested motives or goals, to act contrary to their overall self-interest. Hence, even if dishonor would not be worse for a person than a substantial risk of death, fear of dishonor or hope of honor, glory, or other rewards may nonetheless motivate him to risk death in battle.[17] Here we explain combat participation as a particular species of *irrational* action. This mode of explanation is continued below.

TRAINING-HABITUATION. New soldiers are typically subjected to a training regimen that is designed to make their obedience to the orders of military superiors automatic and unthinking. The purpose of this practice is to habituate soldiers to obedience so that the military operates efficiently and so that soldiers in combat are more likely to obey orders from habit than disobey them from fear. This training is effective to a considerable degree. Undoubtedly, many soldiers go into battle or perform specific dangerous tasks in battle because they are in the habit of doing as they are told by superiors. It is not that they decide to obey; they do not deliberate at all, but simply act as instructed to act.

Are such acts rational? They are *nonrational* in the sense that they are not based on conscious choice or deliberation. They may be *rational* in the sense that they are the natural or predictable outcomes of generally rational prior acts of accepting training in the armed forces. (These prior acts may be rational for the reasons given above when discussing Progressively Limited Options.) At the same time, they can be *irrational* in the sense of being on the whole against the agent's interests and purposes, so

---

[16] See section 2-2.

[17] This observation calls into question the "salience" argument constructed in section 8-3 to rescue Hobbes's second argument that the right of self-defense is inalienable. Since we ultimately rejected Hobbes's argument and its conclusion, Hobbesian philosophy is not affected by the abandonment of the salience argument.

that he would not perform them if he rationally deliberated as to whether he should.

NONEGOISTIC MOTIVES. Predominant Egoism allows that everyone, to some extent, and some people to a very considerable extent, act from nonegoistic motives. There is no doubt that many of those who risk and lose their lives in battle act at least partly from such motives. Love of country, a sense of duty or fair play, or belief in a cause may sufficiently motivate some to fight. The pressures of fighting are said to create very strong feelings of benevolence and loyalty toward one's immediate comrades at arms.[18] Such feelings may well motivate undertaking extraordinary risks to protect one's comrades and retain their respect. And, of course, the psychological atmosphere in an army or society at war is generally such as to encourage, strengthen, or reinforce whatever nonegoistic motives of this kind exist. Everyone is urged to do his part to save the motherland, people are constantly reminded of the sacrifices others have made and are making, grim pictures are painted of how one's society would fare if the enemy prevailed, and so on.

The true explanation of why so many individuals are willing to risk their lives in battle in defense of the State and society contains all four of these elements and probably others. Many of those who risk their lives in battle do so for several of the cited reasons—because their options are few and unattractive, because they are used to following orders, and because they wish to protect their comrades, families, and countries. To the extent that any one of these reasons seems too weak to explain life-risking behavior, the possibility of their combining strengthens the overall plausibility of the account offered. Note further that all four elements in the explanation are consistent with Predominant Egoism, and only two of them—the second and the third—depend, and then only partly, on the fact that individuals sometimes act irrationally. In view of this, the known fact that people are often willing to risk their lives to defend their countries can

[18] See, e.g., J. Glenn Gray, *The Warriors: Reflections on Men in Battle* (New York: Harper & Row, 1959), pp. 47–56.

be readily accommodated within Hobbesian theory without having to revise that theory's motivational assumptions.

But what of the claim that people are *obligated* to defend their countries? This presents a problem for Hobbes, given his doctrine that the right of self-preservation is inalienable. It seems to present a similar problem for our Hobbesian philosophy, for in section 8-4 we suggested that original social contractors would not lay down the right to resist deadly attacks by the State, since an agreement to do so would be essentially pointless in view of people's strong psychological propensities to defend themselves. And it might be thought that surrender of the right to preserve oneself by avoiding battle would be pointless in the same way, thus precluding the possibility that an obligation to aid in national defense could be derived from the social contract.

Ironically, Hobbes's own argument for an obligation to defend the State when such defense is needed does not solve *his* problem, but it does point the way toward solving *ours*. He contends that citizens must defend the State when they are needed, "because otherwise the institution of the commonwealth, . . . was in vain."[19] His suggestion that the social contract cannot fulfill its purpose of protecting the parties to it in the long run unless it obligates them to defend the commonwealth, when needed, from foreign enemies seems correct. But unless one implausibly contends that it is *always* less dangerous to fight than to risk loss of one's country's future protection by surrendering or deserting,[20] the existence of such an obligation does not jibe with Hobbes's view that the right of self-preservation cannot be surrendered.

Hobbesian philosophy, however, rejects the inalienability of the right of self-preservation. It allows that portions of that right can be, and likely would be, surrendered as part of the social contract.[21] Would the parties to the social contract obligate them-

---

[19] *Leviathan*, chap. 21, p. 205.

[20] In which case fighting for the State would always be one's best means of preserving oneself. Our discussion of progressively limited options suggests that this may *often* be the case for parties in battle, but does not commit us to the implausible universal claim that Hobbes needs.

[21] See section 8-3.

selves to one another to defend the commonwealth against foreign enemies when a "certain number" are needed to do so, and when the individuals constituting this "certain number" are selected by a fair or reasonable procedure?[22] It is very likely that they would agree to this surrender of part of their natural right of self-preservation for three reasons. They would realize that the commonwealth was "in vain" and could not protect them in the long run unless supported by an agreement of this kind. They would not view the agreement as pointless, since—for the reasons cited above—fighting for one's country is generally psychologically possible for people, especially, one might add, when those called upon to fight are selected by a fair or reasonable procedure. Finally, the risks undertaken by a social contractor in assuming the obligation to fight when needed and fairly selected are not overwhelming. One may never be needed, or never selected, or never ordered into combat, or may survive combat. Given this, the benefits offered to each social contractor by the mutual partial surrender of the right of self-preservation with his fellows clearly seems to outweigh the personal risks involved.

The generalization of this last point helps us deal with an objection to rule egoism raised in section 9-5. It was suggested there that it is irrational to commit oneself to moral rules—even those based on long-run prudence—since following those rules could, in certain circumstances, lead to one's premature demise. It is true that genuinely committing oneself to moral rules, even Hobbesian ones, can make it more likely that if certain contingencies arise, you will die. Following moral rules may require defending your country in a just war, abiding by the fatal (for you) results of a lifeboat lottery, and so on. It hardly follows, however, that so committing oneself is irrational. The risks of death entailed are generally small, and the benefits involved—protection against many forms of imprudence and shortsightedness, the psychic benefits enjoyed in virtue of one's perception of one's own morality, and so on—are substantial and highly prob-

---

[22] What kind of conscientious objection provision, if any, would be embodied in such a procedure is a question we shall not discuss here.

able. Like the social contractor contemplating surrender of a portion of his right of self-defense or the potential recruit contemplating joining the army, the potential recruit to the system of rule-egoistic moral rules has a good chance of gaining much and must accept only an incremental decrease, if any, in life expectancy.[23] Thus, even in terms of self-interest in the narrowest sense, his commitment to morality may be rational—just as it may be rational to love particular other people, even though this may dispose you to sacrifice your life for them if need be.[24]

11-3. Revolution

In addition to the rights of non-self-incrimination and avoidance of unneeded military service, Hobbes derives a third right of disobedience to the State from the supposed inalienability of the right of self-preservation. This is the right of revolutionaries to resist the State unless offered pardon for their previous rebellious actions.[25] Hobbes is able to posit this right, while holding to a consistent antirevolutionary stance, by assigning different moral statuses to initial and later acts of rebellion. The former are unjust, but the latter are permissible (if no pardon has been offered) because they are necessary for self-defense.

This right to continue rebelling is stronger than other rights of resistance to the State which Hobbes describes in that it is *collective*. Rebels are at liberty "to join together, and assist, and defend one another."[26] The right to resist criminal punishment, by contrast, is clearly a mere individual right. Hobbes emphasizes that one citizen does not, in general, have the right to defend others

---

[23] To the extent that choosing to live morally decreases one's chances of falling into lifestyles with short life expectancies (e.g., criminality, drug addiction) it actually extends one's life expectancy. These factors may outweigh the risks to life that one accepts in committing oneself to moral rules.

[24] For elaboration of the argument of this paragraph, see my "The Reconciliation Project," in *Morality, Reason, and Truth*, ed. Copp and Zimmerman, sec. III.

[25] *Leviathan*, chap. 21, p. 206.

[26] Ibid.

against law enforcement activities.[27] The right of rebels to assist one another is an exception to this general principle.

In "establishing" the right of continued rebellion, however, Hobbes runs afoul of essentially the same problem he faced in deriving the right of non-self-incrimination. His restriction on the "ought implies can" doctrine (section 7-5) implies that even if rebels "cannot but" continue to resist, it does not follow that they can *permissibly* resist. For just as the criminal's situation has been brought on by his past misdeeds, so has the revolutionary's situation been created by his prior unjust acts of rebellion. If we take Hobbes's restriction seriously, then, we cannot accept his argument for the right to continue rebelling.

There are, nonetheless, underlying currents in Hobbes's thought that point to a different and broader conception of justified revolutionary resistance to the State. He writes, "The obligation of subjects to the sovereign, is understood to last as long, and no longer, than the power lasteth, by which he is able to protect them. . . . The end of obedience is protection."[28] This passage clearly suggests that when a sovereign ceases to protect his people their obligations to him disappear. But surely this principle should apply to subgroups within the populace as well as to the citizenry as a whole. If a government seeks to destroy a minority group by genocide, or negligently permits a large part of a group or class to perish from famine, or allows some groups to mercilessly oppress and exploit other groups, the "victim" groups are not being protected and their members are freed of obligation to the government. Should they choose to defend themselves by collective rebellion, they would be acting permissibly.

Nor is this prorevolutionary position supported, in Hobbes, only by the above-quoted passage about sovereignty and protection. As noted in section 6-4, there are other places where Hobbes suggests that rebellion is inevitable, and is to be blamed on the wealthy, if the wealthy consume more than they need while others are deprived of their basic needs.[29] How are these implicitly

[27] Ibid., p. 205; *Philosophical Rudiments*, chap. 6, sec. 5, p. 75.
[28] *Leviathan*, chap. 21, p. 208.
[29] Ibid., chap. 15, pp. 138–39; chap. 11, pp. 86–87.

prorevolutionary principles and statements to be reconciled with Hobbes's explicit antirevolutionary stance? The answer seems to be that Hobbes assumes that the State will act to procure the safety and well-being of all the people by enacting and enforcing beneficial general laws.[30] If so, the basic needs of all will be met and revolt would be imprudent and immoral.

Our Hobbesian view of revolution, sketched in section 6-4, brings these assumptions to the surface and extends them. It is only when all the protections of the satisfactory State are provided that the presumption against revolution becomes so strong as to be virtually incapable of being overridden.[31] When the protections for population subgroups are less than in the satisfactory State, this presumption—based on the costs and uncertainties associated with revolution and its aftermath—is correspondingly weakened and may often be overridden.

For Hobbes, the only limits on sovereign authority are those, such as the right of non-self-incrimination and continued rebellion, that derive directly from the right of self-preservation. Subjects will have rights and liberties other than these, but only as the State chooses to allow them.[32] In our Hobbesian philosophy, by contrast, there are inherent limits on State authority derived from the content of the original contract. The satisfactory State must allow its citizens freedom of speech, thought, press, religion, political participation, and private conduct that does not harm others (see section 5-5). And it cannot ignore merit or practice racial, religious, or sexual discrimination in its hiring and educational policies (see section 5-4). Except on the issue of self-incrimination, then, Hobbesian philosophy is decidedly more liberal than Hobbes himself on issues related to the State's authority

[30] Ibid., chap. 30, pp. 322–23.

[31] Suppose that we give equal consideration to the interests of each present and future generation, as perhaps we should in normative theory but as we did not in the descriptive account of section 6-4. This might increase the chances of overriding the presumption against revolution in a satisfactory State because the potential (weighted) gains are greater. Still, the uncertainties are large enough that a very strong burden-of-proof requirement must fall on the revolutionary challenger of the satisfactory State.

[32] Leviathan, chap. 21, p. 206.

over the individual. Hobbesian philosophy attributes more extensive liberties to individuals as citizens or, potentially, as rebels
than does Hobbes's own philosophy. But as we have seen here
and in Chapter 5, these more extensive liberties can be justified
on the basis of principles and procedures contained in or inspired
by Hobbes's own writings.

TWELVE

LESSONS AND LIMITS
OF *LEVIATHAN*

12-1. *Limits of Hobbesian Theory*

No entirely adequate moral-political theory exists now or is likely
to exist in the foreseeable future. The phenomena to be ac-
counted for are too complex, the values to be expressed are too
various, and the intellectual resources available to devote to the
subject are too limited for a correct and comprehensive theory to
emerge. Hobbesian theory, as presented here, is no exception.
Despite its many virtues and the insights it contains, it has problems, weaknesses, and limitations. Our brief discussion of these
problems will be aided if we distinguish between three different
sorts of shortcomings from which such a theory may suffer. A
theory has *overly restricted scope* if it does not deal with or account for major areas or aspects of the subject matter of which it
is purportedly a theory. An *oversimplified* theory ignores relevant complicating factors within the domain of the theory. An
inaccurate theory is one that yields wrong or unacceptable answers to relevant questions within the area it covers. In general,
inaccuracy is a more serious flaw than the other two shortcomings. Theories with overly restricted scope may eventually be
broadened or conjoined with theories of complementary scope.
Oversimplified theories can be made progressively more complex.
Inaccurate theories, however, must be corrected. Hobbesian theory suffers, to some extent, from defects of each of these three
sorts.

The scope of Hobbesian *moral* theory is restricted to requirements of interpersonal conduct. It thus leaves aside two impor-

tant areas of morality: self-regarding requirements and principles of supererogatory (i.e., nonrequired but morally desirable) conduct. In particular, personal and social ideals, which have a significant role to play in morality, are largely unaccounted for by a theory focused on other-regarding *requirements* of action.[1] Further, since it is at least arguable that sometimes the pursuit or attainment of certain moral ideals should take precedence over particular moral requirements, leaving ideals out of the picture may constitute an oversimplification as well as an overrestriction of moral theory.

Hobbesian *political* theory suffers from similar limitations. Save for treating foreign powers as creating a need for coordinated defense, it basically ignores international relations. While this is primarily a scope restriction, it also is an oversimplification, for other nations and their behavior often have important influences on domestic politics and the social order (or disorder) within a given nation. One would expect, for example, that no detailed descriptive theory of revolution in the modern world could be very successful without taking into account various international factors.

Hobbesian theory also oversimplifies in ignoring various *information problems* in the real world. It primarily treats individuals as rational, aware of one another's rationality, and correct in their perceptions of the background conditions and circumstances of their interactions. But in the real political world, people are often irrational and ill-informed. Equally important, as Hobbes himself recognized, deliberate deception and ideological indoctrination are commonplaces of political life.[2] In largely setting aside these factors, Hobbesian theory grossly oversimplifies political reality. This weakness of descriptive theory, however, is a *strength* of Hobbesian normative theory. To infer normative conclusions from agents' hypothetical choices, we want those choices to be rational, appro-

---

[1] On the role of ideals in morality, see P. F. Strawson, "Individual Ideal and Social Morality," in *The Definition of Morality*, ed. Wallace and Walker.

[2] See *Leviathan*, chap. 13, p. 111, where Hobbes speaks of mastering others "by force, *or wiles*" (emphasis supplied). On the importance of ideological indoctrination, see, e.g., ibid., chap. 18, p. 164; chap. 30, pp. 326–32.

priately informed, not distorted by deception or ideology, and so on. Hence, descriptive oversimplification in these regards is a necessary and fair price to pay for construction of a plausible normative theory.

Because they are modifiable, in principle, without abandoning the main themes stressed in this book, the scope restrictions and oversimplifications so far discussed should not make us question the utility of Hobbesian theory. There remains, however, an apparent inaccuracy in Hobbesian moral theory which constitutes a more serious difficulty. The problem, noted briefly in section 9-5, concerns the moral relationship between members of strong groups and weak groups. Remember that Hobbesian ethics emphasizes that there is a general coincidence between moral and rationally self-interested behavior, with expectations of *reciprocity* by others being the original rational motive for commitment to a moral way of life. Because each individual most profits from the cooperation rather than the opposition and sanctions of others, moral action tends to pay prudential dividends. But one does not necessarily need the cooperation of *everyone* to prosper. Cooperation with enough others with sufficient resources will generally suffice. In particular, when rich strong groups interact with poor weak ones, the latter can often be coerced into surrendering resources to the former without reciprocation and may be in no position to reciprocate any benefits that are provided to them. In these circumstances, wouldn't it be against their own interests for members of strong groups to treat members of weak ones fairly and decently, as morality requires?[3] And if so, doesn't the basic Hobbesian account of morality, based on the concept of reciprocity and the supposed prudence of moral behavior, break down?

Notice that this is essentially a problem for normative rather than descriptive theory. Throughout history, powerful rich groups have not been notorious for their kind and decent treatment of members of weak groups. It is quite likely that this has been

[3] See Bernard Boxill, "How Injustice Pays," *Philosophy & Public Affairs* (Summer 1980): 359–71.

439

because it was, or appeared to be, in the interests of the powerful groups and their members to act this way. Hence, actual group behavior in this regard has generally coincided with the predictions that might be derived from the motivational assumptions of Hobbesian descriptive theory. On the other hand, there is a genuine problem for Hobbesian normative theory here. We could hardly endorse, as a principle of *morality* in the modern world, the imperative that powerful groups and their members mistreat, exploit, and fail to aid weak groups and their members. Yet, according to the present objection, this is precisely where Hobbesian normative theory leads us.

This objection can be answered partly, but only partly, within the confines of Hobbesian theory. No attempt will be made to argue that a coincidence between strong group interests and the decent treatment of weak groups exists in all actual historical, much less all possible, situations. Instead, our defense of Hobbesian theory suggests that in the real world as it actually is at present, the long-run prudential interests of strong groups and their members generally require the decent treatment of weak groups and their members. This suggestion, even if borne out, will not satisfy those who demand a noncontingent guarantee that a moral theory yield correct prescriptions, but it is probably the strongest conclusion supportable without appealing to considerations outside Hobbesian theory. In supporting this conclusion, we shall briefly consider the three most important cases of relations between strong groups and weak groups in the contemporary world: treatment of the domestic poor, impoverished nations, and future generations.

Before discussing these three cases, it should be pointed out that whether there is hope of reconciling group interest and duty depends on what we take the demands of duty to be. If we interpret morality as requiring rich and powerful groups to share so much with the poor and weak as to create absolute equality, there is very little prospect that duty and interest can be reconciled. But it is far from obvious that morality demands this much. What morality does clearly require is that the rich and powerful refrain from actively harming the poor and weak and that the former aid the latter when the costs of giving are small and the benefits of receiving are large. We shall see that with this modest interpretation of the obligations of the powerful, reconciling their obligations with their interests may be possible.

Let us turn to our examples, the first concerning justice within a society. Why should rich and powerful groups in a nation allow the poor opportunities for education, employment, and advancement and provide social welfare programs which benefit the poor, as morality requires? Why shouldn't they simply oppress and exploit the poor? There are several reasons why, in modern times, it is most probably in the long-term interest of the rich and powerful to treat the domestic poor well. First, some rich individuals, and more likely some of their children, may be poor at some time in the future and thus benefit from programs to help the poor. Second, offering opportunities to members of all groups widens the pool of talent available to fill socially useful jobs, which should provide long-run economic benefits to members of all groups.[4] Third, and most important, there is the reason that has impressed social theorists from Hobbes to Rawls: decent treatment of all promotes social stability and cohesion and discourages revolution. This reason is especially important in contemporary times when ideals of human dignity, equality, and justice are known and espoused virtually everywhere, and when revolution is frequently proposed as a legitimate means of attaining such ideals.

Taken together, these reasons constitute a strong case, on prudential grounds, for decent treatment of the domestic poor by a nation's dominant groups. In fact, if we apply disaster-avoidance reasoning, it turns out that the third reason alone shows that good treatment of the poor is prudentially rational, for if the poor find the status quo unacceptable, and apply such reasoning, they may well revolt. In Hobbes's words, "Needy men, and hardy, not contented with their present condition; . . . are inclined to . . . stir up trouble and sedition: for there is no . . . such hope to

---

[4] This argument is the liberal counterpart of the conservative "trickle-down" theory, which claims that direct economic benefits to the rich will indirectly benefit the poor.

mend an ill game, as by causing a new shuffle."[5] The rich, being aware of this, will (if they collectively follow a disaster-avoidance strategy) seek to prevent the poor from falling into such unacceptable circumstances, for the rich thereby maximize their chances of obtaining an outcome acceptable to them—preservation of something resembling the status quo.

What about a wealthy and powerful nation aiding poor, weak nations? Is this in the long-run interest of the former as well as the latter? In a world of advanced technology, international markets, ideological conflicts among powerful nations, and nuclear weapons, it most probably is. In competition with other powerful nations, allies—even poor nations—are useful for political, economic, and military reasons. And economic development of poor nations should in the long run produce economic benefits for richer nations, for example, by providing markets and reliable supplies of various raw and finished goods. Most important, continued poverty in the third world is likely to produce continued turmoil, civil wars, and regional wars between nations. In a world armed to the teeth with nuclear weapons, and with more and more nations acquiring such weapons, the long-run danger of rich, developed countries being drawn into a devastating military conflict begun by a desperate poor nation, or some desperate group within such a nation, is far from negligible.

The above arguments about domestic and international justice suggest that there is, after all, a form of reciprocity between powerful and weak groups because of the interdependencies between the two in economic and security matters. The poor cannot return the aid of the rich in kind, but they can offer their talents, their purchasing power, and so on. If not treated well, they cannot directly punish the rich and powerful, but they can stir up serious trouble for them if they are willing to experience such trouble themselves. Thus they are able, and likely, to return good for good and evil for evil to the rich in the long run, and it will be rational for the rich to act accordingly.

Even this form of reciprocity is not available, however, to deal

---

[5] *Leviathan*, chap. 11, pp. 86–87.

with our third and most puzzling example—the treatment of future generations.[6] Future generations (beyond the next few) are powerless to act upon us, as they will not exist until after we are dead. Yet we have substantial power to determine the quality of their lives by influencing their numbers and the nature of the social and natural environment into which they will be born. Given this absolute asymmetry in power to affect one another, how can it be in our interest to act morally toward future generations? Morality requires us, at a minimum, to leave our descendants with enough resources to allow future people to live decent lives. But this would necessitate having a lower material standard of living than we could obtain by depleting resources and contaminating the environment whenever it is convenient to do so. If future generations cannot punish us for ruthlessly exploiting the earth in this way, does not rational prudence require it of us?

The supporter of Hobbesian theory can come a considerable way toward answering even this objection. One might point out first that misuse of resources and damage to the environment will often produce substantial negative effects within our own lifetimes. So for the most part it is in our own interests to follow conservation policies that will turn out to benefit future generations. This reply will only take us so far, however, for there are policies whose benefits are experienced now and most of whose costs will be borne generations later, for example, building nuclear power plants without having solved the long-term waste storage problem. Also, optimal *rates* of use of scarce nonrenewable resources will vary greatly depending upon how long we care about the resource lasting. Hence, there is a far from perfect overlap between the resource and environmental policies likely to most benefit present people and those likely to ensure a decent life for members of future generations.

A more promising argument begins from the fact that most people care deeply about the happiness of their own children and grandchildren, and hence that their own happiness would be di-

---

[6] As pointed out in Brian Barry, "Circumstances of Justice and Future Generations," in *Obligations to Future Generations*, ed. Brian Barry and Richard Sikora (Philadelphia: Temple University Press, 1978).

minished by contemplating the prospect of these descendants having to live in a resource-depleted world. Further, they realize that the happiness of their children and grandchildren will in turn be affected by the prospects for happiness of *their* children and grandchildren, and so forth. Hence, the happiness of present people is linked, generation by generation, to the prospects for happiness of some likely members of distant future generations. This "chain-connection" argument has considerable force, but it falls short of constituting a full solution to the problem before us because the perceived happiness of one's children and grandchildren is only one component of the well-being or happiness of the typical parent—and the perceived happiness of *their* children and grandchildren is, in turn, only one component of the happiness of one's children and grandchildren. So there is a multiplier effect over generations that quickly diminishes the influence on a present person's happiness of the prospects for happiness of his later descendants.[7] And we must seek some other device to firmly link the interests of living people to those of distant future generations.

The most promising such device is an appeal to our need to give meaning to our lives and our endeavors. One strong reason we have for providing future people with the means to survive and prosper is that this is our best hope for the successful continuation of certain human enterprises that we value (and may have contributed to)—science, the arts and humanities, morality, religion, democratic government, and so forth.[8] Ernest Partridge has argued along these lines that human beings have a psychological need for "self-transcendence," that is, a need to contribute to

[7] We can illustrate this point using arbitrarily chosen and artificially precise numbers. Suppose that my happiness is half dependent upon my perceptions of my childrens' well-being and half dependent on other independent things, and that I assume the same will be true of them and their children, etc. Then one-quarter of my happiness will be determined by the prospects of my grandchildren, one-eighth by the prospects of my great grandchildren, etc.

[8] See sec. IV of my "The Futurity Problem," in Sikora and Barry, *Obligations to Future Generations* (reprinted with minor changes in *Responsibilities to Future Generations*, ed. Ernest Partridge [Buffalo: Prometheus, 1981]), where I discuss reasons for wanting the continuation of the species. Some of the same points apply to assuring future people decent lives.

projects that are outside themselves and that will continue after their deaths.[9] Those without such goals are unlikely to find meaning in their lives, especially during the middle and later stages of life, when people typically reflect on their own mortality. Thus, Partridge says, "We need the future, *now*."[10]

There is a great deal of truth in this argument, but there are some limits to what it can show. It cannot reconcile the interests and obligations to posterity of the narcissist who has no self-transcending goals and is incapable of developing them. However, this need not worry us too much. The self-transcending life may be the happier life for the vast majority who still can live it, and these people have good prudential reasons for doing so. The more important problem is that not all self-transcending concerns need be directed toward the distant future. They may involve goals that do not extend much beyond one's lifetime, for example, the prosperity of one's children or the eventual rise to power of one's favorite political movement. Such goals may give meaning to one's life without supplying reasons to provide for the welfare of distant generations. Perhaps, though, it is a psychological fact that enterprises promising to continue into the indefinite future are better able to provide meaning in our lives or to provide consolation for our mortality.[11] If so, there would be powerful prudential reasons for one's adopting self-transcending concerns of unlimited temporal scope and for protecting the social and natural environments for future generations.

One may find these attempts to reconcile duty and interest, especially in the case of future generations, less than fully convincing. Supporters of Hobbesian theory can take considerable solace in the fact that the question of our duties to future generations is, on practically any moral theory, shot through with perplexities and paradoxes, as the recent literature on the subject has shown.[12] Other recent proponents of hypothetical contract

[9] "Why Care About the Future," in Partridge, *Responsibilities to Future Generations*.

[10] Ibid., p. 217.

[11] The fact that most of us do care a good deal about the future survival and prosperity of humankind may constitute evidence that this is so.

[12] See part 4 of Derek Parfit, *Reasons and Persons*.

theories, in particular, have dealt with the issue by treating the social contractors as members of different generations, thus artificially creating a situation in which agreement on fair principles of saving for the future may be directly required by prudence.[13] But there are two major difficulties with this approach. First, it increases the strains of identification with the parties to the social contract (as discussed in section 10-3) on the part of real people. Unless they already care about fairness to future generations, individuals may reasonably ask why they should comply with principles that would be agreed to in counterfactual circumstances designed to insure such fairness. Second, it seems arbitrary to treat intergenerational issues in this manner without so treating international issues. But so doing would place even greater stress on the motivational efficacy of one's hypothetical contract theory, at least among those not already committed to significant international economic redistribution. Hobbesian theory, with its emphasis on the motivational power of normative principles because of their close links with prudential rationality, cannot readily accommodate these strains and stresses entailed by treating the social contractors as members of different generations.

In the end, then, it must be admitted that the attempt to reconcile strong group member's self-interest with a reasonable moral conception of their duties to members of weak groups is less than fully successful. Self-interest, even long-run rational prudence, does not completely explain our obligations to others under all circumstances. To admit this is not to denigrate Hobbes's vast accomplishments. The many lessons of *Leviathan*, which are reviewed in the next section, are as well worth knowing as its few limits.

12-2. Lessons of Leviathan

It is now time to summarize the argument and conclusions of this book. Chapter 1 focused on method. Our two main conclusions about Hobbes's method were that it is partly empirical, rather

---

[13] See Rawls, *Theory of Justice*, p. 292; and Gauthier, *Morals by Agreement* (Oxford: Clarendon Press, 1985), chap. 9, sec. 6.3.

than purely deductive, and that Hobbes's moral and political theory is essentially independent of his materialist-determinist metaphysics. We promised, in developing our own Hobbesian theory, to sketch descriptive and normative theory separately and to correct some of Hobbes's errors while staying within the structure and spirit of his philosophy.

The beginning of Hobbesian *descriptive* theory, in Chapter 2, sketched a Hobbesian account of human motivation to provide the background for the argument against anarchy. The notorious doctrine of Psychological Egoism, to which Hobbes may or may not have been committed, was described, evaluated, and rejected. In its place was substituted Predominant Egoism, the much more plausible claim that, in conditions of insecurity, self-interested motives tend to determine most people's actions most all of the time.

The core of Hobbesian theory—the three-part argument against anarchy—was presented in Chapters 3 through 6. Chapter 3 developed the first part of that argument. We showed that, and why, rational, predominantly self-interested, and forwardlooking individuals in a groupless state of nature would prefer anticipating (i.e., active defense) to lying low (i.e., passive defense) and would therefore most likely end up in an active war of each individual against every other. The second part of the argument, advanced in Chapter 4, contends that non-State groups cannot adequately solve the state-of-nature security problem. In the course of this part of the argument, we saw that cooperation in the state of nature is possible, but precarious, and that a war of all groups would probably ensue there unless and until a State were formed.

The third part of the argument against anarchy establishes that the problems posed for individuals by the existence of a State—or a State of a certain sort—are not as bad as those encountered in a war of all individuals or groups. This is accomplished, in Chapter 5, by construction of a Hobbesian hypothetical contract theory which indicates that rational predominantly self-interested individuals would agree, under appropriate conditions, on the establishment of what we called a *satisfactory* State. The third part of the argument is completed in Chapter 6, in which certain problems of the State that Hobbes did not sufficiently emphasize are discussed. These problems arise from the difficulty of identifying and apprehending violators of the civil law and from the dependence of political power on the mutual beliefs and expectations of citizens, but they are not grave enough problems to render the satisfactory State less desirable than the state of nature or the likely consequences of revolution. Therefore, their existence is fully compatible with both the Hobbesian argument against anarchy and a scaled-down version of Hobbes's own antirevolutionary position.

Chapter 7 began discussion of Hobbesian *normative* theory with analyses of a number of significant normative concepts, and the observation that Hobbes endorses, but restricts, the "ought implies can" principle. Unfortunately, he does not consistently adhere to his own restriction. In Chapter 8, we saw how this and other problems infect Hobbes's arguments for the claim that the right of self-preservation is inalienable. A more positive note was struck in Chapter 9, in which Hobbes's attempt to reinterpret ordinary morality as a rule-egoistic system was outlined and defended. Hobbes's laws of nature were presented as rational rules of long-run prudence and social peace, containing exception clauses designed to protect agents from the harmful consequences of unilateral compliance. The normative implications of Hobbesian hypothetical contract theory were spelled out in Chapter 10, where it was argued that such a theory can explain why most all residents of satisfactory States are politically obligated. A variety of other grounds of political obedience which may apply to citizens and independents in the satisfactory State and to inhabitants of other States were also discussed. Finally, in Chapter 11, the limits of political obligation were considered. Hobbes's own derivations of certain individual rights from the natural right of self-preservation were questioned, but other more extensive individual rights were said to follow from the Hobbesian social contract, and a limited right of revolution was shown to be consonant with some of Hobbes's own principles.

To put this Hobbesian theory in perspective, it will be useful to point out and review the main ways in which it is different from Hobbes's own theory and certain contemporary theories. A number of significant departures from Hobbes are worth noting. As regards method, Hobbesian theory—unlike Hobbes—makes explicit both the independence of moral and political theory from metaphysics and the rejection of Psychological Egoism. Turning to matters of substance, Hobbes's doctrine of the inalienability of the right of self-preservation, and the consequences he draws from it, are also set aside. Hobbesian theory has no use for Hobbes's version of tacit consent theory, based on the notion of sovereignty by acquisition, and it rejects two key empirical assumptions that Hobbes makes about political sociology—that a sovereign's interests coincide with those of his people and that division or limitation of sovereign power inevitably leads to civil war. As a result, Hobbesian theory presents an account of the content of the social contract that more closely resembles the structure of Rawls's liberal State than the structure of Hobbes's authoritarian commonwealth. On revolution, Hobbesian theory restricts the scope and force of Hobbes's antirevolutionary argument, while drawing out, as Hobbes did not, the potentially prorevolutionary implications of some of his own principles. Overall, Hobbesian theory places considerably more emphasis on individual liberty against the State than did Hobbes, though it is skeptical of some particular liberties that he ascribes to citizens, for example, the right of non-self-incrimination. And in ways too numerous to list, Hobbesian theory develops certain of Hobbes's own arguments and themes more fully than he did himself.

Hobbesian theory differs from recent major interpretations of Hobbes in two ways. On the negative side, it rejects certain of the main interpretive claims put forth by other authors. Gauthier's view that authorization is a central political concept of Hobbes (section 10-1), McNeilly's contention that Hobbes's argument is a priori (section 4-5), and Warrender's interpretation of Hobbes's moral theory as a divine command theory (section 9-3) are all challenged. On the positive side, Hobbesian theory departs from previous accounts in the degree of its separation of descriptive and normative issues, in its detailed development of the three-part argument against anarchy, and in its emphasis on certain liberal elements in Hobbes's philosophy, such as his economic redistributivism and his endorsement of principles favorable to revolution under certain circumstances.

Hobbesian theory is also different from other social contract theories. It views the social contract as yielding conditions of political obligation, rather than principles of social justice or a description of the ideal state. And it does not assume that there must be unanimous agreement on the social contract. Though the Hobbesian social contract resembles that of Rawls, there are significant differences between the two in form and content. Unlike Rawls, Hobbesian theory allows social contractors knowledge of their personal characteristics, takes Hobbes's state of nature as its no-agreement point, and makes use of a disaster-avoidance conception of rational choice under uncertainty. As a result, Hobbesian contractors opt for a guaranteed economic minimum, rather than Rawls's difference principle, and adopt a weaker equal opportunity requirement than do Rawls's contractors.

With these contrasts in mind, we may proceed to summarize the main contributions of Hobbes's moral and political philosophy as emphasized and developed in Hobbesian theory. These "lessons of *Leviathan*" involve four subjects: the problems of anarchy, the functions of the State, social contract theory, and morality.

Hobbes traced the problems of anarchy to (what we now call) the prisoner's dilemma or public goods structure of the anarchical situation, in which personal incentives drive collections of rational individuals to perform acts that are harmful to all of them. His analysis, unlike certain caricatures of it, emphasizes that the motives which lead to trouble in the state of nature are *defensive* as well as offensive and that the structure of the state of nature is troublesome almost as much because it inhibits reliable cooperation as because it encourages violence. This analysis also explains why group formation, short of forming a State, does not solve the problem: rational cooperation within groups is precarious, and the "logic of anticipation" applies between groups in the state of nature as well as individuals. This is both an enlightening and original diagnosis of the problems of anarchy, and one of the major historical sources of the theory of public goods which has been put to such extensive use in modern times.[14]

Hobbes's search for a solution to the problem of anarchy led to his theory of the State. In his view, the State is purely an instrument (albeit a glorious one), a man-made device created to ameliorate the conflicting goals and interests of individuals and allow these individuals to live peaceful, decent, productive, and reasonably secure lives in close proximity to one another. The primary function of the State is to apply sanctions against violators of mutually beneficial rules of conduct, thereby rendering it individually rational for group members to act in a manner that promotes one another's welfare. This proposal about sanctions is one of the classic solutions to prisoner's dilemma/public goods problems of all kinds. As applied to anarchy and the State, it has some interesting corollaries that Hobbes suggests: it matters as much, or more, that there be a reliable sovereign as that there be a certain sovereign or one of a certain kind; revolution is prima facie imprudent and immoral because it impairs performance of this vital sanction-imposing function of sovereignty; and law enforcement is needed as much to render defensive violations unnecessary as to render offensive violations unwise. Hobbes's theory of the State, and his remarks about fear and power, also provide a valuable hint concerning of what State power is constituted—mutual expectations of obedience on the part of citizens. As noted in section 6-2, both the problem of anarchy and the instrument of its solution, the State, are grounded in individual's fears of one another.

We have argued that certain false empirical assumptions led Hobbes to seriously misdescribe the content of the original social contract. Still, some worthwhile ideas emerge from the formal features of Hobbes's social contract theory. One is that *hypothetical* consent, under appropriate conditions, can provide an adequate ground of political obligation. Another is that the legitimate State arises, in principle, from free and equal individuals

---

[14] For a sample of the modern literature on public goods and the prisoner's dilemma, see part 1 of *Rational Man*, ed. Barry and Hardin.

agreeing on rules of mutual restraint to promote their common interests, and institutions to interpret and enforce those rules.

Hobbes also has something to teach us about morality, or at least that part of it concerning how we are required to act towards others. His rule-egoistic account of morality emphasizes that moral requirements must, on the whole, be consistent with the motivational springs of human action, and it explains how and why the prescriptions of morality and long-run prudence generally coincide. The Copper Rule, or nonunilateralist, structure of ordinary practice morality is brought to the fore, and the significant differences between offensive (maximizing) and defensive (minimizing) violations of moral rules are pointed out. Most important, a distinctive function is assigned to morality—that of promoting peace and cooperation among potentially conflicting individuals. And the idea of social peace as a common good or prerequisite of each individual's secure well-being is used to sidestep the "fact-value gap" and to allow the derivation of moral principles from general empirical facts, an account of human nature, and certain assumptions about rationality.

Hobbes's account of morality also stresses the need for moral and legal requirements to work in concert if lasting peace and security are to be obtained. Morality is a mixture of the natural and the conventional. Basic moral rules are *natural*, in the sense of being derivable by reason from the universal common interest in social peace. But their effectiveness as means to security and well-being depends on their authoritative interpretation and enforcement by the legal apparatus of the State. Like morality in general, social justice has both natural components (e.g., principles of basic equality and mutual respect) and conventional components (e.g., specific rules of property distribution), and its realization requires legal enforcement. That morality and justice are effectively and lastingly realizable only within the State is an antianarchist theme of *Leviathan* that is worth taking to heart.

INDEX